The Political Dimension in Teacher Education

The Wisconsin Series of Teacher Education

The Political Dimension in Teacher Education:
Comparative Perspectives on Policy Formation, Socialization and Society

Editors

Mark B. Ginsburg and Beverly Lindsay

 The Falmer Press

(A member of the Taylor & Francis Group)
London • Washington, DC

UK   The Falmer Press, 4 John Street, London WC1N 2ET
USA   The Falmer Press, Taylor & Francis Inc., 1900 Frost Road, Suite 101, Bristol, PA 19007

First published in 1995

A catalogue record for this book is available from the British Library

Library of Congress Cataloging-in-Publication Data are available on request

ISBN 0 7507 0392 x cased
ISBN 0 7507 0393 8 paper

Jacket design by Caroline Archer

Typeset in 9.5/11pt Bembo by
Graphicraft Typesetters Ltd., Hong Kong.

Printed in Great Britain by Burgess Science Press, Basingstoke on paper which has a specified pH value on final paper manufacture of not less than 7.5 and is therefore 'acid free'.

Contents

Contents

Acknowledgments

Many people made this book possible. The contributing authors benefited from each others' comments on earlier drafts of their chapters. Our work also was shaped by a variety of colleagues who attended the panel sessions on this topic we organized at the annual meetings of the American Educational Studies Association (1992), the Comparative and International Education Society (1993), and the American Educational Research Association (1994).

The inspiration for this volume are the many policy makers, teacher educators and teacher education students around the world who have struggled and continue to struggle about and in programs to prepare teachers formally. The political dimension of their — and our — work and lives is the focus of the chapters in this book, and we would be remiss not to acknowledge our debt to them.

One way we seek to repay this debt is by donating the royalties from the publication of this volume to two organizations that in different ways have been engaged in 'political' efforts — through education, teacher education and other means — to change the way power as well as material and symbolic resources are distributed: Educators for Social Responsibility (23 Garden Street, Cambridge, MA, 02138, USA; tel: 617-492-1764) and the United Negro College Fund (500 East 62nd Street, New York, NY, 10021, USA; tel: 212-326-1161). We hope that by our 'political' act we can facilitate materially the future 'political' work of these organizations related to educating teachers and more generally.

We also hope that those who read this volume will benefit, and that they will not only understand better the challenges they face but also be encouraged and empowered to pursue their 'political' goals, particularly those aimed at creating a world in which power and resources are distributed in a just and equitable manner. To quote W.E.B. Dubois (1903, p. 278), we ultimately desire that this 'book is not still-born . . . that from its pages there springs vigor of thought and thoughtful deed to reap the harvest . . . that infinite reasoning [from these pages] may help turn tangles straight.'

Mark Ginsburg would also like to thank Shannon Gallagher, of the Institute for International Studies in Education at the University of Pittsburgh for her competent and good-natured assistance on this and many other projects. He also expresses his appreciation to his spouse (Barbara) and three children (Jolie, Kevin and Stefanie) for their understanding and patience concerning the time he spent over the last few years in particular attending conferences, working in the 'office', and sitting at home in front of the computer screen. His parents (Blanche and

Norman Ginsburg) and his grandfather (Fred Burg) are also in part responsible for any positive contribution this book may make. He also was sustained in this book project by the solidarity shown by those with whom he collaborates in community and university-based social and political action, including the Alliance for Progressive Action, the Pittsburgh Cuba Coalition, the Pittsburgh Peace Institute, and the United Faculty (American Federation of Teachers/American Association of University Professors).

Beverly Lindsay expresses appreciation to Mark C. DeWitt, her assistant and secretary for the Office of International Education and Policy Studies at Hampton University, Hampton, Virginia, particularly for his continuous computer assistance and sense of humor whenever things do not go right. She also appreciates the continuous long-distance assistance from her former secretaries at the University of Georgia, Athens, GA, Margaret A. Williams and Dora M. Ervin, who provided tremendous support when this book project began, especially when she was in South Africa, Kenya and England. The special cultural and intellectual sharing and contributions to Beverly Lindsay's academic and professional development of June M. Parrott and Letha (Lee) See are acknowledged. Both helped her fully comprehend classical and jazz musician Wynton Marsalis' statement: 'I refuse to allow the collective weight of this history that we're living crush my spirit.' And finally she expresses in-depth gratitude to her parents, (the late) Joe Bass Benson Lindsay and Ruth Roberts Lindsay, for their insistence on learning and diligence so she would, as an adult, not bow to hypocrisy.

Reference

DuBois, W.E.B. (1903, 1969) *The Souls of Black Folks*, New York, Signet Classic.

Part 1

Conceptual Introduction

Chapter 1

Conceptualizing the Political Dimension in Teacher Education

Mark B. Ginsburg and Beverly Lindsay

What does politics have to do with it anyway? Why can't we just focus on the academic, professional and technical issues in teacher education — how best to prepare future teachers so they can help children and youth learn and develop? Isn't teacher education complicated enough without trying to place the field in the arena of politics? These and other similar questions, we believe, reflect an incomplete understanding both of politics and of teacher education. The purpose of this chapter (and the book more generally) is to develop our understanding of politics and teacher education so that we can ask more fruitful questions such as: In whose interests does — and should — the political dimension in teacher education operate? How can my colleagues and I become more actively and effectively involved in shaping the political dimension in teacher education toward more equitable and just means and ends?

Programs for educating (developing, preparing or training) preservice as well as in-service teachers can be seen as part of a complex web of policies and practices constructed by individuals and groups interacting at institutional, local, national and global levels.[1] However, the literature concerned with policy and practice in teacher education generally focuses on academic, professional and technical dimensions of such phenomena (e.g. see King 1970; Lomax 1976; Hoyle and Megarry 1980; UNESCO 1982; Yang *et al.* 1986; Tisher and Wideen 1990; Leavitt 1992; Gilroy and Smith 1993). In this edited volume we will highlight the political dimension. In doing so, we seek to build on similar analyses undertaken by other scholars (Singer 1965; Lynch and Plunkett 1973; Goodings *et al.* 1982; Dove 1986; Popkewitz 1987, 1992; Ginsburg 1988; Sharpes 1988; Gumbert 1990). In particular the collection of national case studies in this volume were developed to contribute to our understanding of the political dimension in teacher education by focusing on both policy formation *and* teacher socialization in 'developed' (rich/powerful) *as well as* 'developing' (poorer and less powerful) countries. By comparing phenomena between and within 'developed' and 'developing' societies we are in a better position to conceptualize and develop strategies for intervening in the political dimension in teacher education on a local, national and global level (for a discussion of the advantages and challenges involved in undertaking comparative studies in teacher education, see Lindsay 1990).

Examining the political dimension, we believe, is essential if we are to appreciate fully what does and what does not transpire 1) when teacher education policy is developed and implemented in countries representing various degrees of wealth and power within the world system and 2) when students construct their ideas about teaching, schooling and society in the context of their encounters with the official and hidden curriculum of teacher education programs. If we do not fully consider the political dimension, the ways we think about teacher education will be partial and distorted, and our efforts to intervene in the policy and practice of teacher education will be less effective and salutary.

The Political Dimension

At its core politics is intimately linked to the structural and ideological forms of power, which involves exercising the capacity 1) to get others to do something, 2) not to do something, or 3) not even to consider doing something, such that their action or inaction is contrary to their interests (Lukes 1974). While ideological power is generally associated with '3', ideas may also play a role in addition to structural forms of power (physical force and material rewards/punishments) in relation to '1' and '2'. This conception of power — what Kreisberg (1992) terms *power-over* — is constituted by relations of domination and subordination. In contrast, power can also be conceived as being constituted by enabling relations of mutually supportive action — what Kreisberg (1992) labels *power-with.*

Focusing on the political dimension, therefore, entails examining how power (the ideological and structural forms of power-over and power-with) is distributed and organized among various individuals, groups, communities and societies. However, politics is not only about possessing (or not possessing) power; it is also concerned with the distribution of material resources (food, minerals, raw materials, land, buildings, commodities, financial capital, etc.) and symbolic resources (status, credentials, legitimacy, etc.). The production, reproduction, consumption and accumulation of material and symbolic resources, of course, occurs through the exercise of power (see Ginsburg *et al.* 1992).

It is important to clarify that the political dimension is not limited to considerations of the state, governments, parties, constitutions and voting. All aspects of human experience, from global relations to interpersonal dynamics, whether taking place in the public or the private sphere,[2] have a political dimension (Foucault 1980; Corr and Jamieson 1990). Thus, while the workings of the state receive considerable attention in this volume, we also examine how teacher education is linked with relations of power and resource distributions in civil society,[3] for example, those involving social class, racial/ethnic, and gender relations as they are socially constructed and contested by individuals and groups in homes, neighborhoods, religious institutions, and professional associations and unions.

The Political Dimension in Teacher Education

The experiences of those who participate in the formation (development and implementation) of teacher education policy and those who are involved in the socialization of teachers are no exception to the above-stated point that all human experiences have a political dimension. These educators and other groups work and live within relations of power. Such relations of power are extant in local, national and international policy-making arenas (e.g. in educational systems, states and international agencies), but also in educational institutions, programs and classrooms where (preservice and in-service) teachers are formally educated. Moreover, the processes of forming teacher education policy and of socializing prospective teachers are dialectically related not only to the distribution of structural and ideological power used to control the means of producing, reproducing, consuming and accumulating material and symbolic resources, but also to the distribution of material and symbolic resources *per se*. The actions (and inactions) of educators and others engaged in these processes are constrained and enabled by such relations of power and resource distributions, while at the same time through their daily activity and historical struggles these human beings are engaged in creating, reproducing, resisting and transforming existing power relations and resource distributions. The outcomes of these struggles, furthermore, may preserve or change the status quo and may serve the interests of dominant groups, subordinate groups, and/or human beings more generally.

Below we briefly outline the issues that form the core of Parts 2 and 3 of this edited volume: the formation of teacher education policy and the socialization of teachers. While we have divided the chapters into these two parts, we want to emphasize that policy formation and political socialization of teachers are related components of the political dimension in teacher education. Some of the chapters demonstrate this point directly. For example, in the second part, Paine's and Dembélé's chapters on China and Burkina Faso respectively concentrate on the dynamics involved in the development and implementation of teacher education policy, but also indicate the kind of political socialization of teachers that is envisioned or implied by the various groups involved in these policy debates and struggles. Analogously, Ginsburg's and Burke's chapters on Mexico and Papua New Guinea respectively in the third section delineate how students' political identities and orientations are influenced (reinforced, refined, altered, etc.) in the context of teacher education programs, while also outlining how the formal and hidden curricula of these programs were shaped through policy formation processes occurring at the institutional, local, national and world system levels.

The Political Dimension of Policy Formation[4]

Educational policy formation, like the phenomenon of educational 'reform', can be conceived of as rhetoric and other forms of action about 'education' designed to:

1 change or conserve an education system's size, goals, administrative structure, funding levels and processes, types of organization, curricular content, pedagogical practices, and selection and evaluation criteria and standards;
2 deal with or deflect attention from economic problems;
3 enhance or diminish the quality of people's lives; and
4 legitimate or challenge the power of educational, economic, cultural or state élites (Ginsburg 1991).

The formation of policies governing preservice and in-service teacher education is somewhat more complicated (and more interesting!) because it relates directly as well as indirectly (via schooling) to these dynamics. For example, much recent effort to 'reform' teacher education in 'developed' capitalist societies has been stimulated (at least rhetorically) by concerns to bring teacher education under tighter control of state élites and by desires to prepare teachers differently so that schools will function more effectively in preparing more productive workers (Ginsburg 1988; Popkewitz 1992). Similarly, in the (former) Soviet Union in 1980 the Communist Party launched 'a major effort to secure further improvements in the professional training and political education of future teachers who will be capable of teaching . . . youth for labour in material production' (Grant 1982, p. 56). Teacher education reform in 'developing' countries can be similarly characterized, though the actions are often associated with expressions of concern for providing a cadre of 'qualified' (postsecondary-educated) teachers. In these (and other) instances, concerns about changing teacher education (namely making programs more efficient and effective) are linked directly to societal level concerns (e.g. growing the economy and maintaining legitimacy of the economic system and the state). Concerns about teacher education are also indirectly linked to societal level concerns as these impact on efforts to reform schooling (e.g. making them more effective and efficient in preparing skilled and compliant workers and aware, but not too critical, citizens).

Policy formation in teacher education is political both in the sense of individuals and groups exercising power, but also in the sense of material and symbolic resources being distributed (to individuals, groups, communities, nations, etc.). The following questions draw attention to the political dimension of teacher education policy formation:

1 Where should (preservice and in-service) teacher education programs be located in terms of institutions and communities?
2 From what sources and at what amount should they be funded?
3 Who should be enrolled in teacher education and for how long?
4 To what knowledge and perspectives should students in teacher education programs be or not be exposed?
5 Who should determine the curricular content and the evaluation procedures employed in the programs?
6 Who should be employed as instructors in these programs and how should they be prepared, selected and supervised?
7 Who should administer and evaluate these programs?

While there are academic, professional and technical issues associated with these questions, we hope that it is clear how these questions also bear on the distribution of power and of material and symbolic resources.

Focusing on the political dimension of policy formation in teacher education in the current historical period means considering the functioning of the (local and national) state. We should note, however, that states have not always been intimately involved in the education of teachers. As Dove (1986, p. 187) notes, over time there was a 'gradual extension of state financing and control', although in 'the early days, both in the metropolitan country and the colonies, governments took a laissez faire approach to teacher training.'[5] The increased involvement of or commitment by states to fund, or at least regulate, teacher education was signaled in principle 13 of the 1966 UNESCO 'Recommendation Concerning the

Status of Teachers': 'Completion of an *approved* course in an *appropriate* teacher education institution should be required of all persons entering the profession' (Dove 1986, p. 191; emphasis added).

In considering the role of the state in relation to teacher education, we must understand that the state incorporates more than agencies of local and national governments[6] and that the state is not necessarily unified or monolithic (Dale 1982; McClennan 1984). As Grace (1987, p. 196) observes, 'the state in Education is understood not as a single and unified entity but as a set of agencies, departments, tiers and levels, each with their own rules and resources and often varying purposes.' Moreover, educational policies of nation states are influenced by diplomatic, economic and military actions of other states and international organizations as well as the workings of multinational corporations and philanthropic foundations (Arnove 1980; Berman 1983). That is, international affairs can significantly affect how teacher education policy is developed.

While the state and its constituent governmental and nongovernmental agencies constitute sites of struggle over power and resource distributions, there is not a level playing field. This is because different groups, including educators, have more or less power and other resources to draw on in the struggle, but also because the state embodies (in different ways) contradictions of capitalism, patriarchy and racial formations characteristic of extant national and world system level economic and cultural systems (Ginsburg *et al.* 1988, 1990). For example, in order to survive, the state must

1 find a way to promote capital accumulation (to the advantage of national and global economic élites);
2 facilitate the reproduction of labor power or, in other words, enhance the development of human capital (reducing capital accumulation by drawing of revenue via taxes to provide education, health care, and the like for its citizen-workers); and
3 sustain the legitimacy of the political economy, at times by responding to demands of non-élites (Holloway and Picciotto 1978; Offe and Ronge 1981; Urry 1981; Carnoy and Levin 1985; Brosio 1993).

At least in part because of these apparent contradictions, the dynamics associated with the formation of teacher education policy vary cross-nationally and historically. For example, the capacity or orientation of state élites to promote a particular reform in teacher education, which is driven by a concern to aid economic élites (in accumulating capital) will depend on the level of legitimacy that the state has in the eyes of groups (e.g. workers, including educators) who may be asked to change — perhaps sacrificing some of their own sources of satisfaction in order for the reform to be implemented. Moreover, state élites' efforts to reform teacher education — oriented either to enhance the reproduction of labor power or to increase the legitimacy of the state — will depend in part on having a national economy that is generating and retaining enough wealth to be 'taxed' as a source of revenue to underwrite the costs of the reformed teacher education programs.

In addition, states and state élites are likely to operate differently in nations in the 'center' versus those in the 'periphery'.[7] Their past and present positions in the world system constrain and enable the options for rhetoric and other action open to them. State élites in 'developing' countries not only inherited policies in teacher education developed by colonial powers, but also have tended to develop and (perhaps) implement policies favored by 'developed' (often former colonizing) countries because of continued economic and cultural dependencies (Dove 1986). This does not necessarily mean that actions in the center and the periphery will promote and/or adopt different teacher education policies. Indeed, as we shall see in subsequent chapters, there are remarkable similarities internationally. However, the circumstances in which these policies and practices are considered and (perhaps) implemented may vary by a society's position in the world system. While philanthropic foundations and international organizations may play a role in shaping teacher education in both types of societies, it is primarily in the periphery societies where other nations (through bilateral aid agencies or university-based teaching and research programs) may be influential. Moreover, the relative material deprivation in periphery societies may make them more susceptible to offers of financial assistance (with conditions attached).

Popkewitz (1992, p. 15) reminds us, however, that the 'elements of regulation and contestation in teacher education are not necessarily carried by legislative or coercive functions of the state but in rules, norms and patterns of communication that structure in certain possibilities and filter out others.' That is, we need to attend to ideological as well as structural forms of power — to discursive as well as other practices — that may be used to shape teacher education policy and action. In subsequent chapters we will see how certain ideas about society, education and teacher education — whether the ideas are developed locally or circulated from other locales nationally or internationally — play a role in opening up or closing down certain policies and practices.

The Political Dimension of Teacher Socialization

The political dimension of teacher education operates in the daily practices (curriculum, pedagogy, evaluation, and formal and informal rewards and sanctions) as well as in the policy-making arena. Thus in this volume we also examine the political dimension of (socialization) experiences in teacher education programs. That is, we explore the processes whereby potential and actual teachers are formally and informally prepared to assume active or inactive, conservative or change-oriented political roles in their work and lives.

Research focused on various historical and societal contexts provides evidence that aspects of educators' roles such as the following have an important political dimension: curriculum decision making, pedagogy, student evaluation, research, institutional member (employee and colleague), family member, union/professional association member, and citizen (Ginsburg et al. 1992; Ginsburg 1995). This means that we need to examine the political dimension of teacher educators' action (or inaction) at the institutional and program levels as well as to consider the processes through which students in teacher education programs acquire or develop their political identities and orientations which may influence their future actions as teachers. That is, we need to consider how teacher education not only involves academic, professional and technical preparation, but also socialization for the political roles that teachers play (e.g. Singer 1965; Stromnes 1976; Grant 1982; Ginsburg and Tidwell 1990; Ginsburg 1994).

The concept of political socialization offers some assistance in this latter effort. Political socialization 'has to do with "people oriented" explanations of political events. It is a concept directing attention toward the [behavior,] knowledge, values, and beliefs of the average citizen' (Dawson and Prewitt 1969, p. 5) and concerns 'those developmental processes through which persons acquire [or develop] political orientations' (Easton and Dennis 1969, p. 7). The scholarly work associated with this concept, though, brings with it some potential limitations (see Connell 1987).

Most of the research and theorizing in the field of political socialization, unfortunately, has been based on a narrower conception of politics — one that focuses on public sphere activities in relation to governments and parties. Nevertheless, it seems feasible to draw on work in this field, while maintaining a broader conception of politics as concerned with both the public and private spheres.

Another potential limitation of the concept of political socialization for our purposes here is the tendency for scholars in the field (e.g. Hyman 1959, p. 17; Siegel 1965, p. 1; Dawson and Prewitt 1969, p. 7; Lasswell 1977, p. 75) to focus on how political systems remain stable and are sustained through individuals' accommodation to the status quo or to the interests of dominant groups (see Connell and Goot 1972–73 for a critique of such scholarship). We concur with Kavanagh (1972, p. 28), though, that the 'overall effect of the [political] socialization process . . . may be to change, or even recreate, as well as sustain, the political culture' (see also Langton 1969, p. 4).

A third limitation of much political socialization research is its tendency to rely on an 'over-socialized conception' of human experience (Wrong 1962). This is also a problem for much of the scholarship concerned with occupational and teacher socialization (see LeCompte and Ginsburg 1987; Ginsburg 1988; Zeichner and Gore 1990, for critical discussions of such a functionalist approach to teacher socialization). In the field of political socialization the 'passive reactive model' dominates: 'The individual appears as *tabula rasa* on which society imprints its attitudes, values and behaviors' (Baker 1972, p. 281). For example, Gergen and Ullman (1977, p. 417; emphasis added) state that political socialization practices '*implant* in the individual the particular styles or predispositions that form his or her individual character and that influence, among other things, his or her level of political participation.'

There is, however, a competing approach to studies of socialization, which postulates a more active image of those involved in the process. In this approach '[s]ocialization is not merely the transfer from one group to another in a static social structure, but the active creation of a new identity through a personal definition of the situation' (Reinharz 1979, p. 374; see also Oleson and Whittaker 1968; Bucher and Stelling 1977; Zeichner and Gore 1990). This approach — stressing human agency or the active role that socializees may play in constructing their identities, orientations and practices — can be drawn upon to complement the more passive image in political socialization research. In this case, we view political socialization to be a dialectical process in which future teachers, for example, play an active, but by no means autonomous role. The processes through which they socially construct their political roles are constrained *and* enabled by the structural and ideological context in which they live, while at the same time their activity contributes to the reproduction and transformation of the structural and ideological context.[8]

For instance, Singer (1965, p. 183) observes in the context of Poland during the period of 1956–61 that 'in spite of the indoctrination and political pressure [in teacher education programs] there are still many teachers who . . . have some reservations related to "the new reality" of their environment.' Thus in studies focusing on the political socialization of teachers we need to take seriously the following questions:

1   Are the messages that are transmitted by the socializing agent received by the socializee?
2   If received (consciously or unconsciously), are these messages internalized without any alteration, redefined before being incorporated, or resisted and rejected?
3   Whether or not the formal and hidden curricular messages are received, what other message sources or experiences influence their socialization as teachers?

As we will see in the third part of this volume, the answers to these questions vary among individuals as well as across time and place.

We can further rescue the concept of political socialization if we also consider that not all socialization agents nor even the socialization messages transmitted by single agent are the same or even compatible. Instead, we should be alerted to the potential for contradictions, for example, between and within the formal and hidden curriculum of a teacher education program (Ginsburg 1988; Ginsburg and Clift 1990). Thus, even in the (hypothetical) case where a socializee receives and seeks to internalize all messages from one or more socializing agents or socialization experiences, it is unlikely that we could predict in any simple, straightforward manner what the socializee would believe, think or do. Instead, we would need to examine the complex processes through which individuals (and groups) deal with contradictory elements in forming their identities, orientations and practices.

Teachers (and other people) are involved in various processes of political socialization in relation to a range of socializing agents during different periods of their lives (Hirsch 1971) and there is considerable debate in the literature regarding 'the relative impact of various agents of political socialization' and the 'relative importance of various stages of the age cycle' (Greenberg 1970, p. 6; see also Sears 1991). We are not arguing that the political socialization experiences occurring during involvement in a formal teacher education program — in university and school-level educational settings — are necessarily the most salient for understanding the development of teachers' political identities, orientations and strategies. We only wish to call attention to the political socialization processes that teachers encounter as part of their involvement in formally-organized teacher preparation programs. Such experiences may, to varying degrees, reinforce and/or contradict the political socialization messages provided through other (prior and subsequent) experiences.

Origins and Organization of the Book

This volume was developed as a result of discussions structured around a series of conference panel sessions (American Educational Studies Association, Pittsburgh,

PA, USA, 1992; Comparative and International Education Society, Kingston, Jamaica, 1993; and American Educational Research Association, New Orleans, LA, 1994). The authors of the various chapters represent a diverse group of scholars in terms of their citizenship, institutional affiliations, societal focuses for their research, theoretical perspectives, and methodological approaches. However, through these formal discussions as well as via more informal means of communication, it became clear that we were engaged in related intellectual and practical projects which benefited from such interchange. We also came to believe that our individual struggles to understand and transform teacher education could be assisted by seeking to tie our projects together. We hoped, furthermore, that by sharing the results of our collective work, others (you and other readers) might be assisted in their research and practice in teacher education, and that their (your) reactions to this book would help us move forward as well.

This book is organized around case studies from a variety of societies which analyze the impact of political dynamics on, the politics within, and the political consequences of teacher education. In addition to this chapter, which comprises the 'Conceptual Introduction' part of the volume, there are three other parts. The chapters (summarized below) in the second part of the volume, 'Teacher Education Policy Formation', address the following questions in the context of historical and contemporary national case studies of Australia, Burkina Faso, England and Wales, the People's Republic of China, Sri Lanka, Sierra Leone, South Africa, and the United States:

- Which groups are involved in policy formation and what symbolic, material and power resources do they draw on and in what contexts?
- What goals (in teacher education, education, the economy, civil society, etc.) do they seek to achieve through the policy formation process and in whose interests?
- What rhetoric and other forms of action do they engage in and how are these enabled or constrained by ideological and structural dynamics at the local, national and world system levels?
- What program structures, content and processes actually emanate from policy formation, and whose interests do they serve?

In Chapter 2, 'Teacher Education Policy in England', Maeve Landman and Jenny Ozga briefly discuss the longer history of teacher education policy making in England, prior to presenting a more detailed examination of the more recent period (1979–94). Attention is given to economic and fiscal crisis and the development of an activist Conservative government agenda in teacher education, education, and the society more generally. They emphasize the state's efforts to institute mechanisms of control of teachers and teacher educators through various governmental agencies as well as through the 'marketization' of education and teacher education. They label as a form of 'deprofessionalization' the declining role played by teachers and teacher educators in shaping the organization, content, evaluation, and accreditation of programs to prepare prospective teachers.

In Chapter 3, 'Politics of Teacher Education in New South Wales, Australia', Christine E. Deer, Susan Groundwater-Smith, Robert Meyenn and Judith Parker examine current political and government changes affecting higher education in Australia, particularly as they impact upon teacher education. They discuss the sociopolitical context in which changes have occurred and the consequences and actions arising from the changes at both the national and local levels, with a specific emphasis upon practices in New South Wales. The chapter describes the concerns held by teacher educators both in terms of the prevailing and often competing discourses regarding ownership of teacher education and the ways in which their becoming increasingly politicized has affected the teacher educators (particularly deans) themselves. The authors conclude with a set of principles whereby stakeholders might improve upon and consolidate gains in teacher education in Australia.

In Chapter 4, 'Teacher Education, Reform and the Politics of Knowledge in the United States', Thomas S. Popkewitz focuses on the issue of power and regulation in teacher education. To place the formation of teacher education in context, he examines historically the discursive and other practices associated with the development of mass schooling which helps to link individual identities to the welfare state; the rise of the university-based, social science professional 'experts' as servants of economic and political power; and the construction of school curriculum which regulates what teachers do and which (through a form of 'alchemy') represents a particular selection and organization of knowledge as natural and neutral. Popkewitz then analyzes the contemporary discourses of 'systemic school reform' and 'constructivist' psychologies of education and their embodiment within a particular initiative in teacher education — Teach for America. He shows how graduates of élite higher education institutions, who are being prepared in this program to teach in inner city and rural schools, learn to employ forms of 'population reasoning' which lead them to blame the students (and not schools or society) for the low academic achievement that occurs in such depressed economic settings.

In Chapter 5, 'Teacher Education in Search of a Metaphor: Defining the Relationship Between Teachers, Teaching, and the State in China', Lynn Paine draws on an analysis of documents, interviews and observations to examine how frequent redefinitions of political and educational goals since 1949, and especially in the post-Mao era, have shaped national teacher education policies as well as the practices within teacher education institutions. Different metaphors have been promoted (by government officials, party leaders and educators) during different eras to represent the ideal role (in relation to party and state) for which teachers are to be prepared. Paine draws our attention to the metaphors of 'red' and 'expert' which have been concatenated, but differentially emphasized, during various historical periods, and discusses recent debates concerning teacher education, in part as an extension of these metaphors in what she terms 'nationalizing' and 'modernizing' discourses occurring in the context of changing political economic dynamics in China and internationally. She sees these discourses as contradictory and views them as bankrupt in their capacity to catalyze teacher educators' and their students' commitment to the educational enterprise in the face of declining teacher status, autonomy and financial rewards.

In Chapter 6, 'Social and Political Contexts of Policy Formation in Teacher Education in Sri Lanka', Maria Teresa Tatto and K.H. Dharmadasa discuss how since Sri Lanka's independence from the United Kingdom in 1948, teachers have collaborated with the state in designing and implementing reforms at all levels of education. Teachers' supportive role has been facilitated because of the intensive socialization teachers received through teacher education. In examining how the organization, content and processes of teacher education have been altered over time, the authors point to how teachers and teacher educators have been professionalized as well as proletarianized in relation to the state and other occupational groups. These dynamics occur within a formerly colonized society characterized by egalitarian ideals and interethnic group conflict over the distribution of power and resources, including education and teacher education.

In Chapter 7, 'The Dynamics of Extending an Integrated Rural Teacher Education in Sierra Leone', Kingsley Banya presents a critical analysis of a project housed at Bunumbu Teachers College, which was funded by the United Nations Educational Scientific and Cultural Organization (UNESCO) and the United Nations Development Program (UNDP). The political dynamics of developing the project at Bunumbu and of extending this integrated rural teacher education program to colleges located in urban areas in Sierra Leone are explored. Why Bunumbu was selected as well as how four urban institutions and their communities demanded and why they were granted the resources, despite the project goal of slowing rural–urban migration, are analyzed. These struggles around policy planning and implementation are examined in the context of broader dynamics in Sierra Leone's economic, social and political systems. Particular attention is given to how the distribution of material resources (funds for jobs and buildings) and symbolic resources (status) via the projects was used by political élites to maintain their power within a clientelist–patronage system.

In Chapter 8, 'The Shaping of Secondary Teacher Preparation in Post-Independence Burkina Faso', Martial Dembélé reports on a study that was designed 1) to trace the various institutional and programmatic arrangements for preparing secondary teachers in Burkina Faso from 1960 until the early 1990s and 2) to examine critically the factors and actors that shaped the development of institutions and programs. In explaining why particular institutions for the education of secondary teachers were planned, sometimes implemented, and then phased out at particular times, and why they operated the way they did, he draws our attention to contextual factors (such as economic hardships, political instability, and educational expansion), policies regulating access to secondary teaching, career choices and (non-teaching) opportunities of Burkinabè university graduates, teachers' unions' militant political action (or the government's fear of such).

In Chapter 9, 'Sociopolitical Realities and Teacher Education in a New South Africa', Beverly Lindsay reports on discussions with a range of South Africans (both individuals and organizations) and a review of documents concerned with education in the post-apartheid period. How sociopolitical conditions in (and outside of) South Africa have affected policies concerning higher education, and particularly teacher education programs, is explored. Issues discussed include: 1) the effect of political realities upon the resources devoted to postsecondary institutions and teacher education programs for different ethnic/racial groups, 2) the struggles facing a new nation in designing postsecondary structures, 3) the development of sociopolitical and educational policies designed to ameliorate the education of teachers, and 4) the formation of policy options for social and structural changes.

The chapters (summarized below) in the third part of the book, 'Political Socialization of Teachers', address the following questions drawing on ethnographic studies of teacher education programs undertaken in Germany, Mexico, Papua New Guinea, and the United States:

- What messages about education and society do students encounter in the formal and hidden curriculum of teacher education programs?
- Do these messages encourage an acceptance or a critique of existing social relations in communities, nations and the world system?
- Do these messages convey an image of teachers as active or passive, change-oriented or conservative political actors or are teachers represented as apolitical?
- How do students in these programs interpret and anticipate acting in relation to these messages?
- What features of their current and future contexts serve to enable or constrain certain forms of political activity?

In Chapter 10, 'Student Teaching as Social Reproduction: An Ethnography in Appalachia in the United States', Linda Spatig draws primarily on interview and observational data from a longitudinal ethnography of the process of becoming a teacher in Appalachia, an economically depressed region in the United States. Four themes associated with the student teaching experience are discussed: a practical ('whatever works') orientation, a focus on appearance as opposed to substance, a fragmented mode of thinking about teaching, and an overarching concern with classroom discipline and control. These themes seem to contradict the formally adopted core idea of the teacher education program — critical reasoning. That critical reasoning remains a label for (rather than a pervasive and profound experience in) the program, along with the high level of competition for the few teaching jobs in communities controlled by (or dependent on) a small, but powerful economic élite, help to explain why these student teachers appear more likely to reproduce than to challenge existing inequalities in wealth and power in the Appalachian region or in the nation more generally.

In Chapter 11, 'Preparing Teachers for Gender Politics in Germany: The State, the Church, and Political Socialization', Rajeshwari Raghu reports on a four-month ethnography in one institution in Eichstätt, Bavaria, Germany. The study reveals that the official curriculum is virtually silent on issues of gender and does not explicitly address whether or not teachers should be active politically. The hidden curriculum in the institution, supplemented by messages from government and church officials locally and nationally, however, encourages prospective teachers in this setting to accept existing gender relations and remain passive as political actors. Some students internalize this conservative, inactive message. Others — despite the program and contextual influences — develop feminist perspectives. However, because of concerns to obtain positive recommendations from a church-run, state-regulated university in order to secure employment as a teacher in schools controlled by a state government dominated by the Christian Democratic Party even the male and female students with socialist feminist and radical feminist ideas anticipate being relatively inactive, or at least very discreet, in their political activity concerning gender inequalities and other issues.

In Chapter 12, 'Contradictions, Resistance, and Incorporation in the Political Socialization of Educators in Mexico', Mark B. Ginsburg presents some of the results of ethnographic research focused on one group of students in the Social Studies Education in-service bachelor's degree program at the Escuela Normal Superior Veracruzana (ENSV) in Xalapa, Veracruz, Mexico. The changing nature of the political economy and teachers' corporatist relations with the state and dominant political party are sketched. This provides the context for examining the development of a group of students' political consciousness and action (or, more often, inaction) as they encounter the official and hidden curriculum of the program. Many of the students become more critical in their analysis, in part because of Marxist and other conflict perspectives conveyed in the social science content courses. However, because they fear of losing their jobs and/or distrust existing political parties and unions, the majority of the students are not currently, and do not anticipate that they will become, active in challenging the status quo. It is also noted that neither the formal curriculum nor the students' discussions about social problems draw attention to gender inequalities. In part because of the taken-for-granted nature of gender relations in schools and society, these students seem to organize their work and lives in ways that help reproduce patriarchal structure. For example, Ginsburg shows how while compared to their male counterparts the female ENSV students are more likely to hold conflict (versus equilibrium) perspectives, they are more likely to consider strategies involving consciousness-raising in the 'private sphere' of classrooms and less likely to see themselves as participating in 'public' sphere activities of teachers' unions or political parties.

In Chapter 13, 'Transforming Teacher Education in Papua New Guinea: A Framework for Sustainable Professional Development in Community Teachers Colleges', Clarrie Burke discusses an Australian-based project designed to develop the instructional staff in community teachers colleges. It offers an analysis of how the messages in the official and hidden curriculum of a program encourage or discourage the development of commitment and skills needed to engage in transformative praxis by these college instructors. Burke points to the dissonance experienced by those participating in this program, particularly when they take undergraduate degree courses in Australia in the hope of adapting (versus transplanting) lessons learned as they return to their challenging work in Papua New Guinea (PNG). While instructors from the community teachers colleges appear to develop perspectives and commitments to becoming change agents, at this point it is unclear how extensive and profound such change efforts can be and still retain the support of the political and economic élites in PNG, Australia and the world system.

Part 4, 'Implications for a Transformative Agenda in Teacher Education', contains a single concluding chapter which summarizes and critiques major national and cross-national motifs from the case studies. Recommendations for policy and practice in teacher education are derived therefrom. This final chapter, 'Transforming Teacher Education, Schooling, and Society: Lessons Learned and Political Commitments' by Beverly Lindsay and Mark B. Ginsburg, focuses on how the involvement of teacher educators, teachers, and students in the political dimension of teacher education could help to transform (make more just and equitable) teacher education, schooling, and society.

Notes

1   While concurring with Foshay (1992, p. viii) that 'each of the problems in teacher education is nested in a local culture, a local polity, a local history,' we also consider it necessary to analyze teacher education policy and practice as being constructed within national and global or world system level political, economic and

cultural dynamics. On the importance of examining educational policy and practice within national and world system contexts see Ginsburg (1991).

2   This concern to illuminate the politics of the private sphere (home and family life) as well as the public sphere (affairs of local and national states) is motivated in part to bring more of the political dimension of women's experience into focus. For example, Weiler (1989, p. 14) encourages us to problematize '19th century definitions of the political sphere, [which focused] exclusively on male activities in partisan electoral politics [and ignored] . . . the actions of women who organized and worked in many ways for social ideals.' Similarly, the ('private' sphere) classroom activities of teachers (predominantly females) is less often considered as political than the activities of administrators or teacher organization leaders (more often males) operating in the 'public' sphere of communities (Ginsburg *et al.* 1992).

3   The concept of civil society was introduced by Antonio Gramsci, who 'distinguished between public institutions of the state on the one hand, and civil society on the other — all the private, voluntary organisations such as trade unions . . . churches, community and charitable organizations [and the family]' (Simon 1991, p. 18).

4   Adams (1988) suggests three models of educational policy development and implementation: technical, consensual and political. In this volume we use a broader conception of the term political and thus examine the political dimension of policy formation that occurs through the dynamics highlighted in all three models.

5   This point must be qualified in that often the education of teachers was undertaken by 'voluntary organizations', usually tied to a religious order. Given our definition of the state (see below) as comprising more than government bureaucracies, these voluntary organizations may be considered as part of the state apparatus. Certainly such organizations conducted teacher education in metropolitan and colonial contexts at the pleasure of state (and economic) élites.

6   That is, through struggle parts of what we referred to above as civil society become incorporated in or kept separate from the state. The division between state and civil society, therefore, is fluid.

7   To clarify, the assumption here is that élites and other groups in center and periphery societies are active agents, seeking to understand possibilities and developing strategies to realize them. While recognizing that individuals and groups are not determined by existing social structures and ideologies, we nonetheless wish to highlight how structures and ideologies enable or constrain certain kinds of thought and action in particular contexts.

8   Giddens (1979) discusses this issue in terms of rules and resources both being constitutive of *and* constituted by human consciousness and action.

References

ADAMS, D. (1988) 'Extending the educational planning discourse: Conceptual and paradigmatic exploration', *Comparative Education Review*, **32**, 4, pp. 400–15.

ARNOVE, R. (1980) *Philanthropy and Cultural Imperialism: The Foundations at Home and Abroad*, Boston, MA, G.K. Hall.

BAKER, D. (1972) 'Political socialization: Parameters and disposition', *Polity* **3**, 4 pp. 586–600.

BERMAN, E. (1983) *The Influence of the Carnegie, Ford, and Rockefeller Foundations on American Foreign Policy: The Ideology of Philanthropy*, Albany, NY, State University of New York Press.

BROSIO, R. (1993) 'The role of the state in contemporary capitalist democratic societies: Ramifications for education', *Educational Foundations*, **7**, 1, pp. 27–51.

BUCHER, R. and STELLING, J. (1977) *Becoming Professional*, Beverly Hills, CA, Sage.

CARNOY, M. and LEVIN, H. (1985) *Schooling and Work in the Democratic State*, Stanford, CA, Stanford University Press.

CONNELL, R. (1987) 'Why the "political socialization" paradigm failed and what should replace it', *International Political Science Review*, **8**, 3, pp. 215–23.

CONNELL, R. and GOOT, M. (1972–73) 'Science and technology in American "political socialization" research,' *Berkeley Journal of Sociology*, **17**, pp. 167–93.

CORR, H. and JAMIESON, L. (Eds) (1990) *Politics of Everyday Life*, London: Macmillan.

DALE, R. (1982) 'Education and the capitalist state: Contributions and contradictions', in APPLE, M. (Ed) *Cultural and Economic Reproduction in Education: Essays on Class, Ideology and the State*, Boston, Routledge and Kegan Paul, pp. 127–61.

DAWSON, R. and PREWITT, K. (1969) *Political Socialization*, Boston, MA, Little, Brown and Company.

DOVE, L. (1986) *Teachers and Teacher Education in Developing Countries*, London, Croom Helm.

EASTON, D. and DENNIS, J. (1969) *Children in the Political System: Origins of Political Legitimacy*, New York, McGraw-Hill.

FOSHAY, A. (1992) 'Foreword', in LEAVITT, H. (Ed) *Issues and Problems in Teacher Education: An International Handbook*, New York, Greenwood Press, pp. v–viii.

FOUCAULT, M. (1980) *Power/Knowledge*, New York, Pantheon.

GERGEN, K. and ULLMAN, M. (1977) 'Socialization and characterological basis of political activism', in RENSTON, S. (Ed) *Handbook of Political Socialization*, New York, Free Press, pp. 411–42.

GIDDENS, A. (1979) *Central Problems in Social Theory*, Berkeley, University of California Press.

GILROY, P. and SMITH, M. (1993) *International Analyses of Teacher Education*, double issue supplement of *Journal of Education for Teaching*, **19**, 4–5.

GINSBURG, M. (1988) *Contradictions in Teacher Education and Society: A Critical Analysis*, London, Falmer Press.

GINSBURG, M. (Ed) (1991) *Understanding Educational Reform in Global Context: Economy, Ideology and the State*, New York, Garland.

GINSBURG, M. (1994) 'Aprendiendo a ser Actores Politicos? La Educacion de Maestros en Mexico', *Punto y Seguido*, **7**, pp. 17–20.

GINSBURG, M. (Ed) (1995) *The Politics of Educators' Work and Lives*, New York, Garland.

GINSBURG, M. and CLIFT, R. (1990) 'The hidden curriculum of preservice teacher education', in HOUSTON, W.R. (Ed) *Handbook of Research on Teacher Education*, New York: Macmillan, pp. 450–65.

GINSBURG, M., COOPER, S., RAGHU, R. and ZEGARRA, H. (1990) 'National and world system level explanations of educational reform', *Comparative Education Review*, **34**, 4, pp. 474–99.

GINSBURG, M., KAMAT, S., RAGHU, M. and WEAVER, J. (1992) 'Educators/Politics', *Comparative Education Review*, **36**, 4, pp. 417–45.

GINSBURG, M. and TIDWELL, M. (1990) 'Political socialization of prospective educators in Mexico', *New Education*, **12**, 2, pp. 70–82.

GINSBURG, M., WALLACE, G. and MILLER, M. (1988) 'Teachers, Economy and the State', *Teaching and Teacher Education*, **4**, 14, pp. 1–21.

GOODINGS, R., BYRAM, M. and McPARTLAND, M. (Eds) (1982) *Changing Priorities in Teacher Education*, New York, Nichols Publishing Company.

GRACE, G. (1987) 'Teachers and the state in Britain: A changing relation', in LAWN, M. and GRACE, G. (Eds) *Teachers: The Culture and Politics of Work*, London, Falmer Press, pp. 193–228.

GRANT, N. (1982) 'Communist Countries', in GOODINGS, R., BYRAM, M. and McPARTLAND, M. (Eds) *Changing Priorities in Teacher Education*, New York, Nichols Publishing, pp. 44–64.

GREENBERG, E. (1970) *Political Socialization*, New York, Atherton.

GUMBERT, E. (1990) *Fit to Teach: Teacher Education in International Perspective*, Atlanta, GA, Center for Cross-Cultural Studies, Georgia State University.

HIRSCH, H. (1971) 'Political socialization: Review of the Literature', in HIRSCH, H. *Poverty and Politicization*, New York, The Free Press.

HOLLOWAY, J. and PICCIOTTO, S. (1978) *State and Capital: A Marxist Debate*. London, Edward and Arnold.

HOYLE, E. and MEGARRY, J. (1980) *Professional Development of Teachers: World Yearbook of Education 1980*, New York, Nichols Publishing.

HYMAN, H. (1959) *Political Socialization*, New York, Free Press.

KAVANAGH, D. (1972) *Political Culture*, London, Macmillan.

KING, E. (1970) *The Education of Teachers*, London, Bartholomew Press.

KREISBERG, S. (1992) *Transforming Power*, Albany, NY, State University of New York Press.

LANGTON, K. (1969) *Political Socialization*, Boston, MA, Little Brown.

LASSWELL, H. (1977) *On Political Sociology*, Chicago, IL, University of Chicago Press.

LEAVITT, H. (Ed) (1992) *Issues and Problems in Teacher Education: An International Handbook*, New York, Greenwood Press.

LeCOMPTE, M. and GINSBURG, M. (1987) 'How students learn to be teachers: An exploration of alternative responses to a teacher training program', in NOBLIT, G. and PINK, W. (Eds) *Schooling in Social Context*, Norwood, NJ, Ablex, pp. 3–22.

LINDSAY, B. (1990) 'Comparative teacher education: Illustrations from English speaking countries', in HOUSTON, W.R. (Ed) *Handbook of Research on Teacher Education*, New York, Macmillan, pp. 858–76.

LOMAX, D. (1976) *European Perspectives in Teacher Education*, New York, Wiley.

LUKES, S. (1974) *Power: A Radical View*, London, British Sociological Association.

LYNCH, J. and PLUNKETT, H. (1973) *Teacher Education and Cultural Change*, London, Allen and Unwin.

McCLENNAN, G. (1984) *State and Society in Contemporary Britain*, Cambridge, Polity Press.

OFFE, C. and RONGE, V. (1981) 'Theses on the theory of the state', in DALE, R. ESLAND, G. FERGUSON, R. and MacDONALD, M. (Eds) *Education and the State: Volume 1, Schooling and the National Interest*, Sussex, Open University Press, pp. 77–86.

OLESON, V. and WHITTAKER, E. (1968) *The Silent Dialogue*, San Francisco, CA, Jossey-Bass.

POPKEWITZ, T. (1987) (Ed) *Critical Studies in Teacher Education*, New York, Falmer Press.

POPKEWITZ, T. (1992) (Ed) *Changing Patterns of Power: Social Regulation and Teacher Education Reform*, Albany, NY, State University of New York Press.

REINHARZ, S. (1979) *On Becoming a Social Scientist*, San Francisco, CA, Jossey-Bass.

SEARS, D. (1991) 'Whither political socialization Research? The question of persistence', in ICHILOV, O. (Ed) *Political Socialization, Citizenship, and Democracy*, New York, Teachers College Press, pp. 69–97.

SHARPES, D. (Ed) (1988) *International Perspectives on Teacher Education*, New York, Routledge.

SIEGEL, R. (1965) 'Assumptions about the learning of political values', *Annals of the American Academy of Social and Political Science*, **165**, pp. 1–9.

SIMON, R. (1991) *Gramsci's Political Thought: An Introduction*, London, Lawrence and Wishart.

SINGER, G. (1965) *Teacher Education in a Communist State: Poland 1956–1961*, New York, Bookman Associates.

STROMNES, A. (1976) 'The education of teachers in Norway', in LOMAX, D. (Ed) *European Perspectives in Teacher Education*, London: John Wiley and Sons.

TISHER, R. and WIDEEN, M. (Ed) (1990) *Research in Teacher Education: International Perspectives*, London, Falmer Press.

UNESCO (1982) *Social Change and the Training of Educational Personnel*, Bangkok, UNESCO Regional Office for Education in Asia and the Pacific.

URRY, J. (1981) *The Anatomy of Capitalist Societies*, London, Macmillan.

WEILER, K. (1989) 'Women's history and the history of women teachers', *Journal of Education*, **171**, 1, pp. 9–30.

WRONG, D. (1962) 'The over-socialized conception of man', *American Sociological Review*, **26**, 2, pp. 183–93.

YANG, Z., LIN, B. and SU, W. (1986) *Teacher Education in the People's Republic of China*, Beijing, Beijing Normal University Press.

ZEICHNER, K. and GORE, J. (1990) 'Teacher socialization', in HOUSTON, W.R. (Ed) *Handbook of Research on Teacher Education*, London, Macmillan, pp. 329–48.

Part 2

Teacher Education Policy Formation

Chapter 2

Teacher Education Policy in England

Maeve Landman and Jenny Ozga

This chapter attempts to cover a great deal of ground, as the struggle over the form and content of teacher education has been prolonged and bitter in England. This conflict forms part of an extended war of position concerning the control of teacher education and training within the context of the larger issue of control and definition of teaching and the teacher's role. We feel that this larger issue as well needs to be set within the context of the general political and policy climate in England, which has experienced 15 years (1979–94) of ideologically-driven policy making. The intention of those policies has been to destroy the public sector bureaucracies established by post-war legislation in England to provide education, health, civil and other services on the basis of entitlement (Pollitt 1992). These bureaucracies are believed by the New Right in England, as elsewhere, to operate in the interests of the public servants who work in them (the providers), rather than in the interests of their 'clients'. From this perspective, it was, therefore, necessary to break up these malign, inefficient state bureaucracies, and to challenge the authority and monopoly powers of the providers.

It is therefore necessary to place the policy issue of teacher education against the larger background. The ideological position of the New Right has had direct policy consequences for teachers and for education generally. In particular, the New Right has guided intervention in a sustained program of legislation designed to erode professional autonomy, to regulate and differentiate the teaching workforce, and to enforce accountability from teachers to parents and local school governors. At the same time, this legislative program has opened up education provision to market forces by creating artificial competition among schools for pupils, who carry cost value to the school at point of entry. Marketization of education has been pursued through the creation of different types of provision, from which clients are 'free' to choose. Marketization is also, of course, heavily implicated in the deprofessionalization process, as it privileges clients at the expense of providers (i.e. teachers), increases pressure on teachers to perform well according to simplistic performance measures (examination scores are published as league tables for parents/consumers) and contributes to differentiation, stratification and insecurity in the teaching profession.

Policy in the area of teacher education fits into this picture of deprofessionalization, and within the wider framework of attacking the provider monopoly and of challenging the authority on which its claim to provide services is based. This challenge is fundamental: it concerns the ways in which we understand 'society' and the consequent views we hold regarding state responsibility and citizens'

entitlement. The organization and provision of key services is a profoundly political issue, as is the question of definition and control of the workforce providing
such services. Teachers have always occupied a difficult and ambivalent space
within the bureaucratic model of public sector provision, charged as they are with
allocating life chances, inculcating discipline and preserving tradition, while engaged in activities that encourage criticism of all of these. The space left for
teachers, however, in the new model of market-driven, client-led and state-regulated education provision is not comfortable. We explore the nature of this new
configuration in more detail below, and we discuss the ways in which it is supported by emergent patterns of training.

The Education Policy Context: Market Regulation

England may claim the dubious distinction of leading the world in the scale and
scope of education 'reform', although there is strong competition from New
Zealand (Dale and Ozga 1992) and Australia (Knight *et al*. 1993). For 15 years, the
Conservative government of the United Kingdom has pursued relentlessly a complex and apparently contradictory program of deregulation and central control,
which has affected all areas of education provision. Public sector provision has
been transformed through marketization. Spurred by frustration in attempts at
structural reform, from the late 1980s the speed of change has been accelerated and
the consequences amplified by the use of market forces in education — notably
through the 1988 Education Reform Act, but also in major legislation in 1992 and
1993.

It would be difficult to review comprehensively the extent of the legislation
here. In broad terms, the dismantling of the public sector has been accomplished
by the destruction of sources of power that rival or challenge that of central
government — most significantly through the diminution of the local government of education, and by regulation of the teaching workforce. At the same
time, central government has ensured that the content of education is tightly
prescribed through the national curriculum and its associated program of teacher-
proof assessment.

The operation of the market in education has been accompanied by a reordering of provision and by regulation of curriculum and assessment. Structural changes
are designed to ensure a direct, financial relationship between central government
and schools without any local government mediation. The market is tightly regulated. It is not a means of delivering 'choice and diversity' (Department for Education 1992a), but has been designed to deliver a restricted pattern of provision,
which denies the principle of entitlement and is differentiated and stratified. Markets
in education in England thus serve to reproduce inequalities. By this we mean that
access to choice is restricted; in particular, it is restricted by economic position and
the advantages and disadvantages that brings in relation to academic and future
occupational attainment. Middle-class parents are more often in a position to
choose — and get their children to — distant or inconveniently located schools,
while working-class parents are more likely to be dependent on local provision
that may be reached safely and quickly.[1] Thus the children of middle-class parents
may be more likely to attend grant-maintained (opted-out) schools, whose level

of direct funding by central government has been generous, or the new city technology collges, where, again, the level of resourcing has been high.

The level of resourcing remains high, of course, as attractive schools attract pupils, particularly pupils whose parents are in a position to assist the schools financially. Meanwhile, inner city schools have lost their middle-class parents, and are locked into a spiral of decline associated with declining enrollment and hence income, less successful performance on publicly reported test scores and hence declining enrollment. Moreover, all of this occurs within the context of a reduced capacity for local education authorities to support such schools with financial resources and professional expertise.

The marketization of education in England is significant in its destruction of education as a public service, and the introduction of market forces marks the abandonment of the pursuit of equality of opportunity that was present in the 1944 Act — albeit in the restricted form of 'parity of esteem' for differentiated provision — and that subsequently informed policy for the reorganization of secondary school provision along comprehensive lines in the 1960s. The reestablishment of differentiation and stratification should come as no surprise; patterns of inequality characterize English education and have only been blurred by policy makers' espousal of human capital theory in the 1960s and by the efforts of teachers.

Reforming Tendencies

Do we then see here a coherent policy project, in which the differentiated structures of provision delivered by a steered market are matched by differentiated curricula and a stratified teaching force? Partly, but there are complications. One dimension of complexity is provided by the 'modernizing' tendency of the New Right, who link England's economic decline to the predominance of élitist, academic curricula. The modernizers support changes in curricula and examinations that place much greater emphasis on competences, skills and flexibility. As we will discuss later, in conjunction with this agenda for reform they have taken on the professions and seek to erode the links between higher education and professional training. They wish to establish competency-driven, fragmented and relatively content-free forms of professional training, with a heavy emphasis on process and outcome. The insertion of such a doctrine into training is significant because of the impact that it is thought it will have on the process of schooling.

The modernizers have, however, encountered opposition from those who wish to reassert the primacy of traditional immersion in the revered canon of academic subjects as the informing principle of education (including teacher education). These cultural conservatives associate discipline-based study with moral education, ordered thinking, and the reestablishment of certitude and traditions threatened by progressive education ideologies and cultural diversity. It will be readily apparent that there is some difficulty in reconciling these reforming tendencies. Ostensibly, some resolution may be achieved through separate provision — that is to say, differentiation of the curriculum (in education generally but also in teacher education) — so that traditional academic studies flourish in certain establishments, while others (including the new city technology colleges — see Walford and Miller 1991) produce entrepreneurs, technologists and technicians.

Differentiation between academic and technical studies may also take place within a school, and the recent national curriculum review (Dearing 1994) enables that.

The context is significant, in that developments in teacher education (including initial teacher training) mirror the divisions and debates presented — in crude and summary form — above. It is also a significant ideological battleground for the warring tendencies, as there is an assumption that the model of the teacher placed before pupils will have a marked impact on curriculum choice and on the success or failure of curriculum reform.

Finally, it would be misleading to give the impression of policy for teacher training as emerging from debate between two coherent policy projects struggling for supremacy in the marketized system. The background to the background remains, inevitably, the continuing economic crisis in the United Kingdom; this has persisted, with only temporary indications of weak recovery, and has resulted in very severe constraints on public spending. Scarcity of resources results in targeted provision and supports the case for specialization. The economics of teacher education provide a major factor in the emergence of differentiated, stratified education and training.

Occupational Restructuring

It is important to remember here that the revision of teacher education and training is part of a package aimed at redefining all areas of teachers' work and at restructuring the occupation of teaching. We have indicated the impact of the regulated market on structures of provision, and this was accompanied by a direct attack on organized teachers, heralded by the provocation of a long and bitter pay dispute, and ended by the Secretary of State's imposition of a teachers' contract and the abolition of negotiating rights (see Pietrasik 1987).

The restructuring of the profession has proceeded apace since the Teachers' Pay and Conditions Act (1987) There have been two principal elements to the restructuring: 1) through the use of revised promotion and incentive structures and 2) through the impact of deregulation of employment and devolution of financial management. The first element has been managed through the School Teachers Review Body (STRB), a 'quango' (quasi-autonomous nongovernmental organization) nominated by the Secretary of State for Education that reports directly to him or her while remaining outside the usual mechanisms for public accountability. The STRB has abolished automatic incremental progression in teaching, greatly extended and rewarded management grades, and has attempted to link pay to performance through the introduction of incentive payments, control over which lies effectively with the headteacher (STRB 1993, 1994).

Deregulation constrains union action in defense of employment rights and facilitates redundancy and the use of fixed-term, part-time contracts. Devolution of financial control through local management of schools and grant maintained schools (i.e. schools funded directly by central government and free from local education authority frameworks of planning and financial management) permit employers to vary rates of pay and conditions of employment to suit schools' needs and budgets. All these factors promote managerialism and encourage tractability in the teaching labour force.

The combined effect of these changes is not yet clear. However, historical precedent suggests it may entail strengthened differentiation linked to sector and gender: deskilling of (largely female) primary school teachers, especially teachers of the very young, and increased use of ancillary and auxiliary staff. Overall there is likely to be further simultaneous expansion of management grades, and enhancement of subject status linked to examination performance (the publication of examination grades theoretically permits their use as performance indicators tied to performance pay). The occupational group thus faces the loss of its (often precarious) sense of community and solidarity, and is vulnerable to internal division, to the manipulation of such divisions, and to the erosion of any shared sense of educational mission. Marketization, of course, reinforces these divisive and competitive tendencies.

These changes in the teaching occupation form the context against which we now set out the progress of 'reform' in teacher education and training.

Teacher Education and Training

We said at the outset that education provision in England is characteristically divided, stratified and inequitable, notwithstanding the limited comprehensivization experiment (see Bellaby 1977). Parallel divisions have occurred historically and are currently resurgent in teacher education and training. Essentially, teachers destined for different kinds of school have followed differing training routes, and these differences reflect historically-grounded status divisions that follow from the nature of mass and élite education provision in nineteenth-century England. Mass provision was made by elementary schools that offered a restricted and largely vocational curriculum for pupils up to the age of 14. Secondary provision in grammar schools was available (until 1944) only to those who could pay for it. Elementary schoolteachers were trained in a variety of modes, including the monitorial system — Coleridge's 'vast, moral steam engine' — whereby large numbers of pupils were instructed by one master and a number of unpaid, 11-year-old 'scholar-teachers' (but see Silver 1983, p. 17ff, for an indication of the complexities concealed by this broad summary).

The formal organization of elementary training into college-delivered courses with emphasis on pedagogy and child development accompanied, and may have contributed to, the feminization of this segment of the occupation, particularly in the period after the war of 1914–18 (Grace 1985; Bergen 1987). Elementary training became the fostering of conscious motherhood (Steedman 1985) and was much influenced by the principles of Froebel, Pestalozzi and Montessori (Brehony 1990). Elements of that training reinforced the earlier inculcation of ideas of humility, service and missionary zeal in the elementary teacher.

The separation of training colleges from the rest of higher and further education, and their cloistered nature, reinforced particular characteristics of training; these in turn were strengthened by the increased formal separation of primary (as opposed to elementary) and secondary schooling, following the Hadow Report (Board of Education 1926) and the 1944 Education Act.[2] Inherent in the preparation of primary teachers was a commitment to education as natural development, from which 'child-centred' or 'progressive' primary education evolved, receiving official approval in the Plowden Report (CACE 1967).[3]

It is important to note these points because the permeation of ideas of development and empathy, however imperfectly understood, into teacher educators' 'official' culture had considerable consequences for the nature and status of training. A (heavily gendered) barrier was constructed between primary and secondary teaching and teacher training. As secondary training developed, it was remarkably reliant on discipline immersion and rather limited constructions of teaching 'methods'. Between the two extremes, pedagogy (in the 'science of teaching' denotation of mainland Europe) declined and failed to survive. In political terms, that failure deprived teachers of a powerful discourse with which to defend their professional space and status (Simon 1985).

We have indicated the historical basis of division in routes to teaching, the different status accorded to different routes and their different characteristics. The implications for the current position are developed here. Until relatively recently, the status and gender divisions outlined above remained in place. University departments of education were exclusively concerned with (postgraduate) training for secondary teachers, and primary teachers largely studied for teachers' certificates in training colleges maintained by local authorities or religious foundations. The award of the training certificate for such courses was the responsibility of the Area Training Organization, based in almost all cases in university departments.

The expansion of teacher training in the 1960s brought some blurring of these divisions as certificate courses were lengthened. Following the publication of the James Report (Committee of Enquiry 1972), certificate courses were replaced by three or four-year degree-routes leading to the award of Bachelor of Education (with or without honors) in the drive to produce an all-graduate profession. In the changes that attended this review teacher training colleges became colleges of education, and the nature of provision was broadened to include philosophy, psychology and sociology of education. Incorporation of many colleges of education into the polytechnics produced, in some cases, a powerful combination of liberal education and vocationally-influenced training for undergraduates.[4] Status divisions remained, however, and division generally was increased by the variation in provision. As Whitty et al. (1987) have argued, it is attempting to explain some of the early attempts at the reform of teacher training as motivated by a straightforward desire to tidy up the system. A good deal of messiness remains, however, and in the more recent phases of reform, diversity of routes to training was increased as reformers attempted to diminish the role of higher education by introducing 'licensed' and 'articled' schemes that were largely school-based.

For the purposes of this discussion the main routes into training are as follows: postgraduate and undergraduate. The relevant postgraduate award is the Post-graduate Certificate in Education (PGCE), gained on successful completion of a year's full-time training. It is offered for both primary and secondary level prospective teachers. These courses have been subject to considerable intervention by the Council for the Accreditation of Teacher Education (CATE): in 1984 the teaching year for the PGCE was extended to 36 weeks; in 1992 the period of time spent observing and practice teaching in school was extended to 24 weeks, and schools were given substantial responsibilities for the design and delivery of training, in partnership with higher education institutions. Schools were encouraged to accept these new responsibilities through the transfer of funds from higher education institutions to schools. (We explain the role and status of CATE below.)

The undergraduate routes include obtaining the Bachelor of Education (BEd) degree, which is constructed in a variety of models; some involve discipline/subject-based study concurrently with preparation for teaching; others adopt a consecutive design, with most professional studies following subject study. It is available for primary and secondary training, but the majority of BEd students are intending to be primary teachers.

The BEd may entail study over three or four years, where the final award is an honors degree. In addition, there are a relatively small number of two-year BEd (without honors) awards for intending secondary teachers available to entrants with the equivalent of a year's experience of higher education. These routes were introduced to attract mature entrants to shortage subject areas. In addition to the BEd, a number of higher education institutions (usually traditional university departments of education) have extended their provision into the undergraduate area and offer Bachelor of Arts (BA) or Bachelor of Science (BSc) degrees with qualified teacher status (QTS).

Recent government policy has encouraged a shift of numbers (whose funding and allocation is government controlled) into the PGCE and away from the various undergraduate routes. The reasons for this reflect a conjunction of factors: graduate unemployment, which has boosted applications to teacher training; the speed with which supply can be controlled through the PGCE, rather than the undergraduate programs; and the subject-centredness of the PGCE which makes it more attractive to policy makers than the BEd.

In a circular setting out the parameters of training (discussed below), issued in January 1993, primary training was substantially altered through the duplication of the school-based, subject-centred ethos already promulgated for secondary training in Circular 9/92 (DFE 1992b). In a related policy initiative, the Secretary of State for Education attempted to introduce non-graduate certification for teachers of very young children to follow an apprenticeship mode and recruits were to be drawn from those with experience of children. Fierce opposition to the dilution of the principle of an all-graduate profession led to the withdrawal of that proposal; nevertheless, Circular 14/93 enables the creation of a two-tier system of primary training, and introduces financial penalties for those higher education institutions which persist in offering four-year degrees.

Control Mechanisms: The Creation and Functioning of CATE

Teacher education and training is controlled by the Secretary of State for Education in a number of ways: all of these distinguish preparation for teaching from preparation for other professional and semi-professional occupations, for which political interference is less marked and institutional or occupational autonomy more pronounced.

To teach in the state (public) sector in England it is necessary to have qualified teacher status (QTS). The possession of a degree is not enough; the intending teacher must be a graduate of an accredited course which can confer QTS. Accreditation of courses was, until the time of writing, managed on behalf of the Secretary of State by the Council for the Accreditation of Teacher Education (CATE). The process of accreditation requires institutions to conform to criteria in course content and manner of delivery; course criteria are specified in circulars periodically issued by the Department for Education with explanatory notes from the Council.

Only CATE-accredited courses confer the license to teach (QTS). We shall say something later about recent proposals to dilute the role of higher education in initial education and training and the concomitant growth of flexibility in access to teaching; for the moment we want to examine the role and impact of CATE in relation to the control of teacher education and training.

The first question that requires an answer concerns the need for the establishment of this agency in 1983. What were the Secretary of State's intentions? If we look at the origins of CATE, we need to bear in mind the contextual factors already outlined: diminishing resources, moral panic, growing concern with competition and effectiveness. The moral panic factor is perhaps underplayed in our account so far. The cultural conservatives' agenda for reform was targeted at teachers because they were held to be responsible for falling standards and for an associated decline in moral authority. The publications of various right-wing pressure groups, from the late 1960s onwards, relentlessly attacked teacher trainers' supposed adherence to 'progressive' ideologies and made direct connections between pedagogic practice, family breakdown and rising crime and unemployment (Cox and Dyson 1969; Anderson 1988; Lawlor 1990; O'Hear 1991). In demonizing teachers and teacher-educators, the media played a significant part; isolated incidents were much publicized in a 'discourse of derision' (Ball 1993). It is difficult to convey the full force of these attacks on teachers in England. There were attacks on teachers elsewhere, of course, but in England they were distinguished by their endorsement by policy makers and in their public resonance. The mythology of a well-ordered, hierarchically-ranked society remains strong in the authoritarian populism of post-Thatcherite England.

In attempting to explain the force of the attack on teacher education we are once again obliged to seek illumination from historical precedent. We said at the outset that the nature of teachers' work led inevitably to tensions in their management and control; these tensions have, of course, manifested themselves in teacher selection, recruitment and training. Control of these areas is significant, for obvious reasons. Reform and reorganization of training followed the last great period of expansion and mass provision at the elementary level in the last century and, as indicated above, further adjustments were made during the attempted comprehensivization of secondary schooling and the simultaneous opening up of access to higher education in the 1960s. Latterly, efforts at steerage of the education system through market mechanisms inevitably involve parallel attempts in teacher training, but the particular character of these efforts is shaped by deep concerns about the impact of education, not just on life chances, but on 'common sense' assumptions about society. These attempts at control accompany a predictable moral panic; what is surprising is the crediting of teachers and teacher-educators with such significant transformative capacities. Indeed, the extent of the attack on teachers supports the arguments developed elsewhere that teachers constitute a 'social danger' by virtue of their work (see Lawn and Ozga 1986; Ozga 1990).

Some of the force of the attack is explained by the convenience and facility with which teacher-educators are scapegoated. The deficiencies of British business and industry are more comfortably attributed to inadequate and inappropriate teaching — ascribed to incoherent or subversive training — than to chronic failure to invest or to recognize the shift of economic growth to the Pacific Rim. Conservative politicians cannot, because of their reliance on the constituencies of business and industry, readily impute blame directly to the failure of the established church, nor to inadequate parenting and diminished family values (while these are lamented, education remains somehow primarily implicated). Teacher-educators are an isolated and relatively powerless community; popular and popu-list thinking recognizes no clear claim to expert status, and universities remain equivocal about their education departments. We are, then, an easy target, with no friends at court.

We cannot here explore the extent to which the demonizing of teacher-educators as left-wing ideologues, subverting the social order through infiltration of the education system, has any factual basis; nor is such an exploration relevant to the matter in hand. There is, however, no evidence that unfashionable Marxist meta-narratives are taught as catechism to intending teachers. On the contrary; it is worth pointing out that a very significant proportion of intending primary teachers are trained in colleges supported by church trusts and foundations, and that university departments of education are rather conservative in character and somewhat restricted in the connections they make to critical social theory.

This, then, gives something of the context in which CATE came into exist-ence in 1984; the immediate reason for its establishment may be traced to the inspection visits that led to a report of Her Majesty's Inspectors (HMI) on the efficacy of teacher training as judged by assessment of the performance of newly qualified teachers (Her Majesty's Inspectors, 1987). Although the report was not published until 1987, discussion of evidence from inspection visits apparently identified a number of areas of concern, notably in relation to the quality of subject studies elements of undergraduate degrees, and signaled other issues that were to become themes of the 1980s, namely concern about practical training and the balance of 'theory' and 'practice', and support for longer training periods in schools (Macintyre 1991). The new system of accreditation established by the Secretary of State was put into effect through Circular 3/84 (DES 1984), which specified in some detail the criteria that had to be met before courses could be accredited.

Accreditation procedures began with an extended institutional visit by HMI who then produced a published report. These reports were intended to provide data for CATE, and the senior chief inspector for teacher education acted as an assessor for CATE. Further information was requested from institutions on stand-ardized 'Cateforms', which required them to set out details of how their courses met the Secretary of State's criteria. In the first phase of CATE's operations, the accreditation procedure required senior staff from the higher education institution seeking accreditation to meet a CATE panel in order to discuss or defend their provision. CATE would then send the institution a letter indicating the advice that it would offer to the Secretary of State in relation to accreditation-worthiness. The Secretary of State held the authority to accredit courses, or to refuse accredi-tation and hence authority to confer QTS.

In its later manifestation, CATE procedures required more extensive docu-mentation and the interview at CATE headquarters (which, for most of CATE's life, was located within the Department of Education) was replaced by local com-mittee discussion. CATE local committees included in their membership indus-trialists as well as local teachers and representatives from higher education institutions. The local committee made a recommendation to the central Council, but such recommendations were not binding; moreover, there is anecdotal evi-dence to suggest that particular institutions were favoured with close attention by some members of the Council.

Table 2.1: CATE Objectives for Teachers' Classroom Mangagement Skills

Circular 24/89, paragraph 9	Circular 9/92, paragraph 2
Students should learn the importance of classroom management and different models of classroom organization. Students should be able, on completion of the course, to: • manage children individually, in groups and as a whole class so that work is carried out in a responsible and orderly manner; • differentiate work according to the range of abilities and attainments within a given teaching group or class; • employ a range of teaching methods appropriate to a whole class, groups or individuals; • match teaching methods to learning activity and pay due attention to pace; • establish good working relationships with classes and individual pupils; • communicate clearly and intelligently with pupils orally and in writing; and • evaluate the effectiveness of their teaching in the light of pupils' responses and make appropriate adjustments.	2.4 Newly qualified teachers should be able to: 2.4.1 decide when teaching the whole class, groups, pairs or individuals is appropriate for particular learning purposes; 2.4.2 create and maintain a purposeful and orderly environment for the pupils; 2.4.3 devise and use appropriate rewards and sanctions to maintain an effective learning environment; 2.4.4 maintain pupils' interest and motivation.

Sources: DES 1989; DFE 1992b

This description of CATE's procedures illustrates its bureaucratic, regulatory mode. The circulars are all substantial documents, the criteria referred to is lengthy and detailed, and further elaborated in notes of guidance. In Table 2.1 we present excerpts concerning classroom management to illustrate both the bureaucratic, regulatory nature of the CATE objectives and the shift from the open-ended requirements of Circular 24/89 (DES 1989) to the rather more technical competences of Circular 9/92 (DFE 1992b).

Circular 24/89 was not greeted with enthusiasm by teacher-educators, and there were particularly adverse reactions to the emphasis on subject studies. There was, however, considerable room for negotiation and interpretation within the criteria (Whitty *et al.* 1987) and it was possible to sustain and develop a sophisticated model of the teacher while adhering to the specific criteria. The circular did not entirely remove the teacher from the social context, but provided some recognition of diversity and some recognition of education's role in the challenging of stereotype and prejudice. Paragraph 6.3 of Circular 24/89 (DES 1989) illustrates this:

Courses should prepare students for teaching the full range of pupils and for the diversity of ability, behaviour, social background and ethnic and cultural origin they are likely to encounter among pupils in ordinary schools. On completion of their course, students should have developed:

i　an understanding of the different ways in which pupils develop and learn and the ways in which pupils' work can be planned to secure clear progression;

ii　the ability to set appropriate objectives for their teaching and their pupils' learning;

iii　the capacity to use a range of teaching methods appropriate to the different abilities and other needs of pupils and organise their work accordingly;

iv　the capacity to identify gifted pupils and pupils with special educational needs or with learning difficulties; and to understand the ways in which the potential of such pupils can be developed;

v　skills in the evaluation and recording of pupil performance, including in particular the testing and assessment requirement related to the National Curriculum and, where relevant, the preparation of pupils for public examinations.

Students should learn to guard against preconceptions based on the race, gender, religion or other attributes of pupils and understand the need to promote equal opportunities.

We include such examples not to provide a thorough treatment of the content of CATE-regulated training programmes (see Barton *et al.* 1992) — we cannot sensibly do that in this space, nor do we assume that such detailed content is of interest to an international audience — but to illustrate the complexity of reform. By this we mean that there are two aspects of interest here that have wider applicability in understanding the control of teacher training. First, it is apparent that CATE accepted the location of teaching in social contexts and social relations, despite the rather artificial divisions of criteria into those covering 'subject studies', 'subject application' and 'educational and professional studies'. CATE did not produce a new guide to the official model of a good teacher, but there was a good deal of implicit support for the development of a positive and autonomous model of professional practice. It was up to the teacher-educators to write the framework and construct the connections; some did, though others expended their energies on resisting central control. It was a critical moment in the history of this engagement, but for many it was a missed opportunity.

Second, there is the question of intentionality in the particular practices and procedures adopted by CATE. The bureaucratic, regulatory mechanism produced large quantities of paper and some specific shifts (for example, in the employment by higher education institutions of schoolteachers with recent and relevant experience). There was, however, no necessary connection between the regulations and the practice in the higher education institutions. Many institutional managers were preoccupied with CATE and with ensuring compliance with the criteria, as far as that could be established and monitored. The inspection process increased pressures for compliance, but it was difficult for the centralized system, even in its devolved form, to monitor practice effectively. This was not a system that won hearts and minds. It produced change without innovation, compliance without consent.

Because of the practical limits on CATE's capacity to intervene, two things happened. Good provision of teacher education remained relatively unchanged, as institutions with a clear view of the nature of training and their role in it adjusted to the criteria but maintained their own models of training and of professional practice. The obverse of this was that bad practice also remained relatively un-affected and, indeed, the separation of elements of secondary training may even have exacerbated the isolation of 'methods' and further relieved teacher trainers of the responsibility to engage with the nature of teaching as a societal function.

The Demise of CATE

These strategies were not sufficient to appease the reformers, particularly mem-bers of the influential Centre for Policy Studies. There were indications of tension within CATE, and the pressure increased with the appointment of a long-stand-ing opponent of training, Professor Anthony O'Hear, to membership of the Council in 1989. Policy makers seem to have concluded that CATE was a victim of provider capture — the attack on educators (and, as discussed above, other social service providers) because of the perception that they had captured control over policy making in the field in which they worked — and it is interesting to specu-late on the extent to which their perceptions were accurate. The two major circulars, quoted above, indicate a substantial shift in the direction of reform, and Circular 9/92 (DFE 1992b) was certainly considerably more difficult for teacher trainers to absorb than Circular 24/89 (DES 1989). The context had changed, too. At this time the Secretary of State was a high-profile politician who had already taken on the health service professions. Concern about the costs of the massive expansion of higher education was beginning to be expressed, and public sector borrowing was much reduced. Her Majesty's Inspectorate had been reorganized into the Office for Standards in Education and key civil service personnel with long asso-ciations with teacher training were moved to different areas.

On the face of it, Circular 9/92 (DFE 1992b) shifted the balance of control in training very sharply towards the Council and away from the higher education institutions. The main mechanisms were funding and the requirement that schools play a 'lead role' in training. Other significant shifts indicated by this circular were the reinforcement of the central importance of subject specialism and the construc-tion of the criteria for entry to teaching in terms of competences. The first para-graph of Circular 9/92 (DFE 1992b) conveys the tone and emphasis:

1 Aim of Initial Teacher Training
   1.1 All newly qualified teachers entering maintained schools should have achieved the levels of knowledge and standards of professional com-petence necessary to maintain and improve standards in schools.
   1.2 The planning and management of training course should be the shared responsibility of higher education institutions and schools in partnership.

In many ways the document expresses the determination to locate professional training for teachers within a competence-driven mode and to place the control of that program within the schools and outside higher education. There is also a strong assertion of the centrality of preparation to teach the national curriculum, and a consequent erosion of a focus on the social context of teaching and the teacher's role.

Teacher educators greeted the Circular 9/92 (DFE 1992b) with hostility, though opposition had been drawn by the more extreme proposals of the 'consultation document' which preceded it. Yet even here there is room for constructive interpretation, and some substantial elements of the circular provide a necessary impetus to progressive training practice. This is apparent in the dimension of partnership, for example. The circular expresses a limited and bureaucratic version, with the emphasis on time in school and transfer of resources. That limited version of partnership is open to development by higher education institutions. In particular, the concept of partnership in training requires clarification of roles and has potentially exciting and progressive consequences for developments in pedagogy. Some higher education institutions have recognized this and have moved into proactive developments with schools, devising models of practice that extend well beyond initial training and with productive consequences for continuous professional development and research. At the other extreme, some providers have handed over the cash and delivered the redundancy notices. Once again it is difficult to avoid the feeling that the message of real reform, concealed within the destructive agenda of the government, has been heard too late.

After CATE: The Emergence of the TTA

The system of bureaucratic regulation finally broke down over the issue of training for primary teachers. The government and its advisors wished to extend the school-based model to primary training, and to change the nature of primary teaching by introducing greater subject specialization into the upper classes of the primary school. This is a departure from the convention of the class teacher as generalist, teaching across the range of subjects that constituted the curriculum. There are strongly held views about the appropriate design of primary teacher training, and some well-established difficulties with the conventional model, particularly since the introduction of the national curriculum (with the passage of the Education Reform Act 1988). There is, however, a dearth of research on primary teaching, and there has been little debate; the policy direction stems from the cultural conservatives' adherence to a particular model of teaching and from the desire to reduce costs by importing non-graduates into schools to train in an apprenticeship mode and to take responsibility for the early years of schooling.

This controversial proposal was floated by the Secretary of State without reference to CATE and, as indicated earlier, although it has been formally abandoned in the face of strong opposition from teachers, it was followed by modifications to the funding and design of primary training that allow for two tiers of teaching staff in primary schools, spelt out in Circular 14/93 (DFE 1993). Simultaneous initiatives encourage the use of ancillary staff in roles conventionally sustained by teachers. Earlier we referred to the growth of flexibility in access to teaching; it is clear that this flexibility is achieved through the erosion of the linkage of QTS and graduate status, and should be read as part of the attack upon teachers' occupational solidarity and status.

The latest proposals for 'reform' were implemented through Circular 14/93 (DFE 1993), which also announced the demise of CATE, the suspension of the current system of accreditation and the intention to legislate to establish a new quango (quasi-autonomous non-governmental organization) to fund teacher training. As we write in May 1994, the Bill to establish a Teacher Training Agency (TTA) is proceeding through parliament. Its progress has not been smooth, and part of the proposal has been defeated. It was the government's intention to give the TTA responsibility for funding the main element of educational research, thus separating that research from teaching and from the rest of the academic research community, who are funded through the Higher Education Funding Council for England. The defeat of this proposal is encouraging, but the defense of teacher education as an integral part of higher education has commanded less support, and the Secretary of State has insisted on schools' right to devise training schemes, and to purchase higher education institutions' services to support them as they see fit.

The TTA looks set to take responsibility for allocating funds to teacher training courses, and for funding in-service training. It is very likely that this new quango, whose membership would be appointed by the Secretary of State, will favor the allocation of places and funds to school-based schemes. We cannot predict what will happen, and the account so far indicates the confusion and vulnerability of the higher education institutions and the contradictory agendas of the different reforming tendencies. It is possible that competency-driven models will take priority in low-status schooling, and that apprenticeship modes will reemerge in primary schools and in vocational training.

What we have not discussed is the response of schools to policy that encourages their involvement in teacher training. Obviously, the transfer of funds (or direct allocations by the TTA) is a powerful incentive, but there are competing imperatives, not least the primary function of educating children.

Conclusions

The preceding pages tell the story of attempted control and regulation of a divided, untidy and increasingly demoralized training system. The narrative concludes with the assertion of control through a strengthened regulatory mechanism tied to funding. The TTA will, presumably, avoid 'provider capture' because its membership will exclude higher education-based providers and it will shift funding into training schemes managed by schools. Higher education will still have a part to play while the currency of graduate status remains strong, but the erosion of that status is very probable in primary teaching.

The weapon of financial control is already having an effect as higher education institutions transfer resources to schools — in future from their own core funding — to accompany the shift in responsibilities. Many departments/faculties/schools of education are cutting back on staff, and the situation is likely to worsen as funding for higher education generally contracts. Institutions without strong research funding, and those with expensive four year degree programs, will be particularly hard-hit, losing up to 25 percent of their income in some calculations. There is a strong temptation for university managements to cut their losses and abandon an area that causes very considerable planning difficulties, and which is located insecurely (at least in the traditional universities) where education studies have little academic kudos.

The story above has compressed complicated events into a brief exposition;

we need to take stock here of what this story means for its subjects, and what it tells us about teacher training and about education policy. There are some very interesting aspects of these developments, and here we only begin to uncover a selection. Nevertheless, relating the stark narrative carries with it clear signals of the need to learn from the account, while acknowledging the strength of ideologically-driven policy in contributing to demoralization and disengagement. It is evident that teacher education is a significant policy issue, and that, despite considerable activity aimed at regulation and control, there is still — to put it in negative terms — messiness in relation to recruitment and training. At best, that messiness may be reinterpreted as indicative of resistance to regulation, and of adherence to a model of teacher education that is not reducible to competences or academic subject study.

Direct prescription of content and mode is an inefficient and ineffective policy mechanism, as the national curriculum review concedes. Teacher education and training is vulnerable to the combined effects of financial stringency, devolution of budgetary control to individual schools and enhanced managerialism, and these factors may succeed where prescription failed, expressing as they do the pressure for economy and flexibility in the workforce. This analysis supports approaches to the study of education policy making which give appropriate attention to the contradictory demands on state systems — demands which may briefly be summarized as legitimatory, political and economic (Dale and Ozga 1990).

As well as providing an account of policy making, its intentions and its contradictions, this story operates to expose the deficiencies of teacher education — all its historically-located ambivalence and division, its lack of critical engagement with its own history and development, its failure to provide alternative or extended versions of the official, decontextualized 'good teacher'. Blaming the victim is all too easy, particularly for those, like ourselves, angered and exhausted by efforts to revive professional self-esteem and move it into new modes and definitions in the face of external threat and internal conservatism and failure of nerve.

We hope that we are not merely expressing our frustration; rather, we believe that we are identifying weakness, and some of its causes. There are salutary lessons to be learned about gender and status divisions, and about the need to reconstruct teacher education (and the nature and practice of education studies that encompass and define teacher education). How that could be done is the subject of a further paper; our intention here is to raise for consideration the extent to which we have connived in our own diminishing, and to encourage continued engagement with partnership and pedagogy as vehicles for progressive reform from within.

It may be difficult to identify ways of fostering that continued engagement against a policy context as bleak as the one depicted here. However, we believe that considerable progress may be made by recognizing the extent to which teachers present a policy problem for any system, and by understanding the limited strategies available for their management. At the moment we are in a period of direct rule and regulation, and reform of training is part of that. If we are alert to what is being attempted, particularly through occupational restructuring, we may do our best to work against it. We may do this by avoiding activity that legitimates deskilling — for example, by providing university recognition of shortened and restricted certification programs for teaching assistants. We may also foster genuine partnerships in training with our colleagues in schools, and take the opportunities there to strengthen and sustain a shared occupational culture, so that teachers feel committed to, empowered by, and part of university life. Finally, we need to develop a language — a pedagogic discourse — that enables us to articulate the practice-based expertise that we possess, to link it to theory and to research, and use it to defend what we do. Our colleagues in schools have shown us that non-cooperation (with the national curriculum in its original form) can lead to review and (some) accommodation by the state to professional concerns. If we can win schoolteachers' support, a similar outcome could follow in teacher education. But we will have to work for it, and the narrative we have unfolded is one of the lessons *not* learned from history.

Notes

1 The upper class has tended historically, and continues today, to send their offspring to élite private schools.
2 Prior to the 1944 Education Act elementary and secondary education constituted 'two separate overlapping and contradictory systems primarily for the working class and middle class, respectively' (Ginsburg and Sands 1985, p. 116). Among other things the 1944 Education Act created an articulated system, involving primary, secondary and further/higher education.
3 See Steedman (1985), Brehony (1990) and Alexander (1994) for discussion of the informing principles of 'progressivism' and for assessment of the extent of its impact on teaching.
4 Because of student demand and faculty preference, polytechnics developed a strong liberal arts curriculum, including diploma and degree programs in arts and sciences disciplines.

References

ALEXANDER, R. (1994) *Innocence and Experience: Reconstructing Primary Education*, Stoke-one Trent, ASPE/Trentham Books.

ANDERSON, D. (Ed) (1988) *Full Circle: Bringing Up Children in the Post-permissive Society*, London, Social Affairs Unit.

BALL, S. (1993) 'Policy, Power Relations and Teachers' Work', paper presented to British Educational Management and Administration Society (BEMAS) Conference, Liverpool, 17 April.

BARTON, L., POLLARD, A. and WHITTY, G. (1992) 'Experiencing CATE: The impact of accreditation upon initial training institutions in England', *Journal of Education for Teaching*, **18**, 1, pp. 37–45.

BELLABY, P. (1977) *The Sociology of Comprehensive Schooling*, London, Methuen.

BERGEN, B. (1987) 'Only a schoolmaster', in OZGA, J. (Ed) *Schoolwork: Approaches to the Labour Process of Teaching*, Milton Keynes, Open University Press, pp. 48–68.

BREHONY, K. (1990) 'Neither rhyme nor reason: Primary schooling and the National Curriculum', in FLUDE, M. and HAMMERSLEY, M. (Eds) *The Education Reform Act 1988*, London, Falmer Press, pp. 107–38.

CENTRAL ADVISORY COUNCIL FOR EDUCATION (CACE) (1967) *Children and their Primary Schools* (The Plowden Report), London, HMSO.

COMMITTEE OF ENQUIRY INTO THE ARRANGEMENTS FOR THE EDUCATION, TRAINING AND PROBATION OF TEACHERS (1972) *Teacher Education and Training* (The James Report), London, HMSO.

Cox, C. and Dyson, A. (1969) *Fight for Education: A Black Paper*, London, Critical Quarterly Society.

Dale, R. and Ozga, J. (1990) *Understanding Education Policy* (Module 1. of E333, Policy-making in Education) Milton Keynes, Open University.

Dale, R. and Ozga, J. (1992) 'Two hemispheres: Both new right?', in Lingard, B. Knight, J. and Porter P. (Eds) *Schooling Reform in Hard Times*, London, Falmer Press.

Dearing, R. (1994) *The National Curriculum and its Assessment: Final Report*, London, SCAA.

Department for Education (DFE) (1992a) *Choice and Diversity: A White Paper*, London, HMSO.

Department for Education (DFE) (1992b) *Initial Teacher Training (Secondary Phase): Circular 9/92*, London, DFE.

Department for Education (DFE) (1993) *Initial Teacher Training (Primary Phase): Circular 14/93*, London, DFE.

Department of Education and Science (DES) (1984) *Initial Teacher Training: Approval of Courses, Cmnd 8836, Circular 3/84*, London, DES.

Department of Education and Science (DES) (1989) *Initial Teacher Training: Approval of Courses, Circular 24/89*, London, DES.

Ginsburg, M. and Sands, J. (1985) 'Black and brown under the White Capitalist English Crown', in Hawkins, J. and La Belle, T. (Eds) *Education and Intergroup Relations: An International Perspective*, New York, Praeger, pp. 109–38.

Grace, G. (1985) 'Judging teachers: The social and political contexts of teacher evaluation', *British Journal of the Sociology of Education*, **6**, 1, pp. 3–16.

Her Majesty's Inspectorate (1987) *Quality in Schools: The Initial Training of Teachers*, London, HMSO.

Knight, J., Bartlett, L. and McWilliam, E. (Eds) (1993) *Unfinished Business: Reshaping the Teacher Education Industry for the 1990s*, Rockhampton, University of Central Queensland.

Lawlor, S. (1990) *Teachers Mistaught*, London, Centre for Policy Studies.

Lawn, M. and Ozga, J. (1986) 'Unequal partners: Teachers under indirect rule', *British Journal of the Sociology of Education*, **7**, 2, pp. 225–39.

MacIntyre, G. (1991) *Accreditation of Teacher Education: The Story of CATE*, London, Falmer Press.

O'Hear, A. (1991) *Education and Democracy*, Frome, Short Run Press.

Ozga, J. (1990) 'A Social Danger: The contested history of teacher-state relations', in Cott, H. and Jamieson, L. (Eds) *The State, Private Life and Political Change*, Edinburgh, Macmillan, pp. 189–203.

Pietrasik, R. (1987) 'The teachers' action 1984–86', in Lawn, M. and Grace, G. (Eds) *Teachers: The Culture and Politics of Work*, London, Falmer Press, pp. 168–89.

Pollitt, C. (1992) *Managerialism and the Public Services*, (2nd edn), Oxford, Basil Blackwell.

School Teachers Review Body (STRB) (1993) *Second Report*, London, HMSO.

School Teachers Review Body (STRB) (1994) *Third Report*, London, HMSO.

Silver, H. (1983) *Education as History*, London, Methuen.

Simon, B. (1985) *Does Education Matter?*, London, Lawrence and Wishart.

Steedman, C. (1985) 'Prisonhouses', in Lawn, M. and Grace, G. (Eds) *Teachers: The Culture and Politics of Work*, London, Falmer Press, pp. 117–29.

Walford, G. and Miller, H. (1991) *City Technology College*, Milton Keynes, Open University Press.

Whitty, G., Barton, L. and Pollard, A. (1987) 'Ideology and control in teacher education: A review of recent experience in England', in Popkewitz, T. (Ed) *Critical Studiesw in Teacher Education: Its Folklore, Theory and Practice*, London, Falmer Press.

Chapter 3

Politics of Teacher Education in New South Wales, Australia[1]

Christine E. Deer, Susan Groundwater-Smith, Robert Meyenn and Judith Parker

Critical to an understanding of the politics of education in Australia is an explication of the structural features of the governance of education at the federal and state/territory levels.[2] The federal ministry responsible for the management of education nationally is the Department of Education, Employment and Training (DEET). Closely linked to the ministry is an advisory structure, the National Board of Employment, Education and Training (NBEET) with associated councils servicing higher education, research, schools and training (Marginson 1993). While much of the governing policy is formulated at the federal level the practical concerns of delivery are the responsibilities of the states. Each has its own ministry of education which may be linked to other portfolios. For example, in New South Wales (NSW), the relevant ministry is Education, and Youth Affairs. Currently at the federal level in Australia, the Labor Party is in power although in its 12-year rule it has become increasingly 'conservative' in nature. In NSW, the Liberal/National Party Coalition is in power, and just as the Labor Party has moved to the right so too has the Liberal/National Coalition.

In the public school sector, the employment of teachers, the curriculum and assessment practices, and the allocation of resources are all matters for the state. However, at the state level, there are both government and non-government schools. Public schools receive about 90 percent of their funding from the state, while nearly half of the funding for the non-government schools (private and Catholic system) comes from the federal government (Burke 1992).

So it may be seen that teacher education sits in an interesting, some might even argue, ambiguous position. Teacher education occurs in the higher education sector and is therefore subject to the determinations of DEET. However, those taking teacher education courses will ultimately be employed by state authorities (both government and non-government) who clearly perceive that they have a stake in the teacher education curriculum. For this reason we argue that it is necessary to have an understanding of the political forces being exerted by both federal and state governments (see also Groundwater-Smith *et al.* 1992).

To understand recent changes that have occurred in government thinking regarding education at the federal level, it is helpful to look at the naming of the ministry itself. It is not by chance that the 'mega' ministry, established in July 1987, was called the Department of Employment, Education and Training. The ministry is a prototype of the ways in which notions of economic and human capital are brought together. The topic, employment, is brought into conjunction with the agencies, education and training, with the aim being the improvement of Australian competitiveness in international markets. Categorization, that is 'what goes with what', is not something to be taken lightly. An understanding of how we categorize is central to an understanding of how we function (Lakoff 1987).

It is helpful to consider each component: employment, education and training as a set, or domain, which intersects and interacts with the other two. Thus when we examine the recent changes that have occurred in each domain we can see that they immediately affect and act upon the other two domains. Employment became the site for major initiatives in micro-economic reform in Australia from the mid-1980s. The Hawke Labor government, which came into power in 1983, undertook as a result of an accord between itself, unions and employers, to reform and restructure work practices and conditions of employment. Peak bodies such as the Australian Council of Trade Unions (ACTU) and the Business Council of Australia (BCA) were the key players in this process. There were consequences for education in a number of ways. Education itself was an industry which would be examined in terms of structural efficiency, while at the same time it was also the means whereby the knowledge, skills and attitudes of the potential work force were to be developed.

Similarly, training was also perceived to be fundamental to the process of award restructuring, that is the conditions under which workers were to be classified and paid, based on the assumption that improved skills would lead to higher productivity and greater international competitiveness. Major work was undertaken to review and revise work competencies in order that more systematic training and retraining could occur. A National Training Board was established to prepare competency standards in each industry. It is interesting to note that the metals industry, with its orientation towards the production of goods, was to be the exemplary industry. Some have argued that the intended competency frameworks were not as appropriate to service 'industries' such as education and health (Ashenden 1990).

It was via the competency debate that a closer nexus was forged between federal and state authorities with respect to the senior years of schooling. In 1990 the Commonwealth and State Ministers of Education meeting as the Australian Education Council (normally a somewhat contentious and divisive forum) established a committee to make recommendations on the education and training needs of those engaged in the post-compulsory years of schooling. The committee chair was an executive of a large multinational corporation and members of the ACTU were highly influential in its deliberations (Marginson 1993, pp. 156–7). A major outcome of the committee's work was the identification of key areas of competence essential for the employability of young people.[3]

Just as the economic discourses were paramount at the federal level, so too were they being played out at the level of the states. Changes to school education were designed to make the schools themselves more efficient, both in terms of the 'delivery' of education to the 'consumers' and in the ways in which they were managed such that they would be less costly to the state (Meyenn and Parker 1991, 1992.). The most important stake holders were seen to be employers who would find the 'products' of the school assembly lines attractive and well able to meet their needs and demands. Spiritual, interpersonal, ethical and aesthetic goals were no longer to have the primacy that many advocates for a democratic society believed they deserved (Collins 1991).

Reforms and restructuring in school education in New South Wales follow a pattern which is closely mirrored in other Australian states and is reflective of international trends. While there was to be a major shift from the center, with its historically top-heavy bureaucracy, to the schools in terms of school management, there was at the same time a more centralist policy in regard to curriculum and assessment. A review of school management, undertaken by a leading business man and known as the Scott Report (1990), resulted in devolution to schools of decisions regarding the ways in which they might manage their material and human resources (although a number of caveats still existed, particularly those related to class size). At the same time, a further wide ranging review of schooling processes, from early childhood to postcompulsory schooling was conducted by a former senior conservative politician, Sir John Carrick (1989). Following Carrick's recommendations, legislation was prepared which established an independent Board of Studies charged with the development of syllabuses in the designated key learning areas.

The twin tendencies of devolution and centralism are not as contradictory as they first appear. On the one hand, schools can apparently become more efficient users of their discretionary funds (which are effectively quite small once the salaries' bill has been met), while, on the other hand, the state can regain control over the purposes of schooling which were becoming increasingly pluralistic when school-based curriculum development was in the ascendancy.

The most recent debate in schooling in Australia is one that is as yet unresolved and that is the extent to which the states should cooperate in the formulation of a truly national curriculum. Increasingly, states are aligning their syllabuses with national frameworks and benchmarks. There is an emphasis upon outcomes that have attached to them behavioral descriptors indicating levels of achievement. Behind these ongoing changes (which may or may not be reforms — a word that connotes improvement) is an agenda associated with teacher accountability. In NSW state-wide testing has been introduced in an attempt to monitor the achievement of aspects of literacy and numeracy. While at present there can be no league table reporting of results, there are increasing concerns that the mechanisms are now in place which would allow such procedures.

Accountability and structural efficiency go hand in hand. Both lie at the heart of policy changes, in relation to education, by federal and state governments. The emphasis on all levels is subject to what Yeatman (1991) has called 'metapolicy' status. In other words, the overarching discourses of economic rationalism with their emphases upon economic policies, human capital and commodity production are now driving debates about the conduct of education. As Marginson (1993, p. 56) puts it: 'Education is now seen as a branch of economic policy rather than a mix of social, economic and cultural policy.'

Actions and Consequences

Whether we are concerned with the school sector, the training sector or the higher education sector, the features of policy formulation spelled out here have profound implications for teacher-educators. In this section we shall look more closely at the consequences of government policies, both federal and state, and the actions that have been taken by teacher-educators.

Organization of Teacher Education Prior to 1987

As has been outlined, political forces from both the state and national level affect teacher education. Until 1989, higher education in Australia took place in three types of institutions: the Universities, the Colleges of Advanced Education (CAEs) and the Technical and Further Education (TAFE) colleges. The first of these, the universities, were federally funded for both teaching and research at undergraduate and postgraduate levels. The CAEs were also federally funded (but not for research) and on the whole did not have students studying for higher degrees. In addition, they had grown from teachers' colleges which were part of the state employing authority and thus were instrumental in training teachers to meet the specifications of the employer. In these institutions and in institutions from the state-funded TAFE sector, there was little in terms of a culture of critical discourse.

In regard to initial teacher education the preparation of secondary school teachers took place predominantly in universities, while the preparation of early childhood (preschool) and primary (elementary) teachers largely took place in CAEs. Furthermore, the universities operated autonomously in course development while courses in the CAE sector were under the control of the Higher Education Board with new courses being subjected to detailed scrutiny and other courses being regularly reviewed. The two types of institutions therefore had very different cultures.

Professional Organization for Teacher Education Administrators

Against this backdrop, the New South Wales Teacher Education Conference (NSWTEC), an organization consisting of senior administrators of teacher education from all institutions offering teacher education courses in NSW and the Australian Capital Territory (ACT), was formed in the early 1980s with its membership coming from the 14 CAEs in NSW and the ACT. A number of these were the result of earlier amalgamations. It should be noted that senior staff in teacher education and college administrators were almost exclusively male, a pattern reflecting the school system. Although the teaching profession in Australia has become increasingly feminized, women 'are very much in the minority in positions of authority in the school' (Porter *et al.* 1992, p. 46; see also Turney and Wright 1990). The aim of the NSWTEC was to discuss matters of general interest such as the operation of the teacher education courses that satisfied technical knowledge interests.

In 1987, the six NSW universities offering teacher education courses were invited to join their colleagues from the CAE sector. A further change to the membership came in the interest of gender equity when it was agreed in 1988 that each institution should have two representatives on the NSWTEC, where possible, one of them being a woman. Thus a peak body, the NSWTEC whose membership included all institutions offering teacher education was formed in NSW. The consequence of this changed membership was a change in the prevailing discourse with a greater admission of dissent and critique and a recognition of the need for political intervention.

Unified National System and Teacher Education

Following the formation in July 1987 of the 'mega' ministry (the Department of Employment, Education and Training or DEET) at the federal level came the reorganization of higher education to what is now known as the Unified National System. By 1990 the former CAEs across Australia had been amalgamated in various ways with existing universities or had formed new universities, some with single campuses and others with multiple campuses. As a result there were 11 universities offering teacher education courses in NSW and the ACT. The tensions surrounding these amalgamations showed themselves vividly in 1993 as the University in New England (UNE) with four campuses in northwestern and northern NSW began discussions in order to 'divorce', resulting in the formation of Southern Cross University from 1 January 1994.

The formation of the Unified National System had major consequences for teacher education as many universities found themselves with large numbers of staff and students involved in teacher education. Furthermore, many of these staff were tenured and, having been employed in teacher education for many years with some going back to the time of teachers' colleges, were at the top of their salary scales. They were thus very costly to employ.

Within guidelines set out by DEET, each university is able to adjust its course offerings and not all wanted to have so many students in teacher education. The amalgamations also occurred at a time when the demand for teachers was falling in some states, including NSW, as a result of external forces, such as ministerial directives cutting the number of teachers and changing demography. Changes in school retention rates meant more students stayed on to Year 12 than ever before in the hope of enhancing their career prospects. Further, the federal government cut social security payments to the under-18-year-olds and the increasing recession meant many unskilled jobs had disappeared. Additionally, the demand for teachers of some secondary school subjects such as Legal Studies and Business Studies reflected the great changes taking place in the schools themselves, necessitating revisions of the teacher education courses being offered. Government reports were issued discussing these concerns, for example: *Australia's Teachers: An Agenda for the Next Decade* (NBEET 1990a) and *Teacher Education in Australia* (NBEET 1990b).

In 1990, as a consequence of the amalgamations, the NSW Teacher Education Conference renamed itself the NSW Teacher Education Council in order to reflect its change from a professional organization concerned with the exchange of ideas to an organization involving itself in the political process. Hence with the change in name, the change in membership and the change in federal and state government activity in education, the Council became much more politically active. Regular meetings of the executive were held throughout the year and at least two full day seminars took place for all members. In addition, there was a three-day annual conference. In conjunction with meetings of the executive, other meetings were held with personnel from the Board of Studies (responsible for curriculum development and examination for kindergarten to Year 12), the NSW Department of School Education, the Minister of Education, Training and Youth Affairs, and the two teacher unions (namely, the NSW Teachers' Federation and the Independent Teachers' Association).[4]

The National Organization of Faculties of Education in Australia

The advent of the Unified National System meant that faculties of education across Australia were facing similar difficulties, particularly the decrease in their funding at a time when they had high fixed costs in terms of payments to tenured staff (Deer 1991). As part of the micro-economic reform agenda, employer and employee organizations were encouraged to form peak bodies and in the belief that 'unity is strength' new life was infused into the national organization of teacher educators called the Australian Directors of Teacher Education. This organization of senior teacher education administrators held annual, early January conferences in the summer holidays which were largely a time for social interaction interspersed with some time on current teacher education issues. In January 1990, at the Brisbane Conference, an attempt was made to have gender balance in the membership of the organization in the same way as had occurred in the NSWTEC. This change was met with a very hostile reaction but one member of the new executive was a woman.

In October 1990, members from across Australia met in Sydney with a view to reshaping the group so it could respond more appropriately to federal government's education initiatives. This change was completed at the January 1991 conference and the organization renamed the Australian Council of Deans of Education (ACDE). Its seven-member board consisted of a representative of each of the state groups of deans of faculties of education. In future the annual conference would be held in Canberra, the nation's capital, and the time changed to October. This time and location gave easy access to federal ministers and to staff from DEET. At the national level, deans of education had become more politically active, gaining representation on various working parties that affect teacher education. They were also seen by government and the media as legitimate spokespersons on issues in education in general.

Involvement at the National and State Levels

At the national level, the federal government, which provides the majority of funding for Australian universities, continues to exert its influence. In an attempt to provide more university places for school leavers in 1994, it decreed that each university should not only have to meet specific quotas in undergraduate and postgraduate load (and thus total load), but within the undergraduate entry there would be a specific quota for recent school leavers, namely those who successfully completed the final year of secondary schooling in 1992 or 1993 and had not enrolled in any university course in the interim. However, to meet these quotas some universities had to drop their entry levels for teacher education courses to what some consider unacceptable standards. So, on the one hand, the federal government is advocating career changes and the need for retraining to meet the changing demands of the economy and, on the other hand, it is blocking the entry of mature age students in order to increase the number of school leavers entering universities and thus mask the extent of youth unemployment. The President of the ACDE, in a discussion with policy makers in Canberra towards the end of 1993, gained an acknowledgment of this contradiction but no change was made.

At the state level in NSW, the formation of the NSW Ministerial Advisory Council on Teacher Education and the Quality of Teaching (MACTEQT),[5] a large council of 36 members chaired by the Director-General of the NSW Department of School Education, is clear evidence of the Minister wanting to exert her political will on teacher education although the universities are federally funded. The state funds the schools. The Minister's agenda for this council was set out in an address given at the University of Western Sydney in November 1991, now known as the Macarthur Lecture (Chadwick 1991).[6] The consequences of teacher-educators being involved in Ministerial Advisory Councils is discussed in the next section of this chapter.

The membership of MACTEQT includes 12 teacher-educators who are the nominees of the Vice-Chancellors of each of the NSW universities and the two Australian Capital Territory universities, although the Australian National University has no teacher education courses. There is also a member nominated by the NSWTEC. Other members of the council are nominees of: the Director-General; the Deputy Director-General; the Ministry; the President of the NSW Board of Studies; the Catholic Education Commission; the Association of Independent Schools; the Managing Director of NSW TAFE; the two unions — the NSW Teachers' Federation and the Independent Teachers' Association; the Joint Council of NSW Professional Teachers' Associations; and the Parents and Citizens Association. There are also three teacher representatives from government and non-government schools and nine nominees of the Minister. It is notable that there is no representative of the Ethnic Communities Council or other similar organization in spite of increasing numbers of students in Australian and New South Wales classrooms from a language background other than English.

Readings of the Text of Developments in Teacher Education

There are inevitable tensions as teacher-educators become more involved in the political process, negotiating a role that is at once both spectator and participant (Harding 1937). The tension between the roles of spectator and participant is similar to engaging in explorations of dominant, oppositional and negotiated meanings of text (Parkin 1973; Morley 1980). Cherryholmes (1993) reminds us that we may read educational texts from a number of positions. What is critical is the examination of the consequences of privileging one reading over another. The reading position of this chapter is a sociopolitical one, itself, of course, open to multiple interpretations.

What follows is a specific example of teacher educators being involved in the political process with the attendant risk such involvement entails. The analysis of this example makes more explicit the multiple readings of an educational text.

A major achievement of MACTEQT has been the development of *Desirable Attributes of Beginning Teachers* (NSW MACTEQT 1994). It is no small feat of negotiation that a disparate group of individuals with contesting personal, party-political and institutional agendas were able to arrive at a still point in the interests of describing the complexity of teachers' work and yet making explicit the kinds of knowledge, skills and attributes that are necessary to ensure quality teaching in schools. What could have been a simplistic, atomized statement of competencies (see Walker 1992; Deer 1993) has emerged as a document embedded in an acknowledgment of the pragmatics of the government's right to expect accountability from its public institutions and the rights of other stakeholders, including teacher-educators, to serve their constituencies' legitimate multiplicity of viewpoints.

The *Desirable Attributes of Beginning Teachers* document was launched by the NSW Minister responsible for the education portfolio, Virginia Chadwick, on 4 March 1994 at the first meeting of the year of MACTEQT, and in the presence of representatives of the media. She took pains to explain that the document was not to be seen as a testing instrument, or a template for developing check lists which could be ceremoniously ticked as an indication of achievement. However, a Sydney paper, *The Daily Telegraph Mirror* (claiming a readership of 1.3 million readers a day) sported the following heading: 'New Skill Test — Teachers on Trial'. Such a mischievous headline invites an oppositional reading of the text reconstructing the teacher as technician and the authors as complicit participants in the government's determination to gain closer and more precise control over the processes of schooling.

The price of participation can easily be characterized as complicity in the government's unambiguous agenda of two years ago; that is, define teacher competencies so that teachers, and teacher-educators who 'train' them, can be held accountable in a very public way for the quality of teaching in New South Wales schools. That dominant position, situated in the discourse of professional training, accountability and ultimately control of schools and their curriculum, was that of the Minister. To a considerable extent, that position reflected her frustration over her lack of control of faculties of education located in autonomous universities. Her ideal text, and the one she made clear should emerge, was one that enshrined a check list of key competencies that could be transformed unproblematically and administered to prospective teachers to determine their suitability for employment. Such a text was unacceptable to the Deans of Education (their Vice-Chancellors' representatives on the Council) and through protracted and spirited contestation of these different positions, the present text emerged. It was essentially a negotiated text: one of compromise that recognized and embraced the contesting positions. The oppositional reading of *The Daily Telegraph Mirror* will give legitimacy to the claim of some of our academic colleagues, less intimately involved in the process, of surrendering significant positions of critique in the interests of participation in the political process.

Unless the agenda of the Minister appears to have been entirely muted in the debate, it is instructive and salutary to consider her press statement of 4 March — the day of the document's release. She and the Leader of the opposition Labor Party had been engaged in unproductive sparring over teacher quality in the previous few weeks. In her press release (Chadwick 1994, p. 1), entitled 'Basic Standards for Teachers', she stated:

> [T]he report had been in the making for a year, making a mockery of [the Australian Labor Party] claims that the New South Wales government was not committed to quality teacher standards. It is essential that teachers,

and those that follow them, have the basic standards necessary to ensure that the New South Wales public education system continues to deliver the best education in Australia.

To Be or Not to Be Politically Active

While there are those who are uncomfortable with teacher-educators entering the political fray, we argue that it has been imperative for such participation to occur, not only because knowledge is power and power produces knowledge but because participation is a practice that constitutes a new discourse effecting significant change to the prevailing discourses surrounding teacher education and faculties of education (Ball 1990, p. 173). These textual readings remind us of the value of locating our endeavors in process, to interrupt and interrogate the text and the discourses we are responsible for creating in order to prevent too rapid a closure. Such deconstruction, like participation in political process, is unlikely to be uniformly comfortable; it is more likely to remind us that states of ambiguity and ambivalence may foreground the lack of innocence in the discourses we create (McDonald 1988). As the Labor Prime Minister of the 1970s, Gough Whitlam, once said: 'There are none so pure as the impotent.'

The current climate of educational reform and restructuring within schools and tertiary institutions, and the determination by government for greater accountability of public institutions, have made forays into the political arena necessary. These forays have changed, however, to become genuine attempts to evolve productive partnerships with the other stakeholders in teacher education whose prime *raison d'être* is improving the quality of education in Australian schools. In other words, these productive partnerships have drawn together previously disparate groups which recognize that:

> Collaboration is necessary where parties have a shared interest in solving a problem that none of them can resolve alone. Collaboration makes sense where stakeholders recognize the potential advantages of working together — they need each other to execute a vision they all share, and they need the others to advance their educational interests. (Watson and Fullan 1991, p. 215)

That 'shared interest' is in the name of the learners in schools, the consequential stakeholders whose life chances will be significantly affected by the provision of a well-structured, purposeful curriculum taught with care in a humane and socially just environment (Groundwater-Smith 1993).

Most significantly, the partnerships that are evolving between schools, teacher-educators, employers and unions are ones that are moving beyond consultation and advice towards genuine reciprocity. When reciprocity is obtained, according to Groundwater-Smith *et al.* (1993, p. 4), there is:

- a recognition of interdependence and the unique contribution the various parties bring to the relationship;
- constructive and imaginative problem solving;

- a will to work not only to change but to improve;
- a working relationship which permits risk taking;
- tolerance for ambiguity, uncertainty and dilemmas;
- joint responsibility for the planning, implementation and evaluation of outcomes;
- joint benefits of a commensurable kind;
- organizational structures which facilitate the enactment of decisions;
- well managed communication;
- appropriate resourcing; and
- intercultural understanding.

For teacher-educators, the negotiating of such partnerships has accrued many benefits for their institutions. There is increased relevant and up-to-date knowledge of stakeholders' agendas in relation to education, knowledge that can be translated into appropriate responses and actions in teacher education programs. Such knowledge encourages and allows us to locate our own endeavors and concerns within the broad sociopolitical context and to acknowledge the complexity of current educational agendas.

The sites of conflict between institutions and other stakeholders have been transcended by a sense of collegiality that is beyond boys' club back-slapping and superficial bonhomie. What is needed is the affirmation of the visionary, and sometimes iconoclastic, role of the Teacher Education Council's executive, especially in the early years of its formation. It stood for the value and power of inclusivity above exclusivity, of genuine democratic procedures over hierarchical and status conscious divisions, and inter- and intra-institutional productive partnerships over jealously guarded individual advantage.

Not all of our colleagues have relished these opportunities for engagement in the wider educational community. This is understandable. They have not felt empowered by the commitment to a shared interest partly because they have not been incorporated into, and hence supported by, the collegiality many of us have experienced. At a time of intensification of teacher-educators' work and the uncertainty brought about by changes in their role in the new unified national system, many have felt their career prospects diminished and their previous contributions undervalued. While working with other stakeholders has raised the profile of teacher education and created the conditions necessary to influence political agendas, it has been time consuming and demanding of fundamental shifts in the way we have considered our own institutional histories and culture. For some, however, 'institutional autonomy [has remained] a powerful agent in keeping elements apart'; in the end it is necessary for us 'to yield and listen as well as assert and tell' (Groundwater-Smith 1993, p. 5).

It is no longer possible, if it ever were, to remain complacently isolated and aloof from *real politik*. The social practice of education is unequivocally a political practice and intrusions of government policy are in fact legitimate rights of intervention within the context of a democratic society. The last few years have seen governments of all persuasions assert those rights. Our continuing challenge is to recognize the interdependence of all stakeholders, while at the same time upholding the rights of faculties of education to remain independent within 'autonomous' universities, albeit operating under DEET guidelines. This evolving concern requires delicate negotiation towards partnerships based upon genuine reciprocity.

Understanding and Engaging with Different 'Partners'

The dilemma is the pull of competing discourses and hence the need to balance the legitimate demands of the constituencies the discourses encode. Federally, there is the DEET, as we discussed in the introduction, with its view that education is an industry that could be examined in terms of structural efficiency as part of its micro-economic reforms. For teacher education there were moves towards uniformity (NBEET 1990b, 1992) of programs similar to moves to develop national curriculum frameworks. At the level of the state, particularly in NSW, there is still, although more muted, the discourse of intervention and control, especially of school curriculum and teacher education programs. At both levels of government there is an emphasis on change, efficiency and accountability.

In this context, however, a number of groups have sought to develop a different way of working on educational policy matters. In addition to faculties of education — whose specialist knowledge and skills can certainly contribute to, but cannot be the rationale for dictating the design and implementation of diverse and appropriate programs of teacher preparation — these groups include teacher unions and parents.

A particularly distinctive feature of Australian education in the last few years has been the reorientation of the teacher unions to an involvement in policy formation. It has been less one of industrial adversary and more one of advocacy of the profession. The teacher unions have constructed their agenda of participation in micro-economic reform through enterprise agreements based upon the professional development of teachers. They have been, above all, genuine participants in the development of productive partnerships with teacher-educators.

Perhaps one of the connecting threads through these discourses has been the increased awareness, and hence demand, of parents to assert their claim to be involved in schools in ways that acknowledge their right to influence the nature of their children's education. This can sometimes be characterized as a reactionary emphasis on simplistic notions of literacy and numeracy but such a characterization fails to acknowledge parental rights to demand quality education for their children properly.

The Need to Avoid Simplistic Answers

Why these competing and complex discourses? As Connors (1992, p. 8) points out in her graduation address at the University of Canberra in 1992:

> [T]eachers are common folk. One in every 70 Australians is a teacher. Teachers make up 3 percent of the total workforce — well over 200,000 schoolteachers at the last census — double the number we had 20 years ago . . . Teachers are commonplace because of our commitment to universal primary and secondary schooling . . . The irony is that teaching is too important to pay properly for it, or even to pay for the appropriate length of education and training.

While teaching is commonplace, it is not simple. Yet at both federal and state levels in Australia, governments of all political persuasions continue to seek simple and unproblematic solutions to improving the quality of teacher education and teaching in schools. However, in spite of this government agenda, teacher educators in NSW continue to engage in debates which affirm and even celebrate complexity. This process is without a doubt a political one with political consequences. We propose that the agenda for the future is to move beyond the instrumental towards a more emancipatory set of discourses regarding what is desirable in the formation of teachers in our schools.

Notes

1 Revised version of paper presented at the annual meeting of the American Educational Research Association, New Orleans, 4–8 April 1994. An earlier version of this paper was presented at the annual conference of the Comparative and International Educational Society, Kingston, Jamaica, 16–20 March, 1993.

2 In Australia there are six states: New South Wales, Victoria, Queensland, Western Australia, South Australia and Tasmania, and two territories: the Australian Capital Territory and the Northern Territory. Throughout the remainder of this chapter reference to 'states' should be taken to embody both states and territories.

3 Marginson (1993) goes on to discuss the detail of competency-based standards and frameworks in the workplace. These are complex and the discussions are continuing. Here it is sufficient to indicate that the outcomes will have a powerful effect, particularly on the training agenda. In this chapter we take up the matter of competencies in relation to teacher education as opposed to teacher training at a later point.

4 The Teachers' Federation represents primary and secondary school teachers working in the government sector, while the Independent Teachers' Association represents primary and secondary teachers in the non-government sector. In both cases membership is non-compulsory.

5 According to the *Terms of Reference for the NSW Ministerial Advisory Council on Teacher Education and the Quality of Teaching* (NSW MACTEQT 1992, p. 1), the Council was 'to advise the Minister on matters relating to the pre-service teacher education, induction and ongoing professional development of teachers; matters relating to the quality of teaching in NSW schools; matters relating to the advancement of teaching as a profession; ways of co-ordinating advice from all relevant sectors with an interest and involvement in Teacher Education in New South Wales.' The Minister initially sought the Council's advice regarding: 1) 'the definition of the essential teaching competencies for beginning teachers the extent to which these essential competencies will equip students to meet the educational needs of the full range of students in NSW schools' and 2) '[w]ays in which Teacher Education institutions could report on individual trainee teachers' performance in these competencies' (p. 1).

6 It is important to note that the Minister V. Chadwick is a former secondary school teacher of English and history. She completed her Diploma of Education at the University of Newcastle in the early 1960s.

References

ASHENDEN, C. (1990) 'Award Restructuring and the Future of Schooling', Frank Tate Memorial Lecture, Melbourne: Victorian Institute of Educational Research, October.

BALL, S. (1990) *Foucault and Education: Disciplines and Knowledge*, London: Routledge.

BURKE, G. (1992) 'Resource allocation in education, training and employment programs', in NATIONAL BOARD OF EMPLOYMENT, EDUCATION, AND TRAINING (Ed) *Education and Training: Education Training and Employment Programs, Australia, 1970–2000, Funding and Participation*, Commissioned Report No. 11, Canberra: Australian Government Publishing Service.

CARRICK, J. (1989) *Report of the Committee of Review of NSW Schools*, Sydney: Bloxam and Chambers.

CHADWICK, V. (1991) *Macarthur Lecture*, address delivered at the University of Western Sydney, Macarthur, 6 November.

CHADWICK, V. (1994) 'Basic Standards for Teachers', press release, March 4.

CHERRYHOLMES, C. (1993) 'Reading research', *Journal of Curriculum Studies*, **25** (1) pp. 1–32.

COLLINS, C. (1991) 'Effective Control of Postcompulsory Education or Effective Postcompulsory Education', paper presented to the conference, Educating the Clever Country, jointly sponsored by the Royal Australian Institute of Public Administration (ACT Division) and the Australian College of Education, Canberra, 22–23 July.

CONNORS, L. (1992) 'Teaching's massive task in a mean-spirited society', *Australian Campus Review Weekly*, **2**, 16, pp. 8–16.

DEER, C. (1991) 'Establishing Priorities in Teacher Education: An Example from the University of Technology, Sydney', keynote address at the Australian Teacher Education Association Annual Conference, Ballina, NSW, 7–10 July.

DEER, C. (1993) 'Areas of competence for teachers: The NSW scene', in COLLINS, C. (Ed) *Competencies: The Competencies Debate in Australian Education and Training*, Canberra, Australian College of Education.

GROUNDWATER-SMITH, S. (1993) 'The Transformative Practicum in Teacher Education: Problematics, Pragmatics and Partnerships', paper presented to the Queensland Board of Teacher Registration, South Coast Regional Conference, Gold Coast, 2 April.

GROUNDWATER-SMITH, S., PARKER, J. AND ARTHUR, M. (1993) 'Partnership: Beyond consultation', in WHITE, V. (Ed) *Overview of Schools Research and Reform Proposals*, Sydney, National Schools Project (NSW), Department of School Education, pp. 1–12.

GROUNDWATER-SMITH, S., WALKER, J., ANNICE, C., DEER, C., MEYENN, R. and PARKER J. (1992) 'Political Representation and Political Action: Teacher Education in Australia', paper presented at Annual Conference of the Comparative and International Education Society, Prague, 8–14 July.

HARDING, D.W. (1937) 'The role of the onlooker', *Scrutiny*, **6**, 3, pp. 247–58.

LAKOFF, G. (1987) *Women, Fire and Dangerous Things: What Categories Reveal about the Mind*, Chicago, IL, University of Chicago Press.

McDONALD, J. (1988) 'The emergence of the teacher's voice: Implications for the new reform', *Teachers College Record*, **89**, 4, pp. 471–86.

MARGINSON, S. (1993) *Education and Public Policy in Australia*, Cambridge, Cambridge University Press.

MEYENN, R. and PARKER, J. (1991) 'Education Is Not a Hamburger', paper presented at the Annual Conference of the Australian Association for Research and Education, Griffith University, Queensland, 26–30 November.

MEYENN, R. and PARKER, J. (1992) 'Education Is Not a Hamburger: The Second Bite', paper presented at the Annual Conference of the Australian Association for Research in Education, Deakin University, Victoria, 22–26 November.

MORLEY, D. (1980) *The Nationwide Audience: Structure and Decoding*, London, British Film Institute.

NATIONAL BOARD OF EMPLOYMENT, EDUCATION AND TRAINING (NBEET) (1990a)

Australia's Teachers: An Agenda for the Next Decade, Canberra, Australian Government Publishing Service.

NATIONAL BOARD OF EMPLOYMENT, EDUCATION AND TRAINING (NBEET) (1990b) *Teacher Education in Australia* (Ebbeck Report) Canberra, Australian Government Publishing Service.

NATIONAL BOARD OF EMPLOYMENT, EDUCATION AND TRAINING (NBEET) (1992) *Teacher Education: A Discussion Paper*, Canberra, Australian Government Publishing Service.

NSW MINISTERIAL ADVISORY COUNCIL ON TEACHER EDUCATION AND THE QUALITY OF TEACHING (MACTEQT) (1992) *Terms of Reference for the NSW Ministerial Advisory council on Teacher Education and Teacher Quality*, Sydney, New South Wales MACTEQT.

NSW MINISTERIAL ADVISORY COUNCIL ON TEACHER EDUCATION AND THE QUALITY OF TEACHING (MACTEQT) (1994) *Desirable Attributes of Beginning Teachers*, Sydney, New South Wales MACTEQT.

PARKIN, F. (1973) *Class Inequality and Political Order*, London: Paladin.

PORTER, P., WARRY, M. and APELT, L. (1992) 'The gendered profession of teaching: Visible women and invisible issues', in LOGAN, L. and DEMPSTER, N. (Eds) *Teachers in Australian Schools: Issues for the 1990s*, Deakin, ACT, The Australian College of Education, Canberra, pp. 43–57.

SCOTT, B. (1990) *School Centred Education: Building a More Responsive State School System*, Sydney, Southwood Press.

TURNEY, C. and WRIGHT, R. (1990) *Where The Buck Stops: The Teacher Educators*, Sydney: Sydmac Academic Press.

WALKER, J. (1992) 'A general rationale and conceptual approach to the application of competence based standards of teaching', in NATIONAL BOARD OF EMPLOYMENT, EDUCATION AND TRAINING (Ed) *Issues Arising from Australia's Teachers: An Agenda for the Next Decade* (Schools Council Agenda Papers) vol. 2, Canberra, Australian Government Publishment Service, pp. 93–104.

WATSON, N. and FULLAN, M. (1991) 'Beyond school district–university partnerships', in FULLAN, M. and HARGREAVES, A. (Eds) *Teacher Development and Educational Change*, London, Falmer Press, pp. 213–42.

YEATMAN, A. (1991) 'The "New Federalism" or the Selective Devolution of the Public Sector: From the Welfare to the Competitive State', paper presented to the conference, Educating the Clever Country, jointly sponsored by the Royal Australian Institute of Public Administration (ACT Division) and the Australian College of Education, Canberra, 22–23 July.

Chapter 4

Teacher Education, Reform and the Politics of Knowledge in the United States

Thomas S. Popkewitz

A central focus of educational reform in the United States during the past decade has been teacher education. The reforms assert a progressive rhetoric of educational quality and social equality. New and old slogans abound to mobilize the educational community: national standards to improve the quality of instruction, action research and reflective teaching to promote teacher professionalism, a teacher education that is multicultural, and a constructivist pedagogy that can affect the 'thinking' and 'doing' of teaching. The different focuses about school practices are given sanctity through discussions about the professionalization of teachers — seeking a more effective, technically competent and socially responsive teaching and teacher education. The various reforms are sanctioned by a range of different actors: state governments indicated by their efforts towards 'systemic school reform', schools of education as articulated in the Holmes Reports (1986, 1990), and philanthropic organizations which commission reports about the 'state' of schools and teacher education.

This chapter examines teacher education reform practices as state strategies of regulation and power. I explore two layers of state practices.[1] One is the production of regulatory strategies to steer the organization of schooling through policies. A second layer is the production of particular discursive practices through which the teacher is to organize and act on the phenomena of schooling.[2] This second notion of the state focuses on the construction of particular rules for talking, thinking, speaking, and acting towards the phenomena of schooling and teacher education. The state discourses, I argue, sanction and discipline the 'problem solving' about schooling and teacher education.

By focusing on the discursive practices that discipline teaching and teacher education, I consider contemporary reforms of teacher education as both a continuity and a break with the power relations inscribed historically in schooling and teacher education. The chapter, therefore, initially focuses on particular historical issues of power and regulation embodied in the formation of teacher education in the United States. The constructions of teaching and teacher education in the nineteenth century, I argue, presuppose conceptions of a school curriculum. The conceptions of curriculum embodied a particular organization of knowledge by which individuals were to govern and discipline themselves within the newly formed social arrangements of the modern welfare state. The regulation of the person was not by brute force, but through the inscriptions of the symbolic systems by which one is to interpret, organize and act in the world.

In the second part of the chapter, I juxtapose the nineteenth-century inventions of curriculum and teacher education with contemporary reform efforts. My focus is on three practices that embody central tendencies in the current educational reforms:

1 state strategies to develop 'systemic' school reform;
2 research agendas of constructivist pedagogy in teacher education; and
3 Teach For America, an alternative teacher recruitment/professionalization program.

These seemingly disparate practices, I argue, cohere when their rules of managing and regulating the teacher are examined. The patterns of regulation are not a recapitulation of past practices, however, but express and interpret changing social, cultural and economic patterns in which teacher education and schooling are inscribed.

The State, Scientific 'Reasoning' and the Regulation of Teacher Education: Some Historical Issues

To understand issues in contemporary reforms of teacher education, we need to make a brief excursus to the relations of the state to the educational arena at the turn of the twentieth century. My argument here is threefold. The invention of mass schooling in the late nineteenth century embodied a particular type of problem-solving associated with state tactics of reform. It was in the late nineteenth century that the modern welfare state was formed in the United States (Skowronek 1982). As the state was to produce social progress through rational problem-solving, so were individuals to apply the same methods as they sought personal competence and achievement in everyday life. A mediating institution that linked state reform practices with the dispositions and knowledge of the individual was the social sciences and psychology in the new research universities. The new curriculum theories of this period drew upon the professional discourses found in universities to construct the natural 'development' of the child who was to become healthy, professionally competent in work and self-fulfilled. The problem-solving methods presupposed in the curriculum of the new school were institutionalized in teacher education.

During the nineteenth century the state assumed the functions of schooling that were previously tied to the Church. In certain ways, the formation of the modern mass school re-visioned the regulatory patterns introduced during the Reformation and Counter-Reformation of the seventeenth century. Since at least the Protestant Reformation, schools were institutional patterns that related the state, civil (and religious) authority, and moral discipline.[3] Calvinist theories of social administration maintained the same sense of inner discipline in the theories of school administration (Hamilton 1990). The educational reforms introduced by Martin Luther were to make education a 'disciplining' mechanism in which the individual internalized and acted with the Christian sincerity important to the Reformation (Luke 1989).

We can think of the state construction of the mass school during the United States' Progressive Era (circa 1880–1920) as a joining of the religious commitments of self-discipline with the Enlightenment's faith in reason. Salvation was brought down from the heavenly city of the eighteenth-century philosophers to a nineteenth-century commitment to the progress of the individual through the actions of the state. The Enlightenment made progress as the political reason of the state. Social reform was incorporated as a tactic of the state to improve the social life, health and economic situation of its citizens (Popkewitz 1991). New institutions emerged to take on the functions of securing social betterment. The modern state school, social science and the research university became actors in producing the progressive realization of social ideals.

The construction of the state institutions to secure progress had profound implications beyond its institutional development. A certain type of reasoning takes hold about how to think and feel towards social problems and individuality. Particular forms of 'problem solving' emerged — what Berger *et al.* (1973) call a modern consciousness — that related state tactics of reform, bureaucracy, and industrial technologies to individual 'reasoning' about one's self. The person became a 'citizen' who applied the goals and strategies of the welfare systems as a means towards finding personal salvation. In multiple social arenas, intervention strategies were constructed for individuals to think of themselves and personally to act as healthy, productive citizens and workers. These strategies were tied to rationality and scientific approaches for organizing and planning daily life, such as family health and children's nutrient diet. The problem-solving methods, such as those found in the domestic science movement or in the school curriculum at the turn of the century, were contested, and the outcomes were not determined at the outset. However, the debates and struggles were tied to new institutions of health, labor, education and mental structures that appear alongside the emergence of the new social welfare goals of the state.[4]

Michel Foucault's (1979) notion of 'governmentality' is helpful here to focus on the new principles of regulation that were embodied in state practices. In the nineteenth century, Foucault argues, there occurred a new relation between state governing practices and individual behaviors and dispositions. If the state was to be responsible for the welfare of its citizens, the 'art of governing' had to link the identity of individuals to the administrative patterns found in the larger society.

The word 'police' (and I assume later, 'policy') was used to ensure a downward continuity between the ruler of the state and its populations. In the Middle Ages, governing was an extrinsic activity: the power of the Prince was to protect his geographic principality, with the question of regulation of souls left to the Church in preparing for an afterlife. By the nineteenth century, the meaning of governing involved a state as regulating and coordinating practices of individual behaviors and dispositions. The ensemble of institutions, procedures, analyses, reflections, calculations and tactics that define people as a *populational reasoning* became paramount to the art of governing. Populational reasoning enabled the grouping of people according to certain attributes of social administration. The person could be defined as an individual who 'possessed' some attribute of a *populational* group and then monitored and supervised to control the spread of disease, crime or poverty. The new relation of the state and the individual was legitimated through liberal philosophical discourses about individualism. The idea of social contract was made into a way of defining the mutual pledge of rulers and subjects.

Mass schooling was central to the art of governing. We can think of mass public schooling of the late nineteenth and early twentieth century as continuing the disciplining and regulating project of the Reformation, but producing a break in the systems of knowledge by which individuals were to become productive members of society. The school, a major US reform of this period, encapsulated moral tenets that joined the emerging tasks associated with the modern welfare state and a universalized civil religion associated with Protestantism (see Bellah 1968). The new state school was not only to inculcate virtue but also to remold the pupil to the demands and expectations of an industrialized society with liberal/ political commitments to a democracy. The school was an institutional form designed to resolve the problems of social administration and upbringing pro- duced through multiple transformations; part of this landscape was industrializa- tion, urbanization, immigration, democratic and bourgeois political organizations, as well as intellectual thought that combined utilitarian and pragmatic themes.

The school's 'upbringing' was progressively to produce a healthy citizen and the psychologically disciplined person. The regulation embodied in schooling was inscribed through the systems of ideas, classification and performances by which individuals were to think and know about their 'self' and the world. Curriculum appears during the Progressive Era as systematic attempts to organize and sequence the knowledge made available to children and how children are to effect that knowledge in their practices (Franklin 1986; Kliebard 1986).

The systems of classification inscribed in school instruction were also in- scribed in the programs of teacher education that were being institutionalized at the turn of the century; that is, the missionary character of the church schools in the early nineteenth century were reinscribed and re-visioned in state schools and the training of teachers as the secular purposes of social and personal progress (Herbst 1989). A central element in the reasoning of schooling and of the child was that of populational reasoning; a way for the teacher to monitor the child which is 'carried' into contemporary reasoning of teacher education reform to be discussed later. Teacher education, within this context, was not 'merely' to certify the teacher, but related to the art of governing — its organization of knowledge was to construct the teacher who had dispositions, sensitivities and awarenesses embodied in the changes occuring.

Some readers might object at this point to my emphasis on the state, noting that in the United States there was no centralized state school system and that the formation of the educational sector was different from that of European nations.[5] A US Department of Education existed in the late nineteenth century, for exam- ple, but its main functions were statistical — to track school construction and pupil attendance as well as to monitor the number of reindeer in Alaska. Educa- tional policy and practice, to a large extent until World War II, remained localized. There were strong beliefs about local control of schooling, although an *laissez faire* economic ideology had its death by the end of the nineteenth century (Fine 1956).

My concern with the state, however, is not with the formal administrative apparatus of government, but with relating individual and governing practices through the reasoning applied — the art of governing that I spoke about earlier. Here, we can note that a widespread rationalization of school processes occurred in the United States through non-centralized governmental processes that are in contrast to the processes found in European state formations. Schooling was regulated through local school administration practices and the discursive patterns about teaching and learning. The various state governments, local school administrations and teacher training programs in normal schools and universities developed mechanisms for delivering consistent services, and homogeneous textbooks helped to produce a national curriculum without strong federal intervention (Westbury 1990). The 'cult of efficiency', to borrow a phrase from research on the education of school administrators (Callahan 1962), involved developing a national infrastructure of school control through the incorporation of particular management systems to organize teaching, children and pedagogy in the schools.

The lack of centralized state administration, then, did not mean that there were no regulatory processes as found in the European systems of mass schooling, but that we need to look for them in difference spheres of practice than formal governmental agencies. The development of an infrastructure of schools and teacher education at the turn of the century inscribed particular systems of regulation that responded to and was a part of the urbanization, immigration, industrialization and political democratization occurring (see Herbst 1980, for discussion of teacher education's democratic impulse in the rural United States). That regulation was not one of overt control, such as requirements that children must go to school, although such laws were important to the legitimation of schooling as a knowledge producing institution in society. The regulation had to do with the inscribing of particular ways of problem solving and reasoning about society and the 'self' that were embodied in the construction of mass schooling and teacher education.

Social Science, Universities and Knowledge/Power

Before I more directly examine the constructions of curriculum presupposed in teacher education, I need to focus on a particular invention of the Progressive Era that related mass schooling and state regulation — professionalized knowledge and the social sciences (for detailed discussion see Popkewitz 1991, 1993a). We tend not to consider the social sciences as part of the art of governing as the ideologies of disinterest and value neutrality of science took hold in the early part of the twentieth century. Yet historically the social sciences emerged as social, economic, political and cultural transformations gave rise to new issues of developing competent citizens who would be self-regulating and disciplined.

Scientific rationality and moral responsibility were increasingly tied together as the modern state assumed giving the direction of social and economic progress. The tasks of the social science, as they emerged in the late nineteenth century, were to provide assessments that would guide the social welfare practices of the state (Silva and Slaughter 1984; Ross 1991). The new social sciences at the turn of the century, for example, transformed the initiatives of the social gospel movement among northern Protestant churches into efforts to rationalize and make social institutions efficient in order to instill the necessary notions of civility and ethics for success in the new world in individuals.

At the same time, the discursive practices of social sciences provided rules about the dispositions, sensitivities, awarenesses and behaviors of the person who is to act with reason and purpose in the social arena. The psychologies of the individual and the sociologies of communities and groups were to provide the distinctions and systems of categories by which individual achievement, competence and salvation were to not only to be judged, but to be internalized as an inner disciplining of the 'self' (e.g. see Napoli 1981; O'Donnell 1985).

The social sciences were quickly brought into the newly created structures of the US universities as professionalized knowledge became more important in the organization of modern societies and the welfare state. The university gave the social sciences their institutional home and primary resources for disciplinary development, a situation that did not occur in European countries until later in the twentieth century. The universities also became the 'home' for training the future school leaders and, in the 1950s and 1960s, the home for the professional projects to reform teacher education.

Teacher education merged the disciplining project of schooling with the new legitimating systems of the universities. Teacher education downplayed social conflict by emphasizing the school as a classless institution, where achievement was based upon merit (Mattingly 1975). The focus on individual differences and the seemingly objective methods of social science offered an appealing approach to 'schoolmen' who had to deal with large population increases, issues of urban dislocation, and problems of diverse populations (Powell 1980; Franklin 1986). At places like Teachers College (which would become a part of Columbia University), its science of pedagogy gave concrete attention to the concerns of social harmony. The pedagogical sciences responded directly to concerns about moral upbringing and labor socialization but refocused them as problems of attitude, learning and the skills of individuals as they interacted with their environment.

Curriculum and Technologies of Social Regulation

My final historical point before pursuing contemporary teacher education is to consider the curriculum as tying the knowledge of the teacher to the regulatory patterns that link schooling and the welfare state. We can think of the forming of teacher education in the middle of the nineteenth century as imparting a craft knowledge built upon the practical concerns of teaching. By the early twentieth century, however, the intellectual organization of teacher education incorporated 'scientific' perspectives for organizing the work and dispositions of the teacher.[6] Educational psychology and curriculum theories became important discursive constructions through which teachers (and others) were to assess their competence and achievements.

The idea of curriculum can be viewed as a particular systematic organization of knowledge by which individuals are to regulate and discipline themselves as members of a community/society (Lundgren 1983; Hamilton 1989; Englund 1991).[7] The curriculum theories at the turn of the century were used not only to direct the lives of children, however, but also functioned as lenses by which teachers should define their 'own' competence.[8] The curriculum theories inscribed systems of science as strategies to organize and assess how children understand who they are and what they are in society. Diverse as the ideas of John Dewey, G. Stanley Hall, and David Snedden were, they had in common the attempt to bring professional, scientific knowledge into the school as a way of directing children's thinking as well as their social and physical development. The curriculum was for the construction of the teacher that visioned/re-visioned a person of social commitment, and of individual service and faith.

If I can play with a commonplace word of schooling, the achievements of schooling are in the production of manner and manners as one learns to place oneself in the world. School achievement is only partially that which is formally tested. The discourses of pedagogy, following Luke's (1990, p. 5) studies of classrooms, 'operate not as an abstract set of ideas to be transposed into, inside of, or within mind/consciousness', but as a material series of processes that inscribe attributes of subjectivity into the social body. Models of literacy in schooling, for example, display 'particular postures (correct way of maintaining one's body when reading), silences, gestures and signs of "being in" the lesson that encode particular ways of acting, seeing, talking and feeling of the student' (Luke 1990, p. 18).

I started this chapter with a focus on historical issues that related teacher education to the formation of the state, social science, and curriculum. Central to the discussion was the 'art of governing' in which the regulation of the individual was central. That regulation, I argued, is not 'merely' of certifying the teacher, but of the art of governing as reforms are concerned with constructing the teacher who has certain dispositions, sensitivities and awareness. I related the conception of curriculum in teacher education to the production of regulatory patterns that occur with the rise of the modern welfare state in the nineteenth century and its arts of governing. The courses of professional study that wove together particular curriculum theories, psychologies of the child and school management procedures embodied the new patterns of regulation. My brief excursus into this history of the state, curriculum and social science as regulatory patterns is, however, not to argue an evolutionary process in the deployments of power. Rather it is to provide a sensitivity to certain historical issues of regulation embedded in the current reforms.

Changing Patterns of Regulation: Contemporary Teacher Education Reform

We can think of contemporary schooling and teacher education reforms as embedding the problematic of regulation discussed earlier. The weaving together of the institutional relations of schooling, social science, universities and the state provides an underlying 'motif' in the reform projects. I want to argue, however, that there is a reconstitution of the patterns of regulation occurring as teacher education provides expression to and responds to changes in the social arenas of which schools are a part.

If we focus on the governing patterns of government, we can think of the period following World War II as entailing changing patterns of regulation in schooling and teacher education. Various federal legislation was passed from the 1960s to the present to provide new cadres of teachers for schools in the United States.[9] Specific monies provided to train teachers for inner city schools, for the teaching of science and mathematics, as well as to implement in-service programs related to the development of reform programs were much a part of the curriculum reform movement of the 1960s (Popkewitz *et al.* 1982; Popkewitz 1991, 1993a, particularly Ch. 2).

These changes were not only in training, but in the courses taught as part of certification programs, as federal and state interventions increased the specialization of knowledge within teacher education. In the late 1950s, for example, there was no School of Education at the University of Wisconsin-Madison, just a Department of Education in which specialization was at a minimum. Today, education departments abound as do the internal differentiations that respond to changing mandates of government as well as from social pressures on schools (Popkewitz and Brennan 1994). The differentiations can be found in the development of special educational programs for 'inclusion', construction of courses for the 'at risk' child and psychometrics, as well as the increased subject matter differentiation. The latter has occurred among faculty in the elementary certification programs, previously organized as more child-centered subjects, as teacher education programs respond to current governmental priorities for schooling. The subject matter differentiation embodies a shift to constructivist psychologies to replace behaviorism as a core discipline in designing teaching methods.[10]

State intervention in schools, however, has not only been in the organization of teacher education. There is the production of new categories, distinctions, and differentiations within the teaching of teachers. This was evident during the curriculum reform movement of the 1960s which focused on the 'structure of knowledge' that emphasized a problem solving that defined the world as stable and harmonious, and a school accountable that was instrumental (Popkewitz, 1977; Popkewitz and Wehlage 1977). The regulating qualities of the pedagogical discourses are also evident in current reforms which formulate changes in teaching through constructivist focuses discussed in the following sections. The steering and regulation occurs through the legitimation of certain ways of reasoning about the achievement and competence of teachers.

It is at this juncture of the production of systems of classification that I want to focus on contemporary reform efforts in teacher education. In particular, I relate three seemingly disparate reform efforts. One is called 'systemic school reform' — a slogan to guide the federal government in establishing practices to coordinate and give coherence to the various reform practices. Second are constructivist psychologies which are introduced in the discussion of systemic reform to reorder the ways in which teaching is thought about and practiced, and third, Teach For America, is an alternative, privatized teacher education project to recruit and train teachers for urban and rural schools.

Systemic School Reform

I start this section with a discussion of systemic school reform which, on the surface, seems far removed from teacher education. Systemic school reform is to provide a coherent policy to modernizing schools in the US. It entails making a variety of reforms, implementing practices that have been independently constructed to produce 'successful' schools as part of a concerted national reform program. The practices range from the development of national standards to educational research projects that identify the characteristics of 'successful schools' and the incorporation of 'constructivist' didactics in teaching school subjects and teacher education.

The discourse about 'systemic school reform' has a particularly seductive reasoning. The problem, a Deputy Secretary of the US Department of Education asserts, is to direct further the historical evolution of the school reform movement; the creation of a coordinating mechanism is a natural consequence of the reform movement that has matured from its first wave of school reforms in the 1960s and 1970s and which emphasized back-to-basics. Current reform practices elaborate, refine and in certain instances redefine the mission of the school from the initial reform programs (Smith and O'Day 1990). Central to the second wave of reforms are researchers identifying successful school practices. The problem of the second wave of reform is to coordinate and give coherence to reform programs so successful practices can be incorporated in all of the nation's schools. The role of state practices is to identify 'a coherent *systemic* strategy that can combine the energy and professional involvement of the second wave of reforms with a new and challenging state structure to generalize the reforms to all schools within the state' (Smith and O'Day 1990, p. 235).

At first glance, the rhetorical strategies give preference to a procedural concern for greater involvement in the processes of schooling and to such involvement as having substantive qualities to guide decision making. Democratic and egalitarian goals are made to seem the purpose of such state administration. Multiple historical images of a US millennial dream are to be captured in the reform discourses. In Smith and O'Day (1990), the good school is to maintain a democratic–populist conception of participation. Bureaucracies or élites should not make decisions. The teacher is to act through shared decision making and shared responsibility in determining the educational mission of the school. Parents are to support and participate in the education of their children. For those who seek an intellectually revitalized school, 'systemic school reform' asserts that there should be an intellectual depth and comprehensiveness to school; the intellectual vitality is translated as having 'active student involvement' in learning and 'depth of understanding'. In a society that values expert knowledge and technical competence, a teacher is to be a 'professional' who is guided by national educational standards for achievement and learning but who has the skills and responsibilities to identify the best practices to achieve the educational goals. For those who worry that the school has not fulfilled its obligations to large segments of US society, the 'new' school is to have a system that overcomes the classroom where 'less-advantaged students often lack a surrounding environment that helps them fill in the gaps and draw the connections necessary to construct complex meanings in such situations' (Smith and O'Day 1990, p. 240). Finally, in times of feverish concern about social disorder, the school is also to be orderly, stable, and free of drugs and crime.

As a rhetorical device, 'systemic school reform' seems to leave out no social commitment or ideal as change is outlined for schools in the US. The authors of 'systemic school reform' assert that there is a responsibility to give greater intellectual integrity and coherence to the state's system of schooling. The social and educational inequities that permeate the conduct of schooling do require a rethinking of the assumptions and presuppositions of the organization of instruction. At the same time, democratic commitments to the participation of teachers, students and parents in the processes of schooling do need to be brought to bear in school reform.

Yet when we look deeper into the call for school reform, what seem to be 'truths' to be acted upon, upon examination, are only truths about fragmentation/coherence, participation and standards. The rhetorical flourishes about participation and standards stand within a particular system of reasoning and principles of classification that forms a particular style to the problem solving of schooling. 'Systemic school reform' as a governmental practice gives a political legitimacy *par excellence* to how the problems of schooling and teacher education are defined. 'Systemic school reform' sanctifies certain styles of reasoning and systems of classification for the education of teachers through its tying of school reform discourses with teacher education. The significance of 'systemic school reform' is that it is sanctioned through federal reform discourses, foundational efforts to improve school quality, and unversity/research efforts to rationalize and assess school reform.

Here I want to pay attention to two different practices that are insribed in the discourse of systemic school reform. One links a research tradition of constructivist psychology to teaching methods in teacher education. The second involves the discursive systems through which the teachers of urban and rural schools are constructed. I explore the discursive systems through a study of first-year teachers, in Teach For America. In both instances, I refer to the reform practices as 'constructing the teacher'. By this I mean that the systems of ordering and classification inscribed in the reforms of teacher education are not only about 'expressing' and describing the world — the systems of ideas also construct the objects of the world and self. That is, the discursive practices establish how rules and standards through which the competence and achievement of the teacher in teacher education are to be understood and acted upon. In this sense, we can think of reform policy and educational research as regulatory practices through the standards of reasoning applied to define the problems and solutions.

The Construction of Constructivism as Regulation

In the discussion of 'systemic school reform', the Holmes Reports and constructivist psychologies stand as exemplars for the reconstruction of teaching and teacher education (Newmann 1993; O'Day and Smith 1993). The Holmes Group (1986, 1990) was organized by the deans of leading schools of education, primarily those located in research universities, to reform teacher education programs. Its prescriptions for reform are drawn on a constructivist psychological template to improve the quality of teacher education. The 1990 Holmes Group report asserted that the reform of teacher education 'depends upon engaging the complex work of identifying the knowledge base for competent teaching and developing the content and strategies whereby it is imparted' (p. 46). Further, this knowledge is to give teachers the cognitive resources 'to make pedagogical decisions and to manage productively the hundreds of distinct interactions they will have with pupils each day' (p. 52).

Underlying this faith in remaking the teacher is a faith in educational cognitive psychology to replace an earlier behaviorism. The educational constructivism asserts that knowledge is socially constructed through a symbolic interaction in which there are multiple paths to understanding. That constructivism is brought to bear on the formation of teachers when the Holmes Group's (1990) report asserts that 'the generic task of education' consists of 'teaching students how to make knowledge and meaning — *to enact culture*' (p. 10) and it argues that the real need is for institutional networks and multiple models of reform 'rather than a template for a single conception' (p. 6). The constructivist argument seems altruistic as particular teacher competencies and skills which will establish teachers' professional credentials are identified.

The cognitivist template joins a number of other reform practices through its epistemological rules about how to think about and judge 'good' teaching methods. As stated above, it is the preferred language in the systemic reform discussions about the role of the state in improving the quality of schooling. It is a discourse also sponsored by federal, philanthropic and professional discussions about improving the quality of the teaching of mathematics and science. The National Council for Teachers of Mathematics' (NCTM) efforts to create national curriculum standards, for example, is an exemplar cited in the literature of systemic school reform. It was funded through a combination of federal government and private philanthropic organizations. The language of NCTM reflects standard psychology texts. The National Council for Teachers of Mathematics argues that the selection or shaping of curriculum standards involves children as 'active individuals who construct, modify and integrate ideas' (1989, p. 17).

At a rhetorical level, the active involvement of individuals is a strong democratic commitment. At the same time, we can view the discursive strategies of constructivism as inscribing a particular form of regulation through the dispositions and behaviors that a teacher should have. As applied to teacher education, the 'professional' teacher is to work with knowledge that is contingent and plural. The 'new' teacher and student work as problem solvers. Knowledge is seen as contingent with flexible boundaries that are continually changing. The teacher is to be a 'self-governing' professional who has greater local responsibility in implementing curriculum decisions within boundaries of state goal steering.

As we consider the professional autonomy inscribed in the constructivist paradigm, however, its democratic commitments are functional and politically bound. The reforms reconstitute the tie between the state and the individual, with constructivist epistemology providing a link between state goal-steering and the internalization of goals by which the teacher is to plan, think and act in the worlds of schooling. The pluralities of solutions implicit in the reform practices operate within a larger context of predefined, goal-oriented policies. The regulation of the teacher is not through the explicit defining of results but through the internalization of goals (Popkewitz 1991). In contrast to the curriculum reform movement of the 1960s and 1970s, which sought to rationalize systems (for example, through the teacher-proof curriculum), current reforms seek to regulate by focusing on the thoughts and dispositions of the teachers through which accepted notions of teacher competence are reworked. The potential of the constructivist discourses is to link social changes with people's knowledge of the world in a manner that is to enable them to feel satisfied that the process will effectively attain personal as well as social ends.

The research programs are intrusive as they go directly towards regulating the thoughts, beliefs and dispositions of teachers and students. Without any hesitation about the ethical or political implications of such work, constructivist literature asserts its purposes as 'regulating' and making the teacher feel 'able' and 'inclined' through the internalization of dispositions and sensitivities (Cazden 1986; Newmann *et al.* 1989). The intrusive, regulatory quality is not a reflexive element of the discourse, however. The sense of 'doing' and 'wanting' to be internalized is uncritically accepted as a prescription for action.

What is that sense of 'doing', 'wanting', and 'inclination' associated with constructivism? How is it intrusive and regulatory? It is a constructivism that naturalizes the expert-mediated knowledge that is brought into the school, while searching for the multiple ways that such knowledge can be learned. The construction of constructivist psychology treats science and mathematics as things of logic, rather than as systems of reason that are historically formed and contested practices (for further discussion, see Popkewitz 1991). Mathematics, for example, is taken to be the learning of principles of proof and axioms, and constructivism is to provide alternative and more effective 'problem solving' strategies towards that learning. The problem solving entails learning logical constructs that are stable, but which are best learned by employing multiple teaching strategies. The forms of representations in pedagogical discourses make the systems of classification in science, mathematics and social studies seem to have universal, formal qualities and affinities.

As constructivist methods are brought into teacher education programs, we need to consider that the systems of classifications that children are to learn are themselves systems of appreciation and interpretation that confer values on certain objects and, at the same time, withhold values from other interpretations (see Bazerman 1987; Selzer 1993). For example, I have elsewhere called the transformation of knowledge into school subjects an 'alchemy', as knowledge is transferred from one social field, that of the 'community' of scientists, into another social space, that of schooling (Popkewitz 1993b). The alchemy 'makes' the disciplinary work of science, mathematics and social science, for example, seem as problems of learning, child development and school management. This alchemy enables asking pedagogical questions of schooling without seeing the need to question how the curriculum distinctions of school subjects are themselves representations that are socially constructed. The systems of appreciation and interpretation in constructivism make the world seem unproblematic, as the alchemy makes it seem that thought and reason have no expression outside one's personal 'negotiations' or group learning. The social construction of knowledge, which is a rhetorical construction of constructivism, has no historical or social theory through which to consider how knowledge is socially and politically produced.

The constructivist strategies can be contrasted to twentieth-century scholarship in the history, philosophy and sociology of science. Such scholarship argues that the logic of science is not in its logical formulations of information but in the ways that concepts and generalization emerge from methods, and that the questions and approaches of science entail moral and political concerns as well as those of the sciences themselves.[11] The psychological constructivism, in its irony, obscures the social constructions and power relations embedded in knowledge!

Focusing on the educational literature of constructivism, Carlgren (in press) pursues the limitations of this literature historically. In the previous reforms of teaching, she argues, the teacher was viewed as an 'object of change', as a nonthinking doer. This can be understood, for example, in the curriculum reform movement of the 1960s which sought 'teacher proof' materials that could not be undermined through incompetent instruction. The current reforms have rediscovered the teacher as a thinker as well as a doer, Carlgren argues, but this 'reintroduction of the thinking teacher was, however, connected with a conception of the teacher as a planning and evaluating technical rational "expert" ' (in press, p. 6). The conception of teacher, Carlgren concludes, includes not only a division of teachers' thinking and acting but also a dissociation of means from ends and theory from practice, even though the divisions are both analytically and empirical incorrect.

It is at this point we can extend the critique of constructivism by situating it within larger social transformations. Earlier I mentioned that a potential of the constructivist discourses is to link social changes with people's knowledge of how they feel satisfied that the process will effectively attain personal as well as social ends. This linkage, the French sociologist Donzelot (1991) has argued, is related to changes occurring in labor relations that integrate sentiments and dispositions of work and leisure. In examining the efforts to increase production, Donzelot (1991) argues that there are increasing efforts to break previous psychological ties that define individual identity through fixed notions of work and production. The new approaches accent the relation of the individual's autonomy, capacity to adapt and be an agent of change in a changing world as integral to one's self fulfillment: 'Instead of defining the individual by the work he [or she] is assigned to, [the new psychology] regards productive activity as the site of deployment of the person's personal skills' (Donzelot 1991, p. 252).

The new business entails working conditions that facilitate 'problem solving' — where highly variable customer demands, new technologies, multicentered business structures, and 'horizontal' structures that organize workers into groups concerned with specific projects that do not have the older layers of managements (Fatis 1992). The smaller units are seen to 'empower' workers and to develop flexible, responsive environments that can respond quickly to customer demands.[12]

The individuality of the constructivism is an individuality that is situated in conditions that Donzelot (1991) describes, but conditions that are of culture, the military, philosophy and politics as well as of the workplace. It is a world where complex social relations are restructuring the relation of knowledge, institutions and subjectivities. It is a world of instabilities, pluralities, and a need for pragmatic actions as individuals interact with communication systems. It is a world of contingent qualities of a context that quickly changes situations. The constructivism annuls the arbitrary division between the economic and the social as social relations.

Teach For America and the Construction of the Urban and Rural Teachers

At this point I would like to move the argument about the reform of teacher education to the discourses of schooling in the training of teachers. My focus is on one of the more publicized reform efforts in the recruitment and training of teachers in the US, Teach For America. Conceived in an undergraduate degree honor's thesis at Princeton University, its founder sought to create an alternative teacher education program that brought liberal arts graduates into those areas of teaching where there is the shortest supply — within the poverty of central cities and rural areas in the United States. The program was initiated in 1990 and drew its first 500 recruits from the finest private and public universities in the nation. After an eight-week training at the University of California, Berkeley, the students were placed as full-time teachers in rural Georgia and North Carolina and in the metropolitan areas of Baton Rouge and New Orleans, LA, New York City and Los Angeles.

At one level, Teach For America can be viewed as a non-governmental actor in the reform of teacher education, but the practices of Teach For America draw upon and circulate discourses about teaching, methods of instruction, and conceptions of childhood embedded in urban and rural schooling. The amalgamation of the various state and institutional discourses about teaching and teacher education provide an unspoken horizon in which Teach For America operates. In profound ways, we need to consider the intersection of the various discursive practices through which regulation and power relations are deployed as the art of governing and a meaning to the state in contemporary affairs.

My study[13] of Teach For America focuses on a 'scaffolding' of seemingly disparate and historically different practices inscribed in the daily practices of student teaching.[14] The study was to understand the modes of presentation and styles of reasoning through which the student teachers (corps members) of Teach For America constructed their subjects — that is, how the categories, differentiations and distinctions of schooling defined what is a teacher, a student and learning. In this sense, I speak about the discursive practices as not 'merely' languages but as part of the productive processes of schooling — establishing a 'will to know' through the ways in which the phenomena of schooling are to be grasped, possibilities classified, and objects constructed. The focus of the study, then, was to understand how professional education contains an ensemble of methods and strategies that steer thought, action and self-reflection.

At one layer of teaching practices was an alchemy of school subjects that I spoke about in the prior section. The practices of teaching, like the research strategies of constructivist pedagogy, removed school subjects from their social moorings. The knowledge given as the curriculum was separated from human interests, community norms, and values of social and scientific disciplines. School subjects were treated as having fixed, logical and taxonomic properties that children should learn. The logical properties of knowledge and method were defined as stable and neutral.

By itself, the alchemy of school subjects is important. The knowledge in schooling is made to seem as universal, uncontroversial and neutral. Yet, studies over the past few decades have continually pointed to the various ways in which the 'content' of school knowledge maintains distinctions and differentiations that reflect social interests and therefore are not neutral (e.g. see Popkewitz *et al.* 1982; Ginsburg 1988; Cornbleth 1990; Carlson 1992; Weis and Fine 1993; McLaren 1994).

The alchemies that I speak of must be placed in relation to the pedagogical practices that 'effect' the knowledge of the school subjects. The instructional strategies and the psychological principles had particular implications for children of color and of poverty. With subject knowledge as consensual and stable, norms of the 'good' student stood as an unarticulated but essentially ordered totality from which to understand diversity in schooling. Children of urban and rural schools were 'seen' as having certain social/cultural characteristics which stood in opposition to the privileged norms that were presumed to make the canons of school subjects accessible. The child who sat at a desk in a certain way, who spoke in a certain manner, and who moved and acted in certain ways became the unspoken norm from which principles of personal competence and future achievement were drawn.

The child of color had become the anthropological 'other' — one who stood in opposition to silent norms and who lacked the motivational attributes, behavioral characteristics and personal self-esteem to achieve. The child of color was an oppositional category — the 'other' — about whom a teacher spoke in a psychological discourse about lacking motivation and self-esteem.

The constructions of the oppositions did not occur through explicit discussions of criteria of success but through the particular categories and distinctions that posited oppositions between the 'normal' child and those of children of color. The norms of inclusion and exclusion occurred through talk about learning, classroom management, multiculturalism, and teaching mathematics and science. The teachers, for example, described the pupils in their schools as children who had no discipline at home, whose parents did not read to their children, whose behavioral proclivities made it difficult, if not impossible, to learn properly.

The negative characteristics of children, which were drawn from principles perceived to be universal about social/economic conditions, were brought back into the teaching context through an individualization that explained personal success and failure. The home and community of the child, for example, were first positioned as pathological and the causes of school failures, and then re-visioned in a *doublet* that made the negatives of home and community as psychological principles to help the child overcome the limitations of poverty and community.

The doublets were evident in the practices of learning to be a teacher. The teacher classified children of the urban and rural schools as not able to learn abstractly or to think theoretically. The pedagogical solution was to re-vision the processes by which students could be competent — captured in the slogan of 'hands-on' learning. A child was thus perceived by the teacher as not learning abstract concepts and as having little self-discipline and, as a consequence, the best learning was through 'hands-on' activities that focused on procedures and practical tasks. The 'positive' attributes of the 'hands-on' learning interned child and community as pathological through the distinctions that served as the foundations of teaching itself. Created with noble intents to make the school relevant to children of color, the distinctions of instruction recast the silent norms of diversity-as-opposition into positives that guided and assessed the accomplishments of teachers and children.

One central element in the teaching was a *populational reasoning* that I discussed earlier as a historical construct of the state to manage its territory. Probabilistic attributes of population were to identify particular attributes of the child in need of help. The children were visioned as uniform members of populations in whom particular characteristics are defined as deviant, such as children who are from broken homes, who were crack babies, who have low self-esteem. The population attributes were positioned as individual attributes that described what prevented success in schooling (and society).

The visioning/re-visioning of people as 'populations' was an important element of the reasoning through which student teachers in Teach For America ordered and regulated the child in school. In interviews, they constructed the child as someone who 'can't study', who is 'disruptive', or is 'not read to by his parents' — constructions whose premises were derived from populational reasoning. Student teachers in the program talked about children's 'potential' in the Teach For America schools as a way to 'see' children who were to receive more positive instructional efforts. 'Potential', however, reclassified the probability statements about 'deprivations' of the home and community into signals of 'potentials' the child has and which proper instruction will bring to the surface. In this logic, the pathology of the community becomes a positivity in which the behaviors, proper characteristics, and language of the child as 'other' are rationally ordered and re-visioned in the child through 'relevant' teaching.

The norms of the populations brought a coherence to the teaching through a totalization and a specification so that no action fell outside the grid of normal-ity. The child was the anthropological 'other' who was not the author of the poor achievement or delinquency but the delinquent of a life, a collection of biographi-cal details and psychological characteristics. The social, cultural and economic criteria of populational deficiency were often legitimated through state classifica-tion systems — for example, Title I schools.

As I explored in the historical discussion of teaching and teacher education, populational reasoning is a way of reasoning that emerged with the state reform tactics concerned with administering social welfare (Smith 1990; Castel 1991; Hack-ing 1991). Individuals and events were organized and reclassified in a manner that separated a particular event from its immediate historical situation. Applying the calculus of probability, the state could define social groupings and interests by reference to statistical aggregates of populations. Such reasoning has become a part of the disciplinary talk about children's learning and school achievement, as well as the social/psychological attributes that are deemed causal to school failures.

The notion of population produces a new form of individuality, one in which the person is defined normatively in relation to statistical aggregates which ascribe attributes to the person, and the growth or development of the person can be monitored and supervised. Populations dissolve the notion of the concrete indi-vidual and in its place is constructed a combination of factors of the child who is 'at risk' and in need of remediation (Donzelot 1991). The populational reasoning no longer correlates 'individuality' with some abstract norms or an ideal of a responsible subject. Instead, individuality is related to other members of a popu-lation. The notion of population fixes on particular attributes of social groupings by decentering the totalities of relations among people, things and events. To speak of populations is no longer the state prescribing or describing, however, but it is the populational categories of managing that discipline the teacher as produc-tive practices are sought. As described above in the doublets, the efforts to im-prove instructional efficiency, to psychologically help the child develop self-esteem, and to provide methods of teaching children of diverse backgrounds in the urban and rural schools inscribed classifications of teaching and children that 'made' probabilistic characteristics as internalized attributes of the individual child who was to be 'helped'.

In one sense, the discursive practice of Teach For America may seem far away from the practices recommended within the systemic reform efforts and the constructivist research reform agendas. The efforts to develop greater involve-ment, flexibility and fluidity in what is learned in schooling runs, on the surface, as a counter-measure to the teaching found in the schools where the Teach For America corps members were placed. When we consider the systems of classifi-cation and representation inscribed in the various reform efforts, however, they can be understood as homologous. There is a disjuncture between teachers' knowl-edge of teaching and school content knowledge — the alchemies that I spoke about. The system of ideas that normalizes and disciplines the teacher remains undisturbed in the reform practices as they leave questions about the relation of knowledge and power as unproblematic. Further, the strategies to reform teacher education become more intrusive as the state is no longer in the position of pre-scribing and describing; instead the state deploys populational reasoning to man-age and discipline the teacher as productive practices are sought.

Some Conclusions

This chapter about teacher education in the US began by discussing the problem of knowledge, power and social regulation. I focused on the state as not merely concerned with the administrative/judicial functions of governing. The produc-tive qualities of the state are related to the methodologies and epistemologies through which the subjects of schooling are constructed through pedagogical and evaluation strategies.

To consider the issue of power and regulation in teacher education, I first sought to historicize the problem of teacher education by focusing on the know-ledge that distinguishes and differentiates the objects of schooling — the teacher, the student and the achievement of schooling itself. My approach to the problem of teacher education was to suggest that the discourses embodied in teacher edu-cation are not neutral or descriptive; the amalgamation of discursive practices was viewed as a particular, historically-formed knowledge that inscribes certain ways of acting, feeling, talking and 'seeing' the world.

In this manner, I sought to understand teacher education as social technolo-gies through which the teacher is to become self-regulating and self-monitoring. Technologies that I speak of here are the consecrated practices whereby individu-als are to transform themselves and feel themselves as competent actors within the institutional setting of schooling. The various reform practices, I argued, provide ways in which the teacher can administer the child in school — making the child an object of a field of knowledge that the teacher patrolled. The teacher is a professional biographer whose task is to change the acts of life to the reference points of schooling. In the cases of the constructivism and Teach For America, the technologies operated as a discipline by which to determine administratively what is just and fair, and a political technology to mobilize and utilize classroom prac-tices that were to shape and fashion the 'child'.

It is of this social regulation of curriculum that Foucault (1980) speaks, when he suggests that we reverse the traditional belief that knowledge is power, and define power as embodied in the manner by which people gain knowledge and use the knowledge to intervene in their social affairs. His particular concern is how the individual is governed through the invention of certain forms of scientific discourses about the individual. Foucault called this relation governmentality — the linking of changing sociopolitical administrative patterns to individual behaviors and dispositions. In certain ways Foucault's theoretical interest in the effects of knowledge is important to theories of teacher education.

In sketching a portrait of the reform efforts to reconstitute teacher education through three examples of reform, I also sought to provide a larger context of social transformation in which the reforms occur. Whether I called these changes postmodern, postfordist, or high modern — terms being contested in cultural social theory as well as in education — the 'fact' remains that teacher education and schooling inscribe power relations of the social world through its construction of the teacher.

At this point we can view certain liberal and 'reconstructionist' efforts to reform teacher education as responding to important democratic commitments. Efforts to make teacher education more collaborative — developing a more collegial relationship with teachers, establishing a more responsive relation with parents whose children go to school, and engaging in efforts to develop a multicultural curriculum that is more reflective of the social and cultural diversity of US society — are pedagogical strategies that direct attention to the ethical, moral and intellectual commitments of teacher education in a society fraught with injustices and inequities.

My argument here is not to disregard those commitments; rather it is to suggest that these commitments are often engaged in through discursive strategies that pay attention to the organization of teacher education (i.e. collaboration) and to what and who are represented, but pay little attention to the implications of the rules of representation through which teachers construct their objects of scrutiny and administration. It was this focus to which I have given attention this chapter.

In this sense, we need to be aware of Foucault's admonishment throughout his later writing when discussing the effects of power: all discourses are dangerous, though not necessarily bad. For example, while there are strong and important commitments to participation as central to a democracy, we need continually to interrogate historically the notions of political participation and democracy in the US. Often the rules of involvement inscribed in school reform take for granted the multiple trajectories that construct the rules of participation; these entail, among others, the forming of a political theory that historically merged a strong, late nineteenth-century generalized Protestant view of individual salvation with particular nineteenth-century views of social progress and scientific rationalities (Berkowich 1978). The rules of participation related, as well, to the emergence of capitalism and a bourgeoisie. The rules of participation cannot be assumed as 'natural' to a democracy but need to be continually interrogated as to who is omitted and the silences produced. Thus we cannot celebrate reforms in teacher education as progressive but continually need to historicize our ways of reasoning and acting to make the world 'better'.

Notes

1 My notion of the state is not the Weberian view of the state as an administrative/ judicial institution. For its conceptual development and relation to other literature about the state, see Popkewitz (1991) and Popkewitz and Brennan (1994).

2 In previous work (Popkewitz 1991), I have argued this notion of inquiry as one of a social epistemology; epistemology provides a context in which to consider the rules and standards by which knowledge about the world is formed — the distinctions, relations and categorizations that organize perceptions, ways of responding to the world and the conceptions of 'self'. Social epistemology relates social consciousness and particular cognitive styles to the changing social, historical and institutional conditions in which they arise.

3 While discussions of learning and socialization in the US tend to structure out these considerations of deeper issues of upbringing, philosophically, at least, Marxist pedagogical discussions understood this relation of cognition and affect with political–moral responsibility (Mikhailov 1976; Ilyenkov 1977).

4   The appearances of the institutions entail a historical conjuncture rather than emerging from a grand design. It is the coming together of the multiple developments in multiple arenas of social life that forms what I will later call a break or rupture.

5   State rationalization at the turn of the century occurred in sectors of transportation, labor, banking, industrial relations and the military. The state development in these sectors was to create semi-independent administrative agencies rather than to rule through legislation. The governing policies were a pragmatic response to the existing power of local political parties and the courts that had formed with the new Republic.

6   The Jesuits of the sixteenth century recognized the disciplining qualities of pedagogy as part of the Counter-Reformation (Durkheim 1977). They developed classroom practices that reinterpreted the humanist and secular literature of the Counter-Reformation to assert the values of the Catholic Church. Their strategy was to read texts without historical contexts so as to insert Catholic moral precepts into pagan literature. The schools were expected to promote true faith, service to the state, and the proper functioning of the family.

7   I use the words 'community' and 'society' as distinctions that are of historical significance. The former involves time/space relations that were local; the latter involves more abstract conceptios of self as a citizen of a nation, as a worker, or as an ethnic group within some larger sets of relations. As these abstract notions of society are made part of one's definition fo self, it changes the meaning and relationships in which social relations and identies are defined.

8   It is important to note that most of the discourses about schooling and curriculum were pragmatic, although there was a difference between the instrumental pragmatism of behaviorist psychology and the writings of Dewey.

9   The National Science Foundation (1950), National Defense Act (1958) and the Elementary and Secondary Education Act (1963) were some of the legislative vehicles by which the teacher training and in-service eduation were initiated. Indirect federal influence in teacher education was established in undergraduate and graduate programs through student loans, grants to teachers who taught in federally defined priority areas during the Vietnam War, and funding for teacher institutes concerned with improving university programs and subject-matter teaching. The Borden Act (1946) initiated these projects, with later programs in the late 1960s such as Teacher Corps and Teachers of Teacher Trainers (TTT) providing focus to preservice education and minority educational improvement.

10 This does not occur directly, but through federal and philanthropic research directions that give priority to certain types of problem-solving.

11 For general treatments of these issues, see Bachelard (1984), Cangilheim (1988), Manicas (1987), Tiles (1984), and Toulmin (1990). For discussion about these issues in relation to education, see Popkewitz (1991). In one sense, the work of Resnick *et al.* (1991) seeks to dissolve dualisms of content and method.

12 The changes in business organizations have dual qualities. They produce a revamping of such giant international corporations as General Motors, Sears Roebuck, and IBM. The loss of 25,000 jobs within the giant computer company, IBM, reflects the changing world of work as smaller units with greater self-management are constructed (Meyerson 1992). To cite another example, every three years the world's microchip makers have been able to put four times as many microprocessors on a silicon chip, leading to vast increases in power and miniaturization. Each new generation of microchips creates a new computer industry which overthrows the previous one. Some experts argue that the new model for computer and technological development requires alliances of small, innovative companies, sometimes with government support and sometimes without.

13 The Teach For America study, which I was involved in conducting and on which

I draw in this chapter, entailed a one-year study of the 'socialization' processes and discursive practices during the first year of the program. There were interviews, surveys, and observations of the project during its summer program and in subsequent school placements. A book reporting the study will be published in 1995, tentatively entitled, *The Teacher's Gaze and the Construction of Education: Teacher For America in Urban and Rural Schools*.

14   The phrase 'student teaching' may be misleading here. The graduates from élite colleges who were recruited to participate in Teach For America were provided with an initial training for teaching during a summer session and then worked as full-time teachers. At the end of two years, after acquiring certain course credits and local school documents, they become certified as teachers.

References

BACHELARD, G. (1984) *The New Scientific Spirit*, trans. A. Goldhammer, Boston, MA, Beacon Press.

BAZERMAN, C. (1987) 'Codifying the scientific style', in NELSON, J., MOGILL, A. and MCCLOSKEY, D. (Eds) *The Rhetoric of the Human Sciences*, Madison, WI, University of Wisconsin Press, pp. 125–44.

BELLAH, R. (1968) 'Civil religion in America', in MCLOUGHLIN, W. and BELLAH, R. (Eds) *Religion in America*, Boston, MA, Houghton Mifflin, pp. 3–23.

BERGER, P., BERGER, B. and KELLNER, H. (1973) *The Homeless Mind: Modernization and Consciousness*, New York, Vintage.

BERKOWICH, S. (1978) *The American Jeremiad*, Madison, WI, University of Wisconsin Press.

CALLAHAN, R. (1962) *Education and the Cult of Efficiency: A Study of the Social Forces That Have Shaped the Administration of Public Schools*, Chicago, IL, University of Chicago Press.

CANGILHEIM, G. (1988) *Ideology and Rationality in the History of the Life Sciences*, trans. A. Goldhammer, Cambridge, MA, MIT Press.

CARLGREN, I. (forthcoming) 'Professional cultures in Swedish teacher education', in GOODSON, I. and HARGREAVES, A. (Eds) *Professional Lives*, London, Falmer Press.

CARLSON, D. (1992) *Teachers and Crisis; Urban School Reform and Teachers' Work Culture*, New York, Routledge.

CASTEL, R. (1991) 'From dangerousness to risk', in BURCHELL, G., GORDON, C. and MILLER, P. (Eds) *The Foucault Effect, Studies in Governmentality*, Chicago, IL, University of Chicago Press, pp. 281–98.

CAZDEN, C. (1986) 'Classroom discourse', in WITTROCK M. (Ed) *Handbook of Research on Teaching*, 3 edn, New York, Macmillan, pp. 432–63.

CORNBLETH, C. (1990) *Curriculum in Context*, New York, Falmer Press.

DONZELOT, J. (1991) 'Pleasure in work', in BURCHELL, G., GORDON, C. and MILLER, P. (Eds) *The Foucault Effect, Studies in Governmentality*, Chicago, IL, University of Chicago Press, pp. 251–80.

DURKHEIM, E. (1977) *The Evolution of Educational Thought: Lectures on the Formation and Development of Secondary Education in France* (translator, Peter Collins), London, Routledge and Kegan Paul.

ENGLUND, T. (1991) 'Rethinking Curriculum History — Towards a Theoretical Reorientation', paper presented at the annual meeting of the American Educational Research Association: Symposium on Curriculum History, Chicago, 4–8 April.

FATIS, S. (1992) 'Firms Trim Hierarchies, empower workers', *The Capital Times* (25 December) pp. 4B–5B.

FINE, S. (1956) *Laissez Faire and the General Welfare State: A Study of Conflict in American Thought*, Ann Arbor, MI, University of Michigan Press.

FOUCAULT, M. (1979) 'Governmentality', *Ideology and Consciousness*, **6**, pp. 5–22.

FOUCAULT, M. (1980) *Power/Knowledge: Selected Interviews and Other Writings by Michel Foucault, 1972–1977*, trans. and ed. C. Gordon, New York, Pantheon.

FRANKLIN, B. (1986) *Building the American Community: The School Curriculum and the Search for Social Control*, New York, Falmer Press.

GINSBURG, M. (1988) *Contradictions in Teacher Education and Society: A Critical Analysis*, New York, Falmer Press.

HACKING, I. (1991) 'How should we do the history of statistics?', in BURCHELL, G., GORDON, C. and MILLER, P. (Eds) *The Foucault Effect: Studies in Governmentality*, Chicago, IL, University of Chicago Press, pp. 181–96.

HAMILTON, D. (1989) *Towards A Theory of Schooling*, London, Falmer Press.

HAMILTON, D. (1990) *Learning about Education: An Unfinished Curriculum*, Milton Keynes, Open University Press.

HERBST, J. (1980) 'Nineteenth century normal schools in the United States: A fresh look', *History Of Education*, **9**, 2, pp. 216–27.

HERBST, J. (1989) *And Sadly Teach: Teacher Education and Professionalization in American Culture*, Madison, WI, University of Wisconsin Press.

HOLMES GROUP (1986) *Tomorrow's Teachers*, East Lansing, MI: The Holmes Group.

HOLMES GROUP (1990) *Tomorrow's Schools*, East Lansing, MI, The Holmes Group.

ILYENKOV, E. (1977) *Dialectical Logic, Essays on Its History and Theory*, trans. H. Creghton, Moscow, Progress Press.

KLIEBARD, H. (1986) *Struggle for the American Curriculum*, London, Routledge and Kegan Paul.

LINDSAY, B. (1977) 'Progressive education and the black colleges', *Journal of Black Studies*, **7**, 2, pp. 341–57.

LUKE, A. (1990) 'The Body Literate: Discursive Inscription in Early Literacy Training', paper presented at the XIIth World Congress of Sociology, Madrid, Spain, 8–13 July.

LUKE, C. (1989) *Pedagogy, Printing, and Protestanism: The Discourse on Childhood*, Albany, NY, State University of New York Press.

LUNDGREN, U. (1983) *Between Hope and Happening: Text and Contexts in Curriculum*, Geelong, Australia, Deakin University Press.

MCLAREN, P. (1994) *Life in Schools: An Introduction to Critical Pedagogy in the Foundations of Education*, New York, Longman Publishers.

MANICAS, P. (1987) *A History and Philosophy of the Social Sciences*, Oxford, Basil Blackwell.

MATTINGLY, P. (1975) *The Classless Profession: American Schoolmen in the Nineteenth Century*, New York, New York University Press.

MEYERSON, A. (1992) 'IBM to eliminate 25,000 jobs in 1993 and shut plants', *The New York Times*, 16 December p. 1.

MIKHAILOV, F. (1976/1990) *The Riddle of the Self*, trans. R. Daglish, Moscow, Progress Publishers.

NAPOLI, D. (1981) *Architects of Adjustment: The History of the Psychological Profession in the United States*, Port Washington, NY, Kennikat Press.

NATIONAL COUNCIL FOR TEACHERS OF MATHEMATICS (1989) *Curriculum and Evaluation Standards for School Mathematics*. Reston, VA, National Council for Teachers of Mathematics.

NEWMANN, F. (1993) 'Beyond comon sense in educational restructuring: The issues of content and linkage', *Educational Researcher*, **22**, 2, pp. 4–13.

NEWMANN, D., GRIFFIN, J. and COLE, M. (1989) *The Construction Zone: Working for Cognitive Change in Schools*, Cambridge, Cambridge University Press.

O'DAY, J. and SMITH, M. (1993) 'Systemic reform and educational opportunity', in S.

H. FUHRMAN (Ed) *Designing Coherent Educational Policy: Improving the System*, San Francisco, CA, Jossey-Bass, pp. 250–312.

O'DONNELL, J. (1985) *The Origins of Behaviorism: American Psychology, 1876–1920*, New York, University Press.

POPKEWITZ, T. (1977) 'Latent values of the discipline centered curriculum', *Theory and Research in Social Education*, **5**, 1 pp. 41–60.

POPKEWITZ, T. (1991) *A Political Sociology of Educational Reform: Power/Knowledge in Teaching, Teacher Education, and Research*, New York, Teachers College Press.

POPKEWITZ, T. (Ed) (1993a) *Changing Patterns of Power: Social Regulation and Teacher Education Reform*, Albany, NY, State University of New York Press.

POPKEWITZ, T. (1993b) 'Professionalization in teaching and teacher education: Some notes on its history, ideology and potential', *Teaching and Teacher Education*, **10**, 1, pp. 1–14.

POPKEWITZ, T. and BRENNAN, M. (1994) 'Certification to credentialing: Reconstituting control mechanisms in teacher education', in BORMAN, K. and GREENMAN, N. (Eds) *Changing American Education: Recapturing the Past or Inventing the Future?* Albany, NY, State University of New York Press, pp. 33–70.

POPKEWITZ, T., TABACHNICK, B. and WEHLAGE, G. (1982) *The Myth of Educational Reform: A Study of School Responses to a Program of Change*, Madison, WI, University of Wisconsin Press.

POPKEWITZ, T. and WEHLAGE, G. (1977). 'Schooling as work: An approach to research on evaluation', *Teachers College Record*, **79**, 1, pp. 69–86.

POWELL, A. (1980) *The Uncertain Profession: Harvard and the Search for Educational Authority*, Cambridge, MA, Harvard University Press.

RESNICK, L., LEVINE, J. and TEASLEY, S. (1991) *Perspectives on Social Shared Cognition*, Washington, DC, The American Psychological Association.

ROSS, D. (1991) *The Origins of American Social Science*, New York, Cambridge University Press.

SELZER, J. (1993) *Understanding Scientific Prose*, Madison, WI, University of Wisconsin Press.

SILVA, E. and SLAUGHTER, S. (1984) *Serving Power: The Making of the Academic Social Science Expert*, Westport, CT, Greenwood Press.

SKOWRONEK, S. (1982) *Building a New American State: The Expansion of National Administrative Capacities, 1877–1920*, New York, Cambridge University Press.

SMITH, D. (1990) *Conceptual Practices of Power: A Feminist Sociology of Knowledge*, Toronto, University of Toronto Press.

SMITH, M. and O'DAY, J. (1990) 'Systemic school reform', in *Yearbook of the Politics of Education Association*, London, Falmer Press, pp. 233–69.

TILES, M. (1984) *Bachelard: Science and Objectivity*, Cambridge, Cambridge University Press.

TOULMIN, S. (1990) *Cosmopolis: The Hidden Agenda of Modernity*, New York, The Free Press.

WEIS, L and FINE, M. (Eds) (1993) *Beyond Silenced Voices; Class, Race, and Gender in United States Schools*, Albany, NY, State University of New York Press.

WESTBURY, I. (1990) 'Textbooks, textbooks publishers, and the quality of schooling', in ELLIOTT, D. and WOODWARD, A. (Eds) *Textbooks and Schooling in the United States*, 89th NSSE Yearbook, Chicago, IL, National Society for the Study of Education, pp. 1–22.

Chapter 5

Teacher Education in Search of a Metaphor: Defining the Relationship Between Teachers, Teaching and the State in China[1]

Lynn Paine

Metaphor pervades daily life (Lakoff and Johnson 1980). Because of its pervasiveness, it offers a valuable way to examine how we construct meanings and the conflicts inherent in that construction. This chapter pursues an analysis of metaphor and other discursive strategies in Chinese teacher education as a way of exploring the political dimension of preservice teacher education in that context.

Metaphor is an important part of the discourse of teaching and teacher education in China. As teachers talk about the practice of teaching, as well as the profession, they use metaphor. They talk about teaching as 'gardening', as being 'sculptors' and the 'ones holding the golden keys'.

This pervasiveness of figurative language is perhaps especially striking to me, a foreigner doing research in Chinese. In interviews about educational reforms I began to notice sharp shifts in codes and variations in types of diction or syntactic patterns when teachers moved from policy talk to discussing teaching. There they drew on a repertoire of language very different from that which both they and administrators used in talking about educational policy, reform and school practices. During an initial two years of fieldwork (1982–84) in China, I had interviewed government officials, administrators and teachers about processes of educational reform. Ponderous phrases that stressed the importance of policy, the wisdom of the state, and the groping nature of change had become familiar to me. Then, in a set of interviews about the practice of teaching and sources of teachers' pedagogical decisions, I was caught short. Gone were clumsy phrases about directives and bland details about scope. Instead, teachers spoke in a way much more difficult for me to understand, one rich with literary allusion. The imagery of teaching found both in these interviews and in the extensive body of teacher literature (journals for and by teachers, teacher autobiographies, and published interviews with outstanding teachers) is one rooted in metaphors about culture and art.[2]

Teachers are not alone in using imagery to talk about teaching. Teacher educators in China engage in similar practices. In a widely used teacher education pedagogy textbook, for example, amongst clear efforts to be historical and analytical about teaching, the authors draw on the metaphorical themes of teachers as 'gardeners' and 'molders of the human spirit' (Huazhong Shifan Xueyuan *et al.* 1982, p. 322). Teacher education is referred to as the 'machine tool' which produces parts of other machines; it is the 'mother tool' which forms the crucial pieces in the building of society (Yang and Shao 1990; *ZGJYB*[3] 10 August 1991, p. 2).

Similarly, the state has relied heavily on figurative language to discuss teachers and teacher education. Whether in official policy documents or conversations by government officials, there is frequent use of images to capture the complex role and practices of teachers and their professional education. A long-standing and politically powerful concept of teachers being both 'red and expert' is a case in point (see discussion below).

The particular choice of metaphor, when and how it is used, may well differ with the user and audience. Common threads run across the types of metaphors used by teachers, teacher educators and government officials, however. While much of the traditional rhetoric about teaching and teacher education draws on natural or artistic imagery, contemporary metaphors for teaching and teacher education increasingly represent what Geertz (1980) calls a 'blurred genre', that is, borrowing from other disciplines and applying these sometimes inappropriately. The widely used notion that teachers are 'engineers of the human soul', for example, captures in some uneasy blend the industrial metaphors and nurturing, artistic roots of different image traditions. Like China's educational stance of much of the post-Mao era, the metaphor merges technocratic rationality with art (Habermas 1970).

This chapter begins with blurred genres in metaphor as a point of departure. We need to recognize how metaphors are used to define and mobilize professional practice. Because of their power, we need to interrogate their content and use. As codes, metaphors embed power relations (Foucault 1972). In particular, I see metaphor, especially the blurred genre of contemporary Chinese discourse, as a window on important dilemmas and political conflicts in preservice teacher education and teaching in China in the post-Mao or Deng era. I begin by considering the central metaphor (i.e. red and expert) that historically has shaped teaching and teacher education, and then portray the system of teacher education that has emerged from this historical process. I next describe the dominant characteristics of teaching in China today — as a practice and organization — as well as the criticisms of it. Understanding teaching is necessary for understanding the critiques of and reforms in teacher education. Underlying these critiques are two competing discourses about teacher education: 1) the 'modernizing' view and 2) the 'nationalizing' view. By exploring each and their implications, we are left considering the bankruptcy of current metaphors about teacher education. I argue that teacher education, despite its long and rich metaphorical history, is today in search of a new defining vision, in particular, in search of a metaphor that will help recast the crucial relationships between teaching, teacher education and the state.

To make this argument, I am drawing on extensive field research in China as well as documentary analysis. In a country as large and diverse as China, it seems an act of hubris to talk about 'Chinese teachers'. In a political context where boundaries between 'the state' and the 'Chinese Communist Party' are blurred and at times deliberately obscured from outside view, it is problematic to try to define those terms or distinguish them meaningfully as actors. Finally, in a political economic context changing as dramatically and swiftly as China's, descriptive work that is ahistorical is doomed to be outdated. My fieldwork that began in

1982 certainly persuades me of all three of these points. At the same time, because I have been conducting intensive fieldwork over a long period of time, with repeated and intensive trips to the same sites, I have some confidence about broad patterns. Two years of participant observation in one teacher education institution, followed by three subsequent research trips to that site over an eight-year period, has given me an opportunity to understand how dilemmas of teacher education are worked out in one place. As a part of that research I conducted lengthy formal and informal interviews with teacher education administrators, faculty, students and graduates.[4] My parallel interviews at 21 teacher education institutions in very different regions of the country, combined with my recurrent interviews over the past 12 years with central-level education policy makers, has allowed me to put the experience of my focal institution in some broader perspective. Finally, systematic analysis of education journals and newspapers, as well teacher literature, has helped round out some sense of national developments and tensions.

Still, there are, as I have suggested, real dangers in trying to capture the lived realities of 'Chinese teachers' or 'teacher educators'. This is added reason why a focus on discourse patterns is helpful, since through discursive practices we construct, represent and try to make sense of our world. Discourse is seen here as practices which include but are not limited to text. We create and engage in discourse through our interactions, actions, and decisions (Macdonell 1986; Gee 1990). In making my argument, I try here to stick close either to the field research data on particular sites; to draw on national discourses as represented by widely used newspapers, textbooks, and education journals; or to focus on policy developments. By combining a close reading of text and focused, longitudinal observation of practice, I hope to be able to capture some of what are dominant features of discursive practices in and the discourses of contemporary teacher education in China.

Red and Expert: Capturing Tensions in Teacher Education

The basic metaphor for teaching and teacher education in China, one officially sanctioned and actively promulgated for decades, is that of the 'red and expert' teacher. The image combines politics and economics by suggesting that teaching is a form of moral action with a significant role in economic reproduction. Teachers, in this vision, are servants of the state at the same time they as command specialized, expert knowledge (White 1981). Today these combinations become jarring as the political needs of the state and the demands of the economy collide; for example, the political goals of solidarity and equality often conflict with economic pressures to compete individually for rewards. While the repercussions of this collision are felt in all sectors of education, they are especially powerful for teaching and, hence, teacher education.

Certainly teacher education in all countries is affected by politics and economics. In China, there has been a distinct pattern of such influence caused by the fact that the state has attempted to define the role, knowledge and practice of the teacher. Given China's own turbulent political history, these definitions of teaching have been part of highly politicized debates for decades (White 1981).[5] Such debates have very much influenced teacher education's own history, development and status and contributed to fundamental tensions that have shaped it (Paine 1986).

Tensions have long been central to teacher education in China. In particular, its history has been characterized by a tension between technocratic and political directions (Paine 1986, 1990). Since the founding of the People's Republic in 1949, teacher education has experienced a history of tremendously sharp swings as definitions of teaching, of teacher's knowledge, and of teachers (as a professional group and their role) have changed. At the core of these changes is the shifting prominence and interpretations of the notion that teachers are to be both red and expert. There is potentially an inherent tension in this conceptualization of teaching: 'redness' suggests that the teacher is defined as a moral and/or political actor, while 'expertness' suggests that the teacher embodies technical expertise whose authority rests in knowledge. For decades the state has argued that this concept implies no contradictions, but in the treatment of teachers and in teachers' own actions, it is clear that there have been shifts in the salience of this notion and implicitly, though significantly, in the weighing or balancing of the multiple roles that this slogan attempts to capture.

As a result, teacher education has experienced sharp breaks in its history, as it has stressed at times the moral and/or political dimension of the profession for which it is preparing its students and at other times downplayed that aspect of teaching in favor of emphasizing the academic knowledge that it sees its students as needing. In curricular terms, for example, teacher education institutions for some years abandoned their professional course component (of pedagogy, psychology and teaching methods), decrying this as bourgeois knowledge. At other periods teacher education tried to copy comprehensive universities in transmitting élite academic knowledge (Paine 1990).

Teacher education in the 1980s and 1990s was the product of this disjointed, contested history. By the early 1990s teacher education was situated within a contradictory political economic present. That is, China as a political entity was estranged from the international community in the wake of the repression of the 1989 democracy movement, at the same time that as an economic entity it experienced ever tighter connections to and integration within the capitalist world economic system. Domestically, the early 1990s was a time when 'reform' was a key theme, when the notion of China as a 'socialist market economy' was championed by government leaders as national policy, and when individuals — teachers and teacher educators included — were active participants in a range of market transactions. Teacher education, in short, was working within and responding to a period of tremendous change for China domestically and internationally, a period fraught with paradoxes and uncertainties. Part of the challenge for teacher education during the current period is the need to respond to these circumstances, while drawing on historical traditions, organizational cultures, and an infrastructure which developed over decades of very different models of politics and economics. The introduction of the socialist market economy notion, in the context of the paradoxical juxtapositioning of global isolation and integration, raises questions about the utility of models and metaphors that have been used for teacher education in the past.

The System of Teacher Education

The history of teacher education has produced a system of professional education which is highly specialized and in some ways cut off from other parts of the educational system, particularly élite forms of higher education. Teacher educa-tion in the People's Republic was developed along the model of Soviet sole pur-pose, specialized institutions. As a result, most of teacher education has come to occur in separate institutions: normal schools, which are secondary schools charged with the mission of preparing elementary teachers; normal colleges, two or three-year higher education institutions (offering the *zhuanke* or equivalent of an Asso-ciate's degree) preparing junior secondary school teachers; and normal universities, which prepare senior secondary school teachers.[6]

These institutions work with curricula that are themselves highly specialized and typically very subject-matter focused. The rapid and frequent shifts in na-tional educational policy resulted in teacher education curricula being buffeted about by shifts in the definitions of the teacher's role and descriptions of what teachers needed to know. Shifting teacher education policies meant that teacher education institutions were not able to develop coherent and consistent programs and practices. Teacher education and teacher educators having a lower status than others in higher education further compounded these problems.

Despite the vulnerability and lower status that developed over the years, the scale of China's teacher education enterprise is enormous. By 1990 the system of teacher education included over 3600 institutions of preservice and in-service edu-cation, enrolling 2.1 million trainees. There were over 1000 three and four-year normal schools, 260 normal colleges and universities, and 2000 in-service in-stitutions. At the end of the 1980s there were 1044 normal schools, offering a combination of ordinary secondary education and professional preparation for elementary school teaching and in 1989 enrolling 685,000 students. Normal col-leges and universities include both two and three-year *zhuanke* programs and four-year undergraduate (Bachelor of Arts) programs. In 1989 over 532,000 students were enrolled in 182 *zhuanke* and 78 BA teacher education programs. In fact, teacher education represented one quarter of all university and college students (Chang and Paine 1992).

Teaching and Its Challenges

Who do these institutions serve? Who are the teachers of China, and how can they be characterized? Again, scale alone is significant, particularly in order to grasp the dimension of the challenges facing teacher education. As the 1980s ended there were over 8.5 million elementary and secondary teachers in China (*Zhongguo Jaioyu Nianjian* 1993). The recent changes in politics and economics mentioned briefly above very much affect them. Influencing teachers, these reforms also depend on them. A common argument has been made that the social, economic and technological changes in China require educational reform, and that such reform hinges on teachers. Teachers for a new China, goes the argument, must be highly qualified, able to teach an expanding body of knowledge and new kinds of knowledge relevant to the needs of a modernizing nation, to develop high standards, and to teach in new, more effective ways that support the problem solving and creativity that people see as necessary for technological and economic change (Paine 1992).

The challenge has been to develop this kind of teaching force. Early in the post-Mao years an acute teacher shortage plagued educational reform efforts. As reform continued and teacher education programs — both preservice and in-service — expanded, however, the shortage became less one of absolute numbers and more a scarcity of 'qualified' teachers. Typically, shortages are greater in particular subject areas and at particular levels of schooling. In 1993, for example, nearly half of secondary school teachers (45 percent of junior secondary and 51 percent of senior secondary) were unqualified in terms of their degrees ('Guojia Jiaowei Fuzhuren' 1993, p. 4). This problem takes on special significance because of national policy commitments to introduce compulsory education, to expect that all students' education continue through at least nine years of schooling, and to diversify and vocationalize much of secondary education. The strain on junior high schools (until the 1986 Compulsory Education Law considered part of élite, not mass, education) and vocational schools is thus especially great. For instance, while close to half of secondary school teachers are considered qualified, teachers in agricultural and technical junior and senior high schools were far less prepared: in 1987, only 17.2 and 19.9 percent respectively met minimal standards for amount of schooling (while 30.7 and 40 percent of teachers in 'general' or academic junior or senior high schools did) (*Zhongguo Jiaoyu Tongji Nianjian* 1988, pp. 62–64, 74–75). Even in elementary education, where shortages are less severe, estimates as recent as 1990 described 27 percent as unqualified (*ZGJYB* 25 June 1991, p. 1), and given the large size of the elementary teaching force, this is a serious problem. If you consider the added complications of providing sufficient numbers of qualified teachers for rural schools, for vocational and technical schools, and for schools which now are obligated to extend more years of education to a larger portion of the population than ever before, then the problems of teacher shortages seem to be both serious ones impeding the path of reform and an important challenge to teacher education.

The problems and challenges are not limited to numbers of teachers with appropriate degrees, however. Also central to the success of reforms in teaching and teacher education, critics argue, is the need for new approaches to teaching: in other words, new kinds of teachers. The call is for teachers who can teach very differently, who support the creative thinking, problem solving, and independent work that are now seen to be at the heart of China's technological development. This calls for teachers who do not root their practice in teacher-centered views of instruction.

As daunting as these challenges are for teacher preparation and change, neither ending teacher shortages nor reforming the approaches to teaching solves another central concern of the teaching profession: the status of teachers. Analysts agree that for change to occur within teaching and teacher education, the economic, social and political position of teachers has to improve. Although teaching has at times been highly regarded socially or politically, it has long been a poorly paid profession, and it has remained so in the post-Mao years, in part because of changes in the economy. In a recent study, teachers ranked eleventh out of twelve in occupational wages of professional groups (Yuan 1988).

This long-standing problem of low pay has been exacerbated by market-driven reforms of the 1980s, as all professions and occupations have found other ways to generate income, to rely on bonuses to salaries, and to generate outside earnings. Wage increases teachers received in the reform years did not keep pace either with wage hikes of other groups or with inflation. In many ways, teachers in fact lost ground. They were able to add very little to their earning through bonuses. While 13.4 percent of the total income of people working in state-owned units came through bonuses in 1986, elementary and secondary teachers were only adding 3.4 and 3.2 percent, respectively, to their salaries through bonuses (*Zhongguo Shehui Tonji Ziliao 1987*, p. 101; Wang 1988). Compared to other occupational groups, they were very limited in their ability to cash in on the possibilities of earning outside income (through sideline activities or converting their workplace and skills to a second purpose). Beijing teachers ranked the lowest of 12 occupational groups in their outside income generated (Xiang 1989).

These problems, well known by teachers and the general public, led to a 1987 pay raise targeted only at teachers, but provinces and local governments have in places blocked the distribution of this raise, and what was to be a policy triumph of symbolic and material support for teachers has been diminished by slow and uneven implementation. More recently and more problematic was the well-publicized crisis in 1993 of millions of *yuan* in teachers' wages owed teachers in unpaid salaries (*ZGJYB* 11 January 1993, p. 1). As early as 1991 the central government noted the problem of local governments not paying their teachers, but despite investigation, the problems appeared to have continued and in some places even worsened (*RMRB*[7] 27 August 1993, p. 2). By early 1994 the problem had been addressed in most places, according to government reports, but there remained some regions which had not resolved this crisis (*RMRB* 26 January 1994).

Compounding these very real economic problems for teachers are persistent concerns about the social status and respect afforded teachers. Even though in January 1994 the central government, in response to years of debate and criticism, issued its first Teachers Law that would recognize the importance of teachers, protect their physical safety and guarantee that they would be paid their wages, at the same time mainstream newspapers carried articles about teachers being beaten, assaulted and otherwise shown little respect ('Zhonghua Renmin Gongheguo Jiaoshifa' 1993; *ZGJYB* 1 December 1993, p. 1, 31 December 1993, p. 1). Thus, despite government campaigns, in staffroom conversations, formal interviews, and their actions — such as applying to teacher education programs or making job transfers out of teaching, many teachers acknowledge that teaching is not an attractive profession. Even though job mobility is rather restricted in China, as the economy has changed, many teachers have gladly given up the guarantees of lifetime employment as teachers to seek possibilities out of schools and teaching. Similarly, teacher education programs, despite vigorous recruitment efforts, not infrequently find themselves hard-pressed to attract cohorts filled with students who are committed to becoming teachers. Some programs have even been unable to fill their registration quotas. In one extreme but telling example, a provincial teacher education college anticipated admitting 147 new students, but only one applicant listed it as a preference (*ZGJYB* 9 November 1989, p. 1).

Added to the economic and social barriers influencing teaching are the political problems associated with the teaching profession. Since the crushing of the 1989 democracy movement, the state has once again reasserted the primacy of the political dimension in teaching. It has redefined the teacher's role, stressing their political role, and saying that teachers in a sense must be moral guardians for the state. Of course, the state had never argued otherwise, but in casting about for blame after massive student participation in the democracy activities of the late 1980s, some leaders suggested that schools and in particular teachers may have lapsed in stressing the moral socialization aspect of a child's education. The collapse of the Soviet Union two years later further persuaded leaders to focus on the ideology transmission function of teaching. Li Peng's 1991 speech at the annual Teachers' Day holiday exemplifies this reemergence of an emphasis on the political roles for teachers. Although he argued that 'the key to developing education lies in training and expanding the contingent of teachers with both political integrity and professional competence' (the notion of red and expert), he claimed that the peculiar combination of China's economic openness and political vulnerability argues for putting teachers' ideological functions first:

> Drastic changes have taken place in the current international situation. On the one hand, we face the challenge of a new global technological revolution, while on the other, we face the severe test of upholding and safeguarding the socialist position with Chinese characteristics. Whether China can meet these two challenges successfully is closely connected to educational work. It is hoped that all teachers, cadres, staff members, and workers on the educational front will fully recognize their historical obligation, further strengthen their socialist conviction, heighten their spirit, overcome difficulties, and work hard to continuously improve their political and ideological quality and their professional competence, so as to contribute more to training a new generation of builders of socialism and to ensure that our country will not change its color for many generations to come. (*FBIS*[8] 11 November 1991, p. 17)

My interviews suggest that the state's reassertion of this role makes many young teachers — already less than enthusiastic about their low paid and poorly respected work — feel threatened. Given the history of the Cultural Revolution, they feel vulnerable, and given that for many their motivations for entering teaching had little or nothing to do with its political role, they feel frustrated.

The Challenge for Teacher Education

Together, these aspects of China's teaching profession today pose dilemmas (Paine 1992): how can the country create a teaching force who will be sufficient in numbers and possess new kinds of expertise, who will be better paid and have higher social status, and who will play political or moral socialization roles which are undesirable for many entering it and which may undermine the sorts of new approaches to teaching being proposed? These are real problems for China's teachers, as well as serious challenges to its teacher preparation.

The teacher education system that is to meet these challenges, to respond to this set of criticisms of teaching, has itself experienced a wide-ranging critique in the Deng era. A result of its earlier history of dramatic shifts has been persistent confusion about the goals of teacher education, and this has led to programs with weak goals, ineffective structures, inappropriate curricula and teacher education's poor integration into either K–12 schooling or higher education.[9] Programs, say the critics, suffer from structural overlap and duplication, and the content and structure often represent a poor match with educational needs (Chang and Paine 1992). Particularly strong criticism has focused on the curriculum, which for the most part has been geared towards élite education and away from basic education.

Few teacher education programs, for example, acknowledge the needs of learners in rural schools, which house the majority of China's schoolchildren. Critics fault teacher education curricula for being out of touch with the needs of real schools, focused too much on subject area study to the neglect of professional educational study and practice, outdated in its methods, and offering a poor match between a rigid teacher education curriculum (often top-heavy with required courses taught through lecture formats) and the cognitive creativity and independence that teacher education graduates are supposed to develop in their pupils (Chang 1984, p. 246; Guojia Jiaowei 1988, p. 13; Hu 1989, p. 33).

A second major area of criticism in teacher education concerns its structure. Tight specialization by level of teaching (that is, normal schools for primary teacher preparation, normal colleges for junior high teaching, and so on) restricts teacher education's ability to respond to changes in supply and demand. For example, even though the greatest shortage today is in junior high teaching, only 9 percent of teacher training institutions have this as their training mission; in contrast, 85 percent of teacher education institutions focus on preparing elementary teachers, even though that area suffers the least from shortage and is projected, due to demographic changes, to have a surplus. This high level of specialization within the teacher education system means there is a lack of vertical integration. In addition, teachers often end up being unprepared for the level at which they eventually assume a teaching position. Because of teacher shortages at all levels, schools will often happily accept teacher preparation graduates whose own training was for a different level of schooling, but this muddies the mission of teacher education institutions. Formally, their mission is highly specialized and the curriculum is similarly narrowly defined. While their missions are in fact far more diffuse, however, their graduates unfortunately are not given a comparable breadth of educational exposure.

Competing Discourses

This combination of curricular and structural problems poses a considerable challenge for teacher education. Of course, the challenge is made all the more difficult because of the problems of and demands on teachers and the teaching profession. While the challenges as I have outlined them are fairly widely agreed on, the discourse about them does not represent a single vision of teaching or of teacher education and its relation to the rest of education, the economy, politics and society. Instead, if we analyze these critiques and their related proposals for reform, we see two main discourses, what I suggest are competing discourses: the 'modernizing' view and the 'nationalizing' view.[10] Each tries to construct a view of the world of teacher education, to emphasize some aspects of that world and mask or downplay others, and to assert similarities and differences with other phenomena (Manning 1979, p. 662).

One of these discourses I call the 'modernizing' view. Typically it links its analysis of teacher needs and teacher education reform to ideas of economic and technological development or modernization. A speech to an international pedagogy research conference by Gu Mingyuan, one of the most respected educational researchers in contemporary China, illustrates the assumptions and orientations of this view. Entitled 'Times, Expectations, Education and Teachers', Gu's (1994) speech focuses on education at the end of the twentieth and beginning of the twenty-first centuries and considers how educators today need to take into account this period of dramatic global change — economic, political and social. Countering claims that technological changes will make teachers unnecessary, he argues that teachers in fact will be even more important in the next century, and to fulfill their expanded roles, they will need to satisfy three expectations. His choice of the three and the ordering within these represents a 'modernizing' take on traditional views about the range of relevant competencies teachers need. He suggests that teachers first must have a 'professional consciousness', which includes loving children and a commitment to education. Second is 'strong professional ability', which he sees as having two components — depth of knowledge and 'skill in conveying this to students'. His third expectation is that teachers need 'good psychological character and ideological character. This is expressed in having ideals, having virtues, and being good at dealing with relations between peoples and being able to act as an example' (Gu 1994, p. 18). He argues that all three conditions need to be met, none can be left out, and in this sense he connects to the tradition of calling for teachers to be both red and expert. Yet in his categories that could be considered part of 'redness' he includes psychological and not just political character, and sees these as manifested in terms that are not necessarily political. Just as his speech refers to 'developed countries', so his notion of what teachers need to know and be able to do resonates with many contemporary teacher education proposals in the West.

Those arguing within the 'modernizing' perspective, like Gu, situate their critiques and proposals for teacher education reform within the context of a changing China and a changing world. They implicitly distance themselves from national politics and Party rhetoric and explicitly make connections to the international political economy. Yu Zhongxin, for example, makes the case that the 'outward looking economy' of China's post-Mao period requires a different kind of teacher education (Yu 1989, p. 24) Claiming that too often the call for teacher education to focus on schools has led, perhaps inadvertently, to losing the link to society, he says that in this period of rapid social change teacher education has become 'closed', 'conservative' and 'backward' (p. 24). He proposes instead new operational principles, new management systems, new staffing, and preparing a new or different kind of teacher education student. This new type of student needs to develop, for example, knowledge of foreign languages and technology, a competitive spirit which also allows for cooperation, and independence and a willingness to take risks (pp. 26–27).

This 'modernizing' discourse uses forms of evidence and justification that are part of an international (read western positivist) research community. In making its arguments, it often relies on surveys and other kinds of empirical evidence. Sometimes key concepts it offers as part of its solutions to the challenges of teaching and teacher reform are international (or borrowed from other countries). Thus, for example, in a rural community I observed teachers, and teacher educators busy studying Benjamin Bloom's 'mastery learning' — a concept championed by the provincial education authorities and consequently by the county officials. Teachers in remote villages in this county who had never ventured even as far from their home as the provincial capital were familiarized with Bloom's concepts (significantly, as translated by Chinese interpreters of his thought).

In this case and other instances of this 'modernizing' discourse, solutions to the problems of teaching and, hence, of teacher education tend to be technical and technocratic. There is use of a 'scientific' method to analyze educational phenomena. Rational approaches to attracting teachers and strengthening the teacher education curriculum are put forward. A 1989 study, typical of this genre, proposes reform of the curriculum of teacher education universities on the basis of analyzing the curricula of different majors in nine universities, comparing these with course distributions found in teacher education programs in other countries (especially using statistics from the US, the Philippines, the USSR, and Japan), and conducting follow-up studies of graduates of teacher education programs and the schools which employed them. Based on these data the researcher proposes adjusting the balance of courses in given majors and in professional education and strengthening the quality of that education (Hu 1989, p. 33–37). A similar example of curriculum analyses and reform proposals uses follow-up studies of teacher education graduates and draws explicitly on a western definition of curriculum to start its analysis of the special difficulties of teacher education curriculum (Bi 1989).

Teachers — whether in teaching or teacher education reform proposals — are conceived of as rational actors. While much of the attention focuses on the new kind of knowledge and skills that tomorrow's teachers will need, an equally important thrust of the arguments focuses on such issues as recruitment and admissions. The argument is that developing a new kind of teacher is impossible without getting the right raw material for the teacher education intervention. For example, a State Education Commission report showed a decreasing number of students listing teacher education as their first preference (dropping from 72 percent of admitted students in 1986 to only 55 percent in 1989), an increasing number of women entering it, and a lowering of academic quality.[11] The causes of these trends were seen as rooted in economic and social problems teachers face, their stressful work and poor living conditions, the lack of investment in education, students' antipathy for working in rural schools, changes in people's values, and ineffective admissions procedures. While the authors argued that the combination of teachers' material conditions, ideological education, and admission procedures all required attention and could not be separated, in discussing solutions, those which came first — raising teachers' salaries, increasing investment in education, raising stipends for teacher education students — implied a technical, rational approach towards teachers and recruiting them to the profession (Guojia Jiaowei Gaoxiao Xueshengsi 1990, pp. 68–72).

This 'modernizing' discourse stresses efficiency and effectiveness. In the admissions study just cited, for example, there is great concern about the 'wastage' of teacher education graduates who never enter the teaching profession. Reforms are seen as needed to improve teacher education institutions' ability to function. At a 1988 meeting of the leaders of teacher education universities in the south central region, for instance, university presidents spoke out about how:

> present management systems bind the hands and feet of teacher education colleges and obstruct the development of tertiary teacher education. In the process of real operations, subjective wishes are often far from objective realities, so, on the one hand, education is supposed to respond to society and serve economic construction, but, on the other hand, with old, outdated notions of a pure teacher education character and the constraints of fifty years of the powerful influence of a Soviet model, there

is just the emphasis on matching the ordinary secondary school curriculum. This doesn't match the deep structural changes of the secondary education system and is in sharp contradiction to developing the commodity economy. In addition, because of inflation and economic shortages, tertiary teacher education institutions have difficulty entering the market economy competition. ('Huanan Basheng . . .' 1989, p. 79)

These arguments, like in the case of Bloom's ideas, tend to be connected to and buoyed by an international discourse. The university presidents refer to changes in teacher education in 'advanced western countries' as a way of defending their idea of broadening their schools' mission from being single-purpose institutions and admitting non-teacher education majors. Throughout the period there are many articles that not only bring in occasional references to foreign teacher education but which focus primarily on it, describing its strengths, problems, and development as a way to analyze key issues in Chinese teacher education (Shi 1987).

In the wake of the 1989 repression of the democracy movement and the state's legitimation crisis, however, we can see a shift in the official discourse of teaching and teacher education. While the 'modernizing' perspective remained well represented in journals and interviews into the 1990s, a second perspective, one I call the 'nationalizing' view, also has reappeared. This 'nationalizing' perspective is one with ties to earlier political periods, and calls on the traditions of talking about issues of teachers and teacher education in the language of 'red and expert'. This discourse stresses teachers' moral role and the social obligations of teacher education. It criticizes recent teacher education practices for paying too much attention to teachers' technical knowledge base and neglecting their ideological role. In debates over drafts of the Teachers Law, for example, a National People's Congress Standing Committee member argued that:

> for a while in the past, it had been emphasized that teachers must be academically up to standard while scanty attention had been paid to teachers' political and ideological education. This tendency should be reversed. Currently, the international situation is changing fast, so we should attach importance to this problem. (*FBIS* 3 September 1991, p. 32)

The 'nationalizing' perspective, like the 'modernizing' one, takes international changes into account, yet the interpretation of these changes and their implications for strengthening China's domestic program differs greatly.

Both discourse groups see teacher education reform as demanded by broader social, economic, political and technological changes. Yet the emphasis of that reform is quite different. The 'nationalizing' perspective sees ideological issues, not technical concerns, as central to reform. In a national meeting on teacher education in 1991, for example, the guiding question of the conference was 'how can we do better in putting moral education in the first place and comprehensively improving teacher education in the years ahead?' (*ZGJYB* 25 June 1991, p. 1). In describing teacher education reform that should come out of this discussion, six aspects were identified in order of priority. The first was moral education, while the second was serving rural education. This combination of the moral role of teachers and the social role of teacher education comes through in official discourse that represents the 'nationalizing' perspective. For example, an official in the State Education Commission wrote of the need for normal schools' operation to be rooted in three concepts — 'service, broad education, and the national condition' (Meng 1991, p. 23). Here 'service' is defined as service to basic education (that is, elementary and junior high schooling) and 'broad education' as recognizing education's close link to politics and economics and taking into account the impact of political and economic development on basic education and the associated demands on teachers. The 'national condition' is described as recognizing that China is still a predominantly rural country; the author argues that over 80 percent of normal schools should be preparing their students to teach in rural primary schools. According to this discourse, teacher education needs to turn away from its fascination with élite models and advanced sectors of education and instead focus on serving rural and basic education. This discourse community praises teacher education institutions which have instituted a rural practicum.

At the same time, the 'nationalizing' discourse tends to reject, or at least be very discriminating about, foreign ideas. On the same day that the national newspaper noted the change in Soviet politics after Gorbachev's fall, an article on education quoted He Dongchang, a former Minister of Education, talking to the major educational theory group which represents the source of theory for teacher education. He discussed 'resisting peaceful evolution' (code for what leaders describe as a foreign plot to promote the quiet but dangerous transformation of China through the corrupting influence of bourgeois western ideas) and developing the 'successors to socialism' (*ZGJYB* 22 August 1991, p. 1).

From this perspective, the political dimension in teacher education is foremost, and teacher education, rather than analyzed in terms of rational, isolated individuals, requires a class analysis. A 1991 editorial in the major education newspaper (sponsored by the State Education Commission) makes this point. Interestingly, like those articulating the 'modernizing' discourse, this essay argues for the importance of teacher education. The two perspectives clearly divide over what the important questions for teacher education are, however. In this essay, the authors, after defending the importance of teacher education in terms of its role in supporting education and the development of human resources for the country, argue that:

> education has a clear class nature. For teacher education, the questions of who is to be served, what kind of people are to be trained, and what path they will take have important meaning. The students trained by teacher education colleges will be healthy, young, mature education workers — engineers 'of the human soul'. Their political inclinations, ideological consciousness, moral character and cultural accomplishments all directly influence the next generation. The socialist task asks that teacher education institutions prepare students to possess a firm and correct political direction, deep love for the socialist homeland, a steadfast belief in the socialist system, willingness to serve the people and a noble moral character and good behavior and habits. For this reason, teacher education colleges and universities must adhere to socialist operational approaches and conscientiously make moral education a top priority. (*ZGJYB* 20 August 1991, p. 3)

'Modernizing' and 'Nationalizing' Views on the Professional Education Core

The 'modernizing' and 'nationalizing' discourses share an initial premise about the importance of teacher education and its need for reform. Yet they offer contrasting interpretations of the problems and solutions. What do these conflicting views mean for teacher education practice? As a window on these competing discourses, we can consider the case of the professional education core, especially the pedagogy course, in the teacher education university (or normal university) curriculum.[12] The long-standing problems related to defining the 'teacher education character' are best expressed in how this educational foundation (pedagogy) component is conceptualized, organized and experienced. What is professional knowledge? How should the education core be organized and taught? The answers to these questions illustrate both the challenges facing Chinese teacher education in the 1990s and the competing visions implicit in the responses to these challenges.

For years the required course in pedagogy, typically a semester long course taught in the student's junior year, has been one of the few places where the teacher education curriculum was obviously different from the curriculum of a biology, history, or literature student preparing in a comprehensive university. In the pedagogy course, students who are preparing to become teachers get their first (and generally only) formal introduction to the role of the teacher, educational purposes, the educational system, and other foundation issues that define the relationships between teachers, their practice, society, and the state. The book used for the longest time in normal university pedagogy courses was a translation of a Soviet text by Kairov. Many institutions produced their own text in the 1980s, but these tended to be quite similar, introducing similar issues as the core knowledge for the course.

In the late 1980s this course came to be the center of increasing debate. Students criticized it as boring, dry, and offering material that, they said, using an analogy from eating, 'does not fill you up'. Certainly the student disengagement in this course was striking to me, as I observed each class session for one semester and was impressed by the fact that despite the unusual presence of a foreigner in class, students boldly read newspapers, napped and otherwise showed a lack of interest in the lectures.[13] This student response was obviously a problem for the instructor, who took to calling roll in the large class, even though this took time away from the lecture. Student attendance was nevertheless poor. My experience at my fieldwork institution was obviously not unique. In 1989 even central government officials noted that the professional education curriculum is 'not sufficiently emphasized, has empty theories devoid of content, is unfocused and disconnected, has outdated methods and techniques, too few course hours and lacks necessary investment' (Qiao 1989, p. 40).

By the early 1990s State Education Commission officials were even telling me of their great dissatisfaction with the pedagogy course. The official education newspaper stated:

> the core pedagogy curriculum which is called teacher education institution's special character has presently in some teacher education schools and colleges become 'an adornment class', a 'decorative class' that neither

students want to study nor teachers want to teach. (*ZGJYB* 23 April 1991, p. 1)

The clamor over the perceived weakness of the education core and the pedagogy course in particular produced large numbers of reform proposals. The two major discourses of teacher education — the 'modernizing' and 'nationalizing' views — each have offered suggestions for the improvement of this curriculum. These suggestions illustrate stark differences between the two.

The 'modernizing' perspective has brought its rational and technical orientation to solving the problems of teacher education's pedagogy course and improving the professional education given preservice teachers. Common threads run throughout the proposals for improvement. To address the problem of poor student motivation, these critics propose improving the match between teacher education students and teacher education. They argue for greater curricular flexibility and making professional education, as a piece of the curriculum, more prominent. At the same time they recommend a tighter integration of course components, elimination of redundancy and overlap; for the education core, this means clarifying the boundaries between pedagogy and educational psychology. They argue for making the professional education core more modern. In general these reformers are eager to get away from what they see as the outdated Soviet model of teacher education; often implicit in their recommendations is a kind of rejection of tradition and history. For example, one article focuses on showing how the Soviet model on which China's pedagogy was based is 'traditional educational thinking' (Yan 1987, p. 65). They describe the concept of 'pedagogy' as trapped by its initial framework, one borrowed from the Soviets and overly philosophical and school-focused. In its place they make suggestions informed by research about teacher education and the development of pedagogy in other countries, especially Japan, North America and Western Europe (An 1992).

To provide support for their claims, those articulating the 'modernist' discourse often rely on statistical research. Consider one research paper as exemplifying both the targets of criticisms and the discursive themes of the 'modernizing' perspective. The researchers, in a survey of schools employing graduates of a teacher education university, found that the teacher education students were seen as weakest in their pedagogical knowledge and skills, particularly their 'ability to solve real problems' and knowledge of the 'educational reform situation' — described as reflecting 'mastery of educational knowledge' (Hu 1989, pp. 34–35). A common response to this kind of finding has been encouragement for strengthening teacher education students' practical experiences. Thus, for example, the 'modernizers' call for improving student teaching's administration, placement, content, time, methods, supervision, and financial support (Guojia Jiaowei Zhishu Liusuo Shida Jiaoyu Shixi Yantaohui Jishu 1989, pp. 33–36).

For the 'modernizing' reformers, teacher education in general and the education core in particular needs to be improved by making the curriculum more rationally fit the needs of schools in a rapidly changing China. For these reformers, a historical examination of the pedagogy course suggests that it has 'gotten lost' along the years, and that it has failed to meet the needs or expectations of both researchers, who see it as weak theoretically, and practitioners, who see it as 'cut off from reality or at least not able to give much guidance to educational practice' (Chen 1989, p. 33). A central explanation for the lack of development of the course is political. Critics who write within the 'modernizing' view decry the ways in which political turmoil and an overemphasis on a simplistic Sinification of educational theory has disrupted the development of a critical theory of pedagogy (Chen 1989, pp. 39–40). They envision a pedagogy course informed by international developments in the structure of a changing discipline.

Here the competing discourse of reformers I have called the 'nationalizing' view provides a sharply different vision of goals for and explanation of the problems with China's pedagogy course and professional education more generally in teacher education. For them the goals of the pedagogy course are more explicitly tied to serving national purposes, and the framework which is to inform these goals is Marxist and inevitably linked to the ruling political power. Thus, at a national conference on teacher education in 1991 'nationalizing' participants argued that:

> the revision of the teaching materials for the core pedagogy course must be theoretically guided by Marxism, Leninism and Mao Zedong Thought, develop in depth research on the class nature of education, truly establish with the guidance of Marxist and Leninist thought a socialist education system with Chinese characteristics, research in depth China's national situation, research and summarize China's educational experiences, uphold the principle of theory linked to practice, and face basic education, secondary education, and especially face rural education (*ZGJYB* 23 April 1991, p. 1).

The 'nationalizing' perspective critique of current approaches to the professional core is perhaps best exemplified by an earlier speech by He Dongchang, a Vice-Chair of the State Education Commission, to a national meeting of teacher education institutions engaged in reforming the pedagogy course's teaching materials. He Dongchang, like the 'modernizers', recognizes the phenomenon of student disengagement in pedagogy and even cites a State Education Commission official's view that 'the classes students least like to attend is first politics, second pedagogy, and third teaching [methods]' (He 1991, p. 4). His explanation differs from the 'modernizers', however, who fault outdated approaches and content. Rather, he suggests that what will improve the course is to make it 'reflect more and better the reality of socialist education with Chinese characteristics' (p. 4). He suggests this has been impeded by a fascination with bourgeois ideas. In fact, he begins his speech with a harsh critique of 'bourgeois liberalism' and its influence on courses and texts. Disciplines like pedagogy have not been critical enough of bourgeois social science and are not closely enough connected to China's real situation, he claims. The 'nationalizers' do not exclude all foreign ideas, yet they argue that the main concern of the pedagogy course should be focusing on the present, on China, and on basic education. He Dongchang claims that finding how to deal with foreign ideas in the pedagogy course is both important and delicate work: 'with respect to the West, we can't completely reject it, but also can't completely accept it. This touches on the basic characteristics of socialist education, which are distinguished from capitalist education' (p. 6).

He Dongchang suggests that the 'political orientation and system of thinking' are different (He 1991, p. 6). According to him, Marxism, Leninism and Mao Zedong Thought must be the basis for knowledge in this course and the rest of professional education. Given his starting point, he then is critical of particular concepts and theoretical approaches that have been incorporated into pedagogy. In discussing the bodies of knowledge that contribute to the course, for example, He criticizes psychology as 'not yet a fully mature science' (p. 5). Although he sees it as an important basis for professional education, he makes clear distinctions in psychology as well as other fields between 'correct' and 'wrong' ideas. Notions of correctness are central to the 'nationalizers'' arguments, whether it be appropriately summarizing the experience of Chinese teachers as lessons for preservice teachers or of having a correct view of Chinese history ('He Dongchang Tongzhi . . .' 1992, p. 9). In all cases, however, correctness is determined by the Party, by official definitions, not personal ones.

Much of He Dongchang's and other 'nationalizers'' concern focuses on this question of knowledge — what is the appropriate knowledge for teacher education students? Like others writing in this perspective, however, he also pays attention to questions of purpose — what is professional education for? Here, like in his discussion of pedagogy's theoretical content, He Dongchang puts China's current needs first; that is, he describes the teacher's role, and hence the training they need for that, as linked to national goals. For example, he views the pedagogy course as needing to help teacher education students understand 'why they want to become a teacher?' (He 1991, p. 6) According to him, in answering that question the course should help students develop the sense of responsibility and activism they will need as professionals. A second goal of the course is that it should also help preservice students learn how to be good teachers. Yet it seems significant that for He the first goal — identifying reasons for teaching — is given priority and the reasons are determined by society, not by the individual preservice teacher. The technical issues of how to be a good teacher are treated as secondary and, he suggests, may in fact only be able to be raised as questions in the course, with opportunities to consider them more fully in later practice. Interestingly, in discussing the practicum, which is part of the professional education core, he asserts that its importance is 'not in learning teaching techniques and gaining experience' but in 'understanding why one becomes a teacher' (He 1991, p. 9). Teacher education students can come to understand this through seeing firsthand what society demands of education and how teacher education is needed to support development. In short, in the 'nationalizing' view the professional education core should remind preservice teachers of their social and political roles as teachers and encourage them to see definitions of their role as coming from social or national expectations, not professional and individual interpretations. Pedagogy is fundamentally about ideas, not techniques.

Concluding Thoughts: Bankruptcy in Metaphors

He Dongchang's speech was published in the leading education research journal, *Jiaoyu Yanjiu* (Education Research). There, as in most education journals, readers can find evidence of both discourses. Within a single issue of this journal, for example, one can find articles by 'modernizers' with elaborate tables, reference lists filled with western research, and arguments about the need for teacher education to weigh the costs and benefits of specific actions, as well as those by 'nationalizers' resembling He Dongchang's speech, relying rather less on empirical research and more on a statement of goals connected to a broader and explicit political agenda. These discourses draw on very different data, different conceptual frameworks, and different means of justifying their claims. The results are contrasting visions of the professional education core, of teacher education, and of teaching.

It is not surprising in education research and practice in most countries to find contrasting discourse communities. What is significant in the Chinese case is that prior periods of Chinese education history tended to have one dominant discourse. In the Deng era, however, these two have coexisted, even competed for the attention of policy makers and the energies of teacher educators. The oddly jarring juxtapositions, however, raise questions about the ways in which the teacher education community can unite to find meaningful ways to address the very significant challenges facing them as they prepare teachers for China's schools. Just as teaching has increasingly been characterized by metaphors which represent 'blurred genres' drawn from different disciplines, so now teacher education finds its reforms incorporating eclectic and even contradictory proposals. The state has introduced technical solutions to attract better students, offer a stronger curriculum, and make more efficient graduates' transition to a teaching labor market; it has also relied heavily on symbolic campaigns about teaching and teacher education's ideological calling (Paine 1991). Teacher educators, looking for ways to approach reform, see on a single newspaper page ideas from an article outlining procedures for reducing wastage of graduates and increasing the curriculum's elective options set next to an article affirming the class basis of teacher education (*ZGJYB* 20 August 1991, p. 3).

Metaphors provide codes that can give meaning to action. To the outsider, however, an analysis of the metaphors and other discursive practices that are used to construct teacher education in China today suggests that the two dominant discourses both fall short. At this complex moment in Chinese history, the two main discourses of teacher education still leave unanswered the long-standing question about teacher education's special character. What is that character? If one turns to the 'modernizing' explanation for an answer, teacher education is defined by its need to serve particular kinds of schools efficiently and effectively; it is powerfully shaped by the labor market and the broader economy. Teacher education's special task is to provide expertise. If one looks to the 'nationalizing' explanation for an answer, teacher education is to serve the state's and country's (these being seen as sharing one goal) development needs — particularly in terms of political and moral socialization of citizens.

Neither of these definitions seems to be able to capture the imagination of teacher educators and their students. Instead, increasing numbers of teacher education institutions have set up special non-teaching majors to make money, diluting their focus as a way of competing in what they see as an institutional market. More and more teacher educators have sought to augment their incomes through moonlighting in work outside their field, and teacher education students, lured neither by rational inducement strategies nor by noble propaganda campaigns, continue to enter teacher education only reluctantly and to evade becoming teachers in surprising numbers.

In the early 1980s an essay by a teacher education student showed already the failure of teacher education's mixed metaphors to inspire professional education:

> I stepped foot through the teacher training gate and saw written on a sign, 'Welcome, future engineers of the human soul!' I thought, What engineer? It's only that I've failed my entrance exam and had no alternative but to come to be a so-called 'future engineer'. This is simply self-consolation. (Luo 1983, p. 22)

By the mid-1990s there were rumors of teacher education institutions changing their signs above their entrance gates (and their formal mission), no longer trying to motivate their students towards teaching but pragmatically choosing to jettison their teacher education mission in favor of more training for more lucrative and higher status positions — thus seeking to attract students and the resources that accompany their attendance. Students, teacher educators, and their institutions in the early 1980s had relatively few options, but a decade later the expansion of market practices in the labor force and the commodification of education created far more alternatives, many not conducive to reforming and strengthening teacher education. Teacher education in China, like elsewhere, is located at the nexus of schools, higher education, the labor market and the state. The crisis in China's teacher education is in large part a reflection of its location in this intersection of institutions in transition.

The 'modernizing' and 'nationalizing' discourses fail to capture the dynamics of the situation teacher education faces in the 1990s. Neither is able to draw teacher education forward, and thus we can view them as 'bankrupt'. The term bankruptcy serves nicely here as a metaphor within both the 'modernizing' and the 'nationalizing' views. One can speak of financial bankruptcy in capitalist or market economies, with which the 'modernizers' identify, when for technical or other reasons a person, organization, or society is not in a position to meet debt obligations. One can also refer to moral bankruptcy, when an individual, organization, or society does not have strong enough moral fiber to fend off temptations to immoral behavior — a concern of the 'nationalizers'.

Focusing on ideology and moral socialization to strengthen solidarity and allegiance to a socialist state, the 'nationalizing' view does not speak to a teacher education community deeply affected by a growing commercialization of work and social relations. By ignoring the material changes (or, at other times, downplaying them), this discourse is often discounted by teacher education students I have interviewed as out of touch and ignoring the real issues. In contrast, the 'modernizing' view takes the changing material relations in China very seriously, often seeing greater economic investment and financial incentives as ways to improve teacher education. Yet this general focus on material relations lacks persuasive power when alternatives to teacher education — for students, teacher educators and their institutions — are even more lucrative. In short, these discourses prove morally and materially bankrupt. Teacher education now needs new metaphors of teaching, authentic ones, not 'blurred genres' borrowed from other fields. It needs new discourses to redefine in meaningful ways what gives contemporary Chinese teachers value, where their power lies, what the limits are to that power, and hence what the relationships are between teaching, teacher education and the state.

Teacher education is not only in need of metaphors to give meaning to action, however. Action itself is needed. Inspiring and meaningful metaphors for China's teacher education will only be possible when crucial economic and political relationships are redefined. The challenges facing teachers and teacher education indicate incontrovertibly that their material reality must be changed. In an economic and social context where value is increasingly defined in monetary terms, slogans about teaching as a noble profession or the importance of teacher education will only be empty words, unsuccessful consolation that even entering teacher education students can recognize and dismiss. In addition, metaphors that can constructively shape teacher education reforms will require the state to rethink teachers' power and the autonomy they are now accorded. The problem for teachers and their preparation is not only tight economics, but a stifling political control that limits professional growth and heightens the vulnerability of teaching and teacher education. As a result, teacher education is in search of not only new metaphors, but new conditions — economic and political — that these metaphors can describe.

Notes

1 Research for this chapter was supported by grants from the Committee for Scholarly Communications with China, Michigan State University, and a National Academy of Education Spencer Foundation Fellowship. I would like to thank them for their financial support as well as Brian DeLany, Wang Jian, and Zhang Naihua for assisting me in data collection and commenting on the work in progress.
2 One of the most frequent metaphors combines nurturing with art through metaphors about gardening. In a preface to a collection of teachers' accounts of their teaching, the editor writes: 'Planting millet and planting trees entail what we may call agricultural art or gardening art. This is labor but it is also art. Cultivating people is even harder work, even more exquisite art. Teachers' god-given responsibility is cultivating people, educating people, so they are called "engineers of the human soul"' (Shenyang Shifan Xueyuan Xuebaobianjibu 1981, p. 1).
3 *ZGJYB* is *Zhongguo Jiaoyubao* (*China Education News*).
4 In terms just of the formal interviews in preservice teacher education, I interviewed 75 administrators of teacher education institutions, 44 of their faculty, and 101 undergraduate students.
5 As an example, for a Chinese discussion of three major debates over the notion of 'red and expert', see Shanghaishi Shehuikexue Xeuhui (1992, pp. 125–33).
6 There are increasing numbers of exceptions to this general pattern, as the State Education Commission now allows some elementary teacher education to occur in higher education institutions and encourages comprehensive and other types of universities to prepare some of their graduates to teach in secondary schools. Yet these exceptions remain a small minority of the total of teacher education students and programs.
7 *RMRB* is *Renmin Ribao* (*Peoples Daily*; overseas edition).
8 *FBIS* is *Foreign Broadcast Information Service Daily Reports: China*.
9 Because of the legacy of specialized training and the low status of teacher education, many normal colleges and universities work actively to emulate comprehensive institutions. As a result, say the critics, teacher education programs lose or sometimes even abandon their sense of what makes teacher education special, what the critics call the 'teacher education character' (Chang and Paine 1992).
10 The labels for these two discourses, 'modernizing' and 'nationalizing', are my own construction and not terms commonly used in China to refer to a particular teacher education discourse, 'school', or faction. Readers will note the similarities of these 'nationalizing' and 'modernizing' arguments to the traditions of

discussions about teachers and teacher education being 'red and expert' — with the 'modernizing' view emphasizing the 'expert' aspect and the 'nationalizing' view giving priority to the 'red' aspect. Yet in part because of the particular political economic context of the Deng era, these traditional labels of 'red' and 'expert' are not wholly appropriate to describe the content and style of the contemporary discourses. Tightened links to the capitalist world system give these discourses orientations as well as rhetorical styles which differ from the more traditional 'red and expert' debates. In addition, the crisis of state legitimacy in the wake of the crushing of the 1989 democracy movement makes simple recycling of old political slogans problematic for the state, especially when the goal is attracting and socializing intellectuals to a state agenda. 'Red' thus seems too narrow to capture the rather more complex argument embedded in the 'nationalizing' discourse. Similarly, 'expert' is too widely used a term and one that does not necessarily convey the 'modernizing' discourse's implied and explicit links to a particular vision of modernization, one resting on people developing modern ideas and habits. This chapter suggests that the 'modernizing' and 'nationalizing' discourses operate simultaneously, offering different emphases and priorities for teacher education.

11 According to the analysis, of seven types of institutions which have lately encountered recruiting problems, teacher education tied for last place in the academic level of its applicants.

12 Within the curriculum program for an intending teacher, there have typically been three main types of required courses — courses within one's major, the education or professional core, and other core or general education courses, such as foreign languages, physical education, and military training. Most commonly, this core (which in the 1980s constituted about 5 percent of the curriculum versus 60–70 percent devoted to the major) has been composed of three courses — pedagogy, educational psychology, and teaching materials and methods in one's subject area — and a relatively short (often lasting six to eight weeks) practicum experience (Hu 1989; Chang and Paine 1992).

13 I am grateful to Mark Ginsburg for helping me notice how even in this context of student disengagement from the official (i.e. state-controlled) curriculum and orthodox views of knowledge, students turned to alternatives (such as the newspapers) which were themselves controlled by the state. This small vignette reminds us of the power of the Chinese state to construct the terms of not only the dominant discourse, but also of competing ones.

References

AN, W. (1992) '"Jiaoyuxue" Xueke Chengwei Wenti' (Problems in the Connotation of the Field 'Pedagogy'), *Jiaoyu Yanjiu*, **8**, pp. 36–38, 52.

BI, T. (1989) 'Woguo Gaoshi Jiaoyu Fazhan de Ruogan Wenti' (Some Problems in the Development of China's Tertiary Teacher Education), *Gaodeng Shifan Jiaoyu Yanjiu*, **2**, pp. 28–29, 37.

CHANG, M. and PAINE, L. (1992) 'China', in LEAVITT, H.B. (Ed) *Issues and Problems in Teacher Education: An International Handbook*, New York, Greenwood Press, pp. 71–89.

CHANG, Y. (1984) '"Sange Mianxiang" yu Shifan Jiaoyu Gaige' ('The Three Aspects' and the Reform of Teacher Education), in ZHONGGUO JIAOYU XUEHUI and ZHONGYANG JIAOYU KEXUE YANJIUSUO (Eds) *Sange Mianxiang yu Jiaoyu Gaige*, Beijing, Jiaoyu Kexue Chubanshe, pp. 237–51.

CHEN, G. (1989) 'Jiaoyuxue de Miwang yu Miwang de Jiaoyuxue' (Pedagogy's Loss and the Pedagogy of Loss), *Huadong Shifan Daxue Xuebao (Jiaoyu Kexueban)*, **8**, pp. 33–40.

CHEN, Y. (1991) 'Zhongguo Jiaoyuxue Qishinian' (Seventy Years of Chinese Pedagogy), *Beijing Shifan Daxue Xuebao (Shehui Kexue)*, **5**, pp. 52–94.

FOUCAULT, M. (1972) *The Archeology of Knowledge*, London, Tavistock Publications.

GEE, J. (1990) *Social Linguistics and Literacies: Ideology in Discourses*, London, Falmer Press.

GEERTZ, C. (1980) 'Blurred genres: The refiguration of social thought', *American Scholar*, **49**, 2, pp. 165–79.

GU, M. (1994) 'Shidai, Xiwang, Jiaoyu he Jiaoshi' (Times, Expectation, Education and Teachers), *Jiaoyu Yanjiu*, **3**, pp. 19–21, 28.

GUOJIA JIAOWEI (Ed) (1988) *Gaodeng Shifan Xuexiao Shizi Duiwu Jianshe* (Developing Faculty for Tertiary Teacher Education Institutions), Beijing, Beijing Shifan Daxue Chubanshe.

'Guojiao Jiaowei Fuzhuren Liu Bin Jiu 1993 Nian Zhongxiaoxue Jiaoyu Gongzuo da Benkan Jizhe Wen' (Liu Bin, Vice-Commissioner of the State Education Commission, Responds to this Journal's Reporters' Questions about Elementary and Secondary Education in 1993) (1993) *Renmin Jiaoyu*, **2**, pp. 3–5.

GUOJIAO JIAOWEI GAOXIAO XUESHENGSI (1990) 'Shifan Yuanxiao/Zhaosheng Qingkuang Diaocha' (An Investigation on the Enrollment Situation in Teacher Education Universities and Colleges), *Jiaoyu Yanjiu*, **8**, pp. 68–72.

GUOJIA JIAOWEI ZHISHU LIUSUO SHIDA JIAOYU SHIXI YANTAOHUI JISHU (1989) 'Jiaqiang Jiaoyu Shixi Gaige Tigao Shijian Nengli' (Strengthening Reform in the Education Practicum and Improving Practical Ability), *Gaodeng Shifan Jiaoyu Yanjiu*, **5**, pp. 33–36.

HABERMAS, J. (1970) *Toward a Rational Society*, Boston, MA, Beacon Press.

'He Dongchang Tongzhi Tan Zhongshi Jiaoyu de Jianshe he Fazhan' (Comrade He Dongchang Discusses the Development and Reform of Secondary Normal Education), (1992) *Renmin Jiaoyu*, **5**, pp. 8–9.

HE, D. (1991) 'Zai Quanguo Shifan Yuanxiao/Gonggongke Jiaoyuxue Jiaocai Gaige Yantaohui kaimushi de Jianghua' (Speech at the Opening Ceremony of the Symposium on the Reform of Teaching Materials for the Core Pedagogy Course in China's Normal Schools and Colleges), *Jiaoyu Yanjiu*, **12**, pp. 3–13.

HU, J. (1989) 'Lun Gaige Woguo Gaoshi de "Xuekebenwei Kecheng"' (On Reforming the 'Discipline-Focused Curriculum' of China's Tertiary Teacher Education), *Gaodeng Shifan Jiaoyu Yanjiu*, **4**, pp. 33–37.

'Huanan Basheng (shi) Zhongdian Shifan Daxue Xiaozhang Xiezuo Zhaokai Diwuci Huiyi' (Presidents from Key Teacher Education Universities in the Eight Provinces (and Municipalities) of South China Jointly Hold the Fifth Meeting) (1989) *Jiaoyu Yanjiu*, **4**, p. 79.

HUAZHONG SHIFAN XUEYUAN JIAOYUXI, HENAN SHIFAN DAXUE JIAOYUXI, GANSU SHIFAN DAXUE JIAOYUXI, and JIAOYU JIAOYANSHI (Eds) (1982). *Jiaoyuxue* (Pedagogy), Beijing, People's Educational Publishing House.

LAKOFF, G. and JOHNSON, M. (1980) *Metaphors We Live By*, Chicago, IL, University of Chicago Press.

LUO, R. (1983) 'Shifan Yuanxiao Gonggong Jiaoyuxueke de Jiaofa Chutan' (Preliminary/Discussion of Teaching Methods of the Normal College Core Pedagogy Class), *Kecheng, Jiaocai Jiaofa*, **5**, pp. 21–24.

MACDONELL, D. (1986) *Theories of Discourse*, Oxford, Basil Blackwell.

MANNING, P.K. (1979) 'Metaphors of the Field: Varieties of Organizational Discourse', *Administrative Science Quarterly*, **24**, 4, pp. 660–71.

MENG, J. (1991) 'Renzhen Zhexing "Sannianzhi Zhongdeng Shifan Xuexiao Jiaoxue Fangan (Shixing)"' (Conscientiously Implement the [Experimental] Program for Three Year Normal School Teaching) *Renmin Jiaoyu*, **10**, pp. 23–24.

PAINE, L. (1986) 'Reform and Balance in Chinese Teacher Education', unpublished dissertation, Stanford University.

PAINE, L. (1990) 'Teacher education in the People's Republic of China', in GUMBERT, E. (Ed) *Fit to Teach: Teacher Education in International Perspective*, Atlanta, GA, Georgia State University Center for Cross-Cultural Education, pp. 127–56.

PAINE, L. (1991) 'Reforming teachers: The organization, reproduction, and transformation of teaching', in EPSTEIN, I. (Ed) *Chinese Education: Problems, Policies, and Prospects*, New York, Garland Publishing, pp. 217–54.

PAINE, L. (1992) 'Teaching and modernization in contemporary China', in HAYHOE, R. (Ed) *Education and Modernization: The Chinese Experience*, Oxford, Pergamon, pp. 183–210.

QIAO, Y. (1989) 'Dui Gaodeng Shifan Yuanxiao/Sinianzhi Benke Jiaoyukecheng Gaige de Tansuo' (Thoughts on the Reform of the Education Curriculum in Four-Year Undergraduate Teacher Education Colleges and Universities) *Gaodeng Shifan Jiaoyu Yanjiu*, **3**, pp. 40–43.

SHANGHAISHI SHEHUIKEXUE XEUHUI (Ed) (1992) *Jiaoyuxuejuan* (Pedagogy volume), Shanghai, Shanghai People's Publishing Co.

SHENYANG SHIFAN XUEYUAN XUEBAOBIANJIBU (Ed) (1981) *Teji Jiaoshi Biji* (Notes from Special Rank Teachers), Shenyang, Liaoning People's Publishing House.

SHI, W. (1987) 'Shixi Meiguo Shifan Jiaoyu de Biange Zhi Dongyin' (An Analysis of Changes in Teacher Education in the US), *Jiaoyu Yanjiu*, **2**, pp. 60–64.

WANG, L. (1988) 'Lun Jiaoshi Laodong Baochang' (On Compensation for Teachers' Labor), *Zhongguo Shehui Kexue*, **4**, pp. 83–95.

WHITE, G. (1981) *Party and Professionals: The Political Role of Teachers in Contemporary China*, New York, M.E. Sharpe.

XIANG, Y. (1989) 'Dui Jiaoshi Gongzi Zhidu Gaige de Yixie Shexiang' (Reflections on the Reform of the Wage System for Teachers), *Jiaoyu Yanjiu*, **2**, pp. 15–17.

YAN, G. (1987) 'Kailuofu "Jiaoyuxue" Shuyu Chuantong Jiaoyu Sixiang Fanchou' (A. Kairov's Pedagogy: A Category of Traditional Educational Ideas), *Jiaoyu Yanjiu*, **6**, pp. 65–66.

YANG, L. and SHAO, Y. (1990) 'Fazhan "Muji Xiaoyi" ' (Developing the 'Effectiveness of the Machine Tool') *Guangming Ribao*, 31 August, p. 3.

YU, Z. (1989) 'Waixiangxing Jingji Yu Gaoshi Jiaoyu Gaige' (The Outward-Looking Economy and Tertiary Teacher Education Reform), *Gaodeng Shifan Jiaoyu Yanjiu*, **2**, pp. 24–27, 42.

YUAN, L. (1988) 'Lun Woguo Jiaoyu Jingji Kuique' (On the Shortage of China's Educational Funds), *Jiaoyu Yanjiu*, **7**, pp. 23–26, 31.

ZHONGGUO JIAOYU NIANJIAN 1990 NIAN BIENJIBU (Ed) (1993) *Zhongguo Jiaoyu Nianjian 1990 Nian* (China Education Almanac 1990), Beijing, People's Educational Publishing House.

Zhongguo Jiaoyu Tongji Nianjian 1987 (Educational Statistics Yearbook of China 1987) (1988) Beijing: Beijing Gongye Daxue Chubanshe.

Zhongguo Shehui Tonji Ziliao 1987 (China Social Statistics 1987) (1987) Beijing, Zhongguo Tongji Chubanshe.

'Zhonghua Renmin Gongheguo Jiaoshifa' (Teachers' Law of the People's Republic of China) (1993) *Zhongguo Gaodeng Jiaoyu Yanjiu*, **12**, pp. 5–6.

Chapter 6

Social and Political Contexts of Policy Formation in Teacher Education in Sri Lanka[1]

Maria Teresa Tatto and K.H. Dharmadasa

Introduction

This chapter analyzes the political and social contexts of policy formation in teacher education in Sri Lanka. We provide a brief historical overview of the development and transformation of teacher education from its beginnings to the current reforms. We look at the dynamic relationship between the state, teachers and teacher education against the context of the educational system's structure and different interest groups' actions. Teachers in Sri Lanka have, since independence, been active in shaping the design of education and have played a critical role with the state in facilitating reforms at all levels in the educational system. In this light, we examine the most recent reforms in teacher education and look at political, social and economic forces that have influenced them. We explore the reform of teacher education and its expected effects on the teacher's role. We highlight the responsiveness of teacher education design to societal goals — mostly focusing on unification and preservation of a national identity — and the system's flexibility for constantly implementing new or modifying old approaches as a special characteristic of teacher education reform in its attempts to address the demands of a modern society.

The analysis follows two threads. The first thread uncovers the prevailing tensions between state control and teacher autonomy as state élites along with teachers attempt to shape educational policy in general and teacher education in particular. These dynamics occur as a response to the needs of a new independent society using educational reform, teachers and teacher education as important instruments to advance a modernization agenda. The second thread is shaped by the existing tensions between the development of an educational system that attempts to bring together both a social preservation and a social change agenda emerging from Sri Lanka's colonial heritage held by state élites on the one hand, and by the outside pressures to modernize the economy on the other. This chapter shows how teacher education policy (organization, curriculum and financing) has been shaped by colonial administrators and state élites, as well as teachers, in the context of contradictory relations between teachers and the state within the political economy and educational reform dynamics in Sri Lanka.

Teacher Education and Contradictions in Teachers' Relations to the State

The dynamics of policy formation in teacher education in Sri Lanka can be considered in relation to two dominant paradigms that are often used to analyze education and development: conflict and equilibrium theories (Ginsburg *et al.* 1990). Other authors have struggled to find a synthetic framework based on these two theoretical approaches, but have also recognized the importance of developing valid explanations stemming from both approaches (Paulston 1977; Baker 1988). The view of the authors in this chapter is that no single theoretical perspective can account for the diversity and variety of factors that characterize the complex relationships existing among education and the social, political, economic and individual aspects of teacher education in Sri Lanka or any other country.

We acknowledge that in Sri Lanka, as in many other countries, problems of injustice at the social, political and economic levels are reflected in the present educational system. We recognize that by the very nature of having large economic disparities among population groups and geographical location, relationships of power and domination among the élite and the underprivileged may be legitimized and reproduced through the educational system. We also recognize, however, that impressive developments have been achieved under models looking to benefit large numbers of people in Sri Lanka (such as the impressive 88 percent literacy rate, the highest in developing Asian countries), and in the education of people that enables them to fulfill their basic needs. Efforts such as this may be seen as legitimate attempts to relieve some of the inequalities inherent in the system.

In order to analyze policy formation of teacher education in Sri Lanka it is necessary to conceptualize the role of the state and its interaction with other forces that impact teacher education and teachers in Sri Lanka. Just as the state cannot be considered as monolithic, neither can teachers. The relationship that the state engages in with teachers is affected by economic and social factors and in turn affects teachers differentially according to their characteristics, such as ethnicity, language, socioeconomic status, religion, gender, institutional level, length of experience, and rural or urban place of origin.

The role of the state concerning teachers can be conceptualized as driven by two contradictory forces: *proletarianization* and *professionalization* (Ginsburg *et al.* 1988, p. 319). Teachers are perceived by the State, by others and by themselves as a class of wage earners who are dependent for support and survival on daily employment. Teachers' low status and pay in relation to other professions, as well as their lack of power regarding decisions that directly impact their lives, have prompted teachers' associations and unions to seek to protect their rights, negotiate wages and better working conditions. These actions may reinforce an image of the proletarian character of teachers. Teachers are increasingly being perceived in a number of fronts as professionals, however, who possess — at least in theory — specialized knowledge and status in order to fulfill their role properly. The idea of teachers' professionalization comes accompanied by increased decision-making power, specialized knowledge, better working conditions, improved status and salaries and is thus an effective symbol often used by the state to control or to respond to teachers' demands for better treatment. The relationship that the state holds with teachers is thus mediated by these two contradictory forces (proletarianization and professionalization). Within this context, teacher education has been one of the most effective mechanisms used by state élites — and by teachers — to advance their respective aims.[2]

We look at teacher education as one among a number of forces used to control or 'reward' teachers in a discourse that centers around professionalism as an instrument for change, but that stresses a curriculum that transmits and reproduces the values espoused by the state. The relationship between teacher education and the state is affected by economic dynamics, especially in a time of transition when there is a movement towards incorporating more nation-states into a worldwide system of capitalism. These influences are expressed by an increased emphasis on teacher accountability and in the development of a differentiated teacher corps able to teach the skills necessary to confront the 'needs' of a growing economy.

The relationship between teachers and the state in Sri Lanka has centered around egalitarian issues, particularly the distribution of resources among denominational and government schools, the nationalization of the language of instruction, and the provision of 'free education' (see Jayasuriya 1969, pp. 83–92). The relationship between the state and teachers also touches upon gender lines and illustrates the proletarianization issue mentioned above. In Sri Lanka primary school teachers, a large number of them females, seem to have a congenial relationship with the state. Primary school teachers historically have seemed to be less likely to challenge the status quo and more willing to adopt the values of docility and obedience espoused by the state. Similarly the fact that female teachers tend to stay at the primary level may fulfill the accumulation aims of the state of more work for less pay.[3]

Teachers' relationship with the state is also related to the length of experience of a particular teacher and the urban/rural location in which they work. Teachers with no experience — that is, beginning teachers — whether they have received education or not, serve for a maximum period of three years in 'difficult' schools usually located in remote regions and lacking in resources. Rural teachers' situation is typically less favorable and is characterized by low mobility, challenging work conditions, and reduced possibilities for education and other professional development opportunities.

The debates and struggles around teacher education and other dynamics arising from the relationship between teachers and the state thus must be understood as part of a broader terrain of the political economy in Sri Lanka.

The Political Economy of Sri Lanka

Sri Lanka, an island with about 17.2 million inhabitants[4] mostly living in rural areas, has been an example for developing countries for its success in reaching almost universal literacy during the 1980s.[5] Sri Lanka has a low GNP per capita (US$500), but since independence has allocated a disproportionately large amount of resources to education as well as health — although that trend has decreased markedly since 1983 (Caldwell 1986). The importance accorded to education in Sri Lanka is associated with the concept of 'enlightenment' and the cultivation of the rational mind as the basic principle of Buddhism (Caldwell 1986; Tatto *et al.* 1991). Although Tamils (including Sri Lankan and Indian Tamils) are the largest minority group on the island (18.1 percent) and follow the Hindu religion, Buddhism, the religion of the Sinhalese majority (74 percent), has, since independence from the British, played an influential role in the setting and implementation of nationalistic, linguistic, religious, educational, and health objectives (Caldwell 1986).[6]

Sri Lanka, according to Caldwell (1986 p. 182), is characterized by

> a substantial degree of female autonomy, a dedication to education, an open political system, a largely civilian society without a rigid class structure, a history of egalitarianism and radicalism and of national consensus arising from political contest with marked elements of populism.

Sri Lanka has as well powerful community level groups which work for and support progressive reforms. All these characteristics have contributed to remarkable advances in the provision of education, such as female access regardless of rural or urban locations[7] and the impressive literacy rates reached in the 1980s. Sri Lanka is a socialist democracy and has attempted to provide social services to all its citizens, though ethnic conflict — currently taking the form of a civil war — makes this intention less attainable.

A Historical Overview

The history of Sri Lanka has been marked by pluralism; its most important ethnic groups are the Sinhalese of North Indian origin who came to the island around 500 BC and the Tamils of South Indian descent who settled on the island a few centuries later. According to De Silva (1986), there is no clear account of the indigenous people on the island before the time of colonization, with the Sinhalese emerging as 'the core of the Sri Lankan state system and the Tamils as a distinctive but smaller' and subordinated group (p. 7). The Sri Lankan civilization had a strong agricultural basis on rice and developed one of the most technologically advanced systems of irrigation in the Asian world, giving it a strong economy. Buddhism was introduced around the third century BC and has since then predominated as the religious and cultural foundation of the civilization on the island.

It was not until the fifth and sixth centuries that South Indian Tamils became allies with the Tamils in northern Sri Lanka, carrying out a number of invasions that created tension among the two ethnic groups on the island. Over time, the Sinhalese migrated to the southwest part of the island where they lived separated from the Tamils by a large forest belt. According to De Silva (1986), however, these groups did not operate in isolation of each other and maintained good economic and social relations. Nevertheless, this physical separation, he argues, has contributed to the process of ethnic preservation, and more recently to the development of Tamil nationalism and the ensuing separatist tendencies.

Sri Lanka was colonized by the Portuguese during the sixteenth and seventeenth centuries. The Portuguese were displaced by the Dutch who remained until the end of the eighteenth century. The Portuguese introduced Roman Catholicism in addition to Buddhism, Hinduism, and Islam, the other religions in the island (De Silva 1986, p. 17).

The British colonized the island in the nineteenth and twentieth centuries, introducing Protestantism. The change from coffee to tea and rubber in the mid-1830s introduced immigrant labor from India — with the majority of immigrant laborers being Tamils. This labor force took the character of permanent residents and has formed strong alliances with Sri Lankan Tamils already established on the island. De Silva (1986) points to this alliance as the origin of the separatist movement that prevails up to today. In 1948, the process of independence from Great Britain was finalized with powers devolved to the Sri Lankan people at that time.

Currently, in addition to maintaining relationships with Great Britain, Sri Lanka has maintained a close relationship with Russia. Overall, Sri Lanka has not been closed to establishing ties with other governments, especially in looking for support to develop into a modern socialist democracy. Thus support in developing the Sri Lankan educational system has been received from the Swedish International Development Agency (SIDA), United States Agency for International Development (USAID), and Japanese government aid agencies as well as the World Bank.

System of Governance

Sri Lanka had followed a policy of concentrating administrative and political authority in the capital, Colombo, both under the British rule and since independence. In 1979, under the presidency of J.R. Jayewardene, decentralization was proposed as an important policy to reconcile ethnic conflict. The decentralization schema had the aim to deconcentrate '[p]ower down to the village level, to make the people partners in the planning, organization, and implementation of policy' (De Silva 1986, p. 313). According to observers, the process of decentralization initially confronted a number of financial, legal and constitutional difficulties. It was not until December 1982 that central powers were devolved to the Executive Committees of the District Development Councils. Though some degree of centralization still prevails in the educational system, regarding mostly resources and curricula, by 1985 a number of reforms had evolved as a result or as a complement of the decentralization movement importantly impacting education and the teacher education system on the island.

Political Parties

A plurality of parties reflecting the makeup of Sri Lankan society populate the political spectrum. Though the Communist Party (CP) had been operating since 1919 and the nationalist party Sinhala Maha Sabha since 1920, it was not until universal suffrage was introduced in 1931 by the British, and most importantly the impending independence from Great Britain — consummated in 1948 — that a more formal structure of political parties began to emerge. The first government in the transition to an independent nation was characterized by a nationalist–socialist philosophy, putting forward a number of policies that marked an important departure from colonial dominance and set the tone for the development of the current educational system. The most important political parties, because of their role in Sri Lankan government from independence to the present, are the United National Party (UNP) — a successor to the Ceylon National Congress — which was formed in 1946, and the Sri Lanka Freedom Party (SLFP) inaugurated in 1951. The UNP, a broad-based moderate nationalist party including representation from Tamils, Sinhalese, Sinhalese Buddhists and Christians, was formed by D.S. Senanayake with the goal of '[r]epresenting a fresh start in politics in the direction of consensus of moderate opinion in national politics . . . [a] political party representative of the majority but acceptable to the minorities' (De Silva 1986, p. 152). The SLFP United Front (UF) a narrow-based Sinhalese nationalist party, has attempted to promote policies to strengthen the power/position of the Sinhalese and Buddhism as a religion in the country. The emergence of the SLFP 'as a centrist force' was seen by political observers as a democratic alternative to the UNP (De Silva 1986, p. 157). In a strategic move, the SLFP sought to strengthen its position by forming a United Front (UF) coalition between the SLFP, the Lanka Sama Samaja Party (LSSP), and the Communist Party with its base in Moscow (De Silva 1986, p. 239).

The tendencies and philosophy of these parties have not significantly departed from those that gave them origin. During the period of 1970 to 1977, Mrs Bandaranaike from the SLFP–UF coalition headed a government characterized by being 'anti-Indian and anti-capitalist though receptive to populist pressures and socialist ideologies' (De Silva 1986, p. 282). These tendencies resulted in the dissolution of the UF coalition at the end of 1977, leaving the SLFP government confronting Sri Lanka's worst waves of strikes in 20 years (De Silva 1986, p. 284). As a counter-force, the UNP government returned to power after the elections of July 1977, and attempted to change the atmosphere of distrust that the policies of the SLFP had built during the previous government by 're-establishing minority rights, decentralizing the island's administrative systems, and by seriously addressing the problems of the Tamil speaking people' (De Silva 1986, p. 289). As of early 1994, the United National Party or UNP is in power. The political situation continued to be unstable and the government was being constantly challenged as indicated by recurrent waves of violence which resulted in early 1993 — among other incidents — in the murder of the past UNP president. In the summer of 1994 the SLEP–UF, also known as the People's Alliance, won the elections, returning the Bandaranaike family to power.

The Role of Organized Teacher Labor

In contrast with other countries, teacher unions in Sri Lanka have been many and rarely militant. They were powerful in the policy arena under governments controlled by the Sri Lanka Freedom Party and its left coalition during the years 1956–60 and from 1960–65, and under the government of the SLFP–UF Coalition (lead by the SLFP, the LSSP and the CP) from 1970–78. Under the governments of the United National Party teacher unions were subdued. Because the UNP had their own teacher trade union[8] it did not give other trade unions the recognition or powers they enjoyed under the SLFP and Coalition governments.

Currently, the most important teacher unions in Sri Lanka are the Jathika Guru Sangamaya (National Teacher Union), which has all categories of teachers in it and is controlled by the UNP. The Sri Lanka Nidahas Sewa Guru Sangamaya (Sri Lanka Independent Teacher Services Union) is controlled by the Sri Lanka Freedom Party. There are a number of other teacher unions which are affiliated to socialist parties, including the All Ceylon Teachers Union, National Union of Teachers, Secondary Trained Teachers Union, and Graduate Teachers Union.

The Dynamics of Educational Change

The year 1931 marks a period of rapid change in political, economic and societal dynamics due in great part to the introduction that year of the Donoughmore Constitution.[9] The Donoughmore Constitution 'had the effect of transferring to the elected representatives of the people complete control over the internal affairs of the island' (Jayasuriya 1969, p. 15). Legislative and executive functions were placed in a State Council (which replaced the Executive and Legislative Councils operating until then) formed of seven Executive Committees. One of these was the Executive Committee of Education. The chair of the Committee also served as the Minister of Education with C.W.W. Kannangara becoming the first individual to fulfill this position during the period of 1931–45. The Kannangara Committee — upholding the nationalist–socialist principles and philosophy of the time — had an extraordinary impact on three closely intermingled areas of education in Sri Lanka, which developed over the period of 1939–68 and impacted other areas of educational policy, including teaching and teacher education: 1) the introduction of 'free' education, 2) the abolition of denominationalism in education, and 3) the partial substitution of English in favor of the national languages.[10]

The force behind these three changes resided in an 'egalitarian ideology' held by the leaders of a movement that originated from a number of groups. One group was integrated by members of the Sri Lankan élite who 'had received a high quality education through the English language' (Jayasuriya 1969, p. 83). This group has been characterized by Jayasuriya (1969) as being formed by political personalities and educators espousing a nationalist or a socialist orientation and value system and among whom there was a 'fortunate congruence of interests' (p. 83). The group also included a small number of highly articulate and politicized schoolteachers from prestigious secondary schools in both Sinhalese (such as C.W.W. Kannangara) and Tamil regions. These groups were supported by two additional groups as well: one, a 'second level élite' (or Swabhasha) formed by those who had received a good education in Sinhalese and Tamil languages but who were in turn limited in comparison with those who had received education in English. This group included Swabhasha teachers, Buddhist monks, ayurvedic physicians, and the editors of Swabhasha newspapers who were able to mobilize significant public support for these changes. The other layer of support came from 'the masses' who actively responded to the issues raised by the two élite groups mentioned above. These moves for change were resisted by the sector of the English educated élite who in the words of Jayasuriya (1969, pp. 83–85)

> had been alienated from the roots of their culture, and by those reaction-
> ary groups who saw their vested interests (colonial, social, economic,
> and religious) and their positions of privilege in the public life of the
> country threatened by the nationalist–socialist movement for equality in
> education.

It was not until the early 1970s and again in the late 1980s that another wave of important changes altered the educational scene in as a dramatic way as that beginning in 1931. In April 1971 an insurrection of educated youth, in general the children of the rural poor, woke up Sri Lankan society in what was seen as a manifestation of the social discontent and lack of attention to the basic needs of the population and to the large level of unemployment existing among qualified youth who were demanding work (De Silva 1986).

As a result of the social unrest of the early 1970s, the 1980s was marked by numerous reforms, including education. With regards to teachers, the perpetuation of their dual status (such as 'trained' versus 'untrained'), tacitly supporting the stratification established during the British colonial period, brought about discontent and accelerated a number of important reforms affecting the situation of teachers in Sri Lankan society.

Schooling and the Situation of Teachers in Sri Lanka[11]

Since Sri Lanka gained its independence from the United Kingdom in a transfer of power that occurred from 1946 to 1948 (De Silva 1986), its strategies to promote universal primary education have been admired because of the enormous progress in education they have achieved. However the majority of Sri Lanka's more than 10,000 schools are not seen by local educators as of high quality. One-fifth of these schools lack resources or qualified personnel and are quite small (fewer than 100 students). These schools usually have high drop-out and repetition rates, and few students in these schools pursue advanced studies (Cummings *et al.* 1992). The allocation of schools reflects the composition, regional location and language use of the major ethnic groups on the island. Seventy-three percent of the schools are Sinhalese, 20 percent are Tamil, and 7 percent are Muslim.

Schools are classified according to four groups depending on the orientation of their programs, their resources, and their location.[12] The entrance to the prestigious schools is very competitive and usually those parents willing to pay private tutoring can aspire to have their children enrolled in these schools. The government through the Ministry of Education (MOE) is highly critical of this situation and has taken as a challenge to improve the situation of the lesser schools, and recommended stopping the creation of prestigious schools until more equality could be achieved (MOE 1982, p. 44). However, in spite of these efforts the situation of remote schools and their teachers is often desperate (see Baker 1988).

In Sri Lanka 143,398 teachers work in government schools including primary and secondary schools; of these 43,811 teach in general primary education. About 65 percent of the elementary school teachers are female, while males are more likely to teach upper levels. The majority of teachers (about 81 percent) teach in rural area schools. Eighty-three percent of the teachers are Sinhalese, and the other 17 percent Tamil (MOE 1987). According to the school census of 1989, Sri Lanka had an educated (i.e. certificated) teaching force of close to 56 percent, with the rest of the teachers, though not professionally educated, holding graduate degrees or diplomas (27 percent), general certificates of education at the ordinary and advanced levels and other types of certificates after secondary and high school (17 percent; Tatto *et al.* 1991).

With the democratization of schooling, enrollments at all levels in the school system rose very rapidly; the school-going population (as a percentage of the total population) rose from 13 in 1943 to 18 in 1950, 21.7 percent in 1981 (MOE 1981,

p. i), 24.5 percent in 1988, and 24.9 percent in 1990 (Central Bank of Sri Lanka 1991). Although the overall pupil/teacher ratio in Sri Lanka is quite low (27.6), it varies dramatically with respect to rural/urban location, level, and type (MOE 1987).

Since independence in 1948, the Ministry of Education has sought to implement a range of policies concerned with providing equal and better education at a national level for the people of Sri Lanka. The Ministry of Education Report on Management Reforms published in 1984 summarizes the government goals as follows:

> During the 1960s the international boom of curriculum development influenced our activities and work priorities. The continuing concern of access to schooling was also reflected in the State takeover of denominational schools. Solutions to educational expansion were also sought through partial experiments in the decentralization of education administration. During the 1970s the emphasis shifted to the redesigning of primary school curricula and also the introduction of a new array of pre-vocational subjects. Educational planning received some emphasis though the linkage of plans to implementation of projects was rather weak. The problems and concerns of the 1980s however, require a fresh orientation and a new synthesis. (BRIDGES 1988, p. 3)

In this reorientation the school is seen as formally organized under the rhetoric resembling the human capital approach: 'to raise the level of skills in the population that will support economic growth, provide an adequate supply of expertise, and improve the quality of life of every individual' (MOE 1982).

Under this model the teacher is seen as the major instrument to implement the reform and thus function as a (state-directed) agent of social change. The problem surrounding the teacher is characterized by the state as a complex combination of several elements, such as the methods of recruiting, educating, deploying and retaining teachers. This is in contrast with the most important issues from the teachers' viewpoint which include the poor conditions of their workplace, the rigidity of a centralized curriculum, a lack of professional recognition, and low salaries. These issues are often ignored by the state with the result that teachers may see themselves as oppressed by the system (Baker 1988; Tatto *et al.* 1993).

Nonetheless and congruent with the state's vision, Sri Lanka has been involved since the 1980s in major shifts in the recruitment of teachers, education and employment practices. From 1984, all newly educated teachers were required to take up the first three years of their careers in districts known to have teacher shortages, with the respective district offices in charge of the assignments. Other recent initiatives were directed at improving teacher status by providing credentials, raising salaries, finding ways of stimulating teacher teamwork and providing in-school support to improve teaching practice.

Teachers thus seem to be involved in the 'professionalization versus proletarianization' dynamic characterized by forces attempting to encourage them to become agents of change within a *de facto* centralized bureaucracy resorting to the language and symbolism of professionalization, while in practice little less than half of its teaching force remain without effective access to improved salaries and working conditions. Since the instrument to social mobility has become professionalization through education, teachers who have not been granted/obtained a credential tend to legitimize their lower status in these terms. The granting of credentials through teacher education has served dual purposes. It has been used as a symbolic mechanism to increase teacher status and, presumably, the degree of control they have over their job situation (i.e. increasing possibilities for transfer or promotion), but it has also been used by the state to exert control over teachers — usually newly educated or rural teachers — via coercive deployment to rural/difficult areas for new graduates, although with salaries corresponding to their new credential, and to legitimize inequalities within the educated teaching corps (i.e. different credentials tied to different salaries and working conditions).

The state's rhetorical representation of teachers thus places educators in a strategic yet contradictory position in the dynamic of the school and society. At the same time that teachers are seen as 'a breed of men and women who will conserve all that is best in culture and traditions', they are expected to 'forge ahead as agents of change' (MOE 1982). The following quotations from this document, *Towards Relevance in Education: Report of the Education Reforms Committee, 1979* (MOE 1982) on the role of teachers within the reform framework illustrate different points on the professionalization–proletarianization continuum, and the implied nature of teacher education needed to prepare teachers for their roles. The first quotation depicts teachers as *obedient workers*, part of a hierarchical school structure:

> [T]eacher[s] should be exemplary in [their] conduct. [They] will be disciplined not only because [they are] always under scrutiny but because [they are] a member of a staff under the authority of a principal. [Teachers] will be conscientious and methodical, fired with a sense of commitment, and conform rigorously to a 'regimen of work'. (MOE 1982, p. 89)

Yet this next quotation characterizes teachers as *agents of social change*, though only in a decent and orderly manner:

> [E]ducation and society are constantly influencing each other. In Sri Lanka the interaction has been mostly that of school on community and this one-way traffic is likely to last so long as our people continue to leave education well alone. The teacher stands for decent and orderly progress and is preferred to the more radical type of leader whose techniques are apt to be theatrical and revolutionary. Thus by reason of his [or her] academic status, professional training and locale . . . the teacher ideally fills the role of a catalyst of social change. (MOE 1982, pp. 89–91)

Forming and Reforming Teacher Education

At the time this chapter was written (August 1994), close to 60 percent of teachers at all levels had received some kind of teacher education. In fact, the percentage of teachers who have undergone teacher education increased markedly from 1946 (29 percent), and especially from 1960 (34 percent), to 1989 (56 percent) (MOE 1987). In spite of this major effort, the challenge is still present since close to 40 percent of teachers currently teaching in Sri Lankan classrooms have not received any professional education. Knowing this, however, does not tell us what kind of education they received nor what political dynamics helped to shape the nature of teacher education in Sri Lanka. Below we will address these questions during the pre-independence, immediate post-independence, and more recent eras.

The Pre-Independence Period[13]

The history of teacher education parallels the development of the system of formal education in Sri Lanka. Knowledge in the ancient civilization of Sri Lanka (543 BC) was passed down from father to son in a system of apprenticeship and had its origins in the arrival of Vijaya, who obtained craftsmen of a thousand families of the eight guilds from India (Dharmadasa 1988). With the introduction of Buddhism in the third century BC, the monks became the center of secular as well as sacred education (Mukerjee 1947; Rahula 1956). It is conceivable then that monasteries served as the first centers of teacher training in Sri Lanka. According to this tradition, the constant association between teachers and learners was vital to education, a principle that was very much present in the reformers' agenda to improve the quality of education in the 1980s.

The Portuguese, who controlled the maritime provinces in Sri Lanka from 1505 to 1658, influenced education on the island, but did not have a lasting impact on the education of teachers since they brought missionaries to serve as teachers on the island.

Between 1658 to 1796 the Dutch left their mark on teacher education through the establishment of a seminary in Jaffna in 1690 in order to educate Tamil youth as catechist preachers and teachers. An additional seminary was established in Colombo in 1696. The Dutch introduced the study of Latin, Greek and Hebrew and sent students abroad to be trained for the clergy, who would later become teachers. Less than 50 years later the seminaries were phased out and in 1747 a normal school was started in the province of Pettah but this institution functioned only for few years and ended with the coming of the British.

The strongest influence in teacher education — in addition to Buddhism — came from Great Britain. Initially, the British colonial administration (1802–1948) established the Colombo Academy (with a curriculum including the study of English, mother tongue languages and other subjects common in English seminaries) to educate public servants and later on teachers. In addition to the academy, a monitorial system to educate teachers was established for the first time in the early seventeenth century and was a beginning attempt at school-based teacher preparation. This system prevailed until 1929.

Parallel to this system of education, other attempts to set up more refined methods to educate teachers resulted in the creation in 1842 of the Normal School adjacent to the Colombo Academy with a three-year course of study. The Normal School spread to Galle and Kandy (two important urban centers in Sri Lanka). Diversification of the curriculum to suit the specific needs of the country, as defined by the British colonizers, gave origin to a Normal School for educating Sinhalese and Tamil teachers in 1847.

When in 1858 the Normal School closed down, due mostly to financial problems, terminating the state system for teacher education and leaving a large number of teachers untrained, the missionary schools, which had been developing parallel to the normal schools, were the main organizers of formal preparation for teachers. It was not until 1870 that a normal school was again established. This institution provided courses in subject matter and pedagogy in three languages, English, Sinhala and Tamil, serving the diverse population on the island. During the same period education for English teachers was left to the missionaries. By 1900 there were 15 teacher education institutions in the country: two were under the Roman Catholic denomination, three were Wesleyan, three belonged to the Church of England, one belonged to the American Mission, two were government schools and four were private female schools. Buddhist schools also continued educating teachers. In 1903 the first Teacher Training College was opened and students were admitted to any of three streams: English, Bilingual and Sinhala. The curriculum consisted of principles and practice of teaching, with academic subjects (such as mathematics and sciences) as a secondary emphasis. In the late 1910s, teachers colleges for Tamil and Sinhalese teachers were established. Teachers educated in these teachers colleges were the first recipients of the newly instituted Teacher's Final Certificate.

The system of teacher education spread to the rural areas as well with the creation in the early 1930s of three rural education centers. By 1939 23 teacher training colleges were functioning, providing education in English, mother tongue languages, academic subjects, and rural education. Admission to these education institutions was based on a written examination and an interview. Admission was open to persons who had passed either one of the standard British examinations, namely the London Matriculation Examination, the Cambridge Senior Examination or the Senior School Certificate.

The description of the evolution of teacher education in Sri Lanka signals a series of influences, most importantly from former colonizers, that have shaped the format, the curriculum, and the type of person who received education in these institutions. Though attempts were made to be 'inclusive' by creating three streams (Sinhala, Tamil and English), still the examinations and content of the programs were modeled after those of the colonizers and the 'hidden curriculum' of teacher education supported values alien to indigenous cultures. The programs also reinforced English as a language of instruction, relegating Sinhala and Tamil to 'second class' status. The use of standard British examinations to admit prospective teachers into teacher training colleges was a mechanism used to educate an élite group of teachers who would in turn educate an élite group of pupils. This situation encouraged the creation of, on the one hand, an élite group of teachers who identified with the British culture and who were concentrated in the better-off schools and, on the other, a marginalized group of teachers who taught in the languages of the people, generally in the remote, poorer schools.

Independence up to Recent Reforms

In 1943[14] a major change in the policy governing teacher education came about with the Kannangara Committee, which recommended that all teachers at the basic education level should be educated and given a status in accordance with their educational attainment, qualifications and experience. The committee also made recommendations that the curriculum be divided in four sections (following a model that resembled that in Britain): the study of the theory of education, study of educational psychology, the practice of education, and general and special subject methods. The establishment of actual schools adjacent to the colleges was suggested to allow teaching practice and to complement the type of education envisioned by the Committee.

The Committee also set up the basis for the education of non-graduate and graduate teachers, situating the first in a single type of teacher college and the second in a department in the university. Those teachers that wished to pursue vocational studies were channeled to the Ceylon Technical College. At the same time, the Committee recommended the continuation of grant aid to denominational institutions.[15]

The reform created two-year teacher colleges for primary and secondary teachers. The first year was focused on academic studies in ordinary school subjects, professional studies was the focus of the second year, with teaching practice being carried out in both years.

As a result of independence from Great Britain, the new Sri Lankan state took on the responsibility to finance the education of a large number of teachers who had been until then without teacher education. The number of training colleges under the new modality proliferated and included both the colleges supported entirely by the government and the assisted institutions. A resurgence of indigenous philosophies dominated the development of educational policies as Sri Lanka began looking inwards to find an identity obscured by years of colonization. These policies attempted to encompass language, religion, and ethnic identity considerations.

The nationalist/modernist group in power at that time pursued capitalist ideologies originating from the West, and pressed towards 'modernization'. These views, though resisted by the nationalist/socialist group within the state élite, were advanced in this period. The 'modernist' state envisioned specialized education programs directed at preparing teachers not only in general education but in those subjects needed for the economic 'development' of the country and a changing independent society. Consequently, the education of science teachers was given special emphasis. The principle of 'full pay' education was introduced for selected teachers who enjoyed paid study leave in an effort to improve the quality of teachers. This type of 'arrangement' offered to 'selected' teachers to obtain higher credentials may be seen as an attempt to educate a cadre of teachers who would likely be supportive of the changes introduced by the state to bring about more efficiency and higher levels of accountability into the educational system.

In the early 1960s, the assisted schools and training colleges, which were under the management of religious denominations, came under the centralized control of the Sri Lankan government. The 1960s marks the implementation of a common curriculum in all the training colleges. The concept of teacher training was replaced by the concept of teacher education. In the 1970s the state increased its control over teachers by 1) introducing central regulations, uniformity and accountability to the schools and 2) by increasing the level of 'professionalism' and 'autonomy' — albeit within the guidelines of the state — accorded to and expected from teachers.

In the early 1970s new changes were implemented in teacher education for non-graduate teachers. There was a two-year general course to prepare primary school teachers, a two-year specialist course to prepare junior secondary school teachers, and a three-year correspondence education course for primary school teachers. In total there were 20 general training colleges for primary teachers and eight special training colleges for secondary teachers. By 1975 these distinctions disappeared and all teacher education institutions were considered equal by the state.

Formal teacher education for elementary school teachers[16] was limited until the 1980s to the continuous reform of the traditional British-founded teachers colleges. Some of these reforms were of a curricular character and attempted to address — based on the goals of the indigenous resurgence movement — the different cultural needs for education in Sri Lanka. Teachers colleges having programs for Sinhalese, Tamil and Muslim groups and three streams (English, Sinhalese and Tamil) are examples of these actions. In spite of the rhetoric of equality and professional advancement for teachers, a dual system of education, certification and compensation continued to exist based on the British colonial model, with few teachers having access to formal education and the benefits associated with it. The rest of the teaching force remained, for the most part, without any kind of formal teacher education.

In the early 1980s a new move towards school-based education prompted the extension of the teacher college program for another year, dedicated mostly to teaching practice in schools. This attempt did not have the expected results on improving the education of the future teachers due to the lecturers' infrequent visits to schools and to the lack of qualified teachers to help and guide the student teachers once in the schools. This was one of the last attempts to implement still another layer of reform in the existing teacher colleges already overstretched by lack of personnel and low salaries for teacher-educators. The next stage of reform is characterized by the search for innovations which culminated in the creation of two novel alternatives for Sri Lanka though existent in other countries: a preservice alternative and a distance education mode of instruction. These alternatives, like the teacher colleges developed under close state control, are described in the following section.

The Recent Organizational Reforms

The ideal of teacher education in the rhetoric of the 1980s reform was to bring together two fundamental but seemingly competing perspectives, that of 'laying the foundation for the future while preserving indigenous cultures and beliefs', and 'meeting the country's needs at a particular time' (MOE 1982, pp. 90–91). These two perspectives entail a complex mixture of philosophical principles of education and economic goals for the nation, while delineating the direction of education at all levels. One view can be characterized as a *revitalization* approach and highlights the philosophy of Sri Lankan education guided by 'a concept of people focusing in the uniqueness and dignity of the individual with the teacher providing the kind of environment in which the child will unfold like a flower' (MOE 1982, p. 96). The other view can be characterized by its movement towards *modernization*. Under this approach education is seen as a technical process, 'a view strongly influenced by the western idea of the role of human beings in society with competency as a criterion of achievement and the teacher as a clinician who diagnoses or prescribes what is needed to promote achievement in children' (MOE 1982, p. 96).

The current teacher education programs are a reflection of these two strong and contradictory tendencies and seem to hold a compromise between preserving a centuries old culture and moving along in the path of 'modern development'. Although the advances in education and technology in the West are widely acknowledged, the view guiding Sri Lankan education is deeply rooted in the Buddhist belief that 'there is not true education except within the bond between the teacher and the learner, whether in school or at home' (MOE 1982, p. 97). That educators subscribe more strongly to this Buddhist-based belief creates severe conflict and contradictions with the modernization aims of the state. In fact, one of the guidelines to reform teacher education warns against infatuation with the educational advances made in the West and succumbing to the pressure from the pace of social change. The Ministry of Education report (1982, p. 98) recommends that,

> while there is much that we have learned and can learn from the developed West, let us at the same time look towards our own culture and, before it is too late, identify, appraise and adapt it in enunciating our philosophy of education, in shaping our schools and in formulating programs of education for our teachers.

This has meant the development of programs to educate teachers that attempt to preserve the 'human factor' interaction as opposed to the intensive use of technology, such as television or radio. It has also entailed the encouragement of Sinhala and Tamil as the languages of instruction.

Within this context, in addition to the long-standing teacher colleges, two approaches to educate elementary school teachers have emerged: distance education and colleges of education. As of 1992, teachers colleges, colleges of education and distance education programs were educating 14, 15, and 71 percent, respectively, of the primary school teachers enrolled in teacher education.

The teacher education reform of the 1980s consisted of gradually phasing-in alternative approaches to the long standing teachers colleges, teacher colleges, the three-year (recently reduced to two-year) education program for non-graduate teachers. Eleven teacher colleges began this three-year modality in January 1981. The two newly developed approaches — distance education and colleges of education — stand in contrast with the long-standing teacher colleges, which were mainly designed to provide in-service education to small and select groups of experienced teachers through a traditional curriculum — delivered in a teacher-centered, lecture format — with a heavy focus on knowledge about pedagogy.

Distance education for in-service education was implemented in 1984 to educate non-graduate, in-service teachers. The distance education modality has 30 regional centers; its duration is three years and can be extended to five. This program originated as a response to the limited numbers of teachers that teachers colleges were able to educate and as a way to accelerate the process of education. The distance education program is an innovative approach to in-service teacher education in which a tutorial system brings continuity and support to the future teachers while following a community-based model. Students spend three to five years on a part-time basis using carefully-designed, self-paced instructional materials to develop their knowledge of subject matter content and pedagogy (linked to their continuing teaching assignment).

A preservice teacher education approach began functioning in 1985 with seven colleges of education. This program, which lasts three years, seeks to implement the policy of progressively giving up the practice of recruiting non-formally educated teachers into the teaching profession. At the end of their studies the graduates receive a 'Diploma in Teaching', in contrast with the 'Teacher Certificate' received by teachers colleges and distance education graduates. The preservice program or colleges of education — following a model originated in Britain — is characterized by an emphasis on studying and applying the educational goals of the state, recruitment of young qualified graduates from high school, and provision of a diploma that holds higher status than that of the current teachers colleges or the newly developed distance education. Students study full-time for two years in a student-centered program and then undertake a one-year practice teaching internship.

A brief discussion of how the different forms of teacher education incorporate different ethnic groups is in order. Language of instruction, ethnicity, and religion are all factored in educational planning at all levels on the island. Although the main languages spoken by the people in Sri Lanka are Sinhala, Tamil, English and Malay, only the first three languages are recognized for official purposes as state languages. Sinhalese go to schools and colleges designated as Sinhala medium, Tamils select Tamil medium, and Muslims and Malays have the option to select any of the three official languages for instruction.

As of 1992 there were 16 teachers colleges spread throughout the island. All ethnic groups could attend the three teachers colleges for English teachers, though in one of these Tamil was the medium of instruction. Six other teachers colleges used Tamil as the medium of instruction and there were seven Sinhalese-medium teacher colleges. Of the 30 regional centers for distance education, 23 were Sinhala medium and seven were Tamil medium. Of the eight colleges of education, one is dedicated to Tamil medium, five used Sinhalese as the medium of instruction, and two additional ones admitted students from all language media.

In summary the teacher colleges provide the higher coverage (37 percent) for the Tamil medium, whereas the distance education approach does so for 30 percent, and the colleges of education, the most recently developed approach to educate teachers, covers the Tamil medium in 12.5 percent of them. The proportion of Sinhalese-allocated teacher education programs closely corresponds to the actual population in the island (or 74 percent); this is especially true in the case of distance education. Currently a higher proportion of Sinhalese population attend the more prestigious colleges of education whereas a higher proportion of teacher colleges' resources are allocated to the Tamil medium of instruction. Distance education services seem to cover the population in the island proportionally.

While significantly increasing the opportunities for teacher education and teacher improvement, the current overall strategy still promotes a dual system among teachers. Colleges of education graduates are conceived as an élite group of teachers because of their perceived higher level knowledge of subject matter; the support, personal attention and the amount of resources allocated to these programs; and the more valuable credential they receive at graduation. The diploma in teaching clearly differentiates those teachers who have received preservice education versus those who have been educated through in-service approaches. The diploma is seen as having more prestige and it has had the effect of establishing a hierarchy within the teaching corps. Teacher colleges, just as the distance education graduates, receive a less prestigious credential — a teaching certificate — though associated with possibilities for promotion and a pay raise. In contrast with distance education, however, teacher college candidates are carefully selected, and receive full pay leave during the two years while in the program.

Distance education graduates have the higher personal costs for their education and receive, in relation to both teachers colleges and colleges of education, the least resources from the government (Tatto *et al.* 1993). The distance education approach is, for this reason, quite successful in relation to its costs as far as the state is concerned. It may also be the one that more closely reflects the values and intentions of an indigenous approach to teacher education and is closely in touch with the contextual needs of the teacher, in great part because their candidates are also teaching throughout their preparation and because of the tutorial system built into the program. Nevertheless, a dual status in the teaching profession is still maintained and may in the long run aggravate the problems — teacher discontent and lack of unity — that it currently attempts to prevent.

Conclusion

In summary, teacher education has had to struggle with a colonial educational legacy affecting both the structure of the educational system as well as the content and style of delivery of the instruction given to prospective and experienced teachers without formal teacher education. We have seen that before and after independence the foreign (especially British) models for teacher education have dominated. Since independence the state, in the search for unity and economic development and under a rhetoric of professionalism, has made important advancements in the development of alternative approaches to educate teachers. At the same time it seems, however, such efforts have increased its control over both teachers and teacher education, introduced a dual system in the status of teachers, and increased the contradictions already present in teachers' work.

Sri Lanka represents a case of collaboration between state élites and teachers in the development of educational policy, including teacher education policy, within a framework set by colonial forces. This collaboration has occurred in the context of contradictory relations between teachers and the state and in relation to the dynamics of educational reform and Sri Lanka's political economy.

The rhetoric of teacher education reform has been characterized throughout its evolution by contradictory notions of conservatism and change, revitalization of indigenous cultures and modernization, professional autonomy and state control. Additionally, teacher education in Sri Lanka has been strongly influenced by colonial and foreign forces, though this influence has been tempered by indigenous resurgence movements and teacher activism. Strategies to achieve state control have included the implementation of central curricula (in both schools and teacher education institutions) and the development of policies designed to address teacher deployment and working conditions under the umbrella of professionalism. Revitalization of indigenous cultures and modernization aims have been achieved, for example, through policies regulating the language of instruction, access to schooling, the development of schools and teacher education institutions separated along language, ethnic and religious lines, and the introduction of curricula with emphasis on science and technology.

The state has also implemented policies cast as devolving autonomy and control to teachers. Current changes taking place within the school system — such as the creation of clusters, administrative deconcentration, education of school principals, and the implementation of teacher education programs closer to the school context — have the potential of broadening and enhancing teachers' influence at the local and school level. Additional policies include salary raises and opportunities for promotion to all professionally and academically qualified teachers. Along with this new system of compensation, the state has raised the standard of performance for teachers as part of its policies to improve the quality of education. Congruent with this policy a number of standards of performance have been set up to which teachers are to be held accountable.[17]

The mentioned expectations for teachers send two signals. On the one hand, there is an effort to look at teachers as change agents, who need to think and act independently and to use their own resourcefulness to deal with the constraints imposed by school–community settings. On the other hand, there is a message of accountability, constraint and control. Teachers in Sri Lanka are seen as the state's servants as well as its change agents. Though these signals may create a tension in the role of the teacher, both roles are designed to serve the goals sponsored by the state.

We established throughout this chapter that one of the reasons why Sri Lanka has moved so fast and effectively in the field of education is the close collaboration that seems to exist between teachers and the state. We have also seen that after 1948, as the country attained its independence and leaders of the new nation-state saw the need for promoting economic development and unifying a richly diverse society, teacher education became more relevant as an important instrument to promote the aims of national preservation and unification. Teachers' commitment in the search for a national identity and the input of teachers in educational policy may have served as a powerful catalyst for the close teacher–state collaboration that ensued and prevails until today. The search for national identity, however, especially within a global context espousing western values, has proven difficult for developing countries, and Sri Lanka is no exception. The influence on teacher education policy by Britain, and other foreign countries (e.g. Japan, Sweden and the United States) through their development agencies, is but an example of the prevailing tension between internal and external political, economic and social survival, which constantly challenges the degree to which Sri Lanka can develop a truly indigenous approach to education. Within this context continued teacher input in educational policy plays an important role in the inclusion of indigenous views in the educational agenda.

We have also examined how teacher education policy has evolved under a context of uncertainty within the complex conflicts occasioned by the ethnic, linguistic and religious tensions between the Sinhalese and the Tamil groups on the island (see also De Silva 1986). These ethnic conflicts are reflected in the level of success with which teacher education programs under the different approaches have been implemented. In the Tamil areas for example, the distance education program has been working under severe constraints in comparison with those operating in the Sinhalese areas (Dock *et al.* 1988).

We have discussed the role of teacher education as serving economic aims by recruiting qualified secondary and high school graduates who cannot attain a university education into the teaching profession. This partially addresses the serious problems brought about by unemployment of qualified youth in the country.

We have examined the impact of teacher education reform at the individual level and identified contradictions and dilemmas placed on the teacher, such as calls for change and preservation of indigenous cultures on the one hand, and the calls for autonomy and compliance with control structures set up by the state on the other. We discussed how teachers have actively participated in shifting the political agenda after independence within an indigenous resurgence movement pushing issues such as free education and the language of instruction to the forefront of the policy discourse, while moving forward a modernization agenda. We have also discussed how the state has attempted to create an image of professionalism — not least through teacher education — while maintaining tight controls on teachers' role, performance and working conditions.

Finally we pointed out how the rhetoric of 'professionalism' of the teaching force has supported the creation and legitimation — through teacher education — of a dual system in the teaching force, represented by different certification awards and benefits associated with differential education approaches. We have argued that this differentiation may bring as a consequence conflict within the teaching force itself and weaken the until now unconditional collaboration that teachers have had with the state.

Notes

1   This chapter draws on the research conducted by Basic Research and Implementation in Developing Education Systems (BRIDGES), a collaborative project with the National Institute of Education in Sri Lanka. The project was funded through a collaborative agreement between OBSTUSAID and the Harvard Institute for International Development Contact No. DPE-5824-A-00-5076-00. This research has received additional support from the Department of Teacher Education, Michigan State University, East Lansing, MI. We gratefully acknowledge the comments of Mark Ginsburg in the development of this manuscript.
2   See Densmore (1987) and Ginsburg (1987) for a discussion of how professionalism can be used as a mechanism of control in teaching and teacher education.
3   Teachers' pay has been 'equalized' among those with similar qualifications and positions in specific levels of schools. Therefore, in theory, there is no difference in the salaries between male and female teachers if their qualifications and appointments are the same. However, compared to elementary school teachers, secondary school teachers have the possibility to make more money because of their higher qualifications and the salary attached to specific positions. Females comprise a larger percentage of schoolteachers overall (61 percent compared to 39 percent males), and they constitute an even higher percentage of elementary school teachers. Thus, because of differences in qualifications and teaching positions, female teachers on average are paid less than male teachers.
4   Statistics are as of 1991.
5   In spite of the relatively recent political disturbances on the island, the literacy rate as of 1991 has been maintained at 88 percent (International Bank for Reconstruction and Development 1993, p. 238).
6   The ethnic composition of Sri Lanka's population according to the 1981 Census was 74 percent Sinhalese, 12.6 percent Sri Lanka Tamils, 5.5 percent Indian Tamils, 7.1 percent Moors, and 0.8 percent others. In terms of religion 69.3 percent are

Buddhists, 15.5 percent Hindus, 7.6 percent Muslims, 7.5 percent Christians, and 0.1 percent others. Language groups include Sinhalese, Tamil and Malay (a very small minority group on the island). For educational purposes the official languages of Sri Lanka are Sinhalese, Tamil and English (Wijesundera 1991).

7 The compulsory school attendance age for males and females is 14 years (or the end of the lower secondary education cycle). In 1990, 94 percent of females (compared to 90 percent of males) completed primary school and 77 precent of females (compared to 74 percent of the males) completed lower secondary school. Only 4 percent of male and female young people enrolled in higher education, indicating Sri Lanka's greater emphasis on basic education (International Bank for Reconstruction and Development 1993, p. 294).

8 These unions were all (unofficially) affiliated to major political parties but for official purposes these unions were said to be non-political.

9 The Donoughmore Constitution had its origins in a Royal Commission under the chairmanship of the Earl of Donoughmore. This Commission visited Ceylon in 1927 with the purpose of revising the constitution operating at the time and to make proposals for change (Jayasuriya 1969). The changes introduced by the constitution can be seen as precursors to the adjustments that affected the country in preparation for independence from Great Britain.

10 Ironically, the fight for the official recognition of the vernacular languages as the languages of instruction at the expense of English has had the effect of widening the gap between the two principal ethnic groups in the island.

11 Here we do not attempt an extensive review of schooling; that has been done elsewhere (see Cummings *et al.* 1992). The review of developments in teacher education is more comprehensive because of its obvious relevance to this chapter.

12 According to the Ministry of Education (MOE 1987) the 'Type I AB' schools — about 5 percent of the schools — are recognized as the best on the island and educate students to write the advanced level exams for all subjects. The 'Type I C' schools — about 15 percent of the schools — provide advanced level education in all subjects except science. Type II schools — about 40 percent of the schools on the island — educate students for the ordinary level exams; and type III schools — about 40 percent of the schools — only provide education at the elementary level. In addition to this classification, there is another by location which specifies whether the school conditions are congenial, difficult or very difficult.

13 This section is based on Dharmadasa (1988).

14 Though independence from Great Britain was not consummated until five years later, the period between 1942 to 1948 can be seen as a preparatory phase that set up the basis for the reforms that would occur after independence.

15 At this time similar debates were occurring in Great Britain (see Ginsburg and Sands 1985; Ginsburg *et al.* 1988).

16 We refer here mostly to those teacher education approaches to professionally educate elementary teachers implemented at a national level, and under direct state control. There were other institutions that educated teachers on the island though less comprehensive or short-lived in character. For example, distance education for teachers was implemented by institutions such as 'The Correspondence Distance Education' program for older primary school teachers which functioned from 1972 to 1976; the External Services Agency of the University of Sri Lanka (ESA) which enabled people with a university degree to qualify as teachers; the Sri Lanka Institute of Distance Education (SLIDE) established in 1976 to provide training in management, mathematics, science and technology; and the Open University of Sri Lanka established in 1980 with the purpose of incorporating ESA and SLIDE (Dock *et al.* 1988).

17 These guidelines are used by supervisors, headteachers or principals when evaluating the work of a teacher. Therefore, these standards are not only 'desirable' but

are expected from teachers. They include class organization, teaching ability in the subject, student evaluation, efficiency and discipline, co-curricular activities to increase school–community collaboration, training and professional development, good interpersonal relations, and community development activities. The latter aspect emphasizes the teacher role as a change agent and leader in community development projects. 'This is a role required by national education responses to contemporary socio-economic needs' (MOE 1982, p. 11).

References

BAKER, V. (1988) *The Blackboard in the Jungle: Formal Education in Disadvantaged Rural Areas. A Sri Lankan Case*, Delft, Netherlands, Eburon.

BRIDGES (1988) *Impact of Management Reforms on Cluster Innovation, Principal Effectiveness, Teacher Behavior, and School-Community Relations*, Cambridge, MA, BRIDGES Research Report, July.

CALDWELL, J. (1986) 'Routes to low mortality in poor countries', *Population and Development Review*, **12**, 2, pp. 176–92.

CENTRAL BANK OF SRI LANKA (1991) *Sri Lanka Socioeconomic Data*, Colombo, Central Bank Statistics Department.

CUMMINGS, W.K., GUNAWARDENA, G.B. and WILLIAMS, J.H. (1992) *Management Reforms and the Improvement of Education* (BRIDGES Research Report Series no. 11), Cambridge, MA, Harvard Institute for International Development.

DENSMORE, K. (1987) 'Professionalism, proletarianization and teacher work', in POPKEWITZ, T. (Ed) *Critical Studies in Teacher Education: Its Folklore, Theory and Practice*, London, Falmer Press, pp. 130–60.

DE SILVA, K.M. (1986) *Managing Ethnic Tensions in Multi-Ethnic Societies. Sri Lanka 1880–1985*, New York, University Press of America.

DHARMADASA, K.H. (1988) 'Review of Literature on Teacher Education in Sri Lanka', unpublished manuscript, National Institute of Education in Sri Lanka, Maharagama.

DOCK, A.W., DUNCAN, W.A. and KOTALAWALA, E.M. (1988) *Teaching Teachers through Distance Methods: An Evaluation of a Sri Lankan Programme* (Education Division Documents No. 40), Colombo, Swedish International Development Authority.

GINSBURG, M. (1987) 'Reproduction, contradiction and conceptions of professionalism: The case of pre-service teachers', in POPKEWITZ, T. (Ed) *Critical Studies in Teacher Education: Its Folklore, Theory and Practice*, London, Falmer Press, pp. 86–129.

GINSBURG, M., COOPER, S., RAGHU, R. and ZEGARRA, H. (1990) 'National and world-system explanations of educational reform', *Comparative Education Review*, **34**, 4, pp. 474–99.

GINSBURG, M. and SANDS, J. (1985) 'Black and brown under the white English capitalist crown', in HAWKINS J. and LA BELLE T. (Eds) *Education and Intergroup Relations: An International Perspective*, New York: Praeger.

GINSBURG, M., WALLACE, G. and MILLER, H. (1988) 'Teachers, economy, and the state', *Teaching and Teacher Education*, **4**, 4, pp. 1–21.

INTERNATIONAL BANK FOR RECONSTRUCTION AND DEVELOPMENT (1993) *World Development Report 1993*, New York, Oxford University Press.

JAYASURIYA, J.E. (1969) *Education in Ceylon Before and After Independence 1939–1968*, Colombo, Associated Educational Publishers.

MINISTRY OF EDUCATION OF SRI LANKA (MOE) (1981) *Education Proposal for Reform*, Colombo, Department of Government Printing.

MINISTRY OF EDUCATION OF SRI LANKA (MOE) (1982) *Towards Relevance in Education: Report of the Education Reforms Committee, 1979*, Colombo, Department of Government Printing.

MINISTRY OF EDUCATION OF SRI LANKA (MOE) (1987) *School Census*, Colombo, Department of Government Printing.

MUKERJEE, R.K. (1947) *Ancient Indian Education: Brahminist and Buddhist*, London, Macmillan.

PAULSTON, R.G. (1977) 'Social and educational change: Conceptual frameworks', *Comparative Education Review*, **21**, 2/3, pp. 370–95.

RAHULA, W. (1956) *History of Buddhism in Ceylon*, Colombo, M.D. Gunasena and Company.

TATTO, M.T., NIELSEN, H.D., CUMMINGS, W.C., KULARATNA, N.G. and DHARMADASA, K.H. (1991) *Comparing the Effects and Costs of Different Approaches for Educating Primary School Teachers: The Case of Sri Lanka* (BRIDGES Research Report Series No. 10). Cambridge, MA, Harvard Institute for International Development.

TATTO, M.T., NIELSEN, H.D., CUMMINGS, W.C., KULARATNA, N.G. and DHARMADASA, K.H. (1993) 'Comparing the effectiveness and costs of different approaches for educating primary school teachers in Sri Lanka', *Teaching and Teacher Education. An International Journal of Research and Studies*, **9**, 1, pp. 41–64.

WIJESUNDERA, S. (1991) *Basic Statistics Relevant to Education*, Maharagama, National Institute of Education, Department of Educational Management Development.

Chapter 7

The Dynamics of Extending an Integrated Rural Teacher Education Project in Sierra Leone

Kingsley Banya

Introduction

The allocation of resources (e.g. funding for teacher education programs) within any given society is a political process that sometimes ignores local realities. When a state decides to establish a new institution or experiment with new ideas, it makes a political decision. Some people benefit from such decisions, while others lose; jobs are affected; new values may replace old ones. Political decisions are affected by a variety of factors, including who makes the decision and who is in a position to influence the decision maker(s). Similar power play happens at the international level. The decision to allocate experimental projects in any given country is influenced by considerations other than the realities of the country. This sometimes conflicts with vested interests of various groups at both the local and national levels. Thus, when the United Nations Educational Scientific and Cultural Organization (UNESCO) decides where to allocate an integrated rural development project in sub-Saharan Africa, the decision may partly be based on factors other than technical soundness or degree of need. Political considerations are also likely to enter the calculus of decision making. The project under consideration was no exception.

The problems associated with allocation of resources is exacerbated in developing countries because of their scarce resources, weak economies, and widespread need. This results in keen competition for project resources. The allocation and implementation of a program becomes less of a purely technical matter than:

> the result of a political calculus of interests and groups competing for scarce resources, the response of implementing officials and the factors of political élites, all interacting within given institutional contexts. Analysis of the implementation of specific programs therefore may imply assessing the 'power capabilities' of the actors, their interests and the strategies for achieving them, and the characteristics of the regime in which they interact. This in turn may facilitate assessing the potential for achieving policy and program goals. (Grindle 1980, p. 12)

How the regime handles such diverse interests depends on the type of politics the regime advocates and where its mandate lies. Even authoritarian regimes, however, are intensely concerned with their survival. The maintenance of political peace becomes important to them. Their support is usually found among coalitions of groups, whose interests are taken into consideration when any implementation of policy is attempted. Programs are more likely to be implemented when they do not threaten the interests of groups essential to the survival of the regime. For example, when a government in a developing country decides to build a teacher training college in a particular location, intense pressure is brought to bear on it, to replicate the project in (or otherwise compensate) those areas that were left out, especially those areas whose residents' support is viewed as vital to sustaining those in power nationally.

Whereas in 'developed' countries input at the developmental stage of a policy is vital, in 'developing' countries greater emphasis is placed on the 'output' or implementation stage. Weiner (1962) states that in developing countries organized groups try to influence the administration of policy rather than the formulation of policy. Thus developing countries and sometimes developed ones regard the implementation process as a political stage in which adjustments must occur, in order to maintain the tenuous cohesion of the political community. External pressures both from organizations and individuals help determine how policy is implemented in developing countries. Studies of policy implementation (Smith 1973; Van Meter and Van Horn 1975; Elmore 1978; Fullan 1982) in both developed and developing countries have shown that policy makers are concerned with the nature and scope of changes that they consider desirable, but give little or no attention to the actual conditions under which social services are delivered to those who might benefit from them. Thus the rational approach to change, an if-then-logic, gives way to a more political logic of 'what's in it for me?' or to a 'trading mentality' (Walker 1985; Fullan and Steigelbausers 1991). With reference to sub-Saharan Africa, the World Bank (1990, p. 1) review of the literature on implementing educational policies concluded that:

> As yet little is known about the degree to which public policies are actually implemented in these countries, or about the factors that facilitate or impede implementation. It is now commonly and correctly assumed that implementation is indeed problematic — that the adoption of policies does not ensure that they go into effect — but just how problematic, and with what consequence remains unclear. Also unclear, by extension, is the potential for successful interventions to facilitate implementation. The problem may now be recognized, but its dimensions and the appropriate remedies remain to be established.

This chapter deals with the pressures brought to bear on the government of Sierra Leone by vested interest groups to extend integrated teacher education programs to other teacher training colleges. Case study method was used in collecting data. The method incorporated observation in pilot schools and the college, perusal of related project documents (including previous studies of the program) and focused interviews with project designers, administrators, college authorities, tutors, pilot school teachers, paramount chiefs, and community people. Interviews were conducted in and outside Sierra Leone. Data from interviews, documents and observations were analyzed using an implementation model proposed by Fullan (1982). Data are presented in qualitative form as this gives depth and detail as well as a holistic picture of what happened in the project.

National Context

In order to understand the specific case study on which this chapter is based, it will be helpful to examine the national context of Sierra Leone with respect to the economy, the political system and education.

Economy

The country's economy is an amalgam of traditional and market economies. About 75 percent of the labor force is engaged in traditional subsistence agriculture, which constitutes the largest sector of the economy. The principal food crop is rice, which is cultivated both upland and in the swamps. Rice is supplemented by other foodstuffs such as cassava, yams and maize, which are grown almost everywhere in the country, although better yields are harvested in wet areas. Crops are grown on small plots of one or two acres, using locally produced implements, such as hoes and machetes. Since land is communally owned in the provinces, where the bulk of the arable land is, large modern equipment has not been used until recently, when the government imported large numbers of tractors to cultivate large acreage. Mechanized cultivation has been a failure for various reasons, most notably the unsuitability of the tractors for the terrain (Riley 1970). Integrated rural development projects are currently being implemented to increase food production.

The main agricultural exports are palm products, cocoa, coffee, timber, and passive (a fiber used in making rope). Cocoa and coffee, the principal earners of foreign exchange, are grown mainly in the southeastern areas of the country. Because of the returns on those two products, many farmers have used their landholdings to cultivate them, instead of growing food for local consumption. Increasingly, palm products are being utilized to produce soaps, cooking oil, glycerine and margarine. Timber is also used mainly for domestic markets by forestry industries in the eastern part of the country. The agricultural sector accounts for about 35 percent of the gross national product and 22 percent of total exports.

Mining and industrial activities are the main backbone of the Sierra Leone economy. In 1935 the iron mines at Marampa in the north opened, drawing workers from all over the country and helping to develop a wage labor class. These mines ceased operations as early as the 1980s due to policy disagreements between government and foreign investors.

Rutile and bauxite are mined in the southern region. Gold mines have been opened recently in various parts of the country and the prospects are favorable. Diamonds, however, are the major source of export revenue. Since the 1930s, when diamonds were discovered along the Sewa river and the Kono fields, they have played a prominent role in the economy. The diamonds, mined alluvially, and easily found, have attracted large numbers of people from all over the country and from the neighboring countries, especially Guinea. This uncontrolled influx of immigrants — and reactions by some Sierra Leoneans — has caused civil disturbances and lawlessness, with severe social, economic and political repercussions (Little 1974).

Although minerals account for about 75 percent of exports, the nonrenewable nature of these resources coupled with the depletion of diamond deposits, the deeply embedded culture of smuggling diamonds and gold, and the low prices for diamonds, means that at present, mining cannot provide the solid long-term base for economic development which agriculture could provide (UNDP 1990). The mining sector provides employment for only about 6 percent of the working population.

Political System

From the inception of the Freetown colony or protectorate, there was an expectation that the local people, ex-slaves, were to govern themselves as much as possible. In the legal and bureaucratic terminology of the period, Creoles were British subjects, while Africans were British protected persons. Creoles were allowed token representation in colonial institutions of rule, while protectorate Africans had no such representation until 1924. Africans were governed indirectly through traditional institutions, unlike colony Creoles who were under direct administrative and political jurisdiction of the local colonial oligarchy. Legally, Creoles were subjected to the general principles of British common law, while a three-tier court system (the court of the district commissioner, mixed courts in which paramount chiefs and district commissions jointly presided, and the traditional court of the paramount chief) was maintained in the protectorate. The protectorate was divided into seven districts in the north, three in the south and one in the east. The districts were subdivided into chiefdoms, each with a paramount chief. There are currently 147 chiefdoms. These divisions were primarily based on ethnicity. The ethnicization of local administration was a crucial element in the colonial state's policy of divide and rule. Instead of fostering the assimilation and integration of disparate communities, ethnocultural differences were fetishized and politicized by the colonial administration. This trend continued during and after colonial rule (Hayward 1972).

The principal function of the chiefs was to serve as intermediaries in the colonial states' request for social order and mediated hegemony. This political, administrative and legal dualism in colonial rule in the country contributed in no small measure to shaping the contours of ethnoregional political conflict during and after colonial rules (Crowder 1965). In the Creole colony, a significant milestone was reached in the processes of ethnopoliticization by the passage of the Tribal Administration (Freetown) Act of 1905. The purpose of the Act was primarily to regulate and control the different protectorate ethnic communities in Freetown. Colonial recognition for the institution of tribal headmen in Freetown was granted. Under the provisions of the 1905 ordinance, the governor was empowered to recognize as 'tribal ruler' any 'chief', alimamy or headmen who with other headmen or representatives of the sections of the tribe endeavor to enforce a system of tribal administration for the well-being of members of the tribe, resident or temporarily staying in Freetown (Banton 1957).

This recognition of 'tribal rulers' accelerated the influx of protectorate Africans into Freetown. For example, in 1891 Creoles composed 58 percent of the population of Freetown, while protectorate Africans composed 40 percent. By 1911 the figures were 36 percent and 61 percent, respectively, and in 1947 the Creoles constituted 27 percent against 71 percent for protectorate Africans (Banton 1957). The large influx exacerbated the ethnic tensions between the Creoles and immigrant communities. On the whole the Creoles viewed the migrants as 'unredeemable savages' and asked the colonial government to 'zone the city — and to the swarm of Mendes and other aboriginal tribes, who infest the metropolis from end to end, we should apportion plots of vacant land in one and another of our deserted villages' (*Sierra Leone Weekly News*, 2 October 1900, p 2). The perception of superiority among the Creoles has continued to the present day and has played a major role in the political alliances that the Creoles have entered into with various ethnic groups in the country.

In the protectorate itself the tutelary requirements (hegemony, revenue and security) of colonial state constriction created conditions, as well as induced perceptions, of uneven development between the north and south. This perception later found expression in the emergence and elaboration of a distinctive Temne-led northern political identity — the All Peoples Party (APC) (Corby 1976). In the south and east the Sierra Leone People's Party (SLPP) became the dominant political party. Despite its appeal to other areas of the country, the SLPP remains seen as a Mende party.

A two-tiered administrative system continued in Sierra Leone until 1924, when the protectorate representatives were admitted to the legislative council. The council itself acted mainly in an advisory capacity, the final power being in the hands of the governor. After that date political equality was gradually introduced and claims based on privilege of education slowly declined.

The first major concession from the British was the 1951 Constitution that granted limited self-government beginning in 1953. Further political developments led to the leader of the largest group in the legislature becoming the chief minister, who was charged with the daily administration of the country. The British Governor retained the powers of foreign affairs, law and order. Election to legislature was indirect, with certain seats reserved for the Creoles who lived predominantly in the western area. With further constitutional changes in 1957, an elected legislature was granted and in 1961 the country became independent. Upon independence the country was divided into 12 districts and the western area. This political division has persisted to the present. There are three provinces — the north, the south and the east. These divisions, like previous ones, are based roughly on ethnic divisions (Wright 1965). A district normally comprises a number of chiefdoms. A district, however, is smaller than a province, which normally has three or more districts. The western area coincides with the original Freetown colony.

Sierra Leone is a culturally plural and intensely stratified society; its post-colonial political history attests to and offers interesting insights about the intimate connections between class, ethnicity and state formation. The constant reordering of state–society relations along ethno-clientelist lines has been the bane of Sierra Leone politics since independence. Cabinet posts become rewards to ethnic clients and supporters, carrots to political opponents and a means of silencing restive ethnic communities. As Carew (1985, p. 6) succinctly puts it:

Each time a high office goes to someone in the community his or her tribesmen jubilate openly, culminating finally in a delegation to the head of state to thank him for the appointment of their son or daughter to the high office. All appointments to positions in top statal as well as parastatals are treated in this way.

This means that the individual is seen as an embodiment of the tribe; thus, his or her fortunes are strongly identified with those of the tribe. If the individual succeeds, it is the tribe that has progressed, and if the individual fails it is the tribe that has suffered a setback. The success of ethnopopulism as an instrument of political domination, however, has been largely contingent upon the ability of politicians to translate their access to state resources into tangible benefits for their ethnic constituents. When this expectation of their ethnic constituents is not forthcoming, hostility and rejection ensue. In a country with two major ethnic groups (Mendes and Temne account for nearly 60 percent of the population) and 10 other ethnic groups making the rest of the 40 percent, ethnicity plays a major role in politics.

As the financial resources of the state are depleted because of global economic dynamics or as a consequence of the unbridled venality of the ruling class, however, the opportunities for patronage become more and more limited. The contraction of patronage opportunities diminishes the significance of ethnic politics to processes of domination. The emergence of Temne (the second largest ethnic group in the country) and other northern pirate capitalists under the APC rule was made possible by the systematic plunder and diversion of state resources into private and patronage uses (Hayward and Kandeh 1987).

From the granting of internal self-government to 1967, the Mendes (a Bantu-speaking people who comprise 30 percent of the population) ruled the country. Their political party, the SLPP, embraced not only Mendes but some of the other ethnic groups, especially the Temnes, Kissi and Konos. At one time the SLPP was the only effective party in the country, but when the constitutional talks that led to independence began, the main opposition party was formed — the APC.

Siaka Stevens and most of the other northern politicians, who defected from the United Front (which had been hurriedly put together by Mende, Creole, and Temne leaders to attend the London independence conference) and established their own political organization, visibly lacked the status and material wealth of the SLPP leaders. To overcome this background of relative material destitution and to avoid political marginalization, capturing state power became an overriding objective. From its inception, the APC was an instrument in the class transformation of petty bourgeois elements left out in the politics of independence. Despite its petty bourgeois leadership and ethnoregional base, the APC in opposition had sought to distance itself from the élitism and conservatism of the Mende-dominated SLPP by adopting the rhetoric and slogans of populism and socialism.

Other factors such as the political disaffection and anxieties of the Creoles, the regional deprivation of the north, the abuses and excesses of northern chiefs and the relative openness of the political system at that time combined contextually to favor the emergence of the APC, and the rapacious venality of the state bourgeoisie, as the dominant force in post-independence politics of Sierra Leone. The populist and socialist slogans were later belied by the untrammeled opportunism and parasitism of the APC, as seen by various Commissions of Inquiries after the overthrow of the Momoh regime in 1992.

Education

At independence Sierra Leone inherited from the British colonial government an educational system that was largely academic, theoretical and disconnected from the daily lives of the majority of the population. It did not give cognizance to the daily life and social experience of the people, who lived predominantly in the rural areas (70–80 percent) where their livelihood was closely tied to agricultural productivity. Indeed, years later it can be said that the schools are still divorced from the life and culture of the people of Sierra Leone. Education in the colonial period was closely tied to the state's hegemonic project and initially was limited to Sherbro and Mendeland. The early Islamization of northern Sierra Leone by Muslim emissaries meant that most Christian missions preferred to work among the Mendes and Sherbro who are traditionally animists. By 1938, 80 percent of all schools in the protectorate were in Mendeland (Kilson 1966, p. 77). This educational headstart by the Mendes over other protectorate ethnic groups, and the fact that much of the basic colonial economic infrastructure (such as roads and the railway) were concentrated in Mendeland, gave rise to perceptions of relative deprivation among northern ethnic groups (Hayward and Kandeh 1987).

The consequences of the colonial system of schooling, coupled with cultural, political and economic factors, have reinforced the heavy rural–urban migration of the young (Kilson 1966; Little 1974; Adepoju 1977; Balar 1981; Zachariah 1981). This rural–urban movement has created serious economic, demographic, educational, social and political problems for the government of Sierra Leone. Because independent governments have more or less continued the rigid centralization of authority, no important decision is taken in the provinces without approval from Freetown, (the capitol). Consequently, such simple things as getting approval to teach in a school has meant constant and lengthy travel by the people in the provinces to Freetown.

In an attempt to reverse the trend of increased migration to urban areas, to improve rural productivity and the quality of rural life, and to make the school curriculum pertinent to rural areas, the government of Sierra Leone, in collaboration with the United Nations Educational Scientific and Cultural Organization (UNESCO) and the United Nations Development Program (UNDP), undertook in 1974 a joint project to train primary school teachers for rural areas. This will be referred to as the 'Bunumbu Project'. The initiative for the project was announced in the presidential speech at the opening of parliament on 22 June 1973. President Siaka Stevens (1973, p. 10) stated:

> Emphasis will be made in the integrated approach to social development thereby involving the rural population in a total transformation of the college and a group of primary schools, to be known as the pilot schools, into community schools. A new type of pre-service and in-service teacher training, plus the production of a new primary school curriculum with a rural bias, will be started at Bunumbu Teachers College.

This declaration became part of the five-year Sierra Leone National Development Plan, 1974/75–1978/79, which was extended by an additional three years. Among the aims of this plan were:

1   to accelerate the expansion of primary education, especially as regards teacher education;
2   to make the content of education in all subsectors more relevant to the economic and social needs of the country; and
3   to raise the level of literacy by the provision of better primary and out-of-school education.

The initiation of the project coincided with new political developments within the country. For example, from 1968 to 1973, the APC regime was actively challenged by the only opposition party, the SLPP. Since both parties were ethnically and religiously aligned, Sierra Leone politics and hence patron-clientelism was based on north versus south or Mende versus Temne. To erode the power base of the Mende dominated SLPP in the east, Stevens's APC used the project as incentive for those who would join his party. By providing visible material benefits at the project site and its environs, Stevens was successful in luring some key Mende politicians to the APC. For example, the first African principal of the project, a Mende man, contested elections under the APC banner after he retired from the civil service. By appointing key Mende personalities who were sympathetic to his political beliefs, Stevens was able to make inroads into the opposition stronghold. The project started, therefore, as part of Stevens's patron-clientelism and its continued support was due in large measure because of it. Indeed, one of the key Mende players, Dr. S. S. Banya, became prominent as chairman of the Board of Directors of the project in the late 1970s.

The initial project was based at Bunumbu Teachers College and involved 20 pilot schools within a 20-mile radius. The location seems ideal for a program designed to meet the social, political and cultural needs of rural people. The college is in the heart of the rural area, 270 miles from Freetown, 40 miles from the provincial headquarters in Kenema, and 43 miles from the district headquarters in the town of Kailahun.

Bunumbu was seen as a prospective site to carry out many of the tasks envisaged, and regular meetings were held between the principal of the college and officials of the Ministries of Education and Economic Development. Other developments helped speed the introduction of the project. A presidential speech of June 1973 (see the above quotation) put the government seal of approval on the general sentiments expressed in the White Paper. The project was included in the Sierra Leone proposals for the community program (1973–76) submitted to the UNDP. Earlier in 1973, with an initial grant from the UNDP, a three-person mission from UNDP/UNESCO undertook a three-week feasibility study.

Apart from visiting Sierra Leone, the mission, generally referred to as the 'Honeybone Mission', spent some time at the UNESCO Regional Office in Dakar examining documents related to rural teacher education; the mission also visited a similar teacher training project in Liberia — the Kakata Project. After these activities, the Bunumbu project proposals were made, and subsequently approved by the government of Sierra Leone and the UNDP Resident Representative. The duration of the project was originally intended to be five years, and it was to be undertaken by the Institute of Education and Bunumbu College as chief executing agencies, in close collaboration with the Ministry of Education.

At about this period a nationwide review of education, conducted for the government by the University of Sierra Leone, produced a report sympathetic to the new orientation. The review was undertaken to see whether the current educational system was meeting the needs and aspirations of individuals and the state. One of the recommendations of the review was to make education more relevant to the needs of the rural population.

The problems of Sierra Leone were not limited to education, yet education was chosen as an instrument of redress. The rationale for choosing education over other sectors, such as agriculture, health, social welfare, and transportation, was that schooling was viewed as capable of producing marketable skills with long-term effects on producers as well as consumers. Farmers could be better producers and consumers of goods and services. Also, it was assumed by the project designers that many of the problems of rural living — health problems, poor nutrition, and rural–urban drift — could be solved by a positive change of attitude, engineered by education.

It is easier politically to make education the main strategy since this would place much of the responsibility on individuals rather than focusing on aspects of the political economy that may need to be changed. Political leaders also felt that there was a strong relationship between education and development, namely a greater promise of return on investment in education than in any other sector. Education was expected by the project designers to provide a multiplier effect towards solving some of the problems outlined. Since primary schools play a critical role in teaching children during their formative years, the Ministry of Education viewed it as logical to invest especially in the area of teacher education (Hedd 1981). Teacher education was selected because of the changes it could bring to individuals. In order to involve the other ministries, and thus draw on their expertise and help provide a broader legitimacy for the project, a National Advisory Committee (NAC) was established. The NAC had the responsibility of monitoring events and giving advice and guidance to the college and the ministry on the general operation of the project.

Local Context

While the above activities were taking place on the national level, important developments at the local level led to further implementation of the project. The first African and Sierra Leonean principal of Bunumbu Mr F.S. Ngegba, was appointed in 1971. He came to the post with a wealth of knowledge and ideas from his years as extramural coordinator for the University of Sierra Leone. The extramural department links the university to part-time students all over the country. Correspondence and short-term courses as well as in-service workshops are conducted by this department for the university.

In his previous position he had made invaluable contacts with a network of school personnel. In a society where social relationships tend to be sociocentric, informal networks play an important and useful role. Thus a casual conversation or a chance meeting may influence the shape and formation of opinions and open the corridors of power when least expected. When a decision was to be made about the location of the project, the Bunumbu principal's contacts made that decision a foregone conclusion; all that was needed was official approval. He had contacts both at UNESCO headquarters and in the Ministry of Education. One of the initiators of the project has described in an interview the role played by the principal this way:

> After a while I was appointed member of the Board of Governors, being the resident paramount chief of the college. We decided to meet together to think what best we can do to improve the status of the college. For the first time we met, I met with the late principal, Mr F.S. Ngegba, and one Mr S.R. Allen, who was the PEO [Principal Education Officer] for teacher education, Ministry of Education — now working in Nigeria. We thought of how best we can proceed. The principal suggested that the college should be improved on an agricultural bias, which Mr S.R. Allen suggested should be under elementary HTC [Higher Teacher's Certificate]. This was discussed internally. After some time, proposals were written down by the late principal and Mr Allen, who were experts in that field. The program started, suggestions started, this matter was taken before the UNDP, UNESCO, and the Sierra Leone government (Chief 501).

The principal was fortunate in that most of the senior officials of the Ministry of Education, not only those responsible for teacher education, were sensitive to the problems of Bunumbu.

Nature of the Project

Rural development policies were proposed as palliatives to problems of under-employment and unemployment, lack of productivity in the agricultural sector, a constricted internal market, foreign trade deficits, massive rural–urban migration and shortages of staple food stuffs (Chambes 1974; World Bank 1975).

The concept of integrated rural development (IRD) has given rise to various theories and generated many ideas for development projects (Grabe *et al.* 1975; Grindle 1981; Zachariah and Hoffman 1984). Common to most of the theories and ideas is the complexity and difficulty of defining IRD. A couple of examples illustrate this point. Gebregziabher (1975, p. 3) refers to the IRD as 'consisting of all the things that can most improve the living conditions of the rural masses'. The holistic nature of IRD can be compared to the biblical concept of a deity, as in the idea of God who 'is everywhere, but is found nowhere'. For the purpose of this discussion, Mosher's (1976, p. 10) definition will be used: 'Projects and programs dealing simultaneously with a number of different aspects of rural well being'.

IRD programs, whether established in Asia, Latin America or Africa, are very ambitious, for they seek to cater to all in every field (see Hedd 1967; D'Silva and Raza 1980; Khan 1984). The common theme that predominates in all of them seems to be the effective and rapid integration of children, youth and adults into the social, cultural and economic development of the host country, but without giving them access to all the benefits or opportunities available to élites in urban areas. Whatever the package of activities and services selected, they are viewed to have a synergistic effect on the development of a country, with intentions of improving the living conditions on a permanent basis (Cohen 1987).

For this all-embracing mandate to be achieved, emphasis is placed on concerted interagency and governmental action at the national level. Organic linkage or a functional relationship is formed for better results using the same resources or much better ones with comparatively small additional inputs. In such projects, linkage is not just limited to people, institutions and facilities, like a multipurpose use of a classroom, but to ideas, skills, aptitudes, values, attitudes and school subjects (e.g. an integrated social sciences approach focused on dealing with thematic problems). Linkages form an aggregate, which continually attracts more input. At the local level (i.e. at the project site) through appropriate local community organizations people and things are often meant to speak for themselves. Local people in theory are supposed to participate as full partners in the execution of the project. The projects are thus located in rural areas, and are designed eventually to change the national educational system to reflect the prevailing realities within the country.

The Bunumbu project document underwent many revisions, and the final version was as complex as it was detailed. There were formally stated long-range and immediate objectives. The long-range objectives were:

1 the development of a new, primary curriculum with a rural bias;
2 the expansion of the present functions of the teacher training colleges to include the capability of providing in-service training and educational extension services to village community centers on a request or need basis of serving as educational technology and information resource centers; and
3 the development of a country-wide network of community education centers providing education and training of both a formal and non-formal nature to young people and adults in the rural areas (SL/UNDP/73/009, as cited by Hedd 1981, p. 87).

Although the Bunumbu project was to be largely financed by UNDP, UNESCO, and the Sierra Leone government, there were other sources supporting the project. For example, the Canadian University Service Overseas (CUSO) supplied teachers and the United Nations International Children's Education Fund (UNICEF) provided a water pump and other equipment, both expendable (paper) and non-expendable (vehicles). It was also assumed that the Sierra Leone government would get a loan from the African Development Bank (ADB) to put up the buildings for the student dormitories and classrooms. In fact, the loan was never released as planned. The delay in releasing funds when needed was one of the factors that contributed to the delay in implementing the project.

Political Dynamics of Implementing the Bunumbu Project

The Ministry of Education of Sierra Leone does not give a detailed prescription for achieving goals. A loosely structured approach, encouraged by ministry officials, has evolved since independence, when policy makers tried to be as accessible as possible to those who carry out policies. This practice encourages relative autonomy, with multiple lines of authority, and makes communication with policy makers easier. At the same time, it protects policy makers from bearing the full brunt of any failure, while enabling them to gain political capital from successes. For example, when students protest their living conditions, the college authorities are often blamed, although, in fact, the problem may stem from ministry officials in Freetown not having provided the necessary funds to improve the facilities.

In teacher training, in particular, no rigid structures are set up. Instead, non-routine, non-standardized approaches are permitted. Tutors are quite often in charge of classrooms and what goes on there, because of their alleged specialized expertise to make such decisions. College tutors are generally employed on the basis of specialization in a particular discipline, and teach only that subject. It is assumed by college authorities and by ministry officials that any attempt at rigid supervision may lead to lower staff morale and lower output. Generally, tutors are not viewed as subversive or conveyors of messages that may undermine the regime. Tradition and culture have reinforced the view of tutors as 'professionals' who are competent to discharge their duties without someone looking over their shoulder. Thus, despite the hierarchy within a college (principal, vice-principal, department head), tutors are relatively free to perform their duties as they see fit.

The principal is the administrative as well as the academic head of the college, assisted by a vice-principal and department heads. In theory, the principal reports first to the Board of Governors of the college, and ultimately to the Ministry of Education. However, because of the nature of the college administration, and the fact that the board meets only once a month, the Ministry of Education normally receives reports before the governors. The Board of Governors in turn reports to the ministry through the principal, who acts as secretary to the board. This illustrates another potential source of power of the principal.

The lines of authority described above remained in place for the implementation of the project, although titles changed slightly. For example, the principal became National Director. It is worth noting that no explicit mention is made of the role of students in the organizational structure. The assumption is that the principal and staff deal with students' problems. It is only when the college authorities cannot solve a particular problem — for example, delays in payment of allowances and salaries or serious food shortages — that higher authorities are asked to intervene to pacify the students.

Staffing teacher training colleges in Sierra Leone has been an ongoing problem until quite recently. The job was unrewarding and turnover was high. Bunumbu, in particular, suffered because of poor transportation and the distance from urban areas. Given the bias toward urban life (élite status, etc.) among those receiving enough education to 'qualify' for jobs, the location of Bunumbu thus created an additional problem.

The multipurpose dimension of the Bunumbu project called for a staff that was oriented toward the philosophy of rural education. Yet the relative isolation of the college and the lack of real incentive to work in rural areas militated against having all the qualified staff the college required, before and even after the project started.

An interim measure had to be taken to fill the gap while training programs were started for preparing staff from the local area. The solution was to bring in expatriates. Some expatriates came as UNESCO experts, as well as volunteers from such organizations as Canadian University Service Overseas (CUSO),

Voluntary Service Overseas (VSO), and the US Peace Corps. The staff development program attracted some teachers from other colleges as well as from secondary schools. The expatriates acted as counterparts to Sierra Leoneans in the various subject areas. Their role was initially to train the college tutors and teach their specialties while the Sierra Leoneans went abroad for further studies. The expatriates, while professional in their own rights, also represented the interests of the individual countries and organizations.

By the end of the first phase of the project, the number of staff had doubled from 20 to 40. A majority of the tutors were graduates from the University of Sierra Leone. A few had done graduate work, mainly abroad. There are a large number of Higher Teacher's Certificate holders on the staff, who mainly teach first-year and practical courses. Many other staff expected to go for further studies either within Sierra Leone or abroad.

There are four major conclusions that we can draw from the study of the impact of the project (Banya 1992). First, to a certain extent the project was implemented after many trials and errors. Initially there were difficulties in defining what implementation involved and the roles to be played by those carrying out the project. Second, some of the objectives were achieved, for example, the development of curricula with a rural focus for the pilot schools as well as that of the college. Other objectives were only partially implemented, for example, the transformation of the rebuilt 20 pilot schools into community learning centers. The physical transformation of the schools was achieved but the learning center for adults did not materialize. Third, serious weaknesses and constraints mitigated against the achievements of all the objectives. Some of the weaknesses were the design of the program: lack of clarity of goals; the attempt to achieve many objectives in a relatively short period of time; the failure to specify roles for the groups involved in the project; and the failure of the National Advisory Committee to function properly. Some of the constraints were: the isolation of Bunumbu from the Freetown center of action; lack of trained personnel to implement the program, and the lack of fiscal and appropriate material resources. Fourth, the project had impact (both anticipated and unanticipated) on the community within the 20-mile radius of the college. Some of the effects were: both the teacher's certificate and higher teacher's certificate trainees were given the opportunity to develop their talents in areas additional to academic performance; the construction of the 20 pilot schools improved the conditions under which the pupils study; the 20 village blacksmithing workshops provided much needed technical support for agricultural development in the area; tutors, college administrators, and pilot school personnel have acquired confidence in themselves to tackle the educational as well as the community problems of the area; and Bunumbu has become a semi-urban town, a development viewed with skepticism by many within the community.[1]

Political Dynamics of Extending the Project to Other Colleges

The perceived 'success' of the initial Bunumbu project led to the clamor of other teacher preparation institutions and their communities for similar projects, especially in their desire for additional resources. The Stevens regime came under extreme pressure from the north and west to replicate Bunumbu at the four teacher preparation institutes (two in the north and two in the western area) in those parts of the country. As Stevens had come to power due to massive support from those parts of the country, it was politically expedient for the government to pay attention to their requests. To secure its power base, the Stevens regime sought external funding to extend Bunumbu without any formal needs assessment study. Unlike the initial project at Bunumbu, where feasibility studies were done, the extension of integrated teacher education programs in the rest of the country was carried out by governmental fiat. External funding came from various sources, including the World Council of Churches, International Development Agency (IDA), the World Bank and bilateral governmental agreements. These organizations had their own motives and agendas. For example, the Christian missionaries were interested in extending their influence in the southern part of the country.

As part of the Stevens scheme to consolidate power, every effort was made to give each of the four teacher education colleges some form of an integrated rural development project status even though all are located in urban areas. The extension of the integrated rural development project to other parts of the country should be placed in the context of the state's central role in making provisions for developing human resources, steering the economy, building infrastructure, determining policy towards foreign as well as local businesses, administering commodity exports, allocating mining and import licenses and regulating foreign exchange. Thus, access to the state's decision-making mechanisms has become a fundamental aspiration of both literate and illiterate élites, spearheaded by its more politically committed members (Fashole-Luke 1984). The patron–clientelist results see developmental efforts in one area as a tangible 'reward' that they too must have in their areas.

In Stevens the system found a dynamic player who demonstrated a shrewd understanding of the dynamic uses and intricacies of patronage. From 1968 he cultivated clientelist relations with the leadership and other well-placed individuals of potential opposition. The 1971 unsuccessful assassination attempt and the 1974 abortive *coup d'état* gave Stevens an aura of invincibility and hence a free hand to do virtually anything he wanted. For example, the move toward republican status and hence executive presidency came after the 1971 events. After the 1974 attempted *coup d'état* a one-party system of government was instituted. The imposition of the one-party system is another indication of Stevens's manipulation of power to his advantage. On the issue of one-party system, Foray (1988, p. 6) states that

> the advantages and disadvantages of the one party system carried little weight in the debates preceding the adoption of the system. Neither Sir Albert (Margai SLPP) nor Mr (Siaka) Stevens (APC) would support it whilst not in the saddle of supreme power or whilst in opposition.

Once in power, however, Stevens became an effective political apostate, conveniently and calmly devouring his previous anti-one-party denunciations and pro-multi-party sentiments and elusively and solemnly defending the system of one party. Foray (1988, p. 6) continues,

> there was a difference in approach. Sir Albert, the British-trained lawyer, insisted on scrupulous adherence to legality. Siaka Stevens, the trade

unionist and ex-police constable, the African politician *par excellence*, forced the one-party system through by means of violence, legal as well as physical. I do not think it is too much to assert that in the last three decades, the bane of African politics has been the one-party system with its corollary, the executive president.

Stevens was able to consolidate his hold on power for 17 years until he retired in November 1985.

Stevens's use of the carrot-and-stick approach provided the right atmosphere to extend the integrated rural development project to areas which technically may not have been appropriate sites, but which could be potential areas of political trouble for the regime. Thus Bo Teachers College in Bo (located in Sierra Leone's second largest city) got an integrated rural development project because it is in Mendeland, a stronghold of the opposition party. By providing visible manifestation of what cooperation with his government could bring to an area, Stevens was able to weaken the base of the opposition.

Those areas traditionally neglected in social amenities use all the leverage at their disposal to attract new projects. Thus the establishment of an integrated rural development project brought with it various amenities that a town could not possibly achieve on a piecemeal basis. The fact that the first integrated rural development project was in the Mende area only increased others' wanting the same in their ethnic areas, especially in the Temne area in the north. The other two colleges in the north in Temneland requested and got integrated rural development projects, even though one of these colleges is located in Makeni, the third largest city of the country. The Stevens regime could not afford to neglect its powerbase in the north, and whether colleges needed an integrated rural development project or not, the colleges in the north desired them and got them.

In addition, as discussed above, ethnic identity has always determined recruitment and mobility patterns in both administrative and coercive apparatuses of the post-colonial state. Thus duplicating the integrated rural development project all over the country became part of Stevens's patronage effort to maintain power. In effect, the project was part of the patron–clientelism strategy for élite co-option for the ruling APC (Fashole-Luke 1984). Clientelism offers opportunities for the government to reward its supporters and punish its foes. The integrated development project extension to various colleges was seen as a reward and therefore part of the patron–clientelist strategy of the Stevens regime.

To achieve the goal of patron–clientelism, the Stevens regime used every bilateral agreement with donor countries as well as international organizations to promote the plan for an integrated rural development project for each of the colleges. Stevens's use of the intrigues and intricacies of patronage and patron–clientelism that characterizes the country's politics extended to foreign assistance as well. He courted foreign aid assistance from wherever it could be obtained: the Arab Gulf States, China, the European Economic Community (EEC), the United States and the Soviet Union.[2]

The seductive nature of rural development policies as advocated by the World Bank and other international financial institutions also made it easier for the program to be extended. In the late 1970s and during the decade of the 1980s, integrated development policies were in vogue.[3] This context provided the atmosphere within which the Stevens regime was requesting outside assistance ostensibly to develop the country. In reality, the aid was used more to maintain the power base and legitimacy of the Stevens government.

Conclusion

The modern African state is a legacy of colonial rule, not a historical evolution. The state in Africa, therefore, exists in an overdeveloped relationship with its society. This results in fragile bases of legitimacy and a political culture of ambivalence toward the propriety of impersonal rules and public purpose. From this configuration patron–clientelism has emerged as the mode of governance or neo-patrimonial rule. This provides the context in which the Stevens regime's manipulation of the integrated rural development project must be seen.

What are some of the lessons that can be learned from the development of integrated rural development projects throughout Sierra Leone? Clearly the projects were seen as political rewards for those who supported the Stevens regime. Under a one-party state rule, the leaders need to demonstrate in concrete terms the benefits that accrue from such a system (as opposed to a multi-party system of government) and from a particular party monopolizing power. As indicated earlier, Stevens understood this more than any other politician in the country. He was, therefore, able to use the patron–clientelist strategy to his maximum benefit. As stated earlier, the rapid rise of Dr. S. S. Banya in the political hierarchy of the APC to Vice President and Minister of Finance was due in part to Stevens's use of patron–clientelism to recruit prominent Mendes who initially, at least, were opposed to his regime.

International organizations and foreign government development agencies were willing partners to Stevens's schemes. During the cold war period, donor agencies competed with each other for influence. As indicated, the Stevens regime literally was willing to do anything to get aid from outside. The fact that he could play one organization against another, one ideology against the other, only helped to buttress his position. This also meant that patron–clientelism was further enhanced.

While not minimizing the benefit to the local community where the programs were located, the neo-patrimonial rule makes for potential instability and can be vulnerable on a number of fronts, including foreign manipulation. As Sierra Leone depends more and more on foreign assistance, the country may be forced to compromise part of its sovereignty.

There is an inherent danger of neo-patrimonial rule, especially when it comes to succession. The successor to Stevens, Major-General Momoh, either had to continue the system of government established by Stevens or start a new governance structure. Although President Momoh established a 'New Order Government' upon succeeding Stevens in November 1985, his regime lasted until March 1992, when he was overthrown in a *coup d'état* by junior military officers. The major reason given for his overthrow was that patron–clientelism was no longer functioning effectively within the country. As long as ex-president Momoh was able to provide necessary economic rewards for his supporters and various potential opposition groups, things worked out well. But as the economy deteriorated and external conditionalities increased, Momoh could not deliver the rewards necessary to keep him in power. He was a victim of the new patrimonial rule that characterized the country for 17 years under Stevens's rule as well as changes in the world system — the end of the cold war reduced incentives in the East and West to fund projects in countries such as Sierra Leone.

This was the same period in which integrated rural development was instituted throughout the country. While teacher education programs were only part of this initiative and integrated rural development was only one project through which rewards were distributed, it should be clear that teacher education policy, program development, and funding were and are thoroughly enmeshed in the patron–clientelist politics of Sierra Leone and the geo-politics of the world system.

Notes

1   The project has been affected by the war situation in the eastern part of the country. The building and other college properties have been destroyed. The students and staff were forced to leave for the safety of Kenema, 38 miles away from Bunumba.

2   Sierra Leonean's ratification of the Islamic conference charter in 1982 was done for economic necessity rather than religious conviction. Likewise, the establishment of diplomatic relations with Iran and Saudi Arabia was for economic necessity, rather than a changing ideological disposition. This also explains Stevens's frequent attendance at the annual Franco-African summits. As has been documented by Parfitt (1984) for the case of European Economic Community (EEC) assistance and Riley (1988) for the United States' PL 480 rice program, even foreign aid was dispensed as patronage. It is interesting that countries (e.g. Canada and Sweden) that monitored projects closely and insisted on the use of aid for well defined development activities were never contacted.

3   Whether it is the El Proyecto Especial Integrado sobre la Funcion de la Education en el Dessarrollo Rural (PEIFEDER) of Sicuarri in the province of Canae, Couchis in the heart of the southwestern Peruvian Andes 500 miles away from the Peruvian capital city Lima, or in the vicinity of the countries' capitals, as in the case of the Experimental Pilot Project Integrating Education into Rural Development (EPPIERD) around Islamabad, Pakistan, the projects were readily financed by international organizations with the World Bank spearheading the drive (Banya 1989).

References

ADEPOJU, A. (Ed) (1977) *Migration in Nigeria*, Ill-Ife, University of Ife.

BALAR, J. (1981) *Why People Move*, Paris, UNESCO.

BANTON, M. (1957) *West African City*, London, Oxford University Press.

BANYA, K. (1989) 'Education for rural development: Myth or reality?' *International Journal of Educational Development*, **9**, 2, pp. 111–26.

BANYA, K. (1991) 'Economic decline and education system: The Case of Sierra Leone', *Compare*, **21**, 2, pp. 127–43.

BANYA, K. (1992) 'Educational policy in Sierra Leone: The continuing search for relevance', in LUKE, D. (Ed) *Economic Decline and the Prospect for Adjustment in Africa: The Case of Sierra Leone*, Boulder, CO, Westview Press, pp. 85–111.

CAREW, G. (1985) 'The Multiethnic State and the Principle of Distributive Justice', unpublished manuscript, London, University of London.

CHAMBES, R. (1974) *Managing Rural Development*, Uppsala, The Scandinavian Institute of African Studies.

COHEN, J. (1987) *Integrated Rural Development: The Ethiopian Experience and the Debate*, Uppsala, Scandinavian Institute of African Studies.

CORBY, R. (1976) Western Educated Sons of Chiefs, District Commissions and Chiefdom: The Role of Bo School and its Graduates in the Local Level Development of Sierra Leone. Unpublished Ph.D. Dissertation, Indiana University.

CROWDER, M. (1965) 'An African aristocracy', *Geographical Magazine*, **31**, 2, pp. 183–90.

D'SILVA, B. and RAZA, M. (1980) 'Integrated rural development in Nigeria: The funta projects', *Good Policy*, **6**, 3, pp. 61–69.

ELMORE, R. (1978) 'Organizational models of social program implementation', *Public Policy*, **26**, 2, pp. 85–128.

FASHOLE-LUKE, D. (1984) *Labor and Parastatal Politics in Sierra Leone*, New York, University Press of America.

FORAY, C. (1988) 'The Africans Horton Memorial Lecture', presentation delivered at the Centre of African Studies, Edinburgh University, Scotland, June.

FULLAN, M. (1982) *The Meaning of Educational Change*, Toronto, OISE Press.

FULLAN, M. and STEIGELBAUERS, S. (1991) *The New Meaning of Educational Change*, 2nd edn, New York, Teachers College Press.

GEBREGZIABHER, B. (1975) *Integrated Rural Development in Rural Ethiopia: An Evaluative Study of the Vhilalo Agricultural Development Unit*, Bloomington, IN, University of Indiana International Development Research Center, PASITAM.

GRABE, S. and INSTITUT D'ETUDE DU DEVELOPEMENT ECONOMIQUE ET SOCIAL (IEDES) (1975) 'Upper Volta: A rural alternative to primary schools', in AHMED, M. and COOMBS, P. (Eds) *Education for Rural Development: Case Studies for Planners*, New York, Praeger Publishers, pp. 335–64.

GRINDLE, M. (Ed) (1980) *Politics and Policy Implementation in the Third World*, Princeton, NJ, Princeton University Press.

GRINDLE, M. (1981) 'Anticipating failure: The implementation of rural development programs', *Public Policy*, **29**, 1, pp. 51–74.

HAYWARD, F. and KANDEH, J. (1987) 'Perspectives on twenty-five years of elections in Sierra Leone', in HAYWARD, F. (Ed) *Elections in Independent Africa*, Boulder, CO, Westview Press, pp. 25–59.

HAYWARD, G. (1972) 'The development of a radical political organization in the Bush', *Canadian Journal of African Studies*, **6**, 1, pp. 1–28.

HEDD, G. (1967) 'Sierra Leone: Creating a context', in ADAMS, R. and CHEN, D. (Eds) *The Process of Educational Innovation: An International Perspective*, Paris, UNESCO.

HEDD, G. (1981) 'Sierra Leone: Creating a context', in ADAMS, R. and CHEN, D. (Eds) *The Process of Educational Innovations: An International Perspective*, Paris, UNESCO, pp. 81–105.

KHAN, B. (1984) 'Rural development in Bangladesh. Major issue revisited', *Bangladesh Institute of International and Strategic Studies Journal*, **5**, 4, pp. 45–57.

KILSON, M. (1966) *Political Changes in a West African State*, Cambridge, MA, Harvard University Press.

LITTLE, K. (1974) *Urbanization as a Social Process*, London, Routledge and Kegan Paul.

MOSHER, A. (1976) *Thinking About Development*, New York, Agricultural Development Council.

PARFITT, T. (1984) 'EEC aid in practice: Sierra Leone', in STEVEN, C. (Ed) *EEC and the Third World: A Survey Renegotiating Lome*, London, Hodden and Stoughton.

RILEY, S. (1970) 'No Room for Manuvre? Debt and the Politics of Development in Sierra Leone', in LUKE, D. and RILEY, S. (Eds) *Economic Decline and Prospects for Adjustment in Sub-Saharan Africa: The Case of Sierra Leone*, Boulder, CO, Westview, pp. 112–35.

RILEY, S. (1988) 'No room for maœuvre? Debt and the politics of development in Sierra Leone', in LUKE, D. and RILEY, S. (Eds) *Economic Decline and Prospects for Adjustment in Sub-Saharan Africa: The Case of Sierra Leone*, Boulder, CO, Westview Press, pp. 112–35.

SIERRA LEONE GOVERNMENT (1964) *The Sleight Report*, Freetown, Sierra Leone Government Printer.

SIERRA LEONE GOVERNMENT (1972) *University of Sierra Leone Act 1972*, Freetown, Sierra Leone Government Printer.

SIERRA LEONE GOVERNMENT (1974a) *National Census Report*, Freetown, Sierra Leone Government Printer.

SIERRA LEONE GOVERNMENT (1974b) *White Paper on Educational Policy*, Freetown, Sierra Leone Government Printer.

SIERRA LEONE GOVERNMENT (1974c) *National Development Plan for Education, 1974–79*, Freetown, Sierra Leone Government Printer.

SMITH, T. (1973) 'The policy implementation process', *Policy Sciences*, **4**, 2, pp. 421–56.

STEVENS, S. (1973) *Throne Speech to Parliament*, Freetown, Sierra Leone Government Printer.

UNDP (1990) *Education in Sub-Saharan Africa: Policies for Adjustment, Revitalization, and Expansion*, Washington, DC, UNESCO.

VAN METER, D. and VAN HORN, C. (1975) 'The policy implementation process — A conceptual framework', *Administration and Society*, **6**, 4, pp. 445–88.

WALKER, D. (1985) *Survey of the Status of the Teaching Profession in Africa*, Washington, DC, World Council of Organized Teachers.

WEINER, M. (1962) *The Politics of Scarcity*, Chicago, IL, University of Chicago Press.

WORLD BANK (1975) *The Assault on World Poverty: Problems of Rural Development and Health*, Baltimore, MD, Johns Hopkins University Press.

WORLD BANK (1990) *Implementing Educational Policies in Sub-Saharan Africa: A Review of the Literature*, Washington, DC, World Bank.

WRIGHT, K. (1965) 'Freetown: A Symposium', Occasional Paper No. 2, Institute of African Studies, Fourah Bay College, Sierra Leone.

ZACHARIAH, M. (1981) *Migration in West Africa*, London, World Bank and Oxford University Press.

ZACHARIAH, M. and HOFFMAN, A. (1984) 'Gandhi and Mao on Manual Labor in the School: A Retrospective Analysis', paper presented at the Fifth World Congress of Comparative Education, Paris, France, July.

Chapter 8

The Shaping of Secondary Teacher Preparation in Post-Independence Burkina Faso[1]

Martial Dembélé

This chapter is about the dynamics and traditions that have shaped the development of secondary teacher preparation in Burkina Faso (previously known as Upper Volta). It is based on a study which was designed to trace the various institutional and programmatic arrangements for preparing secondary teachers in this country from 1960 until the early 1990s, and to examine critically the factors and actors involved (see Dembélé 1991).

The concern about the secondary teaching profession in Burkina Faso can be traced back to the early years of independence with the creation of the *Institut Supérieur de Formation Pédagogique*, the first post-secondary institution of the country. Such concern was evidenced again in the attempt to create a *Centre de Documentation, de Formation et de Perfectionnement Pédagogique* in 1982. In 1985 the *Institut des Sciences de l'Èducation* was created at the University of Ouagadougou, and a professional teaching certificate became a prerequisite for entering the profession. Until then, a two, three or four-year general university degree was sufficient for becoming a secondary teacher, with most secondary teachers having entered the profession through this avenue.

Along the way, there were efforts by some university colleges, departments, programs or individual faculty members to create professional education opportunities/experiences for prospective secondary teachers. However, with very few exceptions, all these efforts were short-lived and relatively unsuccessful, and only a very small number of students took advantage of them.

In light of this, I pose the following questions and will attempt to answer them in the rest of this chapter: Why were particular institutions or programs planned at particular times? Why did some planned programs never get implemented? Why did those that were implemented operate the way they did? What were their contributions to the education system? What led to their phasing out at particular times?

My central argument is that how teacher education has been organized in Burkina Faso has been affected by contextual factors, such as socioeconomic, political and educational realities; government policies of access to secondary teaching; and the career choices and non-teaching opportunities of Burkinabè university graduates. In addition, teachers' unions' involvement in Burkina Faso's politics since independence have largely shaped the development of institutionalized forms of secondary teacher preparation in this country.

Looking at Teacher Education in Societal Context

Societies differ in their answers to 'the question of qualifications for teaching' (Avalos 1980, p. 46), and their answers have direct implications not only for the status of teachers, but also for the nature of teacher education — its content, standards, length, location, and level of expenditure. Within the same society, the answer may change over time in response to the combination of changing political, socioeconomic, cultural and educational realities.

Teacher education is an integral feature of the total educational system and of the broader society and culture. As Lynch and Plunkett (1973, pp. 49–51) have argued: 'Teacher education . . . reflects a mass of cultural and structural features both of the educational system to which it is most immediately linked and of the wider society and economy to which it owes its existence.' This is echoed by Taylor (1982), who contends that few good theorists are really interested in teacher education, treating it as something of an epiphenomenon of its ambient system of schooling. He emphasizes that: 'We must examine teacher education in terms of a theory of culture or theories of culture which are broad enough to accommodate a diversity of levels of economic development and types of political organization' (Taylor 1982, pp. 18–19).

Clearly, economic, political and sociocultural conditions have a profound impact on teacher education, and thereby on the method for researching it. Sharpes (1988) rightly claims that 'a combination of political, economic and social realities be factored into any study or program in teacher education in the Third World' (p. 3). Investigating teacher education, therefore, entails looking beyond the institutions and/or programs and their internal technical and psychological processes — examining the context in which the institutions and/or programs operate.

The Context of Teacher Education in Burkina Faso

Burkina Faso was a French colony until 5 August 1960. Located in West Africa, it is landlocked, sharing borders with Benin, Côte d'Ivoire, Ghana, Mali, Niger and Togo. In order to comprehend teacher education policy in Burkina Faso we need consider three aspects of the context in which such policy was developed and/or implemented: political instability, economic hardships, and educational realities.

Political Instability

From 1960 to 1991 Burkina Faso had six presidents, an average of one every five years. This average masks the fact that the longest presidential term lasted 14 years (1966–80), whereas the shortest lasted only nine months (7 November 1982 to 4 August 1983); and four of the presidents succeeded one another between 1980 and 1991 (see Dembélé 1991, pp. 17–41 for more detail).

The army has been at the forefront of the political changes that took place during these three decades; however, the country's political development appears to have been mainly shaped by the civilian political parties in collaboration with their strong allies: the unions. Kabeya (1989, p. 7) argues that the particular nature of trade unionism in Burkina Faso stems from its being composed mainly of civil servants. This is due first to the fact that the state is the main employer of non-agricultural workers, and second, to the fact that industrial workers are not numerous.[2] As a result, the very people who work daily in the civil service are the same who are active in the unions. Civil servants are also the main participants in the political process — an élitist process that has typically marginalized the illiterate masses. Consequently, it is virtually impossible to talk about politics in Burkina Faso without considering the power relations that have always prevailed between the unions and the successive political regimes.

Over the years the unions have maintained a high profile in the country's political life. For example, in January 1966, the first Republic was overthrown by popular demand backed by banned political parties working through the unions, mainly the teachers' union.[3] In addition, civil service unions participated in, or were the organizers of, several other events against the various regimes, including:

- the strike of 15 September 1967 called by the Union of Human and Animal Health Workers (SYNTSHA), followed by a ten-day sit-down strike involving all other unions;[4]
- the strike of January–February 1973 called by the Secondary and Higher Education Teachers' Union (SUVESS), demanding free accommodation, the 'voltaïzation' of all executive positions within the ministry of education, as well their own regrading and tenure;[5]
- the strike of 17–18 December 1975 called by all unions in reaction to the political party, the National Movement for Renewal (MNR), being constituted by the regime in place as 'the sole channel for participation in the country's economic, social, cultural, and political activity' (Kabeya 1989, p. 135);[6]
- the strike of 1 October to 24 November 1980 organized by the primary teachers affiliated with the National Union of African Teachers in Upper Volta (SNEAHV), leading to the downfall of the third Republic on 25 November;
- the series of clashes between the Comité Militaire de Redressement pour le Progrès National (CMRPN) and the unions from early 1981 to November 1982, resulting in yet another military coup (7 November); and
- the strike of 20–22 March 1984 organized by the primary school teachers' union (SNEAHV) subsequent to the arrests of their Secretary General, the Secretary of External Affairs, and the Education Officer — a strike that led to the firing of 1,400 primary school teachers.[7]

To varying degrees, these events have had profound effects on the politics of Burkina Faso. Because of their large memberships and the strategic importance of the teaching profession, the teachers' unions have been a major political actor and all the regimes have had to reckon with them. The overall conflictual nature of the relationships between unions and governments can be attributed to the perceived and actual role of the former. In a context of intolerance for opposition parties, the unions became the prime arena for political expression and participation, literally taking on the role of champions of political rights. In such a context, it is not surprising that many union leaders and/or members are deposed or disenfranchised politicians; nor is it surprising that many of the country's political and administrative figures were union leaders or members at one point in their lives.

It would be misleading to think that the search for political power was the only motive behind the unions' struggles. Although '[a]t its core politics is intimately linked to power, in both its structural and ideological dimensions . . . [it is] also concerned with the control of the means of producing, reproducing, consuming, and accumulating material and symbolic resources' (Ginsburg *et al.* 1992, pp. 417–18). This is especially pertinent in a context of scarcity. In other words we need to understand the economic realities that have underlain the power relations between unions and powerholders in Burkina Faso.

Economic Hardships

In the classification of the World Bank and other international organizations, Burkina Faso belongs to the group of 'low income developing countries'. Besides political instability, several other factors have prevented the country from taking off economically. First of all, there is the negative legacy of the colonial period, especially the dismantlement of the colony in 1919, which led to its being used as a reservoir for cheap and hardworking labor for the more viable colonies (Côte d'Ivoire in particular), and the stagnation of its economy. Second, there is the mismanagement of the first Republic, resulting in an accumulated deficit close to US$5 million at the moment the army took over. Third, and more importantly, there is the heavy reliance on an agricultural sector (cotton production in particular) that has been subject to climatic hazards (notably, a recurring drought since the late 1960s) and to price setting by semi-monopolistic corporations and governments other than Burkina Faso. As a result, the trade deficit kept widening over the years, mainly because of food imports, from CFA francs 0.4 billion in 1960, to 8.9 billion in 1970, 56.54 billion in 1980, and 69.47 billion in 1987.

The economic development (or stagnation) of the country is well summed up in the following by the Conseil National de la Révolution (CNR), which came to power in 1983:

> After 23 years of imperialistic domination and exploitation, our country remains a backward agricultural one where the rural sector occupies over 90 percent of the active population but represents only 45 percent of the GDP and furnishes 95 percent of our total exports . . . Furthermore, the imbalance between exports and imports contributes to the exacerbation of the country's dependence on foreign partners . . . The fact that productive investment efforts are limited leads the State to play a fundamental role in the national economy through supplementing private investment. This is a difficult situation given that the State budget revenues are essentially constituted by taxation revenues . . . What remains then for social and cultural investments? (Conseil National de la Révolution 1983, pp. 17–18).

The answer to this question is of course *not much!* The results are poor performances in sectors like health and education. Actually, these sectors have been among the top priorities of the various regimes that have run the country during those 23 years and beyond, but the political will and rhetoric — even when genuine — has always been confronted with the harsh economic realities described above. One must wonder what education looks like, or more precisely, what happens to the educational system in such a crisis-ridden political and economic context.

Educational Realities

After the granting of independence, many French expatriates left the country. However, Burkina Faso remained under strong French influence in all aspects of modern life, especially in the education sector. The educational system is indeed similar to the French system in most regards. As Debeauvais (1965, p. 82) observed, 'broadly speaking, the forms and the curricula of French education were applied overseas without substantial modification . . . Because the French educational system is uniform and highly centralized, it was easily duplicated overseas.' Burkina Faso operates a 6–4–3 primary and secondary system and a 2–3–3 higher education system, both based on those of France.

Immediately after independence, Burkina Faso set new goals for primary education. 'These goals included awakening in the child of a sense of national belonging, greater emphasis on national history and culture, and equipping the child with skills needed for everyday work and living' (Postlethwaite 1988, p. 166). Yet the country still depended heavily on France for both aid and technical assistance to operate its educational system (UNESCO 1961, p. 561).

Such reliance on external human and financial resources, and the economic hardships that the country has suffered since independence — and before — help explain why, compared to other countries, Burkina Faso has done so poorly in the field of education so far, despite the fact that the total percentage of eligible children enrolled in primary schools more than tripled: from 6 percent in 1960 to 22 percent in 1983. However, internal variations must be taken into account to assess accurately the progress made over these 23 years. For example, the average enrollment rate at the primary level masks the fact that the rates vary between 10 and 60 percent from rural to urban areas (Postlethwaite 1988, p. 167). Low female participation is also masked by this average.

As educational policies seem to have been drafted in general to benefit the urban élite — that is, those who constitute political support – one can argue that the scarcity of educational provisions, and the unequal distribution of academic (or book) knowledge in Burkina Faso is partially a result of political maneuverings. Note, however, that political maneuverings — based on a different ideology and oriented to a different segment of society — also accounted largely for the bringing of education on a massive scale to the rural areas after 1983, resulting in greater increases than before the revolution, especially for girls.

One obvious consequence of expansion in primary education is the pressure put on the secondary cycle. Indeed, the quantitative expansion of secondary education has been quite impressive, given that as late as 1960–61 Burkina Faso had only six secondary level establishments — four of which were private denominational — excluding the three primary teacher education schools.[8] The expansion of secondary education occurred especially during the 1970s and early 1980s, in large part due to the mushrooming of non-denominational private schools in response to the nationalization of Catholic schools in 1969.

Quantitative expansion at the secondary level affected the whole educational system in at least two ways. First, as the number of Baccalauréat (high school diploma) holders increased, so did the demand for places in higher education. Second, to allow for the normal growth of secondary schools, the number of teachers needed to absorb the increasing number of secondary pupils had to increase proportionally. As these teachers had to be supplied mainly by higher education, the development of secondary teacher preparation in Burkina Faso cannot be separated from the development of higher education.

Higher Education and the Development of Secondary Teacher Preparation

As an integral part of the total system of education and the larger society, the teacher preparation enterprise has also been influenced by French practices (see Lynch and Plunkett 1973, for a description of the French system of teacher education). Transferred to the colony, these practices have survived up to the present. The Burkinabè teaching force has been and still is characterized by the differentiation between primary and secondary teachers in many regards. First, the former are called *instituteurs* or *maîtres*, whereas the latter are called *professeurs*. Second, the basic requirement for access to primary teaching is holding the lower secondary school diploma, whereas completion of at least two years of higher education is the basic requirement for access to the secondary teaching profession.[9]

I now turn to look at six notable efforts to develop institutionalized forms of preparation for secondary teachers in Burkina Faso: the *Institut Supérieur de Formation Pédagogique* (ISFP), the *Institut Universitaire Pédagogique* (IUP) as part of the *Centre d'Enseignement Supérieur* (CESUP), the *Institut de Mathématiques et de Sciences Physiques* (IMP), the *École Supérieure des Lettres et des Sciences Humaines* (ESLSH), the *Centre de Documentation, de Formation et de Perfectionnement Pédagogique* (CDFPP), and the *Institut des Sciences de l'Éducation* (INSE).

The Experience of the ISFP

The creation of the *Institut Supérieur de Formation Pédagogique* (ISFP)[10] in 1965 was prompted by the first government leaders' desire and will to replace expatriates by trained nationals in all aspects of the national apparatus, especially in education. However, the special attention given to the preparation of secondary teachers in the design of the institute faded rapidly as a result of economic constraints, political changes, educational expansion, and the career choices and opportunities of Baccalauréat holders and university graduates.

The ISFP was created in a particularly difficult economic and political context. The country's real deficit was getting on to US$1.6 million at the end of 1965 (while the expenditure budget for that year amounted to approximately US$2.8 million), despite the austerity measures in force since 1964.[11] The institute was also created at a period of remarkable expansion at the primary and secondary levels, and that accounts for its main purpose being to prepare educational personnel, as its name suggests. However, such preparation was mainly for lower secondary teachers.

Given the rate of expansion of secondary education (11.7 percent) in the 1960s and 1970s — which was almost twice as fast as that of primary education — it is clear that the ISFP could not possibly satisfy the demand of teachers if professional preparation was a prerequisite for access to the profession. As a result, the normal school tradition, which had underlain the creation of the ISFP, gave way to the liberal arts tradition. According to the latter tradition, 'to be liberally educated and to be prepared to teach are equivalent' (Borrowman 1965, p. 1). As discussed below, the shift in approach to teacher preparation was reflected in the policy regulating admission to the various professional and general education units or tracks of the ISFP. This policy seems to have shaped subsequent policies and practices concerning preservice professional education and access to secondary teaching.

ISFP's *Centre de Préparation aux Enseignements Secondaires* (CPES) opened its doors in 1965 with two major functions: to prepare teachers for junior secondary schools and to monitor the general studies of students pursuing the Licence d'Enseignement. During the 1965–66 academic year, enrollment at the CPES totalled 28 students, including 25 Burkinabè, 21 of whom were males. The program of the first year of studies was essentially academic and geared toward humanities-based certificates. A section for the preparation of junior high school teachers was opened in 1966–67, and admitted for one year of professional preparation the seven Burkinabè students who had failed the certificate exam the year before, as well as 17 new students.

The *Institut Universitaire de Technologie Pédagogique* (IUTP) and the *Centre d'Études Universitaires* (CEU) were created as a result of the restructuring of CPES in 1967. Both the IUTP and the CEU prepared students to become lower secondary teachers in two-year programs, though successful CEU students could qualify to go abroad and pursue the License d'Enseignement, which enabled them to teach in upper secondary schools. The IUTP was thus seen as a lower status, non-academic track, which received older and academically less successful students than the CEU and other units of the ISFP. The students in IUTP were seen as 'failures' and were envious of their colleagues in the academic track. It is then understandable that many of them escaped teaching by transferring to other professional schools or by finding ways to be admitted in the academic track.

The Experience of the IUP as Part of the CESUP

The *Centre d'Enseignement Supérieur* (CESUP) was officially created on 5 May 1969, and began to operate in 1970, replacing the ISFP. The scope of the CESUP reflects the optimism of the late 1960s. In the history of Burkina Faso, these years represent a period of economic vibrancy, and also of relative confidence of the regime that took over in 1966. The tough economic measures taken by the Lamizana administration were bearing fruit. As the economy grew, however, so did its needs for a highly qualified labor force. As Le Vine (1967, p. 26) observed at that time: 'Unlike Senegal, Upper Volta appears not to have an "intellectual surplus". Rather, the picture suggests penury in such areas as teachers, trained technicians, engineers, doctors, and in fact in most areas where qualification implies expertise acquired through training.'

It was in this context of optimism mixed with increasing need of an educated labor force and 'uncontrollable' educational expansion that the CESUP was created. The new higher education center was composed of five units:

1   the *Collège Littéraire Universitaire* (CLU), in place of the CEU;
2   the *Institut Universitaire Pédagogique* (IUP), in place of the IUTP;
3   the *Institut Universitaire de Technologie* (IUT), designed to prepare marketing and business administration personnel;
4   the *Centre Voltaïque de la Recherche Pédagogique* (CVRS); and
5   the *Centre de Documentation et de Perfectionnement Pédagogique* (CDPP).

In contrast with the experience with ISFP, all the units of the CESUP were operationalized. However, in keeping with the topic at hand, I will only focus on the IUP.

This institute was designed to prepare lower secondary humanities teachers for Niger, and both humanities and science teachers for Burkina Faso. At the end of the two-year period 1969–71 22 students had completed the theoretical part of their certificate (CESUP 1971/72), and 51 and 23 students respectively enrolled in 1971–72 and 1972–73 prior to the IUP being closed before the beginning of the 1973–74 academic year.

The officially stated reason for closing the IUP was that the country's needs for the supply of lower secondary teachers had been met — an argument that appears valid with respect to teachers of humanities but not in relation to math and science teachers. I would argue that there were also unstated reasons, namely the desire of the authorities to establish a full-fledged national university, and the political atmosphere that prevailed in Burkina Faso in the mid-1970s.

As implied above, the IUP was part of a bilateral strategy of Burkina Faso and Niger to share the costs of providing higher education, but the 1960s and especially the 1970s witnessed the so called 'one-country–one-university phenomenon' (Wandira, 1977, p. 43). Political and social factors led most African leaders, including those in Burkina Faso, to ignore the financial drain that such institutions would impose on their countries' economies and to establish national universities. According to Zagré (1990):

> The very creation of the University of Ouagadougou [was] an eminently political act. The 1961 cooperation agreement [with France] and the ups and downs of the development of higher education illustrate the strong political will of the different governments to develop this sub-sector of the educational system. (p. 16)

In effect, the CESUP was transformed into the University of Ouagadougou on 4 April 1974.

Beyond the desire to establish a national university, however, the phasing out of the IUP must be examined in relation to the political atmosphere that prevailed in Burkina Faso at that time. A special note needs to be made of teacher organizational activity as evidenced by the 1973 teacher strike — a strike that had a crippling effect on the country's executive power (see Dembélé 1991 for details). Hiring teachers without professional preparation was certainly economical given the financial and human resources needed for such preparation. That may partially explain the phasing out of the IUP, but it can also be argued that it was politically safe to do so. As a matter of fact, considering the active role that teachers played in the downfall of the Yaméogo regime in 1966 and the strike that had recently taken place (in 1973), it seems that the Lamizana administration did not want to build and have to deal with a cohesive secondary teacher corps, which would obviously be politically stronger than its primary counterpart.[12] Quantitatively, their importance lies in their membership, since teachers constitute the largest professional group employed by the government. Qualitatively, their importance has to do with teachers' role in the society at large and in the educative process, and in particular with their ability to mobilize the youth easily for their own purposes (Kabeya 1989).

Furthermore, the creation and closure of the IUP occurred during a period when secondary teachers were pushing for more attention to their profession in order to improve its value and image. For them that meant 1) being offered the opportunity to advance (to climb the professional ladder) like in other professions, 2) having equal salaries with professionals with equal levels of formal education, and 3) having better working conditions. Through their union, the SUVESS, they obtained in the mid-1970s some of the benefits that primary teachers had been enjoying for many years. These included particularly the accommodation allowance and the opportunity to advance professionally.

Despite its short existence, the IUP stands as an important step in that it was the first attempt to centralize and systematize a specialized, separate form of preservice secondary teacher education in Burkina Faso. The second attempt to do so was carried out by the *Institut de Mathématiques et de Sciences Physiques* (IMP), but as the name indicates was limited to the preparation of mathematics and physical sciences teachers.

The Experience of the IMP

As late as 1972–73, and despite the contribution of the IUP, there were only four Burkinabè mathematics and six Burkinabè physics/chemistry teachers in the country. The rest of the teaching staff in these subjects were expatriates, mainly French. In 1972 there was 'a call by the schoolteachers' union, SUVESS, for a reform of the education system and syllabus away from the out of date, arts and law orientated system inherited from the French colonial government' (*Quarterly Economic Review* 1972, p. 15). The following year, teachers in SUVESS went on strike, one of their claims being the 'voltaïzation' of the education sector.

The teacher shortage was later underscored by a study conducted in 1974–75, and it was most alarming in science-based subjects where the demand over a 10-year period was viewed to exceed significantly expected output of trained teachers. The education authorities realized then that France could stifle the educational system by just withdrawing its math and science teachers, especially at a time of unprecedented expansion at the secondary education level. The IMP was created in 1975 in this context. Beyond the attempt to mitigate what was becoming a chronic teacher shortage, however, the creation of this institute must be regarded as a result of the demands of the SUVESS.

The IMP was in some ways a continuation of the science sections of the IUP; it had a two-track program: first, a short track to prepare lower secondary school teachers in a two-year certificate program and second, a long track to prepare upper (and lower) secondary school teachers as well as to provide the basic scientific preparation of engineers and other development agents whose specialization is based on mathematics and physical sciences. The IMP admitted its first cohort of first-year students in 1976–77. The program consisted initially of academic content area study only. However, in keeping with the 29 July 1977 interministerial decree and the November 1977-issued *Plan de Formation des Èlèves-professeurs de l'Enseignement Secondaire* (Université de Ouagadougou 1977b), and to use human and financial resources efficiently, the institute attempted to integrate academic and professional preparations beginning in 1978–79.

The IMP was not able to prepare as many lower secondary teachers as projected — and needed. This was because of three interrelated factors:

1 students' general avoidance of the two-year certificate and thereby of lower secondary teaching;
2 government authorities' reluctance to recognize fully the practical component of their training, thus subjecting certificate holders to a longer probationary period; and
3 the fact that such certificate holders from the IMP suffered the same fate as their seniors of the IUTP and IUP — being assigned to teaching positions outside the capital city, whereas the only place to pursue higher education degrees in mathematics, physics and chemistry was the university in the capital.

Beyond these practical considerations there were political motives for keeping these teachers far away from the main arena of national politics. The 1970s and early 1980s witnessed many instances of student activism as the university population was growing. The IMP students were particularly noticeable in this respect. For example, it was through the student association's demands that enrollment in the short track preparation program for lower secondary teachers became a matter of student choice in this institute. They were also very active during the 1979 university students' strike that led to the boycott of final exams and the dismissal of some students.

Overall, the experience of this institute between 1976 and 1987, when it was amalgamated into the 1985-created *Institut des Sciences de l'Èducation* (INSE), stands out as the most successful of all the post-independence efforts to prepare secondary teachers in Burkina Faso. It could be a model for designing programs for prospective teachers in other subjects, as was suggested in the November 1977 plan that 'although this plan was designed for mathematics and physics/chemistry teachers, it could be expanded to all future educators' (Université de Ouagadougou 1977b, p. 4). This suggestion was obviously directed to the *Ècole Supérieure des Lettres et des Sciences Humaines* (ESLSH).

The Experience at the ESLSH from 1974 to 1989

The programs offered in the various department of the ESLSH were geared essentially toward preparing students for general education degrees, although secondary teaching was identified as the main job opportunity for the graduates. This realization prompted the attempt to mitigate the void created by the closure of the IUP by offering the following courses: history of pedagogical institutions and doctrines; child psychology; and adolescent psychology. Along with courses in philosophy, anthropology, and psychoanalysis, however, the above were noncredit courses, and therefore did not count toward any degree. Because of their status, one may speculate that the majority of students did not take these courses. It was probably in response to this void that some departments, including the departments of English, geography, history/archeology, and humanities decided to offer professional courses or certificates. The experiences of the departments varied significantly with respect to content, form, scope, timing, and time frame. They also encountered various difficulties.

For instance, one of the major difficulties encountered by the department of history/archeology was relative to the availability of experienced secondary teachers willing to receive student teachers in their classrooms. As suggested in the report on the student teaching experience of 1976, their unwillingness to collaborate was mainly due to their lack of professional preparation, and hence their lack of confidence. In one school, an administrative order was eventually used to 'secure' the teachers' collaboration, and naturally that negatively affected the experiences of the student teachers. An equally important difficulty was the result of administrative inefficiency within the university as regards communication with the Directorate of Secondary Education. These difficulties — among other things — led to the discontinuance of this laudable effort to prepare history teachers. A project designed to diversify options within the department was adopted on 2 February 1978, and included a professional preparation option. It remained on paper, however, and a revised project was submitted on 11 November 1981 by a three-person commission.

The commission's reason for discarding the professional preparation option was that the department was having serious difficulties every year in carrying out what was but an initiation to pedagogy. The commission proposed that a memorandum on professional preparation in the department until October 1981 be written and forwarded to the director of the ESLSH. It would support the suggestion for organizing professional preparation for the entire institution with the assistance of the first secondary education inspectors who had just been appointed. This suggestion was certainly related to the *Centre de Documentation, de Formation et de Perfectionnement Pédagogique* (CDFPP), created eight months earlier as a unit of the university (16 March 1981). Although this center never operated, it is important to discuss the context in which it was created, and what it was intended for, because the INSE inherited both its premises and conceptualization, with the difference that the latter is a more ambitious project.

The CDFPP as a Foundation for the INSE

The *Centre de Documentation, de Formation et de Perfectionnement Pédagogique* (CDFPP) was created in response to the growing teacher shortage in Burkina Faso, and in anticipation of quantitative expansion at the secondary level. The necessity to expand secondary education was acknowledged in light of the results of the 1980 secondary school entrance examination. Out of approximately 17,000 candidates, there were places in sixth form (seventh grade) for only 1,500. As only 3 percent of the relevant cohort attended secondary schools in 1981 (*Quarterly Economic Review* 1984, p. 69), a decision was made to increase the number of secondary schools. The normal development of these schools obviously implied increasing the supply of teachers. As observed, however, in *Projet de Construction et d'Équipement d'un Centre de Documentation, de Formation et de Perfectionnement Pédagogique* — the document presenting the CDFPP project:

> To satisfy the country's secondary teacher demand [would] require that most institutes and schools of the University be modeled on the Institut de Mathématiques et de Sciences Physiques (IMP). If that were the case, the University would give the impression of being designed exclusively to prepare cadres for the education sector. The government's decision to create an institution – the CDFPP – designed to harmonize the preparation of prospective teachers for general and technical secondary schools stemmed from the realization of this danger. (Ministère de l'Enseignement Supérieur et de la Recherche Scientifique 1981, p. 3)

It is also noted in the same document that most practicing secondary teachers have not benefited from any professional preparation. To the absence of such preparation for most teachers, one must add the absence of professional support for all of them until the early 1980s. Indeed, as opposed to their primary colleagues, secondary teachers could not count on any support from either pedagogical advisors or inspectors, because there were none. The creation of a category of inspectors had been one of the demands of the SUVESS since the mid-1970s, but it was not until 1981 that the Direction de l'Inspection de l'Enseignement Secondaire (DIES) was created.

> It was in this context that the CDFPP was created, its purpose being to: build a national cadre of teachers and support personnel of high quality for secondary schools, and by the same token to allow these schools to develop normally, thus opening access to secondary education — one that is better adapted to the national realities — to a larger number of students. (Ministère de l'Enseignement Supérieur et de la Recherche Scientifique 1981, p. 4)

To achieve these objectives, the center was to offer both preservice and in-service education to secondary teachers, pedagogical advisors and inspectors. In addition, it was to carry out research in psychopedagogy, study school curricula and develop instructional materials adapted to the schools. The center was expected to start operating as of 31 August 1982 but did not, mainly because its initiators were 'disembarked' as the government headed by the Comité Militaire de Redressement pour le Progrès National (CMRPN) was ousted on 7 November of that year by a regime that was overall dominated by young army intellectuals who were highly critical about past regimes, and therefore wanted to give the country a new direction in all regards.

Another reason for the non-implementation of the CDFPP was related to the appointment of the administrative and teaching staff of the center. There were conflicts over its ownership between the Ministries of National Education and Higher Education — the former as future employer of the center's graduates and the latter as the authority in charge of their education. As a result, the project could not be operationalized. Meanwhile, the preservice professional preparation of secondary teachers remained the responsibility of individual schools, institutes or departments of the university as already discussed.

The idea of the CDFPP remained on paper, but it was physically symbolized by the one-story CFAfrancs 60 million (approximately US$200,000) building that was supposed to house it. The project of centralizing and harmonizing the preservice and in-service professional education of the secondary teaching and support personnel was revived in 1985, resulting in the creation of the *Institut des Sciences de l'Èducation* (INSE).

The Experience of the INSE

In March 1985, a national meeting was held to reflect on the problems and perspectives of higher education and scientific research. It was in compliance with the conclusions of that meeting that the INSE was created. However, the push for an institution devoted to the professional preparation and development of secondary teachers came mainly from the secondary school teachers' union, Syndicat National des Enseignants du Secondaire et du Supérieur (SNESS) — the new name adopted by SUVESS in 1984.

As it appears in the report of the proceedings of its ordinary council meeting held in Ouagadougou from 20–22 May 1983, the SNESS successfully opposed the secondary teacher recruitment tests that were organized in the early 1980s. At an earlier meeting with the authorities of the Ministry of National Education, Arts and Culture on 21 April the union's leaders made the following request, among others: that an *Ecole Normale Supérieure* (ENS) and an *Ecole Normale Supérieure de l'Enseignement Technique* (ENSET) be created in the long term. They also proposed that priority of access to secondary teaching be given to 'those who have undertaken studies for teaching' (SUVESS 1983, p. 13). In practical terms, this statement was clearly a call for 'professionalization' since the restriction of access to a profession to persons who have received a special preparation for engaging in it may be considered a way of enhancing the image and value of that profession in the society.

The SNESS may not have participated actively in the 1985 meeting as it was at odds with the Conseil National de la Révolution (CNR) at that time, but it would not be an overstatement to say that the teachers' demand for professional preparation and development and their claims to professional status through this union were an important item of the meeting's agenda. Among other things, the participants pointed out the shortage of secondary teachers and the need of professional preparation for both secondary and university teachers. As a result, a recommendation was made to transform the CDFPP into the INSE. Five months later (29 August 1985) a decree was passed relating to the restructuring of the university and the creation of the INSE. A 10-member interministerial commission was subsequently appointed to operationalize the project; determine the profile of the instructors; define the content of the program; specify the profile of the institute's graduates; and establish a functional structure of training and research, bearing in mind the country's concrete realities and its political, economic and cultural aspirations within the broad framework of the revolution.

As stated in the January 1986 report of the commission, the INSE was designed to achieve three major objectives:

1 the initial professional education of teachers for both general and technical secondary schools, and the preparation of university degrees in education sciences;
2 the in-service education, and constant follow-up and evaluation of teachers, through workshops, seminars, etc.;
3 the promotion of both basic and applied research in pedagogy and education sciences, and the development of a Documentation, Production and Dissemination Center in the areas of instruction and learning (Badini 1986, p. 3).

The fourth item on the commission's list of tasks was a clear statement of the new regime's intention to control not only the quantity, but also the academic and political quality of the secondary teaching profession. This move must be understood within the broad framework of the revolutionary process in progress since the night of 4 August 1983. The historical importance of this date lies in the fact that it marked the beginning of unprecedented changes in the society at large, and in education in particular.

As opposed to its predecessors, the revolutionary regime headed by the CNR appears to have shown greater interest in education. As a matter of fact, one of the first decisions made by the CNR was to launch an adult literacy and primary education expansion campaign through cost sharing. Another decision was to lower tuition substantially in private primary and secondary schools, thus allowing more enrollments. As stated in the *Discours d'Orientation Politique* (Conseil National de la Révolution 1983), the primary aim of the People's Democratic Revolution was to build a society free of social injustice, age-long exploitation and domination by international imperialism and its local allies. The struggle consisted in fighting those who had vested interests in maintaining the status quo, and making education accessible to those who had been deprived of its 'benefits' thus far. The political slogans that were developed and translated into most local languages and also taught in schools clearly aimed at consciousness-raising about social contradictions, including the unequal distribution of wealth and knowledge, and the jarring disparities in living conditions, depending on one's sex, socio-economic status and/or place of residence.

The CNR was certainly aware of the importance of the teaching profession in the process of building a new society. The regime was also aware of the great impact that teachers' unions had on the country's political life, especially after 1960. It was clear to the new leaders that for any regime to last, it had to have the teachers on its side. Unfortunately for them, the primary school teachers' union (SNEAHV) had already declared war by urging the population to distance themselves from the CNR.[13] The regime perceived that it was left with only one alternative: to control the profession.

The moves to control the teaching profession were manifested in several ways. The first move was the firing of 1400 primary teachers following the 1984 strike organized by SNEAHV. They were replaced partly by the *Instituteurs Révolutionnaires*, and partly by people who were fulfilling their National Service.[14] The CNR-led regime attempted to correct the damage done to the profession, as well as to the educational system, by reinstating most of the strikers during the 1986–87 academic year. In addition, the year before witnessed the creation of the INSE and the *École Nationale des Enseignants du Primaire* (ENEP) — a high status institution to prepare primary teachers.

The second move to control the profession was a direct secondary teacher recruitment test instituted in 1985, pending the full operation of the INSE and in response to a teacher shortage that dated back to the years before and immediately following independence when the vast majority of the teaching staff was provided by French technical assistance. A total of 344 teachers were recruited through this test between 1985 and 1988. It consisted of two exams: subject matter knowledge and politics/ideology. The subject matter knowledge exam certainly aimed at making sure that only academically qualified people had access to the profession. However, as the final grade was an average of the results of both exams, the goal of selecting academically superior candidates was compromised by the political ideology exam, which was actually used to weed out 'reactionaries'.

The third move to control the profession was embodied in the very the creation of the INSE and ENEP in 1985. Indeed, it can be regarded as the CNR's move to build competent and cohesive, yet politically loyal, secondary and primary teaching forces. Access to and practices at both institutions support this argument.

In keeping with the objectives set by the interministerial commission, the INSE was to have three departments: *Département de la Formation Professionnelle Initiale et Permanente, Département ou Unité d'Études* et *de Recherche en Sciences de l'Éducation*, and *Département de la Production*. The institute opened in 1986–87 with only the preservice teacher education section operating. It was not until 30 June 1989 that a decree relating to the recruitment and professional preparation of secondary teachers, pedagogical advisors, and inspectors at the INSE was passed.

The first cohort of the INSE (beginning in 1986) was composed of 34 primary teachers. They were recruited without having to take the subject matter/political ideology exam, as were the group of 35 primary teachers recruited for the second cohort beginning in 1987. In addition, about 30 students who had previously failed their certificate exam at another institution were admitted directly in the second year and therefore became integrated with the first cohort.

From a statutory perspective, all these three recruitments were irregular, in that those admitted were not required to take the subject matter/political ideology exam. The question then is: Why were there no exams required in 1986 and 1987? One could argue that there was no time to organize the exam in 1986 because the education authorities did not realize the gravity of the teacher shortage soon enough. However, this argument falls short, given that there were university graduates seeking jobs. Actually, the reason was essentially economic. It is cheaper to upgrade existing personnel than to hire new people, simply because opting for the latter requires creating additional budgetary posts.

The first prospective teacher recruitment exam was organized on 3 November 1988. One hundred and thirty prospective teachers were thus recruited. In all about 500 student teachers were recruited from 1986 to 1990. There were several different programs organized, and reorganized over time, depending on the academic and professional background of the students entering and the perceived needs of graduates on the job. However, regardless of options, there was a period of theoretical preparation and a period of student teaching.

One of the difficulties encountered by the institute had to do with conflicts over its ownership and management, similar to the case of the CDFPP, but this time involving three interest groups:

- the Inspectorate of Secondary Education, seeking to run the INSE as an *Ècole Normale Supérieure* modelled on the primary program at ENEP;[15]
- the Ministry of Labor seeking to run INSE as an institution of professional training modelled after the *École Nationale d'Administration*; and
- the university as host of the premises of the INSE and also as provider of the majority of the institute's instructors.

A related issue faced by the institute had to do with who the instructors should be: arts and science faculty (large in number); professional teacher educators (a handful); or secondary education inspectors (with no graduate education credentials).

Ownership of the institute was all the more important as it raised the issue of its status. The questions to be dealt with were: What should be the status (professional or academic) of the institute given that it was supposed to offer both professional teaching certificates and purely academic degrees in education sciences? Who should be appointed at the head of the institute: an inspector of secondary education, an administrator of the Ministry of Labor, or a specialist from higher education?

The solution to the question of status could be delayed without much impact on the institute, but the question of administration needed an immediate solution in light of the fact that it was at the basis of the non-implementation of the CDFPP. The first three years of the institute's existence were marked by instability with regard to its administration. A questionable compromise was eventually reached by appointing a French technical assistance person as director. However, the resignation of this person in November 1990 suggested that the difficulties plaguing the institute were still unsolved.

That prompted the holding of two meetings on 6 and 17 November 1990, respectively. The first one was attended by some educational specialists and was essentially devoted to identifying the difficulties of the institute. The second meeting was apparently focused on trying to define the objectives and missions of the INSE. Its participants suggested that a commission of all educational specialists be appointed 'to reflect further on the idea of the Institute, examine, define and specify its short and long term objectives and missions' (INSE 1990, p. 2).

The institute also continued to face problems of recruitment of qualified candidates in certain subject areas — particularly science-based tracks — and of seeing some of those they recruited end up pursuing careers outside of teaching. The immediate solution to these difficulties was clearly beyond the INSE as that involves not only career choices and job opportunities available to university students in science-based tracks, but also the quantitative and qualitative development of these tracks at the secondary level.

In sum the INSE was plagued by many administrative and structural difficulties since it started operating in 1986. The difficult beginnings of the institute were not only due to economic constraints, but to a change in political leadership. As a matter of fact, most of the people who planned the institute were not directly involved in its implementation as the Conseil National de la Révolution (CNR) was ousted on 15 October 1987 by the Front Populaire.

The latter regime set out to 'rectify the revolution', and that meant undoing many of the policies established by its predecessor. Despite the political changes that ensued, the commitment to offer professional preparation to public secondary and primary teachers remained strong. In a sense the secondary and higher education teachers' union's (SUVESS) 1983 proposal to the ministry that priority of access to secondary teaching be given to those who have undertaken studies for teaching was implemented. As opposed to the past, there is now some congruency between the policies of access to the profession and efforts to offer professional preparation to prospective teachers — and it is very unlikely that this will be reversed.

Discussion

As I argued earlier on, the role that teachers' unions played in Burkina Faso's politics since independence, and the policies of access to secondary teaching have largely shaped the development of institutionalized forms of secondary teacher preparation in this country. The unions' role and access to teaching policies must be understood in context, however. In the case of Burkina Faso, the context has been one of political instability, economic hardships, and quantitative expansion of primary and secondary education.

Access policies are very much dictated by economic health to the extent that a country may have ambitions to offer professional preparation to its future teachers, but be faced with 'the practical realities of a school-aged population which certainly outstrips the teacher education resources, and potentially the economic reserves allotted to education as a public service' (Sharpes 1988, p. 11). In such circumstances, the solution is to hire teachers without any professional preparation, or even with inadequate academic preparation. Besides practical considerations, arguments from the liberal arts tradition can be used to justify this solution.

However, access policies can also be highly influenced by political realities. As far as Burkina Faso is concerned, the pre-revolution regimes appeared to be unwilling to build a cohesive secondary teaching cadre. Secondary teachers are far less numerous than primary teachers in most countries, and should a priori be less threatening, as a group, than the latter — at least from a quantitative point of view. It must also be noted that secondary teachers, by virtue of seeing themselves as subject matter specialists instead of teachers in the generic sense, form a less cohesive group than their primary colleagues. However, they have far more years of formal education than the latter, and if one subscribes to the idea that the more education individuals (and their social networks) have, the more power or influence they are likely to have on other people, and the more critical they are likely to be *vis-à-vis* the government (or any authority figure), then it makes sense to think that secondary teachers pose to the powerholders as much threat as — if not more threat than — primary teachers.

In Burkina Faso, because of the existence of normal schools since 1945, primary teachers developed a greater professional identity and are more cohesive than their secondary colleagues. However, because there was only one teachers' union (the SNEAHV) until the July 1972 split — at which point the secondary teachers formed the SUVESS (which was renamed SNESS in 1984) — both groups were involved in the same struggles and actions. Even after the split, the two unions worked closely together and were supportive of each other's actions. Hence, when the SUVESS called a strike in early 1973, it was soon joined by the SNEAHV.

In view of the foregoing, I argue that the pre-revolution regimes were not interested in building a cohesive secondary teaching corps. Interestingly, but not surprisingly, the revolutionary regime tried to capitalize on teachers to advance its principal goal: building a new society. The CNR was clearly interested in building a cohesive and competent, but politically loyal, national teacher corps. That meant having a tight control on the teaching profession through firing uncooperative primary teachers on the one hand, and hiring new teachers at both primary and secondary levels through testing and/or systematic professional preparation in two national institutions on the other. In this respect, the intent to improve schooling through teacher recruitment and/or preparation is inseparable from political motivation. Besides practical considerations and political urgencies, arguments from the normal school tradition can be used to justify these policy options.

Such analysis of the relationship between national politics, economy, educational realities, and the development of institutions of teacher education is useful in that it helps understand why such institutions are created or not, why they survive or not. It can also help understand who has access to them (and ultimately to the profession) and what the curricular orientations of their programs are.

Political decisions are made in light of several factors/forces: economic factors as discussed above, but also social factors, including demographics, the social pressure for/against — or the value that people accord to — the object(s) of such decisions. With regard to education, the case can therefore be made that the demands placed on the system by the size of the population, and also by the degree to which schooling is valued by the population, have a great impact on educational provisions. Educational provisions can be understood in terms of both quantity and quality of school personnel, mainly teachers.

Finally, the kinds of opportunities that are available to university graduates and the status of different professions shape their career choices. Often teaching is something that people fall back on after they have failed to enter more prestigious professions. As a result, it is not typically the candidates of the highest caliber — however conceptualized and measured — who seek entry into the profession, and that has a lot of implications for the standards of both admission in teacher preparation institutions and the educational opportunities they (can) offer. Also, the avoidance of the profession by many people has implications for the sustainability of such institutions. However, when the job market reaches a point where a job is a job, as it has in Burkina Faso, there is a plethora of candidates for teacher preparation institutions given that the education sector is a major employer. As competition becomes tougher, those who have access to the profession tend to be the candidates of the highest caliber. This too has implications for the sustainability of institutions of preservice teacher education and for the character and quality of the educational experiences they offer prospective teachers.

Conclusion

The creation of the INSE marked the resurgence of the normal school tradition in the preparation of secondary teachers in Burkina Faso. It was clearly a move toward a new profile for the profession. However, my assessment (Dembélé

1991) was that the INSE was a rather ambitious project — probably too ambitious — in light of the country's educational and socioeconomic circumstances, and in particular the soaring costs of higher education (see Hinchcliffe 1985, p. 44, Table 11; Jarousse and Rapiau 1988), and the institute's physical and human resource capacities. I argued that chances were that the rapid expansion of secondary education would necessitate alternative routes to the profession, and possibly an unfortunate return to past practices in term of access to the profession. I expressed doubts about the sustainability of the institute, and suggested what I thought would be a more realistic move, that is, to maintain the policy of limiting the number of places available at the INSE, but to recruit teacher candidates at the Baccalauréat level, based on an entry exam. In that case, the professional status of the institute would be maintained, and as incentive, the prospective teachers would receive a pre-salary. The educational program could then integrate both academic and professional preparation and be sanctioned by academic as well as teaching certificates, critically building upon the experience of the IMP.

Recent developments have validated my doubts. Consideration is being given to phasing out the INSE. One alternative institutional arrangement proposed is an *Ecole Normale Supérieure* (ENS). The school would be physically located outside the university, in a city other than the capital. This development raises some interesting issues, one of which is the uneasiness with which teacher education has always sat at the university. To some extent, the *Inspection de l'Enseignement Secondaire* is about to come out victorious from the conflicts over ownership, management and faculty appointment discussed earlier. The request made by the secondary teachers' union (SUVESS and later renamed SNESS) a decade earlier to create an *Ecole Normale Supérieure* would be realized as well.

An important issue that is not part of current debates but that will need to be dealt with in the near future is the issue of the professional preparation of private school teachers. As professional education was transferred from all other constituent parts of the university to the INSE, and perhaps soon to the ENS, university graduates who choose or are compelled to teach in private secondary schools will continue to enter the profession without any preservice professional education. The importance of this issue lies in the fact that private education represents about half of the secondary sector of the educational system in terms of enrollments, and is likely to represent even more under the Structural Adjustment Plan signed in 1991 — a plan that lays emphasis on private investments in all development sectors. If professional education is regarded as essential for improving the quality of schooling — which was one of the reasons for creating the INSE and the ENEP — providing private school teachers with such preparation will become imperative.

Notes

1 This is the revised and expanded version of a paper presented at the American Educational Studies Association conference, 4–8 November 1992, Pittsburgh, PA, USA. I am greatly indebted to Sharon Feiman-Nemser, Mark Ginsburg, Susan Melnick, Lynn Paine, Jack Schwille, and Teresa Tatto for their feedback on an earlier draft of the chapter.
2 Agricultural workers account for between 80 and 90 percent of the population, but they are not unionized.

3   In the absence of a common agenda in 1966, the civilian politicians asked the army to take over temporarily. Aboubacar Sangoulé Lamizana, the army colonel (later general) who was appointed remained in power until 25 November 1980, when he was overthrown by the Military Council for National Progress (CMRPN), headed by Colonel Saye Zerbo.

4   The 15 September 1967 strike was a manifestation of the workers' objections not only to the harsh economic measures taken by the government to recover the economy, but above all to the government's failure to live by its promise of dialogue.

5   The SUVESS was created on 3 July 1972 as a result of a split within the National Union of African Teachers in Upper Volta (SNEAHV). The latter was created in 1949 and was the country's first teachers' union. The split can be interpreted as a differentiation move on the part of secondary and higher education teachers as primary teachers probably constituted a majority in the SNEAHV.

6   Note that General Lamizana had staged a coup against his own regime by dissolving the National Assembly on 8 February 1974.

7   It is worth noting that about a year earlier (20–22 May) the secondary students demonstrated for the liberation of Thomas Sankara who then seized power on 4 August 1983. These demonstrations were in fact organized by the Confederation of Unions (CSV) working through the SUVESS, and in collaboration with a political party, the Patriotic League for Development–African Independence Party (LIPAD–PAI).

8   The first public Cours Normal was created in Koudougou in 1945, followed by that of Ouahigouya in 1948, the Girls' Cours Normal of Ouagadougou in 1955, and the École Normale of Ouagadougou in 1963. Primary teacher education was also provided at two private Catholic Cours Normaux. Prior to 1945, prospective primary teachers received their preparation at the famous École William Ponty in Dakar, Sénégal.

9   An informal assessment suggests that until the late 1980s more than 90 percent of secondary teachers could only claim to have had academic (and not specific teacher professional) preparation. This percentage would certainly be higher for upper secondary teachers since the tendency has been to offer professional preparation only to lower secondary teachers.

10 This institute was developed through reorganizations in 1967 and 1969 and eventually became the University of Ouagadougou in 1974 (Université de Ouagadougou 1977a).

11 Note that these austerity measures contributed to the downfall of the first Republic on 3 January 1966.

12 By 1960 primary teachers constituted a very cohesive group in terms of professional identity. This was certainly due to the fact that the majority of them came to teaching through the *Cours Normaux* or *École Normale*, where they received a two-year professional preparation.

13 The union made this call during its 27th congress (2–7 August 1983). Kabeya (1989, p. 198) argues that the position of the SNEAHV can be related to the fact that it had not been consulted by the new powerholders as they planned the 4 August events.

14 The *Instituteurs Révolutionnaires* were mostly secondary students. Many of them were motivated by political conviction, but for the majority it was a matter of seizing a lifetime opportunity of getting a job in a context where unemployment was on the increase among graduates of all levels of the educational system. They were offered a two-week crash pedagogical training and sent to replace the strikers.

15 Most inspectors were critical about the 'excessive' amount of academic courses offered at the institute at the expense of professional courses.

References

AVALOS, B. (1980) 'Teacher effectiveness: Research in the third world — highlights of a review', *Comparative Education*, **16**, 1, pp. 45–54.

BADINI, A. (1986) 'Rapport des Travaux de la Commission Interministérielle pour la Mise en Pratique de l'Institut des Sciences de l'Education (INSE)', unpublished manuscript, Ouagadougou, Burkina Faso, January.

BORROWMAN, M.L. (1965) 'Liberal education and the professional preparation of teachers', in BORROWMAN, M. (Ed) *Teacher Education in America*, New York, Teachers College Press, pp. 1–53.

CENTRE D'ENSEIGNEMENT SUPÉRIEUR DE OUAGADOUGOU (CESUP) (1971/72) *Livret de l'Étudiant: Année 1971–72*, Ouagadougou, Author.

CONSEIL NATIONAL DE LA RÉVOLUTION (1983) *Discours d'Orientation Politique*, Ouagadougou, Author, 2 October.

DEBEAUVAIS, M. (1965) 'Education in Former French West Africa', in COLEMAN, J.S. (Ed) *Education and Political Development*, Princeton, NJ, Princeton University Press, pp. 75–91.

DEMBÉLÉ, M. (1991) 'Political Instability, Economic Hardships and the Pre-service Education of Secondary Teachers in Burkina Faso: 1960–1990', unpublished MA thesis, Pittsburgh, PA, University of Pittsburgh.

GINSBURG, M., KAMAT, S., RAGHU, R. and WEAVER, J. (1992) 'Educators/Politics', *Comparative Education Review*, **36**, 4, pp. 417–45.

HINCHCLIFFE, K. (1985) *Issues Related to Higher Education in Sub-Saharan Africa*, Washington, DC, The World Bank.

INSE (1990) 'Process Verbal de la Reunion de Travail du 17 novembre 1990 sur la Situation de l'INSE' (Minutes of the 17 November 1990 Working Meeting on the State of IISE), Ouagadougou, Burkina Faso, INSE.

JAROUSSE, J.P. and RAPIAU, M.T. (1988) 'Coûts, Production et Difficultés de l'Enseignement Supérieur au Burkina Faso', unpublished manuscript, Ouagadougou, Burkina Faso.

KABEYA, C.M. (1989) *Syndicalisme et Démocratie en Afrique Noire: L'Expérience du Burkina Faso (1936–1988)*, Abidjan, Côte d'Ivoire, INADES Edition.

LE VINE, V. (1967) *Political Leadership in Africa: Post-independence Generational Conflict in Upper Volta, Sénégal, Niger, Dahomey, and the Central African Republic*, Stanford, CA, Stanford University Press.

LYNCH, J. and PLUNKETT, H.D. (1973) *Teacher Education and Cultural Change*, London, George Allen and Unwin.

MINISTÈRE DE L'ENSEIGNEMENT SUPÉRIEUR ET DE LA RECHERCHE SCIENTIFIQUE (1981) *Projet de Construction et d'Équipement d'un Centre de Documentation, de Formation et de Perfectionnement Pédagogique*, Ouagadougou, MESRS, 21 June.

POSTLETHWAITE, T.N. (Ed) (1988) *The Encyclopedia of Comparative Education and National Systems of Education*, New York, Pergamon Press.

Quarterly Economic Review of Ivory Coast, Togo, Benin, Niger, Upper Volta (1972) 3 (section on 'Upper Volta'), pp. 14–18.

Quarterly Economic Review of Ivory Coast, Togo, Benin, Niger, Upper Volta (1984) Annual Supplement (section on 'Burkina [Upper Volta]'), pp. 65–80.

SHARPES, D.K. (1988) 'Methodological issues in researching teacher education,' in SHARPES, D.K. (Ed) *International Perspectives on Teacher Education*, New York, Routledge, pp. 1–14.

SUVESS (1983) *Travaux du Conseil Syndical Ordinaire du SUVESS* (20–22 Mai), Ouagadougou, Author.

TAYLOR, W. (1982) 'Changing priorities in teacher education', in GOODINGS, R., BYRAM, M. and McPARTLAND, M. (Eds) *Changing Priorities in Teacher Education*, London, Croom Helm, pp. 16–30.

UNESCO (1961) 'Republic of Upper Volta', *World Survey of Education*, **5**, pp. 1355–7.
UNIVERSITÉ DE OUAGADOUGOU (1977a) *Fiche technique sur l'extension progressive de l'Institut de Mathématiques et de Sciences Physiques*, Ouagadougou, Université de Ouagadougou.
UNIVERSITÉ DE OUAGADOUGOU (1977b) *Plan de Formation des Elèves-Professeurs de l'Enseignement Secondaire*, Ouagadougou, November. Université de Ouagadougou.
WANDIRA, A. (1977) *The African University in Development*, Johannesburg, Ravan Press.
ZAGRÉ, A. (1990) 'Pour une Meilleure Adéquation Recherche/Développement, Cas de l'Université de Ouagadougou', Ouagadougou, Burkina Faso, Unpublished Manuscript.

Chapter 9

Sociopolitical Realities and Teacher Education in a New South Africa

Beverly Lindsay

Out of the experience of an extraordinary human disaster that lasted too long, must be born a society of which all humanity will be proud. Never, never and never again shall it be that this beautiful land will again experience the oppression of one by another and suffer the indignity of being the skunk of the world. (Nelson Mandela, Presidential Inaugural Address, 10 May 1994)

South Africa is a nation in a state of flux as it moves toward a new democratic society in a post-apartheid era. This state of flux affects all major social, political and educational institutions — particularly tertiary education, including that for teacher preparation. Moving through a dramatic transition process requires active involvement and participation by all institutions with the overall goal of contributing substantially to the new democratic society which began on 10 May 1994 with the inauguration of South Africa's first African president, Nelson Mandela. Four years after being released from a maximum security prison, where he spent 27 years for his political activities to eradicate apartheid, Mandela was elected by a majority of *all* citizens in the elections of April 1994. Many Africans in exile returned specifically to vote in South Africa, rather than by absentee ballot, for this historic event.

Prior to that historic day, only citizens of English descent or Afrikaners were allowed to vote and to participate fully in government affairs throughout the twentieth century. Indeed, for about 350 years whites had dominated what is now South Africa via colonization and apartheid, so that while whites constituted 12 percent of the population, they controlled 87 percent of the land and its major resources (USAID/South Africa 1993). Only in the 1980s were citizens of mixed black and white heritage and of Asian background permitted to vote and engage in a range of government activities. On 24 May 1994, a new South African Parliament met which represented *all citizens* in its National Assembly (Lower House) and the Senate (the Upper House).

In the case of tertiary (that is, post-secondary) education, full participation by all has been harshly hampered by centuries of apartheid that denied equity to black South Africans in virtually every phase of education. The Bantu Education Act of 1953 and the Extension of University Education Act of 1959 solidified separation by race, especially as separate institutions and different curricula were provided for various demographic groups (Christie 1991; American Council on Education 1992). These acts and many others, initiated in the 1940s and thereafter, set in motion a myriad of sociopolitical and institutional measures that solidified apartheid in education which now necessitate critical examinations of challenges to teacher education and also exacts the formation of innovative policies. Various questions highlight significant concerns regarding the legacies of apartheid, challenges to teacher education in a new nation, and innovative policy options for social and structural changes — the three central focuses of this chapter.[1] Some illustrative questions which help frame this chapter include the following. Who has access to education, particularly teacher education? What fiscal and material resources are devoted to education for various racial and ethnic groups? What quality of education was available to various racial and ethnic groups? Who is involved in the decision making? What fundamental policy issues and subsequent program designs lie at the national, provincial or regional, and institutional levels, particularly for colleges of education?

Legacies of Apartheid

Access to quality primary and secondary education with the possibility of subsequent entrance to teacher education and other tertiary institutions was severely limited by the 1953 Bantu Education Act. As a result of inadequate curricula (which was designed to ensure that blacks remained in subservient positions), resource-poor facilities, under or unprepared teachers and administrators, and subsequent strikes by students and teachers to protest apartheid, consistently less than 40 percent of black students successfully complete the secondary school-leaving matriculation examination. Approximately, 75 percent of coloureds and 95 percent of Asians pass the examination. In contrast, 95 percent of white students pass this examination (Department of National Education 1992).

Due to the poor performance on the matriculation examination, limited space in a range of tertiary institutions, and inadequate finances and facilities, less than 10 percent of the black youth between 18 and 22 were enrolled in tertiary education in 1991 compared to approximately 60 percent for whites (National Education Policy Investigation 1992). Of the black university enrollees, 26 percent were at historically black universities, 6 percent at English-speaking white sites, 1 percent at Afrikans-speaking institutions, and 67 percent at VISTA and UNISA sites (doing part-time and distance education). When distance education and part-time students are excluded, about 84 percent of black matriculants were attending historically black South African institutions (American Council on Education 1992).

African access to colleges of education is somewhat easier than to universities and technikons (the latter grant diplomas after four years of post-secondary study). In 1991, for example, about 16 percent of students in colleges of education were white (in contrast to university enrollments of 51 percent and 62 percent for technikons). About 66 percent of the enrollees in colleges of education were black, compared to 36 percent in universities and 23 percent for technikons (Academy for Educational Development 1992b). The figures for colleges of education reflect those enrolled in primary and secondary teacher preparation; primary colleges include some students who have not passed the secondary school matriculation examination. In addition, there were 69 colleges of education for blacks including self-governing territories and bantustans or homelands.[2] Twelve colleges existed for Whites, two for Indians, and 13 for coloureds (Academy for Educational Development 1992a).

The continuing legacy of apartheid still causes a myriad of other problems in historically black institutions. The absence of fiscal equity among institutions is the most startling illustration. Direct expenditures for black tertiary students are frequently only 8–15 percent of that for white students. In teacher education programs, per capita expenditures are noticeably different among institutions: R (Rand) 15,500 for white students; R8,500 for Indians; R9,540 for coloureds; and about R7,000 for blacks (Academy for Educational Development 1992a). At the pre-college level, expenditures for whites are four times greater than for blacks, three times greater for Indians, and two and one-half times for coloureds (National Education Policy Branch 1991; Robinson 1991).

The absence of rationalization (since institutions are organized strictly along racial lines) means that white and black colleges of education are situated within miles of each other with the white institution well-resourced, while the black sites are unable to provide quality curricula and faculty in a range of subjects. For example, the author observed Soweto College of Education (often regarded as a premier black site) and noted dated curriculum materials and references. The absence of fiscal resources resulted in science laboratories that are woefully underequipped and are not comparable to those of many white secondary schools. In still other instances, black institutions have not engaged in systematic planning and admission procedures as they respond to political demands caused by apartheid. For example, university enrollments have doubled at some sites since 'open admissions' was a response to the political slogan 'admit one, admit all' (Mphahlele 1993b).

Within black tertiary education institutions, few of the senior faculty and administrators have doctorates or other appropriate terminal degrees. The percentage of those with at least a master's degree range from just over 50 percent at some black universities to less than 10 percent at colleges of education. Of those who possess terminal or master's degrees, there are limited opportunities to engage in research and professional development due to heavy teaching loads, poor facilities, and other professional demands. Some faculty stated that they regularly teach 300 or more students each term without any staff or teaching assistants. For senior administrators such as deans, vice-chancellors, and rectors limited, if any, opportunities have been available to acquire managerial training and experience before being thrust into current administrative positions. The results are that insufficient administrative, academic, and research infrastructures exist to provide efficient and effective quality education environments for preservice and in-service teachers.

Deficient professional backgrounds and limited infrastructural capabilities mean that many faculty and administrators have been unable to participate effectively in the ongoing dialogues, debates, research, and formation of education policies and plans for a new nation. Hence the legacy of apartheid continually stifles black participation and involvement in critical decision making, planning, and program implementation for education institutions so that even its professional citizenry are often marginally involved in the transition to a new democratic society.

Challenges to Teacher Education

The challenge is to move toward transformation of the tertiary education sector in general and teacher education in particular. Ever present domestic and international social and political realities affecting education are paramount matters. When analyzing such matters, the fundamental ways of involvement ultimately encompass political and social empowerment by those in tertiary institutions. As explicated in the next sections, the interrelations among empowerment, racial and ethnic groups, political parties, professional education groups, white liberal groups, and international organizations are critical elements of a comprehensive equation.

Social and Political Realities

South Africa is divided demographically and politically into several groups. Eight major ethnic and/or racial groups are the Africans (the Xhosa, Venda, Zulu, Sotho-Twsana, Tsonga), coloureds, Indians, and whites.[3] These groups are traditionally clustered in particular regions. Within the western Cape, there are large numbers of coloureds and small groups of Indians; many Indians are concentrated in Natal. The various African groups are dispersed throughout the nation, with large numbers of Zulus in Natal and southern Transvaal, the Sotho-Tswana in Orange Free State and Transvaal, the Xhosa centered in the eastern and western Cape, and the Venda and Tsonga concentrated in the northern Transvaal. The largest numbers of English and Afrikaners are in the Cape, Transvaal and Natal regions.

To help establish solidarity, many Indians and coloureds have joined Africans in calling themselves black. Thus in the new nation the major groups are blacks and whites. This terminology, while enhancing social and political solidarity, may also mean disregarding the huge discrepancies that exist among blacks, as delineated in the preceding sections regarding access, funding, and types of tertiary institutions. Thus inequities may be perpetuated under the guise of solidarity, if historical antecedents are overlooked.

Several political parties (frequently representing certain demographic groups) harbor long-term mistrust and suspicion among their members and across groups which often spills into the educational milieu. For example, the Pan-African Congress (PAC) and Azanian People's Organization (AZAPO), often regarded as more radical entities than the ANC (African National Congress), were still expressing grave concerns with the tenets of an interim government of national unity until the very days of the April 1994 elections. The Inkatha Freedom Party (IFP) also threatened not to participate in the national elections. In April 1994 much political violence, resulting in hundreds of deaths, occurred in the Natal region (the stronghold of the IFP) and in downtown Johannesburg between the ANC (representing Xhosas and other groups) and the IFP (composed primarily of Zulus). At various historical times, it has been documented that the national government and the Nationalist Party (often composed of Afrikaners and conservative English-speaking whites) funded both the IFP and ANC so these African groups could engage in political violence (Watson, 1994). Normal activities at colleges of education in Natal and elsewhere were halted during extensive political violence.

There is the reality that educational institutions, like other ones, are not immune to political pressures during the periods prior to and immediately after independence. Yet institutional leaders often ostensibly proclaim their neutrality on national political matters. Nevertheless, the 'wars' between rival ethnic groups — symbolized through their political party affiliations — had immediate impacts on educational settings. On the one hand, colleges and schools often became havens of refuge, since there were implicit understandings that some battles would not be waged at educational sites. On the other hand, students and faculty instigated violent political strikes, boycotts, and bans on various educational and social activities, which they believed helped to preserve apartheid. They were beaten, jailed, and killed for their political actions designed to produce a new society.

In various ways, the several political parties and the on-campus organizations and groups are concerned with establishing and maintaining power, which includes empowerment of educators.

Empowerment and Professional Groups

Various professional tertiary education organizations and groups collectively adhere to the three principles espoused by the new interim government — democratic (i.e. one person, one vote), non-racial, and non-sexist (Lindsay 1994). Translating the principles into the tertiary education environment means ascertaining mechanisms for social and political empowerment at institutions and subsequently within the larger society. Social empowerment is concerned with establishing an equitable and effective education system. Political empowerment entails helping education participants — students, faculty, administrators and staff — participate more fully in the development and governance of their institutions.

When active education professionals and students observed the 1993 multiparty conference designed to establish the parameters for the 1994 elections and a transitional five-year interim government, they became aware of and were exposed to potential alternative sociopolitical roles for tertiary education in a new society. Being active players is central to empowerment. This means the development of various policy documents and initial plans for a single tertiary system. In April 1994, for example, the ANC (the major political party which won the largest number of parliament seats in the April 1994 democratic elections) convened a national education conference. ANC officials and representatives of 104 organizations and institutions concerned about the future of South African education discussed the draft *Policy Framework for Education and Training*. This draft ANC document delineates views on policies and methods to transform the education system — including basic and teacher education — and articulates education's roles in the development of a new nation (Loxton 1994).

The document, drafted to a considerable degree by the Education Policy Unit at the University of the Western Cape, stated that the national government should have central responsibility for the provision of higher education and redressing historical imbalances in universities, technikons and colleges (for teachers, nurses and various technical careers). When expanding the tertiary sector, priority should be given to balancing the mix of graduates from various institutions. Strong emphasis should also be given to expanding the college and technikon sectors and programs therein that relate directly to national development policies (Education Department 1994).

In addition to documents and conferences, formal and informal alliances, associations and organizations are being formed at higher education institutions. These collectivities are attempting to formulate their missions, to ascertain how they can respond proactively to the myriad problems which confront them as stakeholders in institutions, and to continue simultaneously their professional and academic responsibilities. For example, the Combined Staff Association (COMSA) includes all university staff ranging from senior professional staff and faculty to custodial supervisors. Balancing the needs of such distinct groups is a challenge. The Union of Democratic University Staff Association (UDUSA), which includes all tertiary staff, is currently neither a union nor a professional association (Moja 1993). Preliminary indications suggest that, at the national level, the movement toward unionization is at the forefront. Determining the central thrust of UDUSA means continued fluidity. Within teacher colleges, the South African Democratic Teachers Union (SADTU), which originally represented primary and secondary school educators, also includes teacher education professionals (Mdaldlana 1991; SADTU 1991). The balance between college and pre-college interests are continual areas of discussions, although there is general agreement on the three main principles — democratic, non-racial and non-sexist — espoused by the government.

UDUSA appears to be an association with potential. It is representative of the large mass of academics who have their ear to the ground, where as practitioners they can register student opinion, staff concerns, and nascent issues. Academicians are in a position to know the challenges of a learning environment: large student numbers, the continual turbulence on campuses, and rejection alternating with acceptance of faculty and staff from various demographic backgrounds (Mphalele 1993a, 1993b).

Transformation and reorientation are the key expressions in the academic environment. Student and staff configurations are in a state of ferment as they have been highly politicized (Vergnani 1993). Although they do not accept government and international financial aid uncritically, they are keenly responsive to what is offered toward the resolution of their perceived educational, political and social shortcomings. The 1993 UDUSA president voiced the hope that programs and projects might help the 'silent majority' of black academics become deeply involved in educational affairs (Moja 1993).

Increasingly, non-government organizations (NGOs) involved in education have emerged, especially in the 1980s and 1990s. Some of these include the Education Foundation, Community Development Trust, Funda Centre, Human Resources Trust, Project for Technical Education Centre for Educational Policy Development, Association for Academic Development, and the like. Many of the struggling NGOs are managed by blacks, while most of the flourishing ones are directed by white liberals. Kagiso Trust and Funda Centre are illustrations of the better-endowed ones that are managed by blacks (Mphalele 1993b; Hartshorne 1991). From a politically-advantaged position the white liberals have been able to procure sustainable funding from the private sector and external agencies because they possess greater credibility than black NGOs. Ironically, fiscal sponsors were impressed by the white NGOs declaration of *intent* to empower blacks. That is, subtle or covert racism still enabled white liberals to garner more private sector and international funding than black organizations.

Empowerment must now include enabling NGOs, which until May 1994 received funding from international organizations and bilateral agency donors which were prohibited from funding government colleges and schools. Whites at the helm must move to provide leadership, administrative, and policy research opportunities and training for blacks. Simultaneously, blacks must empower themselves by moving mentally from dependence to interdependence.

International Organizations

Various governments and international organizations are concerned with furthering sociopolitical empowerment in South Africa. International interventions should be largely linked to the evolving transformation and development strategy oriented to creating and sustaining an appropriate education system for a new nation. Such interventions may contribute to the process by supporting a broad-based constituency for education policy transformation. Bilateral and multilateral donor resources can strengthen the country's research and analysis infrastructures, thereby enabling indigenous professionals to define and carry out policy analysis and planning agendas that make system transformation possible. Capacity building and linkage activities can assist in empowering South Africans themselves to build a more equitable and high quality tertiary system, to which more black men and women will have genuine access.

Combined multi-donor development efforts need coordination by South Africans to ensure success. Only combined efforts can yield long-term and sustained impact on South Africa's multiple development assistance needs. During 1992 and 1993, prominent processes have been undertaken to coordinate donor efforts among the various international governments, private sectors, and foundations via forums and other communication venues. Major donors provide assistance to disadvantaged black South Africans, with over 40 percent of the funding going to education. The major donors include the following:

1 foreign governments, including the United States, Scandinavian countries, Australia, Taiwan, Japan, Canada and the European Community;
2 private sector and multinational organizations (for example, the Anglo-American Chairman's Fund, IBM, Johnson and Johnson, and others);
3 a range of foundations such as the Independent Development Trust and the Urban Foundation of South Africa and most major American foundations such as Ford, Carnegie, Genesis, and Andrew Mellon; and
4 international organizations such as the World Council of Churches (USAID/South Africa 1993).

In 1992, there was approximately US$343 million in external national donor aid commitments to South Africa. The total European Community committed about US$108 million, the United States committed about US$80 million, and Sweden committed about US$57 million — making them the top three donors. Approximately 48 percent of the US funding was directed toward basic/primary and tertiary education (USAID/South Africa 1993). There was very modest direct funding for teacher education. These are notable levels of funding for designated areas based upon input from a range of South Africans. However, it should be recognized that funding is in accord with guidelines or principles approved by foreign governments, their parliaments, congresses, or executive branches (Dean 1993). The boards of directors or their executive officers have also approved funding consistent with the donor organizations' principles and goals.

In early 1993, the World Bank, International Monetary Fund, and United Nations did not operate in South Africa, due to continuing sanctions against apartheid. After the installation of a new government in May 1994, these and other major organizations indicated their intent to become extensively involved in South Africa. Early indications suggest that the World Bank will provide major loans to improve the overall education infrastructure, including tertiary education institutions.

Overall, empowerment can occur via international organizations' supplying fiscal assistance and authentic technical expertise to help provide:

1   access by black South Africans to tertiary education opportunities and resources;
2   equity in the provision of facilities and funding for disadvantaged demographic groups;
3   quality curricula, teaching staff, assessment of students' needs and progress; and
4   strategic planning in light of current and emerging needs.

Addressing such areas means the development and articulation of viable policy options.

Policy Options for Social and Structural Changes

Policy options are concerned overall with equity to ensure fairness regarding access to, the quality of conditions within, and the outcomes or results in colleges of education and other sites. The draft *Policy Framework for Education and Training* states that redressing past imbalances in access and levels of success in various higher education institutions are central policies for a national unitary education system (Loxton 1994).

Policy analysis and planning entails the critical examination of salient issues pertaining to tertiary education with the aim of presenting options, designs and programs to improve black post-secondary education — colleges of education, universities and technikons. Policy analysis and planning is the component that requires the most immediate attention, according to the author's interviews with individuals and focus groups as well as a review of higher education documents. This immediacy stems from the need to promote and assist the ongoing process of defining national, provincial and institutional visions and objectives for tertiary education. South African educators recognize that there are critical issues regarding the role of tertiary institutions in a democratic society, the structure of the system, the rationalization among the components, methods of finance, enrollment and matriculation requirements, and curriculum restructuring.

Some institutions have embarked upon systematic strategic planning for institutional development and transformation, while others have not started or have only recently begun. Black tertiary education institutions are at varying stages of awareness of national and provincial policy analysis and planning. For example, academic and administrative staff at some institutions have participated in national and regional policy forums, such as the National Education Policy Initiative (NEPI), the policy deliberations of the Union of Democratic University Staff Associations (UDUSA), or the development of applied research themes of the Center for Education Policy Development (CEPD). Representatives from colleges of education have not always been engaged in these endeavors, particularly with NEPI and CEPD because these entities have been dominated by university professionals who usually have more technical, policy, research and administrative expertise.

Capacity building is an overarching concern at the provincial and institutional levels. It is the process whereby the qualitative and quantitative conditions within institutions are established and/or enhanced. There is consensus among South Africans that black tertiary education institutions simply do not have the capacity to meet today's demand for access to quality sites. Moreover, the demands for education geared to human resource development needs and evolving social demands in a new democratic society necessitate long-term capacity building. Various options pertaining to comprehensive policy analysis and planning and capacity building are designed for transformation at the national *and* provincial or institutional levels. Synthesis and analyses from numerous interviews, the draft *A Policy Framework for Education and Training* (Education Department 1994) and other documents (Centre for Education Policy Development and Education Policy Unit 1993) indicate that some of the national issues encompass the following:

- forming a unitary education system;
- devising financial resource formulas and equitable distribution mechanisms;
- articulating the roles of various types of tertiary institutions;
- rationalizing a binary system where universities and technikons grant degrees and colleges of education grant diplomas, which could suggest a creative secondary role for colleges;
- rationalizing a system where all tertiary institutions — universities, technikons, and colleges — grant degrees and/or diplomas so that primary roles are evident for all sites;
- restructuring the tertiary sector so that transferability among institutions is possible for degree or diploma matriculants;
- redressing issues of discrimination based on demographic characteristics or gender; and
- conducting national applied policy research.

A national Ministry of Education or comprehensive tertiary education advisory board(s) could ensure that the aforementioned are addressed in depth.

Various provincial and institutional points include:

- fashioning provincial/regional and institutional strategic plans to consolidate resources and avoid duplication;
- providing student and professional access to and quality within various institutions;
- engaging in curriculum development and designing prototypes for subject-specific material to include comprehensive components for national development and unity, based upon the needs of South Africa;

- articulating plans and programs for community outreach and service;
- ensuring that the administrative, academic, and research infrastructures operate in efficient and effective manners;
- contributing to student and professional development for specific careers and subsequent national development; and
- evaluating and monitoring institutional programs for improvement and the identification of emergent areas such as lifelong learning and distance education.

Based upon extensive discussions with a range of South African educators and other professionals, several of the preceding critical areas were elaborated. The colleges' contributing to national development and unity, while engaging in missions central to tertiary education were part of the elaborations. Various educators stated that the development and enhancement of centers or institutes for human resource development could enable educators to engage in a range of cooperative activities. Administrators, faculty, and professional staff could develop and enhance professional skills; initiate institutional or organizational development; promote quality instruction; and facilitate discussions among administrators, faculty, and students to help ensure that all are actively involved in the life of the colleges. For example, black tertiary education professionals generally do not have skills that are comparable to those of white professionals. In a post-apartheid education system, staff at black South African institutions, via professional development at centers or institutes, should become equipped to administer the institutional programs and provide high-quality instruction.

Of particular note were comments regarding the development of centers or institutes for teaching and pedagogical excellence at colleges of education, technikons and universities that prepare teachers. Areas of emphasis included curriculum and instructional development, communication and intergroup skills, student evaluation and cooperation among regional institutions. Within the areas of curriculum and instructional development, discussions focused on developing critical thinking skills and helping students 'learn to learn'. Curriculum development is also needed to build and enhance educational and national sociopolitical and economic infrastructures.

Given the isolation of black South Africans caused by decades of apartheid, linkages among African tertiary institutions and professional organizations *and* those in various nations could be established. Well-designed linkages could promote mutual goals pertaining to the aforementioned policy options and capacity building. For instance, the establishment, operation, and enhancement of research consortia in areas such as policy analysis and planning, intergroup relations and communications skills, innovative prototypes for curriculum development, and innovative paradigms for equitable financial and other resource distributions could be salient concerns. Eurocentric infrastructures and curricula have been at the core of the colleges. Collectively providing structures and curricula steeped in the South African context, yet acknowledging the myriad cultures and education systems throughout the world, could be undertaken by a consortium of colleges. Innovative curricula could be the fertile basis for portraying the diverse ways students and faculty could engage in empowerment activities for a common good rather than continuous acts of protest ostensibly designed to change the system. Cooperative endeavors could be undertaken to help change the perceived and actual 'inferior status' of colleges of education as places where 'students attend because they cannot go elsewhere'. Yet such colleges provide training enabling students to obtain non-teaching positions which pay relatively well. Hence, there has been either limited entrance to school teaching *or* an exodus of qualified teachers from schools thus permitting non-qualified teachers and substitutes to instruct. The latter teach whatever they know, usually without regard to regional and national development goals. Expounding polices to change the status of teaching and retain teachers are essential policy development needs.

Toward Holistic Transformations

A comprehension of the multiple dimensions confronting a new nation, especially the social and political influences which have dominant impacts on teacher education and other tertiary sites, is critical. This chapter highlighted the complexity of education's roles amid multiple dimensions. The complexity is underscored by examining the diverse elements of an equation — one that seeks to explicate how colleges of education can transform their internal components and simultaneously be integrally involved in a new government of national unity. The interrelations among empowerment, racial and ethnic groupings, political parties, professional groups, and international organizations are central factors in the complex equation.

Herculean tasks confront tertiary education, which cannot be daunted in its attempt to devise viable policy options and subsequent structures and programs for teacher education. As an ANC Deputy Education Desk officer stated, 'The present education system is inefficient. It needs to be restructured and reorganized to include new teacher training' (Mabandla 1993) to respond proactively to the challenges of the new nation. What is critically important to restructuring will be the *active involvement* of teacher educators, teachers, students, staff, and organizations which represent such groups in key policy formation and decision making. How to move beyond cultures of protest to cultures of empowerment is both a principal dilemma and a creative opportunity. Engaging in *transparent* or open processes through discussions, forums, debates, research, and policy analyses is an undergirding principle. In essence, holistic transformations (buttressed by empowered stakeholders) can lay the foundations for educational cultures that ameliorate the sociopolitical and economic conditions of a new nation. Thus tertiary and teacher education could contribute to the eradication of an extraordinary human disaster so that a society emerges of which all humanity will be proud.

Notes

1   Much of the material and data for this chapter were primarily collected in 1991 and 1993, when the author was part of international education sector assessments for South Africa. Some data have changed and other material is continually evolving as expected for a new nation. However, the analyses are based upon available printed material, extensive interviews with a range of South African educators and others from the tertiary education sectors, private and non-government organizations, political parties, professional education organizations, and the like. While the assessments were largely sponsored by the United States Agency for International Development, the interpretations and policy options are those of the author.

The author acknowledges and appreciates the critiques of others involved in the assessments.

The author acknowledges that given the fluidity of a new nation, major recent sociopolitical events and likely ones in the near future, conditions are still in flux which can substantially influence major structural and political conditions of teacher education colleges and other tertiary institutions.

2 Bantustans were created by whites in the 1970s and 1980s to further perpetuate apartheid by assigning and restricting blacks' living and working, based on ethnic identification, to various geographical regions.

3 The several African groups existed historically in what is now South Africa. Coloureds are mixtures of Africans and whites (those of English or Afrikaner descent). Indians or Asians originally came to South Africa from the Indian sub-continent as migratory workers. The Population Registration Act (1950) and the Group Areas Act (1950) required the identification of people at birth and specified residential areas where various African, coloured, and Indian/Asian groups must live. Passes or required identification papers were mandatory for movement outside groups' extremely restricted areas (Nkomo 1990). The Population Registration Act and Group Areas Acts were repealed in 1990 and 1991.

References

ACADEMY FOR EDUCATIONAL DEVELOPMENT (1992a) *South Africa: Primary Education Sector Assessment*, Washington, DC, Academy for Educational Development.

ACADEMY FOR EDUCATIONAL DEVELOPMENT (1992b) *South Africa: Tertiary Education Sector Assessment*, Washington, DC, Academy for Educational Development.

AMERICAN COUNCIL ON EDUCATION (1992) *Leveling the Playing Field: Observations on Five Historically Black Universities in South Africa*, Washington, DC, American Council on Education.

CENTRE FOR EDUCATION POLICY DEVELOPMENT AND EDUCATION POLICY UNIT (1993) *PSE Policy Workshop: Draft Policy Proposals*, Cape Town, South Africa, University of the Western Cape.

CHRISTIE, P. (1991) *The Right to Learn*, Johannesburg, South Africa, Ravan Press.

DEAN, L. (1993) Interviews by author and meetings discussions with Leslie (Cap) Dean, Director of the US Agency for International Development for South Africa, July and August.

DEPARTMENT OF NATIONAL EDUCATION (1992) *Annual Report*, Pretoria, South Africa, Department of National Education.

EDUCATION DEPARTMENT (1994) *A Policy Framework for Education and Training*, Johannesburg, South Africa, African National Congress.

HARTSHORNE, K. (1991) 'Education dynamics and the bureaucracy', *Teachers Journal*, **18**, 1, pp. 3–6.

LINDSAY, B. (1994) 'South African education: A system in need of structural transformation', *Journal of Black Studies*, **24**, 4, pp. 462–83.

LOXTON, L. (1994) 'South African Educators Plot a Course for the Post-Apartheid Era', *The Chronicle of Higher Education*, 11 May, p. A24.

MABANDLA, L. (1993) Interviews by author with Lindelwe Mabandla, Deputy Director, Education Desk, African National Congress, Johannesburg and Pretoria, South Africa, August.

MANDELA, N. (1994) 'Presidential Inaugural Address', Pretoria, South Africa, 10 May.

MDALDLANA, S. (1991) 'Presidential Address', Johannesburg, South Africa, South African Democratic Teachers' Union (SADTU), October.

MOJA, T. (1993) Interviews by author with Ms. Taboho Moja, President of Union of Democratic University Staff Association, Johannesburg, South Africa, August.

MPHAHLELE, E. (1993a) 'The Disinherited Imagination and the University's Mission Towards Its Restoration', address for Professor Emeritus Es'kia Mphahlele at the University of Witwatersrand University Opening, Johannesburg, April.

MPHAHLELE, E. (1993b) Interviews by author with Es'kia Mphahlele, Pretoria and Johannesburg, July and August.

NATIONAL EDUCATION POLICY INVESTIGATION (1992) 'National Education Policy Investigation: Post Secondary Education Report,' cited in American Council on Education (1992) *Leveling the Playing Field: Observations in Five Historically Black Universities in South Africa*, Washington, DC, American Council on Education.

NATIONAL EDUCATION POLICY BRANCH (1991) *Educational Realities in South Africa, 1990*, Pretoria, South Africa, Department of National Education.

NKOMO, M. (Ed) (1990) *Pedagogy of Domination: Toward a Democratic Education in South Africa*, Trenton, NJ, Africa World Press.

ROBINSON, R. (1991) 'We lose — and de Klerk won', *Newsweek*, 29 July, p. 8.

SADTU (1991) Program of the First National Congress of the South African Democratic Teachers Union, Johannesburg, October.

USAID/South Africa (1993) *Strategy Concept Paper*, Pretoria, South Africa, US Agency for International Development.

VERGNANI, L. (1993) 'Universities after apartheid', *The Chronicle of Higher Education*, 15 December, pp. A34–A35.

WATSON, R. (1994) 'Black power', *Newsweek*, 9 May, pp. 34–39.

Part 3

Political Socialization of Teachers

Chapter 10

Student Teaching as Social Reproduction: An Ethnography in Appalachia in the United States[1]

Linda Spatig

A great deal has been written about the potentially reproductive and/or trans-formative power of teachers. In addition to purely theoretical discussions linking what happens in schools to the broader social context (e.g. Bourdieu and Passeron 1977), the literature includes numerous empirical studies relating everyday class-room or school practices and experiences to broader social structures. For the most part this literature focuses on social inequalities and the role of the school in either challenging or perpetuating them. For example, Spatig (1988) and Weiler (1988) have examined connections between school experiences and unequal power relations between males and females. In general this literature lends force to, or substantiates, the intuitive belief that what teachers do (and do not do) in their roles as mentors, caretakers, socializers, and transmitters of information is related to the ideas and actions of their students, and through them, to the nature of our society. In addition to their own potential for responding to social inequalities, teachers have the potential for influencing the nature of their students' responses.

This chapter considers these issues in relation to the experiences of six student teachers in an Appalachian setting in the United States. Understanding the rela-tionship between these student teaching experiences and the reproduction or trans-formation of social inequalities requires an examination of power relations in Appalachia generally. Appalachia is a region that stretches along a mountain range from western New York to northern Georgia, including parts of 12 states (New York, Pennsylvania, Maryland, Ohio, Kentucky, Virginia, Tennessee, North Carolina, South Carolina, Georgia, Mississippi, Alabama) and all of the state of West Virginia. It is an area of extreme poverty juxtaposed with rich natural re-sources where inequalities between the poor and the relatively small number of people who benefit from the wealth of natural resources are blatant. Based on his study of a central Appalachian town, Gaventa (1982) has argued that in situations characterized by intense economic and political inequalities the response of those who are deprived can only be understood in terms of historical and current power relations in the local context.

In a sense, his study is an empirical exploration of the three dimensions of power posited by Lukes (1974). Gaventa explains the first dimension of power as the ability of one individual or group (A) to control the actions of another individual or group (B) and the second dimension of power as the ability of A to limit B's access to decision-making opportunities and mechanisms themselves. The third dimension of power, involving A's ideological control of or influence over B, is described as a particularly effective and treacherous dimension of power in that it controls those in powerless positions by influencing or determining their thoughts and feelings. Through this dimension, A is able to control B's ideas about and understandings of the inequalities themselves. This interpretation resembles Friere's (1972) idea that people who are oppressed internalize dominant social values and beliefs (even those that help sustain their position as oppressed people) as a means of escaping the *feeling*, though not the actual circumstance, of powerlessness. Friere has suggested that this internalization process is more likely to occur in situations where inequalities are marked and where the powerless are highly dependent on the powerful. In such situations oppressed individuals and groups are excluded from participation in democratic experiences which, according to Friere, is the basis for critical consciousness.

Gaventa (1982) describes the central Appalachian community, which is the focus of his study, as characterized by particularly glaring inequalities, in the context of the United States nationally. Whereas schooling or teacher education is not a focus of Gaventa's study, he suggests that 'socialization institutions — particularly education and religion' (p. x) have an impact on power relationships in Appalachia, particularly in terms of the third dimension of power — via ideological control or influence.

The Study

The data I have collected about student teachers' experiences in a similar Appalachian community provide the basis for examining such power relations in greater depth. Like Gaventa's findings, those presented here demonstrate the extent to which dominant interests exercise power materially as well as purvey a view of the world that shapes the thinking and actions not only of the powerful within the community, but also of the oppressed. The student teaching data were collected as part of a longitudinal critical ethnography concerning the process of becoming a teacher in Appalachia. The approach implied by the term 'critical ethnography' focuses on the economic and political inequalities that characterize social relations in the world today. This critical approach examines the way that everyday life activities may strengthen or diminish these inequalities.

The critical ethnography focuses on the experiences and ideas of six teacher education students (four elementary education majors and two secondary majors) in a medium-sized state university in West Virginia. I first met these individuals in 1989 when they were enrolled in an introductory teacher education class. As a participant observer, I went through the introductory course with them and then followed them, through observations and yearly individual interviews, during the remainder of their teacher education program. I observed and interviewed them during their student teaching experiences. This included sitting in on university-based student teaching seminars, visiting in local schools where they were placed for student teaching, talking with them (in formal as well as informal interviews) during and at the conclusion of their student teaching semester, and talking (formally and informally) with the university student teaching seminar instructor and school-based student teaching supervisors.

In this chapter, I describe the student teaching experience as it was lived day to day by people who were directly involved in it. Also, I situate these student teaching experiences in a broader social context, addressing ways in which, as well as the extent to which, these student teaching experiences strengthen or challenge prevailing relations of power in Appalachia. Before discussing these student teaching experiences, I provide information about the national context with special attention to the role of teachers in the United States both currently and historically. In addition, I introduce the six student teachers and the Appalachian region in which they have grown up and continue to live. Following a detailed description of their student teaching experiences, I discuss them as expressions of the power inequities and social reproduction processes discussed above.

The United States as Context

The United States, while remaining one of the more affluent countries in the world, is currently struggling with economic problems. Concurrently, teaching, which was once considered a solid middle-class occupation — often a vehicle of upward mobility for working-class women and minorities — is experiencing an economic and social decline. This change, which is part of a shift in the occupational structure in the United States generally, is relevant to understanding the political position of teachers in the United States at the time of this study.

Certified teachers, not unlike those in other occupations, are finding it difficult to obtain and maintain employment in their field because in many parts of the United States there are substantially more trained teachers than there are teaching positions available for them. As is discussed more extensively in the following section, this is particularly problematic in poor and highly rural areas like those in West Virginia. Those who do secure employment as teachers find themselves with relatively low wages and little leverage to use in bargaining for increases.

Historically, teachers in the US, who were not professionalized in the sense of having any standard training, were hired locally and served local interests. In fairly large urban areas, for example, neighborhood schools (often attended primarily by one ethnic group) were staffed by teachers who were, for the most part, members of the same ethnic group. Beginning with Horace Mann and the Common School movement, the teacher's role became increasingly defined centrally (formally at the state level, but through more private, voluntary arrangements[2] at the national level) and standardized, particularly in terms of the type of education required for certification. It has been argued that this centralization served to professionalize teachers and to increase their autonomy *vis-à-vis* lay members of the local community (Kaestle 1983).

While the centralization of teaching may have served to assist teachers in their striving for greater autonomy and power, the increasing emphasis on teacher competence and accountability has served to undercut their occupational autonomy. It has been argued that recent reform movements with their focus on prescriptions related to the methods and mechanics of teaching are a form of occupational deskilling (Ginsburg 1988; Spring 1990) which actually proletarianizes teachers, leaving them with even less autonomy, power and status than ever.

The Student Teachers in Appalachia

The six student teachers I studied are white; three are women and three are men. For the most part, they grew up in lower middle-class families in small towns and rural communities near the university. Several of them described their earlier school years in terms of traveling long distances on buses to attend consolidated schools. In some cases, they are first generation college students, though two-thirds of their fathers and one-third of their mothers have college degrees. In four families, one or both parents have, or used to have, education-related jobs. For example, Celia, who grew up in a small town of about 2000 near the city in which the university is located, has a father who is a high school art teacher and a mother who is a secretary. In this section, I weave together information about these six individuals and their families with information about the Appalachian region generally.

My Mom, She Raised Us

In individual interviews, in addition to talking about their parents' occupations, the student teachers talked about roles and relationships within their families of origin. They described their lives and their families in terms of the strength, courage and hard work it takes to survive during difficult times. Mothers and grandmothers often were described as strong family caretakers, both financially and emotionally, and many fathers and grandfathers were described as struggling economically, as emotionally and sometimes physically absent and, in many cases, as alcoholic (Spatig 1991).

For example, Nina described her father as an unhappy man who drank too much and hated his job with the Ohio River Company. He had given up a teaching job so that he could earn more money. A returning student with college-aged children of her own, Nina described how her family did not have enough money to send her to college when she was younger:

> I remember 'cause Mom did take me to the bank . . . and Dad would have had to take out a personal loan and Dad just wouldn't do it. And that's the only thing I ever held against my dad. Because I was the only one in the family that had the grades and had the ambition to go to college and I wanted to go . . . I think he just thought I was a girl and I would just get married and that it would just be a waste.

Similar stories of family difficulties were told by male students. Nate, for example, talked about family problems during his high school years.

> When I went through high school, I kind of didn't go — didn't apply myself . . . almost failed tenth grade. We had some hard times as a family — were on welfare — just poverty sort of, so it carried over to school. My mom and dad, they split up. And he was an alcoholic . . . I was growing up around it so, you know, [I thought:] 'He's a drunk and he let us all down.' Now I just forgive him. It's like a sickness. He couldn't help it. My mom, she raised us. When they split up, I was like four . . . She

raised four sons. She worked for Avon. She's done pretty well for us, working and everything.

In an effort to use these six individuals as cultural informants, I asked each of them to talk with me about their perceptions of Appalachia which they described as family oriented, religious, proud and poor. These four themes overlapped as these student teachers wove their descriptions of Appalachia and their own life experiences within it. For example, Celia talked about how much she admired her grandmother who was a first grade teacher:

> I am real, real close to her. She's a really strong person. She's really a good Christian; that's where all my church influence came from. She's just really strong. She took care of my grandpa during his illness for a long time.

Along the same lines, Nina described the strength with which her grandmother faced difficult life circumstances:

> The person I'd most like to be like is my other grandma because like my papaw left her when she was real young and she had like eight kids and she raised them by herself; and I mean she was so impressive . . . She raised eight kids by herself and she worked and she cleaned houses.

Nina's mother, who worked on the production line of an industrial plant, faced similar hardships:

> She put up with my dad. He walked out on her after 32 years. My dad was a drunk. It wasn't a good marriage but mom was one of those [who says:] 'I've got five kids. I'll tough it out.' Mom did what she had to do. I can remember she worked five days a week and came home and cooked. And then on week-ends all she did was clean house and do the clothes.

The student teachers did not mince words when discussing the hardships and problems characteristic of Appalachia. Stephen described the people of Appalachia in this way:

> I would say that for the most part they're conservative, God-fearing people. [There is] low income, a lot of unemployment; drugs is on the increase; [there is a] high . . . [rate] of teenage pregnancies. The state's in shambles, as far as the West Virginia part of Appalachia.

While James was similarly straightforward in describing economic conditions in the area, he expressed pride in relation to what he saw as the region's more positive features:

> It's not an area most people would like to be, unless you've grown up here all your life. But you go anywhere else . . . and you won't find friendlier people, people that are willing to help each other. And we have four seasons. But it's a [de]pressed area right now and I don't see it

getting any better . . . My economics teacher last year put it best. He said we are a third world state. We ought to quit looking at ourselves as first world and start looking at ourselves as third world . . . One hundred thousand people have left [the state of West Virginia] in the last 10 years and it will be that or more in the next 10 years.

Other student teachers were equally forthright in discussing the adverse economic circumstances in Appalachia and they also were equally quick to express pride in Appalachia and a sensitivity about the way in which the region is often stereotyped. For example, when Celia talked with me about Appalachia, she began by saying:

First, it really, really makes me mad. People go around and think we don't wear any shoes. And I even have a textbook that has an awful picture in it of a family in Charleston; and I tell you the truth, I've never seen any person in Charleston that looked like that. I don't think we're like that. I think we're diversified; I think every area is.

Data from other sources suggest that the experiences of these young people and their perceptions of Appalachian poverty are not atypical. As reported by the West Virginia Bureau of Employment Programs (Fleishman 1994), the current unemployment rate in West Virginia is 11.6 percent, the highest in the nation, and almost double the national average of 6.7 percent. The same report indicated that unemployment is substantially higher in the more rural counties of the state. For example, Wyoming County's unemployment rate was listed at 20 percent and 11 other counties have rates between 16 and 20 percent. Another indication of the state's economic difficulties is the percentage of people receiving public assistance. As of 1991, the state average of individuals receiving public assistance, such as Aid to Families with Dependent Children (AFDC), and non-public assistance food stamps was 19.4 percent. This can be compared with a 1988 national average of 12.4 percent receiving public assistance.

It is likely that the level of economic depression in Appalachia is related to the rural character of most of the communities in the region. In West Virginia, which lies totally within Appalachia, two-thirds of the population reside in rural areas where unemployment is higher and per capita income is lower even than the state average. The tendency for poverty to be exacerbated in rural regions holds true nationally and internationally as well. O'Hare (1988), for example, reports that in 1986 whereas 62 percent of rural poor adults in the United States worked at least part-time, their earnings were so low that the individuals remained below the poverty line. Shapiro (1989) argues that a rural family with working parents is about twice as likely as an urban counterpart to be poor. Furthermore, the rural poor are more likely than the urban poor to hold jobs, but their wage levels keep them in poverty. According to O'Hare (1988), the poverty rate in rural America is increasing at a high rate. Not surprisingly, studies show that people living in rural areas are likely to experience the ill effects of other conditions associated with poverty, such as malnutrition, substandard housing, poor health and high rates of disabilities (Shotland 1988; Lazere *et al.* 1989; Podgursky 1989).

Despite these grim statistics, it could be argued that rural Appalachia is *not* poor because it has tremendous wealth in the form of natural resources, particularly coal. However, most of the *people* of Appalachia *are* poor; for the most part they do not own or benefit from the region's wealth of natural resources. These are enjoyed primarily by a relatively small number of land owners, many of whom do not live in Appalachia. This is described by Gaventa (1982) who calls central Appalachia a 'region of poverty amidst riches; a place of glaring inequalities'.

According to Reid (1990), the major limitation to rural economic growth is the lack of demand for highly educated workers, not a shortage of workers. Economic growth in rural communities often means new minimum wage jobs which offer limited benefits to the poor. Amount of education cannot fully explain the persistent differences in rural and urban poverty rates. Reid (1990) and Shapiro (1989) report that differences in rural and urban high school graduation rates have narrowed over the past decade, while the poverty gap has widened. In fact, the greatest discrepancy in urban and rural poverty rates is among those with more education. This discrepancy gives those with more education an incentive to leave rural areas.

These findings are consistent with the experiences of the student teachers I studied. In their earlier years in the teacher training program, they expressed a strong desire to remain in the area in the future, but they also indicated an awareness of the difficulties associated with this choice. In Lisa's words, 'I just don't want to move away from West Virginia; but I don't want to be poor the rest of my life either.' As the student teachers involved in this study completed their programs and graduated they began to look for teaching jobs. At the time of writing this chapter (June 1994) — two years since these student teachers graduated, only one has secured a full-time teaching position; she is a Headstart teacher, working in a rural area in Ohio, earning $5.75 an hour. The other five are working as substitute teachers.

The remainder of the chapter focuses on the student teaching experiences of these six young people who have grown up in Appalachia, a place they love despite the hardships they have experienced. I begin with a brief description of the teacher education program of which student teaching was one part.

The Teacher Education Program

The student teachers were enrolled in the College of Education during an interesting time, programmatically. In 1989, the college began preparing for its National Council for the Accreditation of Teacher Education (NCATE) evaluation by engaging in a self-study which increasingly became focused on determining a conceptual theme or framework for the teacher preparation program overall. In May 1990, the college faculty voted to endorse *critical reasoning* as the organizing theme of the knowledge base in the program.

A booklet distributed to college faculty in December 1990 defined critical reasoning in the following way:

> Critical reasoning is the active process of inquiring, identifying, refining, and judging divergent patterns and perspectives. Critical reasoning encourages students to develop their own value positions on the basis of critical study and their own reflections.

The booklet also included four readings which represent a range of ideas about critical reasoning. Two articles address critical reasoning in relation to social context, with a focus on power relations. For example, in one of these articles Smythe (1989) argues that a reflective stance involves recognition of the historical, theoretical and moral nature of teaching and advocates a more activist notion of reflection, reflection that is not limited to passive deliberation and contemplation. Other readings were selected from the literature on cognition and information-processing. For example, the booklet included an article by Paul (1986) which contrasts didactic and critical teaching by listing 21 differences between the two approaches.

Subsequent writing on the knowledge base was less inclusive of this range. The conceptual framework ultimately was described in a way that is somewhere between the critical pedagogy literature and the literature in cognitive psychology. This is evidenced by the statement on critical reasoning that was placed in the College of Education Student Handbook when it was revised in the spring of 1992. The handbook opens with the following straightforward statement about the importance of critical reasoning in the college: 'As College of Education faculty, we believe that our primary goal is to cultivate the *critical reasoning* capacities of prospective and practicing educators. Because this is the central focus of all our programs, we want to introduce it to you at the outset.' The handbook goes on to list and briefly discuss five themes that characterize critical reasoning. The themes, which are a means of explaining the idea of critical reasoning to incoming students, address the importance of:

1 examining a variety of perspectives on any issue;
2 cultivating independence in thought and action;
3 inquiry, both in terms of developing an inquiring attitude and in terms of learning how to use a variety of inquiry and research methods;
4 making reasoned value judgments in light of alternatives; and
5 relating theory to practice in deliberate ways.

The handbook statement concerning critical reasoning concludes by saying: 'In sum, our goal is for you to become critical thinkers so that you, in turn, will become educators who will be able to work with students in such a way that they will learn to think well, that is, to think both carefully and critically.'

The brief description above is intended to give the reader a sense of one aspect of the formal programmatic context at the time these students were engaged in student teaching. While the college had officially adopted a critical reasoning conceptual framework, the student teaching experiences of these students, described below, did not seem to be characterized by a focus on critical reasoning.

Student Teaching Experiences

Based on an inductive content analysis of observation and interview data obtained during and immediately following the student teaching semester, several issues are salient. One is related to a practical, pragmatic, 'whatever works' orientation to teaching which was evident in the content of university seminar discussions, in the classroom practices of the student teachers and in their reactions to the student teaching experience overall. A second issue concerns a focus on appearances as opposed to substance, which was evident, for example, in an emphasis on the appearance, rather than the content, of bulletin boards and learning centers. A third issue relates to the fragmentation characteristic of thinking about teaching. Lesson plans, bulletin boards, handouts, speakers, and behavior management techniques were dealt with as isolated ideas, materials or skills related to teaching. Fourth, there was an overarching concern with classroom discipline and control. The way this issue was addressed intersects with the other themes in the way that classroom management was discussed: in isolation from other aspects of teaching, in relation to what specific techniques work and with respect to what makes the teacher and her or his class appear orderly.

The Dark Side of Teaching: Classroom Discipline and Control

As I coded the student teaching data, the most notable issue, in terms of both frequency and degree of emphasis, was related to classroom discipline and control. One student teacher referred to this as 'the dark side of teaching' which he believed university professors tend to avoid. Whereas this student teacher felt inadequately prepared (by his university program) in the area of discipline, my data from the student teaching semester show preponderant attention to issues related to discipline. I think it is fair to say that discipline was considered the most important issue addressed in student teaching. The university student teaching supervisor told me, 'We hit discipline very early; it's extremely important.' She went on to explain how she tells student teachers 'that there is no learning that can happen in a classroom if everybody is going every which way and yelling and even running around the room.' She was particularly concerned that student teachers maintain order because she believed they should be trying to impress both her (as the student teaching supervisor) and local school personnel with their ability to control a classroom. She expressed concern about what people would think if they walked by a student teacher's classroom that was noisy and (by definition) out of control.

Given the programmatic context, in terms of the college's focus on and commitment to critical reasoning, I was surprised about *how* classroom discipline was approached. As the above examples suggest, discipline tended to be thought of in terms of quiet and control. Quietness seemed to be the hallmark of a well disciplined class. One student teacher described her classroom teacher as an 'excellent disciplinarian. I mean, the kids in her class . . . know exactly when to be quiet.' Also, fieldnotes of classroom observations contain countless examples of student teachers trying to make sure their students are quiet.

We need to quietly get our readers out . . .

There doesn't need to be any talking . . .

Break is over now. You need to be quiet . . .

When everyone is quiet, I have an activity . . .

When everyone is seated and quiet, I'll give you directions.[3]

In an interview, one student teacher talked with me very explicitly about the importance of students being quiet. He was criticizing a teacher in the field for being too lax in disciplining her students. He described her as being more comfortable than he was with students interacting. In explaining his own views, he said, 'I'm more like — I'll give [students] time to talk or I'll give [them] certain activities where [they] can interact, but mostly if I'm teaching, [they] need to be quiet.'

Overlapping with the issue of quiet are the issues of control and compliance. A teacher-controlled classroom with obedient, compliant students was equated with good discipline. The fact that teachers should control their classes was taken for granted by the student teachers. Their only question was about *how* they could gain and maintain the control. One student teacher described a supervising teacher's classroom in this way: 'The kids were running wild . . . He didn't have control . . . His attitude was like — wasn't a very good teaching attitude.'

This desire for control also was evident in observations of student teachers interacting with students in the field as well as in discussions with them about the observations. Most examples involve a student teacher exacting compliance from students by threatening or administering punishment of some kind. The following excerpts from classroom fieldnotes provide examples:

> Jason, sit down. Justin, quit it. Just sit. Put it on the floor. The next person I call down will not go to the computer room next week at all. [. . .]
> At one point [a student teacher] told a boy to move from his seat to a table in the back of the room. The boy didn't move. He just sat there looking down. The room got quiet as students anticipated the student teacher's response. He said, 'You need to come back here so you'll learn more.' The boy said 'no', still looking down. The student teacher said, 'It's your choice. Move or get detention.' The boy silently got up and moved to the back table.

Overlapping with the focus on ensuring that students are quiet and obedient, there was a tendency to think about discipline in terms of specific behavior modification strategies that are effective in ensuring quiet and control. For example, every elementary student teacher was required to design or choose a behavior modification strategy to use with their students during student teaching. As I was interviewing the university supervisor, she gave me an example of a 'good' strategy. It consisted of a cord with paper ducks (each of which has a child's name on it) draped across the wall. As she described it: '[I]f the child chooses to disobey the rule . . . then their duck goes upside down. Next time [the child disobeys] the duck comes off. If the duck comes off, the child gets detention.'

Show and Tell: Appearance Versus Substance

The second theme concerns a focus on form and appearance over substance. I titled this theme 'Show and Tell' because one of the requirements of the university's elementary student teaching seminar was that each student teacher bring two 'show and tells' to share with fellow seminar students. In most cases, 'show and tells' were little tidbits of information, helpful hints, ideas — things with little substance that could be communicated to classmates relatively quickly. As examples, the university supervisor brought several 'show and tells' to the seminar. One was a one-page handout called 'The Teacher's Prayer', which begins 'God grant me wisdom, creativity and love.' She distributed it to the student teachers, read it aloud and commented on how beautiful it was. There was no further discussion of it. Another of her 'show and tells', which was shared around St Patrick's Day, consisted of a sheet of lined green paper with a leprechaun in one corner and shamrocks around the edges. These were simply passed out as she commented about how cute they were.

Another example of the greater emphasis on form than content is related to the supervisor's use of videotaping in the seminar. She videotaped each student teacher in her or his public school classrooms. In the seminar sessions, the videotapes were shown without the sound so that we got only a picture of the classroom. As the video panned around the classroom, the supervisor pointed out what she considered positive features; these frequently focused on the physical appearance of the classroom. For example, in one video, she drew our attention to a 'gorgeous bulletin board'. Then she pointed out that the learning center table had red paper on it, commenting, 'Isn't that pretty? . . . Where did you get your big cardboard to make that?' Another videotape showed a classroom with chairs arranged like seats on an airplane, as part of a unit on transportation. The supervisor interjected, 'Isn't that darling? They even had flight attendants . . . This is what I call creative, sparkly teaching.'

In addition to 'show and tells' and videotapes, another example of this emphasis on form over content relates to the way lesson plans and curricular units were treated. For example, in discussing requirements for the student teaching seminar the university supervisor explained to me that she instructs the student teachers about:

> how to do the lesson plan and how to set up a unit . . . They crank out a hundred million of them [lesson plan sheets], punch holes and put them in a notebook. And they know it's like the American Express Card; they should never leave home without it. If they do, I [get very upset], because I go in and the first thing I ask is to see their log, and they better be caught up. If not, then I make a notation of that and discuss that with them. They have to keep their daily lesson plans on a special log sheet and they write a lesson plan for each day, for each subject, so that after . . . [their student teaching assignment is over, the log should be] about an inch thick.

In relation to curriculum, what was discussed frequently and emphasized was that daily lesson plans be done using a particular format, that they be done on time and that a certain number be done. I heard little discussion concerning the substance or content of the plans — let alone critical analyses of them.

Doing Whatever Works

The third theme is a 'whatever works' orientation to teaching that is related to the idea of learning through experience. In discussing their teacher education experiences, student teachers expressed the view that most of what they learned about teaching had come from life outside the College of Education. It is similar to what Britzman (1992) talks about as the myth that experience makes the teacher.

One student teacher told me that his teacher education program had provided him with no major insights or understandings about teaching. He said, 'Life has been my best teacher.' What the student teachers repeatedly said they learned from life, from being in the real world of the public schools, was *what worked*. In terms of discipline, for example, one student teacher discussed positive reinforcement techniques she studied at the university and then tried in her second grade student teaching placement:

> It works great . . . in second grade. Second graders are much easier to discipline than first graders . . . But, you know, not just giving them things. Just saying 'I like the way you're ready . . . Thank you for being ready for me to go on' . . . They really respond to this a lot.

Another student teacher told me that she learned in her teacher education program that ability grouping should not be used in teaching reading. She did not remember the reasons given for not using ability grouping. She went on to say that she agreed with this until she went out there (in the real world) and saw that teaching the class as a whole group 'didn't work'. When I asked in what sense it did not work, she responded focusing on discipline and control issues: the class was too hard to keep on task and under control as a whole group.

Another student teacher, in critiquing his university professors, spoke about how important it was for them to have recent classroom experience in order to know and teach about what works:

> Well, I guess they [professors] have to be in the classroom. They have to know what's going on. They have to know what works for the majority of classrooms and I guess they have to know the new learning styles that are going to work . . . They just can't sit on their soap box and preach to you what's going to work.

The same student teacher went on to explain that ultimately each individual teacher must try something to see if it works for herself or himself. His advice for student teachers and new teachers was to: 'Try it. If it works, use it. If it didn't work, you know, try something else. You know, you could try most of their [professors'] opinions in the classroom and see how they work for you.'

The university supervisor also seemed to adhere to a 'whatever works' philosophy of teaching. In a seminar discussion about a classroom discipline strategy in which the children wear hats, the supervisor described it as a 'neat little behavior modification thing. If you misbehave, you lose your hat. If it works, use it.' Another example of this theme is the university supervisor's comments when I asked her about the extent to which she was able to integrate critical reasoning into her student teaching seminars. She said that using critical reasoning 'didn't work too well' because student teachers are required to follow the public school curriculum guides which in many cases are not oriented to critical reasoning.[4]

Whereas there was much attention given to nostrums for what works, there was a noticeable lack of critical analysis of what works. I heard little discussion concerning what works for whom, under what circumstances, for what purposes, and so on.

Students' Previously Held Ideas

The sections above describe six Appalachian students, from lower middle-class families residing in a very poor region within a relatively affluent nation, and the teacher education program in which they were enrolled. At the time of this study, these individuals were involved in student teaching, the final stage of an undergraduate teacher education program which was officially organized around the theme of critical reasoning.

It is also important to look closely at what these student teachers brought to the program, in terms of their own previously held ideas about teaching. These ideas are related to the nature of their responses to program messages, both the critical reasoning messages and the messages stressing the mechanics and methods of teaching.

Interview data collected from these students earlier in the teacher education program suggest that the student teaching messages discussed above (in terms of discipline and control, appearance versus substance and a whatever works orientation) may have strengthened ideas the students held prior to student teaching, and perhaps prior to beginning the teacher education program in 1988. I asked students, in individual interviews conducted fairly early in their program, to discuss their ideas about teaching and the kind of teacher they hoped to be someday. Their responses focused on teacher characteristics and specific instructional methods, as well as ideas about and techniques for disciplining students.

Data from interviews conducted toward the end of their programs, at the conclusion of student teaching, suggest that the teacher education program's influence may have been minimal — except perhaps to reinforce their prior views. As mentioned above in the section concerning a 'whatever works' orientation, the student teachers themselves tended to downplay the role of their teacher education program in terms of impacting their ideas about teaching. Similarly, my interview data show very little change in students' ideas about teaching over the course of the program. Student responses at the end of their programs also focused on teacher characteristics, specific instructional strategies and techniques for disciplining students.

For example, Celia, an elementary education major, said in an early interview that she wanted to be a bubbly, happy teacher with lots of energy who can help young children learn how to share and play together. She also elaborated on positive discipline techniques she hoped to use, involving brief periods of time out in the same room. At the conclusion of student teaching, she made almost identical remarks, stressing her desire to be a 'bubbly, happy, high energy, enthusiastic, positive teacher like Mrs. Drew', a preschool teacher whom she had observed as part of her teacher education program.

Similarly, Justin, a secondary social studies major, said in an interview early in his program that he wanted to be a teacher who is 'upbeat', who always opens class with something interesting. He talked about wanting to do some lecturing, but also to use other teaching techniques. At the conclusion of student teaching his comments again focused on teacher characteristics, lecturing and other teaching techniques:

> The way I've always thought it out would be like Monday and Tuesday I would maybe lecture a little . . . and Wednesday I would maybe lecture a little more or something and then I'd get into maps . . . And Thursday would be the review and then what questions they had. And every day I'd have time for questions . . . I don't want it to be droning through lecture notes. I want it to kind of be upbeat . . . And then Friday I was thinking [I'd] have a test — every week.

As the above examples illustrate, the comments about teaching students made at the end of their program were fairly superficial and did not seem to be informed by a great deal of reading and thinking about educational issues. I would expect to get similar responses from individuals who had not received formal instruction about teaching.

Students' previously held ideas about teaching, as expressed in interviews early in their program, seem to derive largely from their own experiences as students as well as from experiences working with children in church school settings, camps and so on. The programmatic messages sent to them as student teachers were, for the most part, consistent with their prior understandings. The focus on discipline and control, the emphasis on methods and techniques rather than on curricular substance, did not challenge the students' previously held perspectives about teaching. The official college position on critical reasoning was the major programmatic factor that might have served to challenge or significantly modify the students' prior understandings. However, based on observation and interview data from the student teaching semester, this message did not appear to have been received, if it had ever been clearly and strongly transmitted.

Student Teachers' Experiences with Critical Reasoning

Whereas the college's official documents stressed the importance of critical reasoning in all programs, the formal and informal programmatic messages these student teachers received stressed the development and use of techniques for behavior management and for the well-organized and attractive delivery of state-mandated curricula. There was little encouragement to examine or reflect on these techniques, except in the sense of questioning the extent to which they work in the classroom. In terms of management techniques, the focus was on whether they worked in the sense of keeping students quiet and obedient; in terms of instructional techniques, the focus was on whether they looked good and whether they successfully met state curricular and achievement guidelines. In the student teaching portion of the program, as it was experienced every day by these particular students, both formal and informal programmatic messages were highly inconsistent with critical reasoning as it was discussed in official college documents.

When I asked the student teachers specifically about critical reasoning I discovered that four of them had never heard of it and the other two disagreed with it. Lisa told me, 'I really don't even know what it is. I don't really understand. I saw signs about it and wondered what it was all about.' Nina and Stephen, on the other hand, did have a sense of what it was about (based on teacher education course work prior to student teaching) and rejected it. For Nina, this rejection was related to her beliefs about human nature:

> I get so tired of listening to this stuff [about] critical reasoning because that goes against my philosophy altogether . . . I really feel like if you're a human being, you're born with the ability to do critical thinking. I don't think it's necessarily something that can be taught. It's an inborn quality and that's what makes us different [from other animals] . . . So I just don't see it.

She believed that one of her professors was emphasizing the importance of teaching children to think critically, and Nina just did not believe that thinking was something that could be taught. Stephen's objections to critical reasoning, which were also of a philosophical nature, related directly to his beliefs about Christianity:

> I had problems with that [critical thinking] . . . I think it's good that you teach a child to sort out right from wrong. But then once the child starts thinking, 'Well, if I don't think it's right, then it's not right' . . . Some things are right and some things are wrong — period. It's not a question of whether you can justify [it in] your own mind . . . The school system would disagree with me but I would go back to the Bible and God says [what's] right from wrong . . . It's not a question of how you feel about it. It's just a question of whether the Bible says it's right or wrong.

These Student Teachers as Reproducers or Transformers

As stated earlier, one of my intentions in this chapter is to discuss connections between the experiences of these student teachers in Appalachia and power relations more broadly. One way to address that issue is to look at how the student teaching experiences might be likely to impact the socially reproductive or transformative potential of these prospective teachers.

I have come to believe that the situation is sufficiently complex to make it difficult, if not impossible, to identify such connections with very much certainty. These six individuals are located in a relatively affluent nation where there is widespread expectation of upward mobility through individual effort and ability. At the same time, they have grown up, and continue to live, in a region that is characterized by high levels of unemployed or poorly paid people. As described earlier, they know poverty personally, in terms of having uneducated (or undereducated) parents; unemployed (or underemployed), alcoholic fathers; and mothers and grandmothers who worked 40 or more hour weeks at minimum wage jobs and then came home to cook, clean and wash clothes for the family. In almost every case, overcoming major obstacles has been necessary in order to enter college, let alone complete their college education.

What is the relationship between these conditions and experiences and the reproductive and transformative potential of these student teachers? It seems to me that these individuals' experiences in these national and local contexts have a conservative impact, encouraging acquiescence rather than resistance in the face of social inequalities. Whereas the students have grown up in communities characterized by glaring power and wealth inequalities, similar to the central Appalachian community studied by Gaventa (1982), they have successfully completed a four-year college program. For some, that should enable them to maintain the social class status of their original families and it may put the others in a position to achieve some degree of social mobility. My study of them leads me to believe that it is unlikely that they will challenge the current social system in which they have achieved some moderate success, even though (or perhaps because) it has been the result of a great deal of struggle. Given their desires to find teaching jobs in an area where there is a surplus of teachers, strategic compliance is more likely.

In relation to this, the third dimension of power, as discussed by Gaventa (1982), is significant. In the third dimension of power A controls B by controlling B ideologically, influencing his or her ideas and beliefs. As discussed above, the student teachers were keenly aware of the economic depression characteristic of Appalachia, calling it a third world region, an 'economic basket case'. They discussed the poverty in Appalachia in general terms as well as in terms of their personal family experiences of being on welfare. However, they stopped short of thinking of the poverty in political terms, in relation to the intensely unequal power relations characteristic of a region of which much is controlled by wealthy absentee landowners. Also, they did not make connections between these economic disparities and schooling.

This non-political thought is illustrated in comments made by the prospective teachers when I talked with them about their political orientations and about their views on the 1990 West Virginia teacher's strike which took place while they were enrolled in the teacher education program. Three of these individuals described themselves as 'not political', two called themselves political 'middle of the roaders' and one described himself as a 'conservative'. Those who considered themselves non-political emphasized their lack of interest in and knowledge about current events. For example, Lisa said, 'I'm not political at all. I haven't the slightest idea about anything that goes on . . . I never read the newspapers unless it's Dear Abby.' These 'apolitical' individuals expressed mixed feelings about the teachers' strike. For example, Justin, who said that he 'could see both sides' of the teachers' strike, explained that if he had been a teacher he 'would not have voted to strike, but [h]e would not have crossed the picket line.' Similarly, the conservative individual said that he understood the necessity of the strike (in light of West Virginia teachers' experiences with pay and benefits) but that he would not have voted for the strike.

Only one of the six prospective teachers was strongly supportive of the striking teachers. This individual, who described herself as neither liberal nor conservative, but 'middle of the road', stated: 'I think they should be paid more. They were justified [in striking]. They had no other choice. If I had been teaching, I would have voted to strike and just not gone to work. People that crossed the picket lines got on my nerves.' The other 'middle of the road' individual, who called herself a 'political independent', was opposed to the teachers' strike, saying that she was not a union person and that strikes create a 'no-win situation for both teachers and students'.

What role did this teacher education program play in the nature of these prospective teachers' ideas about the current social system and the role of teachers within it? Whereas data from this study do not allow me to answer that question fully, they do offer some ideas worth considering. My experiences with these undergraduate students suggest that their student teaching experiences, and perhaps the teacher education program overall, did little to increase their awareness or understanding of social inequalities and the school's role in maintaining or changing them.

These individuals were completing the final requirement (student teaching) in an undergraduate teacher education program officially organized around the notion of critical reasoning.[5] As discussed earlier, the college's stated primary goal was to 'cultivate' thinkers who possess the knowledge and skills necessary to engage actively in the process of inquiry, thinkers who are aware of diverse perspectives and have the ability as well as the inclination to examine those perspectives carefully with an eye toward making 'reasoned value judgments in light of alternatives'. While the college's official documents stressed the importance of critical reasoning in all programs, most of the formal and informal programmatic messages these student teachers received were the antithesis of critical reasoning. Instead, the messages stressed the mechanics of teaching, specifically, the importance of using teaching techniques that are effective in terms of maintaining attractive, well-organized classrooms with quiet, compliant students.

It can be argued that a critical reasoning approach has the potential to encourage students to become more aware of, and responsive to, social inequalities. For example, Greene (1988) suggests that teachers encourage students to see social conditions as problematic, facilitate classroom dialogue, and take initiatives to discover 'humanizing possibilities' in an effort to encourage students to be 'awakened' in order to see clearly and name social inequalities which form obstacles in their own lives. According to Greene, this kind of awareness is necessary for individuals to be willing to resist identified obstacles and work toward envisioned alternatives.

In an earlier phase of the longitudinal study of these students, I examined students' responses to a social foundations class in which the instructor focused on social inequalities and the school's responsibility for perpetuating or eliminating those inequalities (Spatig and Bickel 1993). I found that students' ideas about the role of education in society *were* impacted, at least temporarily, by their experiences in the course. In interviews conducted at the end of the class, students explained how the course opened their eyes to various perspectives on issues that previously had not been considered or had been taken for granted. While they knew about ability grouping, for example, prior to this class few had thought about it as an obstacle in their lives or in the lives of certain groups. This is consistent with Greene's (1988) assertion that while individuals often experience the 'weight of cultural reproduction', they are not aware of it, do not see it or name it as such; thus, they think of it as normal and, in effect, have no choice or freedom in it.

The fact that the College of Education had adopted a critical reasoning approach certainly could be seen as a factor increasing the transformative potential of these future teachers. However, the students experienced this approach in only one or two classes, if at all. For the most part, their teacher education program focused on the mechanics of teaching as discussed above in the description of student teaching experiences. This focus strengthened the students' previously held ideas of teaching in terms of personality characteristics and techniques for transmitting information and maintaining classroom control.

Student teachers' previously held ideas about teaching consisted of common-sense, taken-for-granted ideas based on their experiences as elementary and secondary school students. They did not talk about teaching in terms of social reform or transformation. If Gaventa (1982) and Freire (1972) are right about the potentially conservatizing impact of a context characterized by particularly intense inequalities, this is not surprising. Appalachia continues to be a region of harsh poverty. Recently, a journalist commented that these are the worst times Appalachia has seen in 40 years, causing mass migration from the area: 'Family upon family is being split apart as one of the oldest — and most misunderstood — cultures [in the United States] is in danger of being wiped away' (Fleishman 1994, p. 1).

In this study the student teaching experiences, and to a large extent the entire teacher education program, failed to offer a challenge to these prospective teachers' previous understandings of social inequalities. While this is probably not unlike teacher education in most other US contexts (for example, see Ginsburg 1988; Britzman 1992), it has particularly harmful potential consequences in Appalachia. Facilitating an acceptance of the status quo in a region characterized by intense poverty (in relation to a wealth of natural resources owned by a few people and in relation to an affluent national context) and glaring power imbalances, is particularly disturbing. With the exception of the social foundations class, these teacher education students were not encouraged to question, or even be aware of, the political dimension of Appalachian poverty and the role of schooling and teachers. As such, the student teaching experiences, as well as most of the teacher education program in general, fostered the socially reproductive, rather than transformative potential of these prospective teachers. The teacher education experiences neither encouraged these future teachers to play an active role in social reform efforts (let alone to participate in more radical social movements) nor oriented them to encourage such a response in their own students. This is particularly disheartening in Appalachia where poverty is intense.

I am not suggesting that the student teaching experiences, or the teacher education program overall, were the major determinants of the orientations of these prospective teachers. As discussed above, these individuals came to the professional training program already holding certain ideas about teaching, ideas that formed the basis for their active responses to teacher education experiences. They left the program with these same ideas. The program experiences, for the most part, did not encourage students to examine their own ideas about teaching critically, nor did it encourage them to consider their role as teachers in terms of supporting or resisting the social inequities that they have confronted — and will continue to confront — in classrooms and communities in the Appalachian region of the United States.

Notes

1 A previous draft of this chapter was presented at the annual meeting of the American Education Research Association, New Orleans, LA, 7 April 1994.
2 Until World War II the United States government did not play a major role in education or teacher education. Since it is not mentioned as a federal responsibility

in the US Constitution, education is a matter left (for the most part) to the states to regulate and finance. While the federal role has increased since 1945 — arguably even more so since 1983 — there has always been a national level process of shaping education and teacher education. The organizational players in this process have been private voluntary organizations, including those of teachers (both unions — the American Federation of Teachers and the National Education Association — and subject area groups), administrators, parents, school board members, and teacher educators. In addition, private, voluntary accrediting bodies (e.g. the National Council for the Accreditation of Teacher Education or NCATE), private businesses (notably textbook publishers and the Educational Testing Service, which produces and administers exams, such as the National Teachers Exam, which many states use in screening prospective teachers), and philanthropic foundations have played important roles.

3 These kinds of comments also were directed to the student teachers themselves by the university supervisor during the weekly student teaching seminar, as indicated in the following excerpt from my fieldnotes: 'Tina has a question. Let's all be quiet while she asks it . . . You keep talking and we'll stay longer.'

4 Note how this instructor's concern for 'what works' encourages her to devalue the major concept around which the teacher education program is organized — critical reasoning.

5 It should be noted that the program's official emphasis on critical reasoning was decided upon — in the context of an impending NCATE review — after these students began their undergraduate degree programs. That this decision was made by the College of Education faculty only two years before these students undertook their student teaching may be part of the explanation why critical reasoning was not pervasive in the program.

References

BOURDIEU, P. and PASSERON, J.-C. (1977) *Reproduction in Education, Society and Culture*, Beverly Hills, CA, Sage Publications.

BRITZMAN, D. (1992) *Practice Makes Practice*, Albany, NY, State University of New York Press.

FLEISHMAN, J. (1994) 'Families Gutted as Appalachian Culture Goes Downhill', *Charleston Gazette*, 16 January, pp. 1, 5B.

FRIERE, P. (1972) *Cultural Action for Freedom*, Harmondsworth, Middlesex, Penguin Books.

GAVENTA, J. (1982) *Power and Powerlessness: Quiescence and Rebellion in an Appalachian Valley*, Chicago, IL, University of Illinois Press.

GINSBURG, M. (1988) *Reproduction, Contradiction and the Socialization of Teachers: A Critical Sociology of Teacher Education*, London, Falmer Press.

GREENE, M. (1988) *The Dialectic of Freedom*, New York, Teacher's College Press.

KAESTLE, C. (1983) *Pillars of the Republic: Common Schools and American Society, 1780–1860*, New York, Hill and Wang.

LAZERE, E. LEONARD, P. and KRAVITZ, L. (1989) *The Other Housing Crisis: Sheltering the Poor in Rural America*, Washington, DC, Center on Budget and Policy Priorities and the Housing Assistance Council (ERIC Document Reproduction Service No. ED 320 753).

LUKES, S. (1974) *Power: A Radical View*, London, Macmillan.

O'HARE, W. (1988) *The Rise of Poverty in Rural America*, Washington, DC, Population Reference Bureau (ERIC Document Reproduction Service No. ED 302 350).

PAUL, R. (1986) 'Critical Thinking and the Critical Person', unpublished manuscript (ERIC Document Reproduction Service No. ED 273 511).

PODGURSKY, M. (1989) *Job Displacement and the Rural Worker*, Washington, DC, Economic Policy Institute (ERIC Document Reproduction Service No. ED 325 281).

REID, J. (1990) 'Education and Rural Development: A Review of Recent Evidence', paper presented at the annual meeting of the American Educational Research Association, Boston, MA, 16–20 April.

SHAPIRO, I. (1989) *Laboring for Less: Working but Poor in Rural America*, Washington, DC, Center of Budget and Policy Priorities (ERIC Document Reproduction Service No. ED 319 566).

SHOTLAND, J. (1988) *Off to a Poor Start: Infant Health in Rural America*, Washington, DC, Public Voice for Food and Health Policy (ERIC Document Reproduction Service No. ED 323 075).

SMYTHE, J. (1989) 'Developing and sustaining critical reflection in teacher education', *Journal of Teacher Education*, **49**, 2, pp. 2–9.

SPATIG, L. (1988) 'Learning to manage the heart: Gender relations in an elementary classroom', *Educational Foundations*, **2**, 2, pp. 27–43.

SPATIG, L. (1991) 'Gender and Teacher Education in Appalachia', paper presented at the annual meeting of the Comparative and International Education Society, Pittsburgh, PA, 16–20 March.

SPATIG, L. and BICKEL, R. (1993) 'Education for freedom: A case study in social foundations', *Educational Foundations*, **7**, 1, pp. 51–64.

SPRING, J. (1990) *The American School 1642–1990*, 2nd edn, New York, Longman.

WEILER, K. (1988) *Women Teaching for Change: Gender, Class and Power*, South Hadley, MA, Bergin and Garvey Publishers.

Chapter 11

Preparing Teachers for Gender Politics in Germany: The State, the Church, and Political Socialization

Rajeshwari Raghu

In all societies existing gender relations are characterized by structural and cultural inequalities between men and women (Chafetz 1984). Gender inequalities can be explained in part by differing biological functions (Orthner 1974) and by power relations (Connell 1985b). However, gender inequalities are not solely the result of biological or structural determinants. Gender-role socialization and, more generally, social and or cultural practices in the education system, families and the broader society need to be considered in understanding how gender inequalities are maintained or altered over time (Romer 1981). Our attention to educational practices, moreover, warrants an investigation of how teachers — as key actors in education — develop their orientations to and strategies for addressing existing gender relations.

This research was designed to investigate the processes involved in the political socialization of preservice teachers, particularly with respect to their preparation for playing active or inactive roles in the politics of gender. The study thus focused on how preservice teachers come to think of themselves as political actors in relation to gender issues and how they develop, among other things, what is termed 'political' orientations towards their future work (Blase 1987, 1991; Carlson 1987; Sultana 1989). The research addressed the following questions:

1 What messages do students encounter in the Catholic church-sponsored, state-regulated teacher education program in Eichstätt, Bavaria about: a) the nature of gender relations and b) how teachers should deal with gender issues in their activity in classrooms, schools, and community?
2 How are students' views of: a) gender relations and b) teachers' roles in gender politics developed in the context of this teacher education program?

Theoretical Issues

In seeking to conceptualize the phenomena under study, I focus on the church and state as political institutions, teachers as political actors, and the political socialization of teachers.[1]

The Church and State as Political Institutions

As Ginsburg and Lindsay discuss in the first chapter of this volume, the state is a key political institution. In most contemporary societies the state is both the locus of power and a site of struggle over the distribution of material and symbolic resources, especially in relation to education. One should remember, however, that secular states are a relatively recent institutional development in the longer human history. Historically, the 'church'[2] wielded power and was a site of struggles over such resource distributions. Today, organized religion continues as an important political institution. While some societies (e.g. Mexico and the United States) have sought to formalize a separation of church and state, other societies are organized in ways that explicitly link the state to religious organizations (whether Christian, Islamic or Jewish). These different situations indicate that both the church and state are political institutions; each (in different ways) can either provide ideological and structural support for the other or function to challenge the other's legitimacy (Robbins and Robertson 1987).

In cases, such as Eichstätt, Bavaria, Germany, although there may be tensions, the church and state function symbiotically. For instance, the state government of Bavaria, which is controlled by a conservative Christian party, funds and defines the parameters in which a Catholic-organized and staffed university operates. Not only are all university faculty and students formally subject to state *and* church regulations and authority, but those students seeking to become teachers depend on validation from the church-sponsored university in order to take state-regulated exams, which are prerequisites to obtaining teaching positions controlled by the state. In such a context, teacher education students engaged in constructing the identities and orientations as political actors face a fairly united front and relatively homogeneous messages about political issues, such as gender relations and what, if anything, teachers should do to reinforce or transform them.

Teachers as Political Actors

Teachers are key political actors in all societies (Freire 1973, 1985). They have been known to use classroom strategies — directly or indirectly, individually or collectively — to shape or change certain aspects of society (Thomas 1983), for example, the nature of gender relations. Teachers may also influence students' ideas and practices with respect to gender through their modeling of behavior in classrooms, schools and the communities (Valli 1986). Experimenting with non-sexist pedagogies in the classroom (Weiler 1988), challenging patriarchal relations in the workplace (Connell 1985a; Weis 1990) and empowering students for a 'project of possibility' (Simon 1987; Giroux 1990) are some of the activities that may serve as models of how students might also confront existing, unequal gender relations. Teachers can also model activities that conserve existing gender relations, such as discriminating against girls in the amount of attention directed to their intellectual work and using in an unproblematic way curricular materials that primarily depict men as power figures in the 'public sphere' and women as care-givers in the 'private sphere'.

If teachers are political actors in classrooms, schools and communities and if their action or inaction can serve to reproduce or challenge existing gender relations, then it becomes important to understand how teachers develop their conceptions of existing gender relations and their orientation to perpetuate and transform them. Clearly, teachers learn these things, like other people, through their socialization in families and schools (Anyon 1980; Romer 1981; Valli 1986). However, teachers also experience a more formal and specialized form of occupational socialization. Although, as Lortie (1975) states, considerable socialization of teachers occurs prior to entering teacher education programs, experience in such formal preparation programs may be influential in the development of teachers' conception of gender relations and their orientation to preserving or transforming gender norms and practices.

Political Socialization of Teachers

The prior question, however, is how teachers come to construct their roles socially in particular ways so that their performances within the school and community serve to reproduce or to challenge both culturally and structurally existing gender relations. Relevant to this question is the concept of political socialization, whereby future teachers learn about and develop orientations that may influence their future practice as 'political actors' (Lacey 1977). These processes of socialization may serve to preserve traditional political norms and institutions or inculcate values different from the past (Hyman 1959).

Teacher preparation can be seen as designed to prepare the 'good' teacher who will help develop the 'good society' (Doyle 1990), including the preferred form of gender relations. In teacher preparation all individuals (teacher educators and prospective teachers) are enmeshed in a set of power relations. These power relations — within higher education institutions, professional fields, and society more generally — are what comprise the context for the development of preservice teachers, and they serve to shape the nature of the political socialization of teachers.

The political socialization of preservice teachers can be attained through formal and informal processes (Zeichner and Gore 1990). The formal processes involve exposures to values, worldviews and practices through the prescribed, official curricula (Lynch and Plunkett 1973; Popkewitz 1987). The informal processes involve preservice teachers encountering messages in the hidden curriculum, the social relations of teacher education and the political environment in which the teacher education operates (Eisner 1985; Ginsburg and Clift 1990). The hidden curriculum in this context is comprised of institutional policies as well as the practices of the teachers, administrators and others connected with the institution. Some of the messages in the hidden curriculum include student expectations, classroom behavior, student evaluation, and student–teacher interactions inside and out of the classrooms (Lawton 1976; Rosser 1988). Also, teacher education needs to be investigated in the context of messages conveyed by existing national political and economic dynamics (Hewitson *et al.* 1991).

Political socialization in a passive, functionalist model portrays students as being socialized in the socially approved behaviors and attitudes necessary to support existing political systems (Thomas 1983). The active model of political socialization, in contrast, stresses how social actors actively construct their identity and orientations in the social and cultural context, characterized by contradictory messages. From this perspective, not all of the various institutional and societal-level messages (mentioned above) are perceived and internalized by prospective teachers; indeed, they may actively filter or reject some of the messages and seek out or develop alternative ideas (Ginsburg 1988; Ginsburg and Clift 1990). It is the latter, active model of socialization that informs this study, although I recognize that students' active construction of their political identities does not mean that they will be critical or change oriented.

National Context of the Research

Germany as the research setting is important because of the nature of its political systems that has influenced educational policies, both directly and indirectly (Hearnden 1974; Pauwels 1984; Brehmer 1987). Under different political regimes in Germany teachers have experienced political as well as professional training to suit the prevailing dominant group, its ideology and values (McInnis *et al.* 1960). For example, during the Weimar period the republicans attempted to eliminate monarchist tendencies in teachers through various government directives, curriculum prescriptions, and (re)education efforts (Samuel and Thomas 1949). During the Nazi period teachers were called upon (and socialized) to instill fascist values concerning race and genetics (McIntyre-Stephenson 1971). After World War II East Germany tried to purge the fascist elements from the teaching force and as a result many of the teachers were expelled or forced to resign from their profession, while others seen as more reliable were subject to (re)education programs (Fishman and Martin 1987). Now in the reunified Germany the state is trying through analogous initiatives to eradicate 'communist' elements from the educational system in the eastern zone. Clearly, all these processes were and are directed at forcing teachers to fit the prevailing state's model of the 'good teacher'.

With respect to gender relations, the German system has always been discriminatory against women in some form or other (Brehmer 1987). Women experienced inequalities in every political era in the spheres of education, economics and politics. For example, élites during the Weimar period, despite their democratic credo, did not reform women's education due, at least in part, to the pervasiveness of the old nationalist elements in the Republic (Samuel and Thomas 1949). The Nazi period witnessed a further degradation of women as it implied and advocated the housewife and mother image as one of the anchors in women's education (Frick 1934). In East Germany, 'democratic school reforms' were adopted after World War II, but women continued to carry the dual burden of working outside the house and doing unpaid domestic work (Tappendorf 1975). In West Germany policies stipulated 'protection of women's reproductive capacity', which indirectly worked to perpetuate inequalities between men and women. And some public policies categorized certain public tasks as 'heavy' and detrimental to women's reproductive organs, thus restricting women's opportunities to certain forms of paid work (Schöpp-Schilling 1985; Kolinsky 1989).

Institutional Setting

The institutional setting for this study was the Katholische Universität Eichstätt in the state (*lander*) of Bavaria in Germany. This is a private Catholic university whose chancellor is the local bishop. The state sponsors and subsequently employs the teachers; therefore, it alone decides and directs the university on how many students will be admitted to each strand of the teacher education program. Although the faculty as well as the administrators are state civil servants, most of them are Catholic and some of them are also priests from a seminary affiliated to the university. Of the approximately 3000 students at this university, about 550 were preparing to teach in *Grundschulen*, *Hauptschulen*, *Realschulen* and *Gymnasia*.[3] The students from all the four strands of the program are integrated during the time of their course work. However, each student has to follow a handbook prepared by the State Education Department and take courses as per the requirements of the types of school for which he or she is preparing to teach. Program requirements range from six to eight semesters of course work, though the students may spend more time in other departments before they decide to take the state examination. At the end of the course work or program, the students take the first state examination. After passing this examination, the students are involved in a practice-teaching internship, varying in length from 18–24 months depending upon the supervisors and the interns. Following the internship they take the second state examination, which also concludes preservice teacher preparation. From then on they would be considered as *Beampten* or civil servants.

Research Method

Data for this research were collected in the summer of 1991, using ethnographic methods (Bogdan and Taylor 1975; Schwartz and Jacobs 1979; Bogdan and Biklen 1982). The ethnography involved participant observation in classrooms, the cafeteria, the student union, the town's main church, the auditorium in the town where the students gathered informally, and the walkways along the river. Interviews were conducted with 45 male and female students at both the beginning level or junior students and the senior students (who had completed all course work requirements in the *Grundschule*, *Realschule*, *Hauptschule* and the *Gymnasium* strands of the program, but had not taken their state examination. The ethnography also involved content analysis of textbooks, class materials, bulletin board messages, and other relevant documents. Spradley's (1979, 1980) domain, taxonomic, componential and theme approaches were used to analyze the data. Data analysis began in the field, with opportunities to check initial interpretations with informants or against subsequent observations and documentary analysis, and was concluded during the write-up phase of the research (for details see Raghu 1992).

Prospective Teachers' Conceptions of Gender Relations

Analyses of observation and interview data indicate that the preservice teachers who entered this teacher education program did so with preconceived notions of gender relations derived from the way they had been socialized previously both at home and in schools. Of the 45 male and female students who were interviewed, 21 were categorized as conservatives, 12 as liberal feminists, three as socialist feminists, and nine as radical feminists.[4]

Conservatives — the largest category of students (21 of the 45) — viewed the existing gendered division of labor at homes and in workplaces as logical and appropriate. Unequal gender relations, according to the conservatives, are so arranged to keep society functioning effectively and efficiently. To the conservatives, a woman's place is with the family and children. Biological and physiological differences between the sexes were seen by conservatives as determining the kind of work men and women should perform at home or outside the home. As one student stated: 'Women cannot do *heavy* work. We should leave that for men.' In this sense, the conservatives were non-feminists as they accepted and advocated existing gender arrangements based on their perceptions of the implications of biological and physiological differences between men and women.

Twelve (of the 45) informants, who identified attitudinal differences stemming from sex-role socialization as central to a division of labor, were labeled as liberal feminists. Though mildly criticizing the advantages and opportunities that men had over women, they also pointed out that the government policies have been and can continue to be changed so that the sexes are treated 'fairly'. One student noted: 'As teachers we both will get the same salaries.' They also advocated attitudinal changes of both sexes. As another student noted: 'Our parents treat boys and girls differently. We need to change that.'

Three (of the 45) students, who problematized gender relations in terms of patriarchal ideology and power relations between men and women, were categorized as socialist feminists. While socialist feminists viewed existing gender relations critically and saw them as created and maintained through cultural practices, they located much of the blame for the oppression of women (and the exploitation of working-class men) on the nature of the economic system. For example, one student discussed the correspondence of domestic chores to their roles in the workplace: 'Traditionally women were expected to stay at home. And if they do go out to work, they are not taken seriously in the workplace. They have to accept men as boss. Women perform similar tasks, such as making coffee or cleaning up.'

The radical feminists — comprising nine of the 45 students — also problematized gender relations like the socialist feminists. They agreed that social and cultural practices worked to sustain unequal gender relations in the societies. The radical feminists challenged the notion of 'natural' acceptance of gender distinctions; instead, they pointed out how unequal gender roles are constructed through the institutions of marriage, heterosexuality, and motherhood. As one student noted: 'As soon as we are 20–21, our parents start talking about marriage. Then they talk about having children.' The radical feminists also did not believe in alienating themselves from men or other women. They believed that they could construct their own peaceful world, without having to compete with men. They also emphasized taking advantage of being 'women' for peaceful change through nurturance and by 'educating men'.[5] In this sense, the radical feminists celebrated 'being a woman'.[6] A radical feminist asked: 'Why should we fight with men? We can live harmoniously among ourselves.'

The difference between socialist and radical feminists is that while the former were for struggling, reevaluating, redefining, and reclaiming equality, the latter projected an alternative political mode, a peaceful solution, by promoting women's causes, feminist art, music and culture.

Plans for Political Action as Teachers

The prospective teachers' plans for political action centered around the classroom and field activities, specifically shaping the curriculum and organizing co-curricular and extracurricular activities. As to the questions whether teachers can and should be bringing gender issues to the attention of their students or otherwise addressing gendered norms and practices, these prospective teachers' responses varied in accordance with their conception of existing gender relations. In general, liberal, socialist and radical feminists, but not the conservatives, considered teachers to be key 'political' actors, who should and can play important roles to minimize, if not eradicate, inequalities between men and women. For conservatives, existing arrangements between men and women are beneficial to both males and females as well as to the society as a whole; thus the teacher's role was seen to involve socializing boys and girls for their respective appropriate roles. However, obtaining and maintaining a teaching position — and thus pledging allegiance to the state and its ally the Catholic church — seemed to be the primary concern with all future teachers. At this point most of them did not want to upset their opportunities of being a civil servant, and hence most of them (regardless of their view of existing gender relations) anticipated being cautious about addressing gender issues in their activities in classrooms, schools and communities.

Plans for Political Action by Conservatives

Whether in classrooms or schools, the conservatives said they did not anticipate addressing gender issues. They planned to maintain the status quo as they did not believe in disturbing present gender arrangements. They were comfortable with the current situation, and they thought that the current gendered division of labor worked well in the home and the community. As one conservative informant stated: 'Feminists are bad for the society. They ruin the harmony in the families. We do not need that. We like the way it is. Men should be doing certain things and women have their places.'

When asked how they might seek to address gender issues in their work and lives, the conservatives stated that they basically anticipated being 'good' teachers. This involved two decisions, both focused on how they would operate out in the relatively isolated, 'private' sphere of the classroom: 1) deciding to teach the state-prescribed curriculum 2) deciding not to get involved when 'something' did not concern them personally. One conservative responded: 'I want to teach my subject.' Another explained: 'I do not want to disturb anything, because I believe it is better that way.' Others seemed annoyed at my questions about their plans for dealing with gender issues, replying 'Leave me alone, don't bother me. I don't want to be rude to you!' or 'Remember, my main concern is to graduate and get a job.'

When queried specifically about plans for any 'political' activities outside the classroom or school contexts, one female conservative mentioned that she might do some 'social work' as part of her duty towards helping people on humanitarian grounds. Generally, however, most conservative females and many of their male counterparts did not have much in mind about public involvement. What they did say, moreover, clearly articulated their belief in a traditional gendered division of labor. Both male and female conservatives labeled certain activities as 'indoor' (e.g. cooking, housecare, childcare) or 'outdoor' (e.g. attending public meetings or participating in protest demonstrations). They argued that women should not engage in 'outdoor' activities because this would take women's time away from their families, thus causing marital disharmony. According to conservatives, union and professional organizational activities should be 'left to the men'. As one student commented: 'Women should not be spending too much time with unions. It is men's work.' Conservatives believed that even for men such organizations were not so much a basis for engaging in 'political' work as they were outlets for social and recreational activities, such as sports, hobbies and special interests. 'Oh yes, all men are expected to be members of some professional organization', was a comment from a conservative man. Conservative men also had another concern — not being labeled an extremist. As one male student mentioned: 'If my activity is considered as radical by some people, it will jeopardize my career as well as my promotion prospects.'

Plans for Political Actions by Liberal Feminists

The liberal feminists' focus for political action was 1) to socialize boys and girls for equal opportunities and 2) to integrate both sexes in all activities. For instance, they showed concern to avoid the practice by teachers of addressing boys and girls differently, with girls called by their first names and boys by their family names. This practice, according to the liberal feminists, socialized boys and girls, respectively, for higher and lower positions in the social hierarchy and not for equal opportunities. Liberal feminists also indicated that they planned to integrate boys and girls in all activities, which would involve assigning similar classroom tasks to both sexes.

Attitudinal change was the main agenda in the liberal feminists' future classroom practice, which would discourage the present practice of expecting and promoting different roles for boys and girls. However, their plans for promoting attitudinal change were not without an element of apprehension. They were uneasy about the reaction of boys if asked to learn the things that traditionally were learned by girls. As one of them put it: 'I don't know how the boys will accept this.'

As to curriculum decision making or curriculum delivery, the liberal feminists stated that textbooks and curricula will have to be delivered as prescribed by the state. This, they anticipated, could not be changed dramatically by the teachers. However, they anticipated making space to emphasize that both boys and girls had equal opportunities through equal appreciation, evaluation, and role expectations.

The liberal feminists also planned to use extracurricular activities to address gender issues. For instance, they wanted to refrain from separating boys and girls during field trips — a practice that was seen as unnecessarily creating gender divisions. Liberal feminists also planned to use field trips as occasions for countering assumptions that boys naturally assume leadership roles, while girls naturally take the back seats. As one liberal feminist student observed: 'Mixing boys and girls might create opportunities for girls also to lead the groups.'

With respect to community-based 'political' activities, liberal feminists, particularly women, expressed caution concerning their future plans for addressing gender issues in ways that might be interpreted as a significant challenge to the status quo. Like the other categories of women, the liberal feminist females were generally hesitant to join professional associations or unions or to participate in protest marches or demonstrations. They preferred to keep a 'low profile' in such activities, which they identified as outside the parameters of their expected roles as women. However, they did anticipate membership in unions, which used collective bargaining to enhance teachers' salaries, but only as part of 'a group with other women'. Group activities gave them protection against being negatively evaluated by the society and their own family members.

While women liberal feminists preferred to be 'inconspicuous' and cautious, their male counterparts did not seem to be as concerned about being noticed by others as members of unions and professional associations. As was the case with the male conservatives, male liberal feminists indicated that such memberships were often expected of them. For the most part, liberal feminist men did not see any problem in being actively engaged in unions and professional associations. 'In fact, I am already a member of a teachers' association,' stated one liberal feminist man.

Like their conservative sisters, the liberal feminist women did not anticipate participating in public debates to address gender issues. Some liberal feminist females, similar to some of their conservative sisters, saw themselves devoting some time for 'social work', like helping women from third world countries. For liberal feminist males, they stated that they might participate in public debates, but not specifically to address gender issues. Both male and female liberal feminists felt that school and classroom activities provided adequate opportunities for their 'political' work to address gender issues.

Plans for Political Actions by Socialist Feminists

Socialist feminists' plans for political actions to challenge existing gender relations involved: 1) acting in ways that empower girls *and* boys, 2) problematizing the gender-biased content of textbooks, and 3) participating in formal organizations.

Socialist feminists hoped to transform gender relations at home, in education, in the economy and in politics. They anticipated engaging in activities that would empower boys and girls to think critically about and actively challenge existing gender relations. Socialist feminists identified many areas in classroom teaching and curriculum decision making for their 'political' actions. Both male and female socialist feminists were enthusiastic about using classroom activities to influence their students to think about and act to challenge gender issues. They anticipated making space in the formal as well as co-curricular and extracurricular activities to address gender politics.

Women and men holding a socialist feminist perspective, however, differed in their preferred curricular and organizational contexts in which they would address gender issues. While the man tended to emphasize social studies, the women stressed practical subject areas, such as home economics and wood shop, as the most appropriate curricular areas for focusing students' attention on the problematic nature of men's and women's roles. For instance, the male socialist feminist explained: 'In history classes we can talk about women who have contributed but are not mentioned in the texts.' Female socialist feminists said they anticipated challenging the practice of training boys and girls in practical subject areas that traditionally have been earmarked, respectively, for men and women. For example, a female socialist feminist commented: 'Gender tracking for the division of labor starts in such classes; we have to do something about it.' Another observed that although normally in practical subject areas 'boys elect to learn carpentry work and girls automatically join cooking lessons, I would like to change this practice.'

Like their liberal feminist peers, the socialist feminists (male and females) also wanted to change the practice in schools of addressing boys by their family names and girls by their first names. As one female socialist feminist explained: 'When boys are addressed by their family names, they think that they are superior to girls. I want to change this attitude.'

Socialist feminist women anticipated using cultural activities and sports to equalize boys' and girls' roles. This was possible through elocution, debates, singing, and play-acting. 'We can write different parts for boys and girls [not gender stereotyped, as is the practice now] for plays,' noted one respondent.

Women in the socialist feminist group do not plan to be associated with feminist groups or other such organizations to address gender issues. Like the conservatives and the liberal feminists they were concerned about the repercussions of being involved in such public forms of political activity. They might, however, be willing to be associated with groups that addressed other social issues, but not specifically gender issues. Most of them were hesitant about the negative connotation associated with the term 'feminist'. One female socialist feminist student stated emphatically: 'I may want to work for women's causes, but I do not want to be called a feminist.' The male socialist feminist also did not anticipate addressing gender issues through political organizations or any feminist groups. However, he did state: 'If it is necessary, yes, I will do it.'

Unlike the women in the conservative and liberal feminist groups, the socialist feminist women would join the teachers' associations or unions, but only to strengthen efforts for better salaries and working conditions for teachers. The socialist feminist man proposed to be actively engaged in union activities, though again not specifically to address gender issues.

Socialist feminist women also planned to participate in community activities, but mainly to engage in 'social work' efforts, not to debate about or engage in struggles concerning women's issues. Some spoke with interest about the possibility of developing a women's center, where issues about women's situation could be openly discussed. Some also identified the plight of women who were brought into the country by German men as one concern that would mobilize them to public political action. They planned to address this situation of exploitation of foreign women by German men by speaking at public forums, writing letters to the editor, and organizing photo exhibits. The male student with a socialist feminist perspective also criticized this practice, but did not volunteer what actions he might take to stop this practice.

Plans for Political Actions by Radical Feminists

The radical feminists identified different areas and strategies to influence children to think about and act in relation to gender issues. Their plans included: 1) creating critical awareness in students, 2) celebrating being a woman, 3) demonstrating concern for harmony, and 4) participating in activities through formal organizations.

The radical feminists recognized that empowering their students to think critically about gender relations was very important. They believed that being a woman is not a handicap, but a powerful experience that men lack; hence they located their strength in being women. The reason as they saw this is that 'women have a different kind of strength.' As one of them noted:

> Women can perform several tasks at the same time. We do not need physical strength. We can have children, work full-time, and also participate in national politics. Look at the women in the Green Party. All those women are highly educated and have children.

This is a message that radical feminists planned to convey to their students. As one female radical feminist noted: 'I plan to tell the children that there is no difference in being a boy or a girl. We [women] can equally accomplish what men can.'

The radical feminists concurred with the other feminist groups in relation to the textbooks provided by the state. They did not see how they could change or alter the curriculum, but stated that they would make space in the way they taught the content, presenting the curriculum in a different way. As one radical feminist pointed out: 'We have a lot of opportunities while teaching religion. There are many stories which we can tell.' Like their socialist feminist counterpart, men with a radical feminist perspective planned to use social science subjects for change efforts. Women placed their emphasis on religion or language classes. As one female radical feminist student noted: 'In library reading and language classes, we can influence students to read about problems associated with women.' Another noted: 'I will be teaching music, and art. I can make sure that boys and girls learn the same instrument or express the same themes in their art work.'

Radical feminist women planned additionally to raise consciousness about gender relations through extracurricular and co-curricular activities. Debates, school speeches, bulletin boards, drama and singing were some areas they proposed to use to influence children to think critically about gender relations. According to one student: 'I think songs and plays will be very effective for raising gender-related awareness.' Unlike the conservatives and the liberal feminists, who preferred the cloak of participating in a group, the radical feminists planned to become active addressing social issues in this manner even if others did not initially join them.

The radical feminists agreed with the socialist feminists that a women's center would be helpful for women to deal with gender politics. Unlike the socialist feminists who did not have a concrete idea of what they wanted to do in the women's center apart from debating, the radical feminists stated that they would have used the center for peaceful projects. Some suggestions were that they could encourage communicating a feminist perspective in art, music and literature. The radical feminists were quite clear about not proposing highly confrontational measures for dealing with problems of gender inequalities. They wanted the center to offer men (and women) an opportunity to understand the problems from a feminist perspective.

Unlike the women from the other gender perspectives, radical feminists (some of them) planned to affiliate themselves openly with feminist organizations. One of them stated that she was already a member, while another was a member but was uncomfortable publicizing this fact.

Men in the radical feminist group did not have any problem being active through professional associations or unions. This was partly because they wanted to express solidarity with the group, in addition to performing 'outside' work that was expected of them as men. Radical feminist women also regarded membership in unions as men's work, but were going to join anyway. However, they stated that they did not anticipate being as active as their male counterparts.

Male radical feminist students stated that they anticipated active participation outside the school in public debates and community activities. Radical feminist women were willing to participate in street politics, lobbying and demonstrating, which was not the case with other women. Some would be directly engaged, and others not so directly. Women also planned to organize exhibitions and distribute leaflets to address women's issues. Some of them were already engaged in such activities. Among the radical feminists, men anticipated some intensity in their work, but women pointed out that they (as women) would be handicapped because of family obligations. As one of them expressed it: 'We may want to be very active, but we will have time constraints, due to familial ties.'

Messages Encountered in the Teacher Education Program

Given the range of views evinced by students in this teacher education program, it is important to examine the messages transmitted by the official and hidden curriculum of the program that these students may have perceived and accepted or rejected. Here the focus will be on both messages concerning the nature of gender relations and messages concerning the political roles teachers can or should play.

Messages About Gender Relations

Students received messages about gender issues directly from the church and the state as well as indirectly through the faculty, some of whom were priests and all of whom were state civil servants. One of the direct messages they encountered from the church was that they were expected to maintain the traditional values. The indirect messages transmitted by the faculty and the priests were the approval/disapproval of male and female behavior, both on and off campus. In short they had a well-defined social script according to which they were expected to act.

Because the church managed the university, conservative religious values tended to permeate the personal lives of students (and faculty). For example, the three groups of feminist students whom I interviewed referred critically to the church's view on matters relating to divorce and abortion. A divorce could cost a student his or her admission. Therefore, many of the students learned to keep their personal lives concealed (living with their partners, having children before marriage or a possible separation/divorce) to comply with the church's wishes. The conservatives, however, did not think that the church should behave differently. They were particularly happy that the church discouraged divorces, which helped to maintain social stability.

One of the direct messages from the state was that gender issues were not important, in that the state-prescribed curriculum was generally silent on women's issues. When gender relations were portrayed, this was done in a way to portray traditional male and female roles in a taken-for-granted manner. For example, in an art class the students were discussing an earlier assignment, which involved evaluating the form and content in the drawings done by kindergarten children. Some of the drawings showed a 'mother' with big eyelashes pushing a shopping cart or walking with children. The instructor remarked that little boys know how to distinguish a male and a female face and, hence, this one has added 'eyelashes' to his 'mama'. He also mentioned that children spend most of their time with the mothers and notice what they do during the day. He seemed to accept the fact that mothers (not fathers) were expected to spend time with the children.[7]

The gendered division of labor in schools is also portrayed unproblematically. For instance, in one of the methods classes an instructor identified female teachers with small children. He seemed to suggest that women are most suited to handle small children in *Grundschule*. His comments seemed to signal the care-taking roles of women extending to elementary schools, suggesting that children found emotional security in female teachers. Such suggestions seemed to indicate that nurturing and women were closely connected. At the same time such messages about women being ideally suited to nurture young children also communicated that the reason males should be in the *Grundschule* program was so that they could manage women teachers in the elementary schools. As one student noted about a faculty member's 'surprise' to find males in this program: 'It may seem that [the professor] is encouraging men to be *Grundschule* teachers, but in reality he is trying to tell all of us [women] that there is a potential administrator sitting amongst you.'

That males are more likely to occupy dominant positions was also communicated by the fact that the faculty members and the senior administrators were predominantly men, while female faculty members were mostly junior in rank, and depended on male votes for promotions. That the church was also dominated by men — for example, all priests were male and during religious processions men led and women followed behind — was also a powerful message perceived by at least some students. For example one woman noted: 'Men are protected by the church, and they know that they can continue to enjoy freedom, power, and status.'

Furthermore, male instructors, particularly those who were priests, seemed to elevate the position of men in the classes. As one female student commented, while pointing to a male student: 'He is in one of my classes. A priest teaches this class. [The priest] never looks at girls. [The priest] gives more importance to boys, even lets them ask more questions.' Women students expressed in interviews that such favoritism toward male students, especially by faculty who were priests, tended to build men's confidence and undermine women's confidence.

Messages About Teachers' Political Action

There was little attention in the official curriculum concerning the role of teachers as political actors. Rather the emphasis in the program was to prepare students to be skilled in what were portrayed as professional and technical activities. The content of the lectures and workshops focused on the methods of teaching, use of teaching aids, use of psychology with children, and classroom management. As one student observed: 'The professors teach us how to control the class and discipline the students.'

The hidden curriculum transmitted similarly depoliticized messages. The students stated that they had been influenced by their professors as models to remain silent on controversial issues. As one of them observed: 'The professors do not discuss women's problem in the class. We don't know if we can discuss it at all.' Even outside the classrooms the faculty rarely discussed with students social issues, such as the nature of gender relations. The religious conservatism of the faculty, their peers and others also have influenced them to be cautious in their approach to dealing with any problems. As one liberal feminist male student noted: 'I have to be careful. The priests, prospective priests and my friends observe me all the time. In this Catholic university, we have to accept and support the religious beliefs. Otherwise I will be in trouble.'

Everybody connected with the university, directly or indirectly, was expected to be mutually in agreement with the control of the church and the state at all occasions, including being present during church services at the beginning and end of the term. Under the circumstances, it is clear that the ideological state/church apparatus[8] is not limited to the academic sphere, but also encompasses personal lives.

Pressure toward conformity to church and state authority also occurs for students in the teacher education program at Eichstätt during their practice teaching and internship period. During practice teaching the interns' zeal dies or is negated as they are constantly supervised for 'negative behavior'. Future employment opportunities depended on the supervisors' review; hence most of the students observe caution while they practice teach.

Program Influence on Students' Perspectives and Orientations

How did the students deal with the messages in the program? In what ways were they influenced, if at all? Were their perspectives and orientations reinforced or challenged and changed?

In general the senior students who had spent between six to eight semesters in course work did not think that either their views about gender relations or their plans for engaging in political action on issues of gender in school and communities had changed much during the course of their experience in the program.[9] Some changes were nevertheless reported. For example, women in particular stated that they had matured progressively and come to understand better the problems of the society, including those linked to gender relations.[10]

Conservatives stated that the program had helped them to strengthen their views on their roles as men and women, in the school, as family members and as members of the community. Some conservative women stated that their roles as teachers should correspond to their roles in their families. As one conservative female student advocated: 'Teaching in *Grundschule* is like [having responsibility for] childcare at home.' The conservatives made it clear that they were not so concerned about any change in their gender perspectives, because their main focus was to be efficient teachers. They seemed to prefer a role that corresponded to their roles at home.

The students with various feminist perspectives certainly did not find much in the official or hidden curriculum to reinforce their views about the nature of gender relations. While the conservative messages encountered in the program did not encourage them to rethink how they viewed gender relations — indeed, some found themselves strengthening and refining their perspectives in the face of such conservative messages — their program experiences discouraged many of them from becoming active in trying to change gender relations. For example, one radical feminist student, although committed to having a women's center as a site for promoting a feminist agenda, expressed her doubt about ever having such a center. The reason that she gave was: 'Things are too tightly controlled by religious-based values of the university and the state. This is difficult to happen.'

Conclusions

To understand why these prospective teachers developed their political identities in the way they did one needs to consider the ideology and structural power of the state and the church. In this case, the state controlled the curriculum, professional licensing exams, and teaching positions. The church managed the university, supplied priests as some of the faculty members, organized religious and cultural activities, and performed a surveillance function over students' (and faculty's) public and private lives. The messages of conserving traditional values and not challenging the status quo are further strengthened by the fact that the state government is dominated by the conservative Christian Democratic Party.[11]

Thus it is not surprising that the largest category of the students (21 out of 45) were what I labeled as conservatives, who did not plan to change the status quo with respect to gender relations or more generally. Instead, they projected their 'political' role as teachers to consist of performing their duty as state employees to deliver the state-sponsored curriculum. However, despite the fact that the church-controlled, state-sponsored teacher preparation program at Eichstätt was conservative, not all students were conservative in their perspectives on gender relations or in their plans for 'political' actions concerned with gender issues. Some, like the liberal feminists, were mildly critical of existing gender roles and desired to change people's attitudes to achieve more equitable and less biased arrangements. They did not see much space for themselves to change gender relations directly, but saw their role as treating boys and girls more equally and promoting gender-neutral attitudes so that in the future gender inequities would be reduced or eliminated. The socialist and radical feminists strongly criticized existing gender relations, and planned to 'redefine' gender relations through current efforts but mostly in their future activities. The socialist feminists critiqued existing gender relations but were apprehensive about the consequences of challenging the power of the church and the state. Like the liberal feminists, the socialist feminists anticipated that they would mostly engage in classroom and extracurricular school activities to raise gender issues among students, in the hope that they would create a future society less characterized by patriarchal and other forms of social inequalities. The radical feminists planned to engage in peaceful, non-confrontational, but more often overt and community-based political strategies.

The conservative students did not really face the dilemma of how to change things without sacrificing 'success' (graduating and getting a good teaching position), since their perspectives and orientations were in line with those in positions of authority within the church and the state. To varying degrees, however, the feminists who faced this dilemma preferred to 'go with the flow' for the present. Most of the liberal, socialist and radical feminists sought to resolve this dilemma by what Lacey (1977) terms 'strategic compliance'. That is, they decided for the most part to maintain silence (by not speaking and not acting publicly on their critique of existing gender relations) until they got into their future positions as teachers, when they believed they would be less closely controlled by the church/state or any authority structure. While the liberal, socialist and radical feminists may be correct in predicting a different orientation in the future, it may be that their positioning *vis-à-vis* the church and the state will continue even after the program is finished and they have obtained their coveted teaching positions. Most of the students were Catholic and after certification they are likely to continue to exhibit their allegiance to the church, at least because they will be employed in Bavaria, a Catholic state. As all teachers in Germany are state employees, the student–state relations will continue even after their teacher education is completed. Time will tell how they play out their 'political' roles as teachers, though if the university faculty and schoolteachers with whom they came in contact during their teacher education program at Eichstätt are any indication, one should not expect these students to become very active politically in transforming gender relations in Germany.

This study leads me to believe that people committed to developing teachers' understanding of and orientations to transform gender relations must strive to incorporate in the official curriculum a focus on gender relations analyzed from various, including different feminist, perspectives. Instead of the silence I observed at Eichstätt, gender issues should be highlighted in relation to various aspects of the study of teaching and schooling: curriculum, pedagogy, evaluation, administration–teacher relations, etc. Attention should also be given to gender relations in the home and community and how they are connected with the schooling process. It is critical to give future teachers an alternative source of visions and empower them with conceptual tools to reflect critically on issues of gender. Moreover, by linking analyses of gender issues to the conservative and potentially transformative activity of teachers in schools and communities, teacher education program curricula can help future teachers to orient their practice to reflect their value commitments actively.

It is also necessary that attention be given to messages conveyed through the hidden curriculum, which may be even more influential than the official curriculum in socializing prospective teachers. Inactive participation in gender politics at Eichstätt resulted from the way male and female instructors performed their roles. First, male and female students need to be given the same kind of attention inside or outside of classrooms. Equal encouragement needs to be given in terms of career choice, and traditional views (men make good administrators and women are best suited to be teachers in *Grundschulen*) are not transmitted in an unproblematic manner.

Second, the gender ratio of faculty and administrators needs to be addressed. Heavy concentration of males as administrators and senior faculty in the teacher preparation program at Eichstätt was interpreted as perpetuating and legitimating power in male hands. Struggles over whether males and/or females should be appointed and promoted at the university not only may change the gender ratio of faculty, but the process of struggle itself could model for future teachers the kinds of institutional level political action in which they may need to participate.

Third, faculty need to be models as agents of transformative political action in educational institutions and the community. This entails being engaged in individual and collective struggles for progressive causes and making such involvement more explicit to the students. If faculty merely encourage students to be active, while appearing to remain uninvolved, it is likely that students will see the contradiction and follow the safer path of low profile or non-involvement which is the case now.

Notes

1   This chapter only briefly summarizes the literature on teachers as political actors and the political socialization of teachers because the issues are discussed in more detail in Chapter 1 of this volume.

2   The term 'church' is used here to represent all forms of organized religion, whether they be associated with churches, mosques, synagogues, temples, etc., as places of worship.

3   *Grundschulen* are elementary schools; *Realschulen* and *Hauptschulen* are both 10-year, terminal, secondary schools; and *Gymnasia* are academic high schools leading to university education.

4   The breakdown of students' conceptions of gender relations was remarkably similar for males and females as can be seen in the table below:

Sex	Conserv.	Lib. Fem	Soc. Fem.	Rad. Fem.	TOTAL
Male	11	6	1	5	23
Female	10	6	2	4	22
Total	21	12	3	9	45

5   'Educating men' did not correspond to socializing like the liberal feminists, but to consciousness-raising or creating awareness.

6   Being a woman was considered to be more powerful than being a man. For one thing the radical and socialist women thought that while women could live without men, the same was not true for men.

7   The content of the school textbooks, which the interns encountered during their teaching practice, contained similar messages portraying the non-problematic nature of the existing gendered division of labor. For example, an illustration in one of the textbooks showed a 'mother' shopping and the 'father' working outdoors. These were not problematized in the text, nor for that matter by the classroom teachers or student interns.

8   This concept, which represents an extension of Althusser's (1971) 'ideological state apparatus', signals how at least in this case the church and state operate symbiotically to promote a world view that preserves existing unequal social arrangements.

9   The junior students were new in the program. Most of them were either in their first or second semester and hence could not contribute to this issue as much as the seniors. Most of the junior students were still in the process of experiencing

the program effects, and expressed that '[w]e have not taken many classes yet' or '[w]e do not know yet.'

10   Interestingly, some the women commented that by participating in this research their views on gender issues had changed, becoming more critical in observing social relations between men and women. As one of them remarked: 'Your research has set us thinking. Before this we never paid much attention to how men and women are treated in schools or at work. We just accepted it, as how it is supposed to be. Now we have started questioning.'

11   It should be noted that for many students the the church's management in their daily lives was not resented, but on the contrary was welcomed. Indeed, many of these future teachers opted to study at the Catholic University of Eichstätt because the university's religion department had a good reputation.

References

ALTHUSSER, L. (1971) 'Ideology and ideological state apparatuses', in ALTHUSSER, L. *Lenin and Other Essays*, London, New Left Books, pp. 127–86.

ANYON, J. (1980) 'Social class and the hidden curriculum of work', *Journal of Education*, **162**, 1, pp. 67–92.

BLASE, J. (1987) 'Political interactions among teachers: Sociocultural context in the schools', *Urban Education*, **22**, 4, pp. 286–309.

BLASE, J. (Ed) (1991) *The Politics of Life in Schools*, Newbury Park, CA, Sage.

BOGDAN, R. and BIKLEN, S. (1982) *Qualitative Research for Education*, Boston, MA, Allyn and Bacon.

BOGDAN, R. and TAYLOR, S. (1975) *Introduction to Qualitative Methods*, New York, Wiley-Interscience Publications.

BREHMER, I. (1987) 'Women educators in German speaking europe: The middle ages to today', in SCHMUCK, P. (Ed) *Woman Educators: Employers of Schools in Western Countries*, New York, State University of New York Press, pp. 105–20.

CARLSON, D. (1987) 'Teachers as political actors: From reproductive theory to the crisis of schooling', *Harvard Educational Review*, **57**, 3, pp. 283–307.

CHAFETZ, J. (1984) *Sex and Advantage: A Comparative Macro-Structural Theory of Sex Stratification*, Totowa, NJ, Rowman and Allanheld.

CONNELL, R. (1985a) *Teachers' Work*, Sydney, Allen and Unwin

CONNELL, R. (1985b) 'Theorizing Gender', *Sociology*, **19**, 2, pp. 260–72.

DOYLE, W. (1990) 'Themes in teacher education', in W.R. HOUSTON (Ed) *Handbook of Research on Teacher Education*, New York, Macmillan, pp. 3–24.

EISNER, E. (1985) *The Educational Imagination*, New York, Macmillan.

FISHMAN, S. and MARTIN, L. (1987) *Estranged Twins: Education and Society in the Two Germanies*, New York, Praeger.

FREIRE, P. (1973) *Education for Critical Consciousness*, New York, Herder and Herder.

FREIRE, P. (1985) *Politics of Education*, South Hadley, MA, Bergin and Garvey.

FRICK, W. (1934) *Die Deutsche Frau im Nationalsozialistischen Staate*, Berlin, Langensatz.

GINSBURG, M. (1988) *Contradictions in Teacher Education and Society*, New York, Falmer Press.

GINSBURG, M. and CLIFT, R. (1990) 'The hidden curriculum of preservice teacher education', in HOUSTON, W.R. (Ed) *Handbook of Research on Teacher Education*, New York, Macmillan Publishing Company, pp. 450–65.

GIROUX, H.A. (1990) 'Teacher education and the ideology of social control', *Journal of Education*, **162**, 2, pp. 5–27.

HEARNDEN, A. (1974) *Education in the Two Germanies*, Boulder, CO Westview Press.

HEWITSON, M., McWILLIAM, E. and BURKE, C. (1991) 'Responding to teacher education imperatives for the nineties', *Australian Journal of Education*, **35**, 3, pp. 246–60.

HYMAN, H. (1959) *Political Socialization*, New York, Free Press.
KOLINSKY, E. (1989) *Women in West Germany: Life, Work and Politics*, Oxford, Berg Publishers.
LACEY, C. (1977) *The Socialisation of Teachers*, London, Methuen.
LAWTON, D. (1976) *Class, Culture and Curriculum*, London, Routledge and Kegan Paul.
LORTIE, D. (1975) *School Teacher: A Sociological Study*, Chicago, IL, University of Chicago Press.
LYNCH, J. and PLUNKETT, D. (1973) *Teacher Education and Cultural Change*, London, Allen and Unwin.
McINNIS, E., HISCOCKS, R. and SPENCER, R. (1960) *The Shaping of Post War Germany*, New York, Praeger Publications.
McINTYRE-STEPHENSON, J. (1971) 'Women and the professions in Germany, 1930–40', in NICHOLLS, A. and MATHIS, E. (Eds) *Germany, Democracy and the Triumph of Hitler: Essays in Recent German History*, London, Allen and Unwin, pp. 175–213.
ORTHNER, S.B. (1974) 'Is female to male as nature is to culture?' in ROSALDO, M. and LAMPHERE, L. (Eds) *Woman, Culture and Society*, Stanford, CA, Stanford University Press, pp. 66–88.
PAUWELS, J. (1984) *Women, Nazis and Universities*, New York, Greenwood Press.
POPKEWITZ, T. (Ed) (1987) *Critical Studies in Teacher Education: Its Folklore, Theory and Practice*, London, Falmer Press.
RAGHU, R. (1992) 'Development of Teachers as Political Actors in a Private German University: How Pre-Service Teachers Anticipate their Contribution to Preserving/Transforming Gender Relations', unpublished doctoral dissertation, University of Pittsburgh, PA.
ROBBINS, T. and ROBERTSON, R. (1987) *Church–State Relations: Tensions and Transitions*, New Brunswick, NJ, Transaction Books.
ROMER, N. (1981) *The Sex Role Cycle*, Old Westbury, NY, Feminist Press.
ROSSER, P. (1988) 'Girls and boys and the SAT: Can we even the score?' *NEA Journal*, January, pp. 48–49.
SAMUEL, R. and THOMAS, R. (1949) *Education and Society in Modern Germany*, London, Routledge and Kegan Paul.
SCHÖPP-SCHILLING, H. (1985) 'Federal Republic of Germany', in FARLEY, J. (Ed) *Women Workers in Fifteen Countries*, New York, Industrial and Labor Relations Press, pp. 124–37.
SCHWARTZ, H. and JACOBS, J. (1979) *Qualitative Sociology*, New York, The Free Press.
SIMON, R. (1987) 'Work experience' in LIVINGSTONE, D. (Ed) *Critical Pedagogy and Cultural Power*, South Hadley, MA, Bergin and Garvey, pp. 155–78.
SPRADLEY, J. (1979) *Ethnographic Interviewing*, New York, Holt.
SPRADLEY, J. (1980) *Participant Observation*, New York, Holt.
SULTANA, D. (1989) 'Are there any critical educators out there? Perspectives on teachers and transformation', *Critical Pedagogy Networker*, **2**, 4, pp. 1–8.
TAPPENDORF, L. (1975) 'Gleichberechtigung und Förderung der Frauen in der DDR', *DDR Komitee für Menchenrechte, Schriften, und Information*, **1**, pp. 6–25.
THOMAS, R.M. (1983) *Politics and Education: Cases from Eleven Nations*, New York, Pergamon Press.
VALLI, L. (1986) *Becoming Clerical Workers*, Boston, MA, Routledge and Kegan Paul.
WEILER, K. (1988) *Women Teaching for Change: Gender, Class and Power*, South Hadley, MA, Bergin and Garvey.
WEIS, L. (1990) *Working Class Without Work*, New York, Routledge.
ZEICHNER, K. and GORE, J. (1990) 'Teacher socialization', in HOUSTON, W.R. (Ed) *Handbook of Research on Teacher Education*, New York, Macmillan, pp. 329–48.

Chapter 12

Contradictions, Resistance and Incorporation in the Political Socialization of Educators in Mexico[1]

Mark B. Ginsburg

Much of the literature about teacher education internationally focuses on academic, professional, and technical dimensions (see Ginsburg and Clift 1990; Zeichner and Gore 1990). In contrast, my concern here is to highlight the political dimension, that is to examine the political socialization of educators in formal preparation programs. In this chapter, which builds on the theoretical discussion in the first chapter, I sketch the national, state-level, and institutional context prior to reporting on findings of a longitudinal, ethnographic study in a *licenciatura* (bachelor's degree) program at the *Escuela Normal Superior Veracruzana* (ENSV) in Xalapa, Veracruz, Mexico. The research at this and two other institutions[2] was designed to address five main questions:

1 How do female and male students[3] in a teacher preparation program view society in terms of political economic and social problems?
2 What are they currently doing or do they anticipate doing to deal with these societal problems *in* their work activity?
3 What are they currently doing or do they anticipate doing to deal with these societal problems *outside* of their work settings?
4 Why are they oriented to engage in or refrain from certain strategies for addressing societal problems?
5 To what extent and in what ways have their views about society and their (in and outside of work) strategies for dealing with social problems been influenced during their various experiences while enrolled in the program?

These research questions were investigated using ethnographic methods (Spradley 1979, 1980; Goetz and LeCompte 1984; Bogdan and Biklen 1992). The study involved fieldwork focused on students in one of ENSV's teacher education programs that requires attendance in classes during six summer sessions. Participant observation in and outside of class sessions occurred during July–August 1989, July–August 1990, July 1991, and July–August 1992. The primary focus of the research was on one group of students enrolled in ENSV's first cohort (1987–92) of the Social Science Education program and the instructors with whom they interacted. In 1989 this group (then in their third summer of the program) along with a first and second-year group were each observed during one full day of classes. In 1990–92 participant observation focused on the focal group of students (during their fourth through sixth summers of the program) for varying numbers of days.[4]

Class sessions and interaction between classes were observed and fieldnotes were written up; occasionally presentations or discussions in class were audiotaped. These data provided evidence of 'messages' in both the formal and hidden curricula. Written materials (assigned readings, handouts, etc.) used in classes as well as other written materials the group came into contact with were also reviewed to identify their messages about society and educators' role as political actors. Participant observation also took place in the afternoons and on weekends away from the ENSV campus. Of interest here were group and individual activities related to the program (e.g. studying or team project work) or more informal interaction that provided opportunities for conversations to obtain information and to establish and maintain rapport.

During the participant observation fieldwork in 1989–92, discussions and informal interviews with students, teachers, and administrators were conducted. In addition, during the summers of 1990–92, a questionnaire containing a set of open-ended questions was used to collect data on the students' previous educational and work experiences as well as their ideas about the societal problems, in-work and outside work strategies for dealing with such problems, and perceived influences of program experiences.

Domain, taxonomic, componential, and theme analyses of the data (Spradley 1979, 1980) from fieldnotes, taperecordings of classes and interviews, and the gathered written materials were carried out both during the study and subsequently. This involved some collaboration with Mexican colleagues as well.

Context of the Study

The following discussion draws upon observations, fieldnotes, interviews, and document analyses as well as literature in order to situate the program experiences and students' views within the historical and contemporary contexts of the nation (and global relations) of Mexico and the state of Veracruz institution, ENSV.

The National Context of Mexico

Mexico achieved its political independence from Spain in 1821 — after 302 years of Spanish colonial rule. However, Mexico's national political identity and culture is more often represented as linked to the 1910–17 revolution through which the 'dictatorship' of Porfirio Diaz was ended and a constitutional 'democracy' was established.[5] Based in part on 'the ideology of the Mexican Revolution':

> 'National culture' functions as the great mediator in the class [and associated ethnic group] struggle . . . [by transposing] real social actors to a realm where they shed most of their original contradictory features, transforming them into characters who serve the sham of national unity. (Bartra 1989, p. 68)

National unity has also been symbolized by a strong, central state apparatus (even in a federal system of government) and through the emergence and (until recently) uncontested dominant role performed by a single, 'all-incorporating' political party. Here I refer to the *Partido Revolucionario Institucional* (PRI), which originated as the *Partido Nacional Revolucionario* (PNR) in 1929 and was reorganized along corporatist lines and renamed the *Partido Revolucionario Mexicano* (PRM) in 1934 before being named PRI since 1946.

Two points should be made about this notion of national unity. The first is that this strong sense of national identity and culture operates in the context of — but deflects attention away from — Mexico's continued economic and cultural dependency in relation to Europe and the United States.[6] As Bartra (1989, p. 65) notes, 'national culture' in Mexico not only functions by 'rising above social classes', but also by 'establishing itself through the expression of global interests of the dominant class'. The point is that discourse of Mexican nationalism, even when laden with reference to US imperialism, has not always been associated with élite efforts to counter the economic and cultural penetration and domination by primarily US-based multinational corporations (Cockcroft 1990).

The second point is that the unified national identity and culture seems to function ideologically to rise above or smooth over conflicts and contradictions based on gender. Thus *machismo* (a Latin American cultural form of sexist ideas and practices) as well as patriarchal social structures (through which male power and privilege is consecrated) are rendered invisible or, at least, unspeakable as men and women are incorporated into a unified national people and society. However, as Cortina (1989) explains, the reality of gender relations in Mexico (as in other countries) should be understood differently:

> The family obligations of women . . . housework, child care, social net-works, and informal economic activities to complement the family economy . . . bind up the free time that women might otherwise have for greater professional responsibilities, union participation, and other [pol-itical] activities outside the home . . . The differentiation of roles between men and women and the time demands of the social and economic as-pects of family life both reinforce and are reinforced by the centralization of institutional and political processes that hinder the advancement of women. (pp. 373–5)

Education has been a key means through which national culture, or what Estrada and La Belle (1981, p. 287) term a 'comprehensive national ideology', has been promoted and legitimated. This has occurred both through ideologies trans-mitted through the official curriculum and free textbooks (Perissinotto 1974; Lechuga 1984) and through ritual performances (e.g. weekly ceremonies saluting the Mexican flag and singing the Mexican national anthem). An ideology of na-tional unity (i.e. based on a belief of sharing in the definition of and benefits from political and economic 'development') has also been reinforced by the meritocratic ideal. This idea is enshrined in the beliefs that the state will provide expanding opportunities for education to all citizens, that all groups have an equal chance to be successful in school, that those who succeed in school will be rewarded with commensurate adult status and power, and that they will use such positions to benefit all Mexican citizens.[7] By propagating the meritocratic ideal coupled with achieving real expansion of education provision since the revolution, state élites also have to a certain extent been able to perpetuate and legitimate the Mexican nation-state by 'coopting political unrest and in keeping the political support of the largest and most powerful labor organization in the country, the teacher's union' (Morales Gomez and Torres 1990, p. 52).

Relations between teachers and the state and the prevailing image of teachers in Mexico has varied widely within this century:

1   as orators, advisors and leaders in the struggle during the 1910–17 Mexican Revolution;
2   as self-sacrificing missionaries seeking to 'redeem' the uneducated and to commit them to the goals of the revolutionary and secular state during the 1920s;
3   as community organizers of peasants and workers oriented to bring about progressive social change through collective action in the 1930s; and
4   as apolitical professionals focused on techniques for motivating students and transmitting the curriculum since the 1940s (Alba 1969; Gonzales Navarro 1975; Aguilar and Retamal 1982; Imaz and Salinas 1984; McGinn and Street 1984).

This latter image has been associated with a 'corporatist' relationship (see Lehmbruch and Schmitter 1982) between organized educators and the Mexican state, in which educators along with other sectors obtain some benefits and influence in exchange for supporting or at least not seriously challenging state and party élites (Torres 1991).

Still another image is the one projected by the 'Movimiento Magisterial' (Teachers Movement), which began in 1979 but surged to the center of educational politics in 1989 (Arriaga 1981; Street 1989; Campos *et al.* 1990; Torres 1991). Here teachers are participants in 'independent' grassroots efforts (connected with the *Coordinadora Nacional de Trabajadores en Educación* or CNTE) to challenge the austerity package imposed by the International Monetary Fund (Noriega 1985; Cockcroft 1990), at least as it affects teachers' salaries and funding for education, and the corporatist nature of the Mexican state and ruling political party (PRI), in terms of its control of the national teachers' union (*Sindicato Nacional de Trabajadores en Educación* or SNTE).[8] In this recent period, when Mexico has been facing a major economic and debt crisis — a crisis which has exacerbated social inequalities and undermined the legitimacy of the state and PRI — teachers have also been active more generally in public sphere politics. Some teachers' participation with other citizens in political parties, both on the right (*Partido Acción Nacional* or PAN) and on the left (*Partido Revolucionario Democrático* or PRD), has provided a serious challenge to the monopoly that the ruling party (PRI) has held for approximately 60 years.

Teacher education — as a focus for policy making and an institution of political socialization — has not been detached from the dynamics of teacher–state relations within the national and global political economic context.[9] For example, even before the revolution the development of teacher education programs was linked to the politics of gender relations. As Cortina (1989, p. 357) reports: 'In

Mexico, the creation of public institutions for training teachers at the end of the nineteenth century was accompanied by a new rhetoric of opportunity for women [who] quickly became a majority of students in normal schools.' While they still comprise a sizeable majority of teachers, especially among those working at the preschool and primary school level, women are grossly underrepresented among in positions of authority either in the national government, *Secretaría de Educacion Pública* (SEP) or the national teachers' union (SNTE).

The development of teacher education programs has generally been linked to efforts to expand the provision and improve the quality of schooling, which (as we noted above) has at least in part been designed to perform certain political functions. Thus teacher education institutions and programs have been organized to socialize teachers for the kind of political roles that state élites and/or union leaders conceived for them.[10] The creation of the *Universidad Pedagógica Nacional* (UPN) in 1978 provides an interesting case. In one sense, UPN's creation reflects a long-standing proposal from SNTE leaders and rank-and-file members for a postsecondary level program for preparing teachers. At the same time it was part of the Jose López Portillo administration's plans to wrest control over the education of teachers from the SNTE-dominated normal schools (McGinn and Street 1984; Noriega 1985; Morales Góemez and Torres 1990). SNTE responded to this move by the state by using its strong influence in the appointment process basically to block access to jobs of UPN graduates. Over time SNTE gained in its influence on UPN's internal affairs, while the in-service teachers attending UPN became increasingly politicized in the context of Mexico City as the teachers' movement strengthened. In this context, the Lopez Portillo administration — in line with other efforts to deconcentrate the educational system administratively (see Pescador 1988) — moved to decentralize UPN's programs onto campuses at various sites outside of Mexico City.[11]

Part of the effort to decentralize this professionalized form of teacher education involved the transforming of normal schools from upper secondary to higher education institutions, which took place in 1984. Interestingly, the 1984 policy document that specified this change characterized teachers as 'change agents, upholding the ideology and principles of the constitution' and seeking 'social justice' and a 'democratic life for peace and liberty' (SEP 1984, pp. 7–10). We need to be cautious, though, to not read too much into such calls for teachers to be change agents. For example, in 1989 the Salinas de Gortari government's 'modernization' program for education in Mexico similarly portrayed teachers as agents in 'the process of social modernization . . . contributing to the transformation of the economic, political, social and cultural reality of the nation' (SEP 1989, pp. 63–64). In the same document, however, there is a concern expressed to increase the national coordination of the operationally decentralized teacher education programs and to ensure that such programs conform to SEP norms and curriculum. Moreover, the type of change agent role, rather than being one linked to social movements operating autonomously from the state, may be more in line with helping to prepare students to cope with or fit into changes being directed by state and economic élites. For example, one of the objectives of the modernization project is listed as 'improving the capacity and ability of the working teacher, favoring their functioning within conditions of accelerated social change' (SEP 1989, p. 67).

The Institutional Context: ENSV

The *Escuela Normal Superior Veracruzana* (ENSV) is located in Xalapa, the capital of Veracruz, a state which has a relatively vibrant economy (though the benefits are unequally shared) and is strongly dominated by PRI and SNTE. Although by August 1992 (compared to 1986, when the last gubernatorial election took place, or even 1989, when the field work began) PAN and especially PRD were more visible and made a stronger showing in the gubernatorial election, the PRI candidate 'officially' (critics argue 'fraudulently') won by a large majority. CNTE began visibly to organize a challenge to the SNTE leadership in Veracruz during 1990, but this never reached the level of intensity as was witnessed, for example, in poorer states, such as Chiapas, Michoacan, or Oaxaca. The power of PRI and SNTE is manifest generally, and in Veracruz very openly and extensively, through the party and union officials gatekeeping functions for jobs, promotions, etc.

ENSV began offering programs in 1987 to provide working teachers and educational administrators in the state of Veracruz with a level of teacher education commensurate with an undergraduate degree (*licenciatura*). As noted above, in 1984 preservice teacher education was moved to the college level for those entering the field, and ENSV was one of institutions developed to provide an opportunity for practicing educators to upgrade their credentials and enhance their knowledge and skills as teachers (and receive some increased remuneration). The inaugural ceremonies for ENSV on 6 July 1987 signaled, though, that ENSV was not merely an academic, technical, or professional initiative, but had a political dimension as well. In his speech at those ceremonies the then Governor of the State of Veracruz called attention to an important role played by teachers, including those about to enter ENSV programs: 'The teacher is the natural agent of social change and transformation. For him/her the importance of each day is to better prepare oneself to mold the consciousness of children and youth . . . To educate is revolutionary work' (Gutierrez Barrios 1987, p. 6). The Director General of Secondary Education in Veracruz made clear that this was seen to be government-directed change in stating that ENSV 'synthesizes the thought and action of the Government of Veracruz' (Pina Sanchez 1987, p. 13). The words of ENSV's first Director reemphasized the idea of teachers as agents of change (though perhaps in directions determined by state élites):

> In epochs of crisis, education imparted by the state acquires its greatest force . . . For this we must work hard to ensure that our teachers have a better professional level, that elevates their capacity as agents of social transformation and their critical conscience for fulfilling their function. (Aguilar Schroeder 1987, pp. 15–17)

The *licenciatura* (or bachelor's degree) program at ENSV involves six summers, each consisting of two three-week semesters of intensive course work (*fase directa* or direct phase). During the rest of the year (*fase abierta* or open phase), while many are working as school teachers etc., the students are expected to study and are evaluated at intervals.

During the annual six-week direct phase the students are expected to attend classes five days a week from 7:00 a.m. to 2:30 p.m. The degree programs are organized by subject areas (English, mathematics, sciences, social sciences, and Spanish), and although students in all subject areas take the same 'basic' course work (in addition to specialized course work in their subject area), their classes throughout the six-year program are taken only with a class group identified with a specific subject area.

For the open phase students receive packets of photocopied course materials at the end of each direct phase that correspond to the courses to be offered the following summer. They are expected to do the readings and assignments outlined in the packets. Periodic evaluations of their progress are made by ENSV officials throughout the school year. At the beginning of each direct phase completed assignments are to be turned in to the instructors of the respective courses to be graded.

The official structure and titles of the courses in the ENSV program, as well as the content of the materials used in them, contain a predominance of messages and representations that stress a technical and individualistic role for teachers. The program follows closely the centralized system guidelines for teacher education programs and can thus be expected to embody many of the assumptions reflected in the state's functionally derived representation of teachers as needing to be professionalized with skills, knowledge, and techniques that advance the dominant version of socioeconomic modernization. However, conflicting messages and representations formed a significant part of both the official and especially the hidden curriculum at ENSV. With respect to the official curriculum in the Social Science Education program there was also considerable attention given to critical (Marxist, but not feminist) perspectives on historical and (less often) contemporary national and (sometimes) global political economic dynamics. The hidden curriculum contained messages of instructors generally *un*involved in institution and community-level political debates and struggles (including those associated with the teachers' movement) along with messages of student 'representatives' negotiating with individual instructors and ENSV's administration concerning evaluation practices and the quantity (but not the content) of the curriculum (see Tidwell and Ginsburg 1991).

ENSV Students' Views and Orientations

The findings presented here derive primarily from the students' responses to the open-ended questions on the questionnaires administered to the focal group in 1990, 1991 and 1992. Following the structure provided by the research questions outlined above, we will examine their views about societal problems, strategies they would employ in dealing with these problems in and outside work, their rationales for their strategies, and perceived influence during the program.

To elicit their views I asked students to respond to the following questions or statements:

1990:   Do you believe that teachers can or should be agents of social change? Why and how?
1991:   Please indicate two major economic, political, or social problems that we must try to resolve. For each problem (mentioned above) describe

what things you try or would try to do to resolve them in your
work . . . [and] outside of work.
1992:   Describe the things, if there are any, that you would try to do in your
work . . . [and] outside of work to promote important social changes.

Views of Society and Its Problems

From their responses it is clear that these students,[12] most of whom were working
as schoolteachers or educational administrators, viewed Mexican society as less
than ideal, as having a number of serious problems that needed attention. While
there was a shared sense that Mexico was beset with problems at the local, state
and national levels, the students reflected different perspectives in describing the
various problems. These perspectives are categorized in terms of the distinction
between order or equilibrium and conflict perspectives (see Horton 1966; Paulston
1977). Thirteen of the 39 students included in this analysis seemed to adopt what
might be termed an order or equilibrium perspective, within which they identified problems that had arisen in a basically salutary system and that would require
technical adjustments or reforms. In contrast, 16 students appeared to approach
their discussion from a conflict perspective, within which they identified problems
representing more serious or fundamental flaws in the political or economic system
that would require systemic changes to really address them. Finally, 10 were categorized as 'eclectic', meaning that they seemed to give voice to both perspectives.
    Female ENSV students were proportionately more likely to evidence a con-
flict perspective. Over half of the females (eight of 17), but one-third of the males
(eight of 22), were so categorized. Females (five of 17) were also disproportion-
ately overrepresented compared to males (five of 22) among those students identified as having eclectic perspectives. In contrast, male students were proportionately
more likely to evince equilibrium perspectives (nine of 22) than was the case for
female students (four of 17)
    Equilibrium and conflict perspectives were clearly contrasted in ENSV stu-
dents' comments on economic, political and educational problems.[13] The most
frequently mentioned category of problems (by 25 of the 39 respondents)[14] was
economic. From an equilibrium perspective some students mentioned social and
economic problems generally, unemployment, inflation, or external debt. These
were described as problems requiring local community or national government
efforts to change certain practices or policies that had caused the system to experience such disequilibrium or problems. For example, Hidalgo saw the problem of
unemployment as a consequence of not giving enough 'opportunities to private
companies in medium-sized towns to modernize' (1991); Nicolas stated that people could address social and economic problems by 'improving [material] conditions in neighborhoods . . . [and] searching for better jobs' (1991); Anita saw
unemployment and inflation resulting from individuals not 'preparing themselves'
sufficiently to engage in productive work (1991); and Angelina (from the equilibrium aspect of her eclectic perspective) discussed external debt as at least in part
stemming from 'economic habits of the family' and people not being 'productive
enough in [their] work' (1991).
    From a conflict perspective economic problems were more often described in
terms of inequalities, whether between social classes, rural and urban dwellers, or

developed and underdeveloped societies. In contrast to those exhibiting an equilibrium perspective, for students with a conflict perspective the problem was not seen primarily as a question of a government policy needing technical adjustment, people needing to work harder or obtain more training. Instead, economic problems resulted from certain groups being the target of 'marginalization and exploitation . . . [and] violations of human rights' (1991), as Pancho explained it. Vincente referred to 'misery' and 'poverty' and the need to 'struggle for the redistribution of wealth' (1991); Chavo spoke of the need 'to struggle to obtain better economic conditions for the most disfavored members of the population . . . [and] to demand more economic resources for the rural areas' (1991); and Xochi conceived Mexico's economic problems as resulting from 'the Mexican government, which is subservient to [the United States] . . . has squandered our financial resources obtained through the work of the most vulnerable sectors . . . and does not permit [fundamental] social change' (1990). Thus the role of government was mentioned by ENSV students with conflict perspectives; the focus was not on policies needing to be improved, but on structural problems in the political system. For example, Tomas discussed the 'situation of the economic crisis in Mexico . . . that affects deeply the people', noting that although the government is giving openings to leave the crisis, 'no change is considered that would change political structure.'

It is not surprising, therefore, that equilibrium and conflict perspectives were also evidenced as ENSV students commented on political problems — the next most frequently mentioned category of problems identified (by 22 of the 39 respondents).[15] From an equilibrium perspective the problem was defined as Mexican citizens not exercising their suffrage right, or as Mauricio put it: not 'having the participation of all the [adult] population in the elections' (1991). According to Eddy, the problem is that the Mexican people are reneging on their 'citizen obligation to select our government officials. The problem in Mexico is absenteeism — the great majority of people do not vote and are not interested in political topics' (1991).

From a conflict perspective, nonvoting was an acknowledged feature of the political landscape, but the central issues were lack of 'democracy', 'corruption' by government officials, 'imposition' of the system on the population, and 'lack of government credibility'. Pilar, for instance, expressed Mexico's political problem in terms of PRI being the 'party of the state' (1991); in other words, Mexico basically has a one-party system in which PRI dominates through its control of the government (corporatist state) apparatus, including the electoral process. Pancho also criticized the corporatist nature of Mexican politics, in his case noting that the fact that 'the unions serve the state . . . [is] one of the greatest setbacks for workers' security or welfare' and proposing that the 'arbitrariness and favoritism [*charrismo*] of union leaders must be denounced' (1991).

Equilibrium and conflict perspectives were represented among the 18 ENSV respondents who focused on educational problems[16] in their responses to the 1991 questionnaire items.[17] From an equilibrium perspective, for instance, Inez viewed illiteracy as primarily a technical problem of 'needing more schools and teachers' (1991). Arturo similarly saw educational problems as deriving from the inadequacies of the preparation or training possessed by educators, stating that he would deal with this problem personally by 'improving my teaching and preparing myself more' (1991).

In contrast, from a conflict perspective, educational problems were seen to have a political as well as a technical dimension. For Violeta, the problem of illiteracy in Mexico stemmed from a lack of public 'consciousness of the problem' that restricts students, teachers, and others in the community from doing something 'to help resolve the problem' (1991). Similarly, Marina noted the problem of 'the lack of commitment of the great majority of teachers to act as agents of social change', in discussing the need for community-based projects to address the problem of student dropout that would 'not have students conform with what is already established' but rather would encourage students to work with others 'to change the world' (1991).

Within-Work Strategies

Given the above discussed differences in perspectives on economic, political, and educational problems, one might expect that the strategies proposed or currently being pursued by these ENSV students would also be different. This was the case. The differences are apparent when we examine the categories of work-related strategies for dealing with social problems:

1 raising students' consciousness;
2 developing students' knowledge or skill;
3 changing student–teacher relations; and
4 interacting with colleagues.

Of the 39 respondents, 32 mentioned consciousness-raising as a strategy for dealing with social problems or bringing about social change. Male (18 of 22) and female (14 of 17) students were equally likely to mention this within-work strategy. However, ENSV students with at least some elements of a conflict perspective were more likely to suggest consciousness-raising (15 of the 16 conflict perspective and nine of the 10 eclectic perspective students), although a majority (eight of 13) of those with an equilibrium perspective also identified with within-work strategy. The link between societal perspective and this proposed strategy for addressing societal problems is also apparent in that consciousness-raising (and the associated pedagogical approach of 'critical didactics') seemed to mean different things to ENSV students depending on their societal perspective. For those with a conflict perspective consciousness-raising was to foment social change,[18] while those with an equilibrium perspective more often spoke of consciousness-raising in order to motivate students to participate in a society that was seen to being undergoing change. Both sets of students celebrated the value of critical thinking, but the conflict perspective students sought to combine critical thinking with action (to engage in praxis) to undertake systemic change, while the equilibrium perspective promoted critical thinking so children would become better participants within existing (or evolving) systemic arrangements. To illustrate, the following are students identified as having a conflict perspective:[19]

> . . . raise the consciousness of my students so that they will have a more critical understanding of the social reality in which they live [and so that they will help] bring about change in the structure and superstructure of our system. (Calvino 1991)

> . . . ensure that students are not only aware of [social inequalities] but that they also act to demand their rights. (Carla 1991)

> . . . raise the consciousness of students in order to break the system that subjugates them and represses the liberty of human beings. (Marina 1990)

The above statements about consciousness raising can be contrasted with those made by students reflecting an equilibrium perspective:

> . . . have students be more conscious and realistic about their expectations for the future and be oriented to be better students and citizens, inculcating in them the value of our history, patriotic values, family values, and that they can be competitive with the best. (Eugenio 1992)

> . . . raise students' consciousness so that they can be critical and value things, such as the traditions of the people to have a better country and family. (Fernando 1992)

Another category of strategies also focused on curricular and pedagogical components of the teacher's role in classrooms. This category, referred to by 18 students, involved strategies to develop children's (and/or teachers') knowledge and skill in order to make them more productive or self-sufficient. Students with at least some elements of an equilibrium perspective (nine of 13 equilibrium and six of 10 eclectic perspective students) mentioned developing knowledge and skill more so than did those with a conflict perspective (three of 16).[20] The connection between these students' societal perspectives and their use of this strategy may also be understated by these ratios. This is the case because all of those with a conflict perspective who mentioned the knowledge transmission strategy did so in combination with consciousness-raising oriented to social change efforts, which was not the case for those holding an equilibrium perspective. Thus, transmitting knowledge was not proposed by students with a conflict perspective as a technical solution unrelated to a broader system-change-oriented approach. For example, Calvino, exemplifying a conflict perspective, suggested that he wanted to teach students so that they could 'integrate themselves into the productive apparatus but with a broad vision [and heightened "consciousness"] of the social reality in which they live' (1990). In contrast, Juanita, evincing an equilibrium perspective, expressed her view of teachers as change agents in terms of 'having the students achieve significant learning for their proper development in relation to societal changes that are occurring' (1990).

Another classroom strategy for dealing with social problems was mentioned by only two respondents, one of whom had a conflict and the other had an eclectic perspective. This strategy consisted of involving students more actively and democratically in decision making in the classroom about content to be studied, assignments to be undertaken, etc. Gilda (from a conflict perspective) mentioned such 'participative methods', the topic of her thesis, as being 'necessary for encouraging students to work with their peers on issues related to their social reality' (1992). Based on conflict elements in his eclectic perspective, Arturo stated that teachers 'cannot achieve changes that are not based on examples' and that in order to end authoritarian relations in schools and society teachers must develop 'more democratic relations between teachers and students as well as among all members of educational institutions' (1992). That only two ENSV students focused their attention on shaping such messages in the 'hidden curriculum' is interesting, given that the issue of 'democracy' in ENSV classrooms was a major issue of discussion among ENSV students and frequent focus of struggle between instructors and students at ENSV (see Tidwell and Ginsburg 1991).

The final within-work strategy for dealing with social problems to be discussed here — interacting with colleagues — was also only mentioned by students with a conflict perspective (four of 13) or an eclectic perspective (two of 10). Sometimes this strategy involved efforts to raise colleagues' consciousness so that they might in turn raise the consciousness of other students, etc. Carla mentioned trying 'to influence [her] colleagues to make their curriculum more relevant' (1992) and Pilar noted that she would 'try to make her colleagues more aware of [economic inequalities]' (1991). Others saw working with colleagues as a strategy for collective struggle with educational or other government officials. For instance, in discussing the problem of the 'imposition of the system', Yolanda revealed how she would 'try to work to unite colleagues to be strong enough to oppose certain norms or rules' (1991). That three female students are quoted above signals their greater proclivity (five of 17) to promote this strategy than their male counterparts (one of 22).

Strategies Outside of Work

When asked what they would do outside of work to deal with social problems or to promote social change, ENSV students mentioned the following categories of action:

1 involvement in community projects;
2 consciousness raising focused on community members;
3 speaking out in public or contacting officials; and
4 electoral work.

Nineteen of the 39 ENSV students referred to some form of involvement in local community projects,[21] with a larger proportion of men (13 of 22) proposing involvement in community projects than that of women (six of 17). These respondents included roughly equal proportions of students from the three perspectives: seven (of 13) equilibrium perspective, four (of 10) eclectic perspective, and eight (of 16) conflict perspective. The nature of the community projects varied, however, in relation to the students' societal perspective. From an equilibrium perspective, for example, Edmundo expressed a commitment to 'promote community development . . . to protect the environment[22] and promote improvements for all' (1992) and Nicolas stated in 1991 that he would seek to deal with social and economic problems by 'working with the neighborhood to improve conditions . . . [and] search for better work, better relations'.[23] In contrast, from a conflict perspective, Pablo mentioned working in the community to 'exit or escape from the crisis in which we find ourselves' (1991) and Luis viewed his community project work as involving 'forming a defense front to counter or challenge the government's noncompliance with its obligations' (1991).

The next most frequently mentioned outside-of-work strategy was conscious-ness-raising in the community. In contrast to the case for involvement in com-munity projects, females (six of 17) were somewhat more likely to suggest consciousness-raising in the community as a strategy than were males (five of 22). Moreover, a greater proportion of conflict perspective students identified con-sciousness-raising as an outside-of-work strategy than representatives of the other societal perspectives. Of the 11 (of 39) respondents identifying this strategy, one (of 13) was an equilibrium perspective and three (of 10) were eclectic, while seven (of 16) were conflict perspective students. Consciousness-raising activities in the community were often associated with involvement in community projects (with eight of the 11 listing the former strategy also listing the latter). Thus not only was consciousness-raising in the community less likely to be anticipated by stu-dents with an equilibrium perspective, but the consciousness-raising engaged in or proposed by students with a conflict perspective was more likely to be associated with structural change (as opposed to reform or narrowly conceived 'improve-ment') projects in the community. For example, from her conflict perspective, Gilda said she was committed to 'trying to change mental structures to be open to changing the system . . . [and] to provide opportunities for new political lead-ers so they can change the social structure' (1991).

ENSV students with a conflict perspective were also more likely to discuss speaking out in public forums or contacting public officials.[24] Of the seven stu-dents mentioning this form of activity only one held an equilibrium perspective. This was Inez, who discussed 'doing surveys' about drug addiction and 'talking with local elected officials' about what she discovered (1991).[25] The six other students (four with conflict and two with eclectic perspectives) were oriented to speaking out or contacting officials in a more challenging manner. As Pancho relates, he is committed to 'defending the integrity and customs' of indigenous people and 'denouncing their marginalization and exploitation' (1991). Or as Joel describes both his current and his anticipated future actions: 'writing in local newspapers about the problem of the distribution of wealth and of the bias [in favor of the PRI] of the government' (1991). This 'public' form of political activity, moreover, was more likely to be identified by males (five of 22) than females (two of 17).

The final area highlighted (by seven of the 39 ENSV students) as an outside-of-work strategy, electoral work — building party membership and encouraging people to vote — also appeared to have a male bias to it. Marina was the only one of the 17 ENSV female students to mention electoral work, while six (of 22) male students referenced this type of 'public' political involvement. Furthermore, given the range of ideological perspectives represented among political parties in Mexico, we should not be surprised that these students reflected a range of perspectives: five (of 16) conflict, one (of 10) eclectic, and two (of 13) equilibrium. At the same time we should note the higher proportion of conflict perspective students men-tioning this outside-of-work strategy for dealing with societal problems.[26] From a conflict perspective, Chavo could relate his commitment 'to engage in political proselytizing so that people know how bad the situation is and so they can con-tribute to bringing about change' (1991) and 'to organize [people] to confront this situation, but in a positive manner' (1992). Also from a conflict perspective, Marina commented that she would 'encourage people to vote, but not only against the

Table 12.1: 1992 voting behavior of ENSV Students with different perspectives

Perspective	PRI	PRD	? Party	Not Voted	No Answer
Conflict	3	7	3	1	2
Eclectic	2	2	1	2	3
Equilibrium	2	2	1	3	3

official party [PRI] but also . . . to elect candidates who are not afraid to pursue real changes' (1992). In contrast, Huberto, reflecting an eclectic perspective, noted that he would seek to achieve some of the social changes he desired to see through 'interacting in my community, doing political work, and participating fully [within PRI] in the center of . . . the political arena' (1992). What is worth noting, however, is that the two equilibrium perspective students (Mauricio and Eugenio) who mentioned such political activity did so not in relation to PRI (or PAN) but in connection with environmental parties: the Mexican Ecologist Party and the Greenpeace Party.

Other evidence suggests that electoral work was not a major focus of these students' 'political activity'. The final phase of fieldwork at ENSV coincided with the campaign and the election for governor of the state of Veracruz. Although a few students brought campaign buttons, etc., to distribute to fellow students, the level of such activity was minimal. Moreover, although 23 (of 29 responding) indicated that they voted in the election, only three students reported on the questionnaire, administered after the election, that they had been active in the campaign — two for PRI and one for PRD.[27]

Political party support in the 1992 governor's election, not surprisingly, was associated with ENSV students' societal perspective. As can be seen in Table 12.1, based on data collected on the 1992 questionnaire, those with a conflict perspective were more likely to support the *Partido Revolucionario Democrático* (PRD), the main opposition to the *Partido Revolucionario Institucional* (PRI), the national governing party that won the election according to the official results.[28]

With respect to gender, the profile of male and female ENSV students' political party support in the 1992 governor's election was almost identical, both when examined in general or when examined within societal perspective groups.[29] With only 18 of the 39 students responding to this question and indicating the party they supported, however, this finding masks what appears to be an important gender difference in political party affiliation. This gender difference is evidenced by ENSV students' responses to the item on the 1991 questionnaire concerning their membership in or support for political parties. As can be seen in Table 12.2, while the ratio of PRI to PRD support is equal for males and females (two to one for both gender groups), female ENSV students are less likely than males to belong to or support either the governing party (PRI) or the main left opposition party (PRD). The lower proportion of females (nine of 17) in comparison to males (18 of 22) supporting either party obtains mainly because: 1) female ENSV students (four of 17) were more likely than their male counterparts (two of 22) to respond that they did not belong to or support any political party and 2) only females (two of 17) identified an 'other' party (*Partido Ecologista Mexicana*) that they supported.[30]

Table 12.2: 1991 Party identification of ENSV students by gender and societal perspective

Gender	Perspective	PRI	PRD	Other	None	No Answer
Male						
	Conflict	3	5	0	0	0
	Eclectic	3	1	0	0	1
	Equilibrium	*6*	*0*	*0*	*2*	*1*
	Total Male	12	6	0	2	2
Female						
	Conflict	2	1	1	3	1
	Eclectic	2	2	1	0	0
	Equilibrium	*2*	*0*	*0*	*1*	*1*
	Total Female	6	3	2	4	2

Constraints on 'Political' Activity

As discussed above, ENSV students in the Social Science Education program evidenced varying degrees of commitment to or involvement in different forms of what I would term 'political' activity, both in and outside of work. Four ENSV students expressed a general sense of hopelessness and powerlessness in explaining why they were less active than they recognized they might wish to be. As David stated concerning outside-of-work strategies for dealing with societal problems (lack of work and corrupt politicians): 'I cannot do anything, unfortunately' (1991). Or as Anita commented: 'Unemployment is a problem that is focused on another level; it's not in my hands' (1991).

Others were more explicit about the constraints to their political activity. The most frequently mentioned constraint concerned the existing government and dominant political party (PRI). This type of constraint was identified by 17 of the 39 ENSV students, representing approximately equal proportions of females (eight of 17) and males (nine of 22) and a somewhat higher proportion of students with a conflict perspective (nine of 16) compared to those with eclectic (three of 10) or equilibrium (five of 13) perspectives. Four of these students (both conflict and eclectic perspective students of both sexes) mentioned constraints on their social change efforts in their work, focusing on the control exercised by the central government over what they teach or how they perform their administrative roles. Angelina, for example, commented: 'In the social [studies] area I would not be able to do much because we are submerged by an autocratic government that does not think about social change' (1992). Similarly, Julio explained why he as an educator might not be able to be an agent of social change: 'Our system is not entirely free. We are to educate by indoctrinating and repeating the information [determined by the government]' (1990).

With respect to the outside-of-work strategies, all 17 of these ENSV students mentioned how the government and the dominant party (PRI) functioned to limit dissent or opposition. For example, from an equilibrium perspective, Fernando explained part of the reason he did not vote in the 2 August 1992 governor's election: 'I'm not interested because [elections] have become a joke since PRI always wins' (1992). From her eclectic perspective, Teche similarly confided why she did not vote:

> No political participation interests me because they do not present alternatives to the economic, social and political situation in which we live. The imposition of Chirinos as a [gubernatorial] candidate of PRI by [Mexican President] Salinas bothers me. Political centralism is at its highest point. (1992)

From a conflict perspective, Elena commented on the 1992 state governor's election and the 1988 national presidential election that she was 'greatly disillusioned when the results did not reflect how [she perceived] people actually voted . . . If no democracy exists, then it's not worth voting' (1992).

   Other explanations of limited activity ranged from international dynamics (mentioned by one male and one female students with conflict perspectives) to personal factors (cited by two females and one male, representing all three perspectives). In terms of international dynamics, for example, Xochi discussed the problem of US intervention in Mexico's affairs under the guise of curtailing drug trafficking: 'We cannot do anything. I only hope that the [US's] inclination toward drug addiction ends up destroying [US] society' (1991). Personal factors noted as reasons for not being more active politically in or outside of work included not having the time, knowledge, skill or personality for activism. Pilar, for instance, commented: 'I do not like to go to political party meetings or to mobilize people. I do not have the strong personality of a leader' — a statement contradicted somewhat by her involvement in class negotiations with instructors over workload and evaluation issues.

Influence of ENSV on Students

To what extent are the ideological perspectives, favored strategies, and rationales for them the result of what the students brought to the ENSV experience and/or what they encountered while enrolled in this six-year program? Directly assessing how much the students changed during this time is hampered because the study began in the third year of their program and more in-depth data on their views etc. were not collected until their fourth summer at ENSV. Nevertheless, some changes are observable across administrations of the questionnaire and many of the students reported how their ideas and (less clearly) their practices were shaped by their experiences in the program.

   When asked about the influence of ENSV in 1991 and 1992 three students (interestingly, one conflict perspective and two equilibrium perspective students) reported that the program had very little, if any, influence on their ideas or practices. The rest identified one or more ways in which they perceived they changed or were influenced by their experiences during the program, via readings, lectures, class discussions, or more informal interaction with instructors and (more so) peers.[31] At the same time many students (both those who did and did not perceive program influences) seem to agree with Benito and Xochi, who respectively noted that their work experiences and information they encountered in the media during this time period may have had more of an impact on them than the formal (and perhaps the hidden) curriculum of the program.

Thirteen of the 39 ENSV students acknowledged that they had learned about and developed increased capacity as a classroom instructor. These 13 were represented by a somewhat greater proportion of females (eight of 17) than males (five of 22), but approximately the same proportion of equilibrium perspective (six of 13) as conflict perspective (six of 16) students.[32] Societal perspectives were related to the nature of what they learned. Those with an equilibrium perspective (regardless of their gender) made reference generally to skills and techniques that they had learned and believed would improve their effectiveness, while those with a conflict perspective usually emphasized their exposure to and capacity to engage in what many of them termed 'critical didactics'. For example, Juanita stated that 'peers helped me to understand better the practice of teaching' (1992). From her conflict perspective, Violeta noted that while at ENSV, she 'personally and academically learned a lot about teaching and learning . . . and had been encouraged to try to get the students to be more reflexive . . . and know better the reality in which we live' (1992).

On a more general level 20 students reported that their experiences during their enrollment in ENSV resulted in their social consciousness being raised, which entailed alerting them to the range and severity of societal problem and orienting them to become actively involved in social change efforts (of the different types discussed above). A somewhat greater proportion of females (12 of 17) than males (12 of 22) mentioned such program influences. The consciousness-raising influence of the program was also more likely to be noted by conflict perspective (12 of 16) than eclectic perspective (five of 10) or, especially, equilibrium perspective (five of 13) students.

Nevertheless, all categories of students appeared to have undergone some degree and form of consciousness-raising while enrolled at ENSV. This meant that someone like Mauricio, who toward the end of the program still seemed to exhibit an equilibrium perspective, could remark about his program experience: ENSV 'provided me with a chance to reflect on social change and the need for such' (1991) and '[ENSV] has taught me to be reflexive and involved, to form a critical sense; I have transformed my manner of thinking' (1992).[33] It also means that Pancho, whose conflict perspective was well established before I began my fieldwork during the third summer of his program, viewed the program in similar terms: 'the influence at ENSV on my form of thinking and acting has been radical' (1991); the readings and other experiences at ENSV 'have been fundamental in changing my thinking, which was very conformist' (1992); and [now I have a] 'strong commitment to work for change to improve the life of my students and others' (1992).

The nature and outcome of such consciousness-raising, however, seemed to have varied by the societal perspective. This is apparent, for instance, when examining the statements of Alberto (equilibrium perspective) and Gilda (conflict perspective). Alberto reported that the program influenced him to 'search for an equilibrium, firstly between each person and the others' (1991), while Gilda described being influenced during the program by exposure to 'some Marxist economic theory, complemented by the contribution of [instructors] immersed in the material' (1991).

Two other students, Teche (eclectic perspective) and Linda (conflict perspective), are important to discuss because changes in their thinking (and perhaps action) were not only remarked on but are evidenced in how they responded to items on the questionnaires during the course of the study. In 1990 Teche remarked that as a teacher 'I would pursue [social change] but it is difficult to do so.' In 1991 she expressed the desire to engage in more consciousness-raising in her teaching, while she suggested that outside of work: 'I need to participate more actively in political issues, but in ways that are congruent with my thinking.' At this point she also explained that ENSV has 'definitely influenced me. I have recognized, ratified, and rectified certain ideological schemes' (1991). By the end of the program, though, we see her continuing struggle with the ideas she has encountered, her understandings of the social context, and who she is as a person. With respect to her work situation she informed me: 'I am very ambitious to try to bring about social change . . . [through the] teaching of social sciences' (1992). When asked about social change strategies outside of work, Teche confided 'paradoxically, I'm not interested in social and political militancy' (1992). Her comments about the influence of the program seem to reflect this paradox of working for social change in the classroom but not being engaged in social change efforts outside of work. She indicated that ENSV 'has influenced my critical thought, helping me to remember and reevaluate technical–methodological aspects involved in the practice of teaching' (1992).

Linda seems to have been struggling with similar issues, though ending up with a somewhat different perspective and orientation to action (especially outside of work). She commented in 1990 that teachers are and should be agents of social change 'always when they know the field and the propitious moment to do so.' In 1991 Linda expressed commitment both in her work to 'raising students' consciousness to prevent [government] corruption' and outside of work to 'try to be productive, honest, and conscious of social problems.' She also related that ENSV 'has influenced me by showing that we . . . can achieve personal improvement in order to help those around us economically, politically, and socially' (1991). Toward the end of the program she retained her commitment to consciousness-raising through her teaching: 'make students more aware of our reality, make them feel that we can be change agents for our community' (1992). Linda stated that outside of work, 'I would begin with myself and my family to be more active in what is referred to as contributing to education and in the terrain of politics. I would start at the level of my community and then expand the focus' (1992). She concluded by noting that the most important aspect of her experience at ENSV was the 'modification of my form of thinking with respect to my work. [ENSV] also awakened me to become more engaged with the problems of society' (1992).

Conclusion

This examination of the views and experiences of students in a teacher education program in Mexico not only indicates how important the political dimension is in teacher education, but also how complex the processes of political socialization are in one setting, let alone across contexts.[34] We have seen how perceptions of societal problems and the strategies for dealing with such problems varies among students in the program as well as — at least for some students — over the course of their enrollment in the program. Here we have focused on differences among male and female students of different societal perspectives.

Male and female students in the Social Sciences Education strand at ENSV undoubtedly brought with them differences in perspectives and orientations to political action derived from previous experiences. Their ideas, however, seem to have undergone some changes during the six year program. Overall, the program seems to have encouraged them to devote more attention to societal problems — political, economic and educational. These problems (and their solutions), though, can be viewed from different perspectives, all of which received some attention in the program. While some students' perspectives on these problems appeared to change during the course of their involvement at ENSV, it appears that the messages encountered in the program's formal and hidden curriculum were just as often filtered through (and thus acted to reinforce) relatively stable societal perspectives. Thus we organized the presentation of the findings around how students with conflict, eclectic, and equilibrium perspectives viewed societal problems and strategies for dealing with them.

The conflict perspective students were more likely to see the local and national problems faced by Mexico to be fundamental, requiring systemic changes. In contrast, those with an equilibrium perspective focused on how individual attitudes and behaviors would need to be changed so that the problems could be overcome. This difference between conflict and equilibrium perspective students is reinforced by the fact that the former gave more emphasis to political and economic problems, while the latter more often stressed educational problems. Eclectic perspective students, as noted, combined elements from both of the other two perspectives.

In terms of in-work strategies for addressing these problems, equilibrium perspective students focused more attention on developing children's and teachers' knowledge and skill, whereas conflict perspective students were not only more likely to mention consciousness raising but also tended to define the goal of such efforts as fomenting social movements to promote social change (versus preparing people to adapt to changes taking place — as those with an equilibrium perspective often framed the strategy). Conflict perspective students tended to give more attention to intervening in the hidden curriculum of their primary or secondary school classrooms, highlighting the need to democratize decision making in classrooms and to engage in collaboration with teacher colleagues in dealing with problems.

The outside-of-work arena for political action was more often a concern for those ENSV students with a conflict perspective. This may in part reflect the fact that the ideas of equilibrium perspective students are more in tune with those of the government and governing party (PRI), thus reducing the perceived need to engage in active participation to shape political discourse and action that already reflects many of their views and concerns. Certainly conflict perspective students more often mentioned the existing government and PRI as a constraint in their efforts as teachers to be change agents. However, there also appears to be a more general difference between the two groups. Equilibrium perspective students tended to view the teacher's role as limited to classroom or school level activity defined as their job, with outside-of-work political activities only being required (or advisable) when necessary to support directly such in-school efforts. In contrast, more conflict perspective students conceive of the teacher's role as involving social change efforts both in *and* outside of school. Hence while students with both perspectives were equally likely to refer to involvement in community projects, conflict perspective students were more likely to see themselves engaged in speaking at public forums, contacting government officials, and participating in electoral campaigns. Moreover, the types of community projects identified by conflict perspective students were more oriented to systemic change (versus refining, extending, or strengthening existing institutions) than was the case among those with an equilibrium perspective.

It is important to remember that conflict, eclectic and equilibrium perspectives were held by male and female students. Thus we examined the importance of gender in ENSV students' views of societal problems and the strategies they proposed for dealing with such problems. First we noted that males were more likely to evidence equilibrium perspectives, while females tended to exhibit conflict or eclectic perspectives. This perhaps reflects differences in their previous experiences in homes, schools, and communities, where females (in comparison and in relation to males) would have been more likely to find themselves in subordinate or oppressed situations, what Horton (1966) claims is an experiential basis for the development of conflict perspectives. We should note that neither female nor male ENSV students referred to gender relations or women's subordination in discussion of major economic, political, and cultural problems — perhaps reflecting the success of the ideology of national unity in smoothing over conflicts and contradictions based on gender.[35] Nevertheless, women students' experience of status and power deprivation may translate into a more generalized orientation to view social relations from a conflict perspective. It may also be that, in the context of the existing gendered division of labor in households, schools, and communities, conflict perspective females would be more motivated and able to negotiate space in their lives to add to their lives six summers of intensive coursework plus assignments during the rest of the year.

Some important gender differences were also noted with respect to strategies to be pursued in dealing with societal problems. In the work setting male and female ENSV students were equally likely to mention consciousness-raising, but females gave more emphasis to developing students' and teachers' knowledge and to collaborating with colleagues to address various societal problems in school. The latter finding may reflect female ENSV students' stronger sense of — and concern for — interpersonal networks and community, something that seems to be more often associated with women than men educators (Weiler 1988).

Outside-of-work strategies were referenced more often by male than female ENSV students, although there was a slightly higher proportion of women mentioning consciousness-raising activities in the community. Men were more likely than women to see themselves actively working on community development projects, speaking at public forums, contacting public officials, and participating in electoral campaigns. This greater tendency by male ENSV students may stem from both their having on average less extensive responsibilities in the 'private' sphere of the home and family and their receiving greater cultural support for participation in the 'public sphere'. In contrast, female ENSV students may have less life space, because of greater household and family responsibilities, while at the same time having to confront the cultural (and structural) blocks against women's active participation in the public arena. We observed that women ENSV students were more likely to identify personal factors (including lack of time available, but also perceived lack of ability or interest) as constraints limiting their active involvement. We also noted that women ENSV students' projected political involvement outside of work was concentrated in consciousness-raising — an activity that represents a direct extension of the 'private' sphere, household and classroom roles that have come to be conceived as in line with cultural notions of femininity (Corr and Jamieson 1990). Moreover, female ENSV students were less likely than their male counterparts to belong to or strongly identify with either the governing party (PRI) or its major challenger (PRD), perhaps signaling some degree of inhospitality toward women in such organizations. For example, it may be that in general the power-over (versus the power-with) aspect of power (see Kreisberg 1992) that dominates in existing political parties makes them seem less congenial to women.

If it is critical to identify the political implications of the decisions that educators make on a daily basis (Ginsburg 1995; Ginsburg *et al.* 1992), then it is essential that we analyze the political socialization processes that we and other colleagues in universities, schools, churches, families, the media, and other institutions organize for preservice and in-service teachers as well as ourselves (Ginsburg 1988). We must remember that the political is personal *and* the personal is political. We need to reflect on our own and others' activity, and we need to consider seriously the political implications of what we do. The choice is not about being 'political' or 'apolitical' or about being involved or not being involved in political socialization, but about pursuing strategies of political socialization (and other forms of political activity) that are relatively active or passive; autonomous or heteronomous *vis-à-vis* other groups; conservative or change-oriented; focused on individual, occupational group, or larger collectivities' goals; and allied to dominant or subordinate group interests. This chapter hopefully moves us to a fuller understanding of these issues, at least as they were worked out in the Social Sciences Education strand of the ENSV program in Xalapa, Veracruz, Mexico.

Notes

1 This chapter is a revision of a paper presented to the Comparative and International Education Society annual conference, Kingston, Jamaica, 16–19 March 1993. I would like to thank Gilda Rodriguez Gabarron Holly for her help in clarifying the meaning of some of the responses to the open-ended items on the questionnaires, Hugo Zegarra for his assistance in reviewing some of the relevant literature, and Monte Tidwell for his collaboration on various aspects of the overall project. The research was in part sponsored by the Center for Latin American Studies Faculty Research Grant and the School of Education Faculty Research Grant programs at the University of Pittsburgh.
2 In addition to focusing on ENSV the larger research project also included fieldwork in a primary teacher education program at the *Escuela Normal Veracruzana* (Ginsburg 1992, 1994) and in a program designed to prepare secondary teachers, counselors, and administrators at the *Universidad Veracruzana* (Ginsburg and Tidwell 1990).
3 In this chapter gender was the only characteristic of the students that was systematically examined in analyzing political perspectives and current or ongoing political activities. In subsequent analyses marital status, having children, large or small city residence, and number of years and institutional level of teaching experience may also be examined.
4 During the summer of 1990 a group of third-year students were also observed by another researcher (see Tidwell and Ginsburg 1991) during two days at the end of their fifth three-week semester and during the entire three weeks of their sixth

semester that summer. Formal, semi-structured interviews were conducted with a representative sample of students and instructors during a fourth week of ethnographic fieldwork. Although these data are not drawn on in detail for this paper, they do provide a more sustained, in-depth look at another group of students during one phase of their program.

5   There is considerable disagreement among scholars (and others) regarding whether the Mexican Revolution should be seen as a continuing process or one that reached closure either in 1917 or the 1930s (see Ross 1975). While *campesinos* or peasants and other workers who played important roles during the revolutionary war (and subsequently) and even though some significant economic and political changes occurred, I would basically label this as a bourgeois revolution, in that it 'did not produce radical changes in the class structure of society' (Morales Gomez and Torres 1990, p. 10). One also needs to problematize the labeling of Mexico as a democratic polity since there continues to be questions both with respect to procedural and substantive definitions of democracy. For instance, concerns about inequities in the distribution of both political power and the material benefits derived from economic activity featured strongly in the January 1994 uprising which took place in Chiapas, Mexico by the Zapatista National Liberation Army (Hernandez 1994; Taibo 1994).

6   It is important to observe that the North American Free Trade Agreement (NAFTA), or as it is labeled in Spanish, *El Tratado de Libre Comercio* (TLC), which went into effect on 1 January 1994 (the same date the Chiapas uprising was launched) does not mark the initial penetration of US-based corporate capital into Mexico. Rather it opens a new era of intensified capital penetration — one arguably not seen in the post-revolutionary period. However, the US and Mexico had a free-trade agreement, at least for border states, which was initially established in 1861 and expanded during the first years of Porfirio Diaz's 'dictatorship' in 1877.

7   Loaeza (1984) argues that the original sense of education as an institution that promotes opportunity and social solidarity has been substantially weakened after 1970 when education's contribution to individual social mobility began to decline.

8   SNTE was formed in 1943 with the intervention of PRI and government leaders as part of a more generalized effort to unify the organizations of workers in order to link them in corporatist relations with the Mexican state (Alba 1969; McGinn and Street 1984; Morales Gomez and Torres 1990).

9   It is interesting to note that before the 1910–17 revolution 'Mexican teachers were sent off to the United States for training and told to observe the North American behavior as a model of *order* and development' (Estrada and La Belle 1981, p. 292; emphasis added).

10 Here I am not arguing that the programs necessarily functioned politically to socialize teachers in the way that political élites or union leaders desired, but only that those in power had political socialization in mind as they planned and struggled over the content and organization of teacher education.

11 One of the explanations for the decentralization initiatives promoted by PRI and the Mexican state — initially by the Lopez Portillo administration in 1978 and reemphasized by the Salinas de Gortari administration a decade later — was that it was a strategy to weaken organized teachers (McGinn and Street 1984; Ornelas Navarro 1984; Prawda 1992). Interestingly, the strategy could serve to undermine the power of both 1) the *Vangardia Revolucionaria* (VR), which dominated the national teachers' union (SNTE) and thus had considerable influence in the *Secretaría de Educacion Pública* (SEP), and 2) the CNTE-led dissidents, whose objectives included unseating the leader of the VR and SNTE, Carlos Jongitud Barrios, as well as challenging the corporatist nature of the Mexican state. (Note that in the 'victory' of the teachers' movement in 1989 only the first objective and a moderate salary raise was achieved.) By administratively decentralizing responsibility (if not

authority) for education and teacher education PRI and state élites could reduce SNTE's nationally organized influence on policy making, while simultaneously keeping localized the growing presence of the CNTE-led dissident teachers' movement to the states where CNTE had already established a significant presence.

12 The names of the students have been changed to protect their identity and ensure confidentiality of their responses.

13 Other problems mentioned by ENSV students (with the number of students noting each) included: drug addiction and alcoholism (four); problems of sexuality, such as abortion, promiscuity, and pornography (four); contamination or destruction of the environment (four), and negative effects of television (two). These 14 individual students (one student mentioned two of these other categories of problems) were proportionately more likely to have equilibrium perspectives (seven of 13) than eclectic (four of 10) or conflict perspective (four of 16). Female ENSV students (seven of 14) were somewhat more likely to mention these other categories of 'major social economic, social, and political problems' than their male counterparts (seven of 22).

14 ENSV students with conflict perspectives (12 of 16) were proportionately more likely to mention economic problems than either equilibrium (eight of 13) or eclectic (four of 10) perspective students. ENSV students referencing economic problems also included a slightly higher proportion of males (15 of 22) than females (10 of 17).

15 These 22 students mentioning political problems were proportionately more likely to have conflict perspectives (12 of 16) than either eclectic (six of 10) or equilibrium (three of 13) perspectives. Males (12 of 22) and females (10 of 17) were almost equally likely to mention economic problems.

16 Although not surprising that educators would refer to 'educational problems', it should be remembered that the questionnaire item to which they were responding refers to 'major economic, political, or social problems that we must try to resolve'. Thus a focus on education problems for ENSV students (as with some educational reformers — see Ginsburg *et al.* 1991) may serve, consciously or unconsciously, to deflect attention from broader and more fundamental economic and political problems.

17 Those with conflict perspectives (three of 16) were much less likely to mention educational problems than either eclectic (seven of 10) or equilibrium (eight of 13) perspective students. In terms of gender, male ENSV students (11 of 22) were somewhat more likely to mention educational problems than their female counterparts (seven of 17).

18 ENSV students who evidenced a conflict perspective, however, recognized the fine line between consciousness-raising and indoctrination. For example, Joel expressed that, as agents of social change, teachers 'can and should use critical didactics to offer to students the liberty to decide for themselves about their social surroundings' (1990). Similarly, Pilar urged that such consciousness-raising efforts to promote change be moderated. This was based on her experience as an undergraduate student at the *Universidad Metropolitana*, which she described as 'a period of crisis' for her because it 'undermined the credibility of all of [her] values, beliefs, and interpretations of the world' (1990). In 1991 Pilar also shared about these 'terrible experiences' but reported how she shifted (somewhat) away from a strongly anti-capitalist, anti-imperialist perspective — which had been enough in evidence that her 'mother told [her] to quit being a student because [Pilar seemed like she] was going to become a guerilla'. Interestingly, this was when the (former) Soviet Union invaded Afghanistan in 1981.

19 Some students evidenced conflict elements of their eclectic perspectives when discussing consciousness-raising. For example, Barbara stated that teachers can

and should be agents of social change because they 'have the difficult task of creating a critical consciousness in [students] about the need for changes in the social reality' (1990) and Huberto commented that teachers can and should be agents of social change by helping 'students to reflect, think for themselves, and analyze the situation from different points of view' (1990).

20 That the only three conflict perspective students mentioning this strategy were women contributes to the fact that females (nine of 17) were somewhat more likely to identify this strategy than males (nine of 22).

21 The number of students oriented to community projects could be increased to 23 if we were to include the four additional respondents who mentioned adult literacy work (either in the school or the community). These four (three male and one female) ENSV students were comprised of one with a conflict, two with an eclectic, and one with an equilibrium perspective.

22 Environmental concerns were also mentioned by Carla (with a conflict perspective), Lily (with an eclectic perspective), and Eugenio and Mauricio (with equilibrium perspectives).

23 In response to the 1992 questionnaire, however, Nicolas responded 'for the moment, no' to the query about outside of work activities to promote social change.

24 Interestingly, those with a conflict perspective also were more likely (four conflict to one equilibrium perspective students) to mention self-improvement (increased knowledge or skill) as an outside-of-work strategy for dealing with social problems or promoting social change. The prominence of conflict perspective students across all the categories of outside-of-work strategies reflects the fact that the equilibrium perspective students either did not mention any such strategies or only mentioned one (versus two or more for many conflict perspective students).

25 Three other ENSV students mentioned a research role for dealing with social problems — two exhibiting a conflict perspective and one an eclectic perspective. Note the difference between Inez reporting her results from a survey of drug addiction with Luis's plan 'to do an investigation of the Mexican political system, since it is one of the most corrupt and one in which the people's will is less often respected' (1992).

26 That a slightly higher proportion of conflict perspective students (compared to eclectic or equilibrium perspective students) identified involvement in electoral politics as an outside-of-work strategy for dealing with social change, along with the earlier reported tendency for conflict perspective students to identify political problems, suggest that students with other perspectives may see less need to intervene personally in electoral politics for their social change goals to be addressed by the state and national government.

27 Some caution has to be made in interpreting the limited involvement in this campaign, in that the 7:00 a.m. to 2:30 p.m. class schedule five days a week, not to mention readings, preparation for presentations, projects, and other assignments made it difficult to free up much time during the last three weeks of the campaign. Indeed, one student in the group, Joel, opted out of the program during the entire summer of 1992 in order to take an active role in the PRD candidate's campaign. Also, we should observe that some of the students were away from their electoral districts while attending ENSV, because they resided and worked in other regions of the state than Xalapa.

28 The data on voting obtained on the 1992 questionnaire understates the equilibrium perspective students' support for PRI because only five of the 13 ENSV students with this perspective could be categorized with respect to party support. As is demonstrated in the table below, based on response to the 1991 questionnaire item about party membership or support, equilibrium perspective students were very likely to be members or support the PRI. In 1991 conflict perspective students were somewhat more likely to report membership in or support of the

PRD, though there was greater evidence of identifying with PRI than was the case in their responses to question about voting for governor in 1992.

*1991 party membership/support of
ENSV students with different perspectives*

Perspective	PRI	PRD	Other	None	No Answer
Conflict	5	6	1	3	3
Eclectic	5	3	1	0	1
Equilibrium	8	0	0	3	2

29 Among the 17 female ENSV students, four voted for the PRI and five voted for the PRD candidate. Among the 22 male ENSV students three voted for the PRI and six voted for the PRD candidate. These small gender differences in the proportion of students voting for PRI versus PRD are not emphasized because of the substantial number of ENSV students (eight females and 13 males) who either did not respond to this question, did not vote, or voted but did not indicate the party they supported.

30 Note that two males and two females did not respond to the question about party membership or support.

31 Perceived lack of influence is distinguished here from the notion, expressed by Hidalgo and Julio, that their views or ideas were strengthened by the program.

32 One of the ENSV students referring to his developing teaching skills during the program had an eclectic perspective.

33 Mauricio's involvement with ecological concerns may, in fact, indicate a shift away from an equilibrium perspective.

34 Cross-national and historical comparisons (Ginsburg and Raghu 1992) as well as cross-institutional comparisons are needed. In line with the latter type of comparison, the investigation at ENSV (see also Tidwell and Ginsburg 1991) constitutes part of a larger study involving concurrently two other institutions in Xalapa, Veracruz, Mexico: *Escuela Normal Veracruzana* (see Ginsburg 1992 and 1994) and the *Facultad de Pedagogía* at the Universidad Veracruzana (see Ginsburg and Tidwell 1990).

35 For example, when I raised questions about gender relations in schooling and society, male and female ENSV students would often deflect my queries by saying that they were based on North American and western European cultural notions that were not relevant to the Mexican context.

References

AGUILAR, P. and RETAMAL, G. (1982) 'Ideological trends and the education of teachers in latin America', in GOODINGS, R. BYRAM, M. and PARTLAND, M. (Eds) *Changing Priorities in Teacher Education*, London, Croom Helm, pp. 140–59.

AGUILAR SCHROEDER, P. (1987) 'Discurso', in ESCUELA NORMAL SUPERIOR VERACRUZANA (Ed) *Ceremonia Inaugural de Cursos*, Quetzalcoatl, Veracruz, ENSV, pp. 15–20.

ALBA, V. (1969) 'Mexico', in BLUM, A. (Ed) *Teacher Unions and Associations: A Comparative Study*, Urbana, IL, University of Illinois Press, pp. 200–32.

ARRIAGA, M. (1981) 'El Magisterio en Lucha', *Cuadernos Politicos*, 27, January–March, pp. 79–101.

BARTRA, R. (1989) 'Culture and political power in Mexico', trans. Susan Casal-Sanchez, *Latin American Perspectives*, **61**, 16, pp. 61–69.

BOGDAN, R. and BIKLEN, S. (1992) *Qualitative Research for Education: An Introduction to Theory and Methods*, Boston, MA; Allyn and Bacon.

CAMPOS, J., CANO, A., HERNANDEZ, L., PEREZ ARCE, F., ROJO, C., SALINAS, G., STREET, S., TAIBO II, P., VARGAS, R., and VAQUEZ, P. (1990) *De las Aulas a las Calles*, Pueblo, Informacion Obrero.

COCKCROFT, J. (1990) *Mexico: Class Formation, Capital Accumulation, and the State*, New York, Monthly Review Press.

CORR, H. and JAMIESON, L. (Eds) (1990) *Politics of Everyday Life*, London, Macmillan.

CORTINA, R. (1989) 'Women as leaders in Mexican education', *Comparative Education Review*, **33**, 3, pp. 357–76.

ESTRADA, L. and LA BELLE, T. (1981) 'Mexican education', in IGNAS, E. and CORSINI, R. (Eds) *Comparative Educational Systems*, Itasca, IL, F.E. Peacock, pp. 285–324.

GINSBURG, M. (1988) *Contradictions in Teacher Education and Society: A Critical Analysis*, London, Falmer Press.

GINSBURG, M. (1992) 'Learning to Be (A)political Actors: The Education of Teachers in Mexico', paper presented at the American Educational Research Association annual meeting, San Francisco, 20–24 April.

GINSBURG, M. (1994) 'Aprendiendo a Ser Actores Políticos: La Educación de Maestros en México', *Punto y Seguida*, 7, pp. 17–20.

GINSBURG, M. (Ed) (1995) *The Politics of Educators' Work and Lives*, New York, Garland Publishing.

GINSBURG, M. and CLIFT, R. (1990) 'The hidden curriculum of preservice teacher education', in HOUSTON, W.R. (Ed) *Handbook of Research on Teacher Education*, New York, Macmillan, pp. 450–65.

GINSBURG, M., COOPER, S., RAGHU, R. and ZEGARRA, H. (1991) 'Educational reform: Social struggle, the state and the world economic system', in GINSBURG, M. (Ed) *Understanding Educational Reform: Economy, Ideology and the State*, New York, Garland, pp. 3–47.

GINSBURG, M., KAMAT, S., RAGHU, R. and WEAVER, J. (1992) 'Educators/Politics', *Comparative Education Review*, **36**, 4, pp. 417–45.

GINSBURG, M. and RAGHU, R. (1992) 'Teacher Education as Political Socialization: Cases of Germany and Mexico', paper presented at the World Congress of Comparative Education, Prague, Czechoslovakia, 8–14 July.

GINSBURG, M. and TIDWELL, M. (1990) 'Political socialization of prospective educators in Mexico: The case of the University of Veracruz', *New Education*, **12**, 2, pp. 70–82.

GOETZ, J. and LECOMPTE, M. (1984) *Ethnography and Qualitative Design in Educational Research*, New York, Academic Press.

GONZALEZ NAVARRO, M. (1975) 'The ideology of the Mexican revolution', in S. Ross (Ed) *Is the Mexican Revolution Dead?* 2nd edn, Philadelphia, PA; Temple University Press, pp. 177–87.

GUTIERREZ BARRIOS, C.F. (1987) 'Discurso', in ESCUELA NORMAL SUPERIOR VERACRUZANA (Ed) *Ceremonia Inaugural de Cursos*, Quetzalcoatl, Veracruz, ENSV, pp. 5–9.

HERNANDEZ, L. (1994) 'The New Mayan War', *NACLA Report on the Americas*, **27**, 5, pp. 6–10.

HORTON, J. (1966) 'Order and conflict theories of social problems as competing ideologies', *American Journal of Sociology*, **71**, May, pp. 710–13.

IMAZ, C. and SALINAS, S. (1984) *Maestros y Estado*, Vols I and II, Mexico City, Editorial Linea.

KREISBERG, S. (1992) *Transforming Power*, Albany, NY, State University of New York Press.

LECHUGA, G. (1984) 'Introduccion', in LECHUGA, G. (Ed) *Ideología Educativa de la Revolución Mexicana*, Xochimilco, Universidad Autonoma Metropolitana, pp. 9–18.

LEHMBRUCH, G. and SCHMITTER, P. (Eds) (1992) *Patterns of Capitalist Policy Making*, Beverly Hills, CA, Sage.

LOAEZA, S. (1984) 'La Educacion Nacional entre 1940 y 1970', in LECHUGA, G. (Ed) *Ideología Educativa de la Revolución Mexicana*, Xochimilco: Universidad Autonoma Metropolitana, pp. 97–111.

McGINN, N. and STREET, S. (1984) 'Has Mexican education generated human or political capital?' *Comparative Education*, **20**, 3, pp. 323–37.

MORALES GOMEZ, D. and TORRES, C.A. (1990) *The State, Corporatist Politics and Educational Policy-Making in Mexico*, New York, Praeger.

NORIEGA, B.M. (1985) *La Politica Educativa: A Traves de la Politica de Financiamiento*, Mexico City, Universidad Autonoma de Sinaloa.

ORNELAS NAVARRO, C. (1984) 'La Educacion Técnica y la Ideología de la Revolución Mexicana', in LECHUGA, G. (Ed) *Ideología Educativa de la Revolución Mexicana*, Xochimilco: Universidad Autonoma Metropolitana, pp. 33–63.

PAULSTON, R. (1977) 'Social and educational change: Conceptual frameworks', *Comparative Education Review*, **21**, 2–3, pp. 370–95.

PERISSINOTTO, G. (1974) 'Educational reform and government intervention in Mexico', *Current History*, May, pp. 208–11, 226.

PESCADOR, J.A. (1988) 'Mexico', in POSTLETHWAITE, T.N. (Ed) *The Encyclopedia of Comparative Education and National Systems of Education*, Oxford, Pergamon, pp. 482–5.

PINA SANCHEZ, R. (1987) 'Discurso', in ESCUELA NORMAL SUPERIOR VERACRUZANA (Ed) *Ceremonia Inaugural de Cursos*, Quetzalcoatl, Veracruz, ENSV, pp. 10–14.

PRAWDA, J. (1992) *Educational Decentralization in Latin America: Lessons Learned*, Report No. 27, Washington, DC, World Bank.

ROSS, S. (1975) *Is the Mexican Revolution Dead?* 2nd edn, Philadelphia, PA, Temple University Press.

SECRETARIA DE EDUCACION PUBLICA (SEP) (1984) *Plan de Estudios, Licenciatura en Educacion Primaria* (*Plan of Studies, Licenciatura in Primary Education*), Mexico City, SEP.

SECRETARIA DE EDUCACION PUBLICA (SEP) (1989) *Programa para la Modernizacion Educativa: 1989–1994* (*Program for Educational Modernization: 1989–1994*), Mexico City, SEP.

SPRADLEY, J. (1979) *The Ethnographic Interview*, New York, Holt.

SPRADLEY, J. (1980) *Participant Observation*, New York, Holt.

STREET, S. (1989) 'El Magisterio Democrático y el Aparato Burocrático del Estado', *Foro Universitario*, January–April, pp. 7–24.

TAIBO II, P.I. (1994) 'Images of chiapas: Zapatista! The phoenix rises', *The Nation*, **258**, 12, pp. 406–10.

TIDWELL, M. and GINSBURG, M. (1991) 'Teacher Education and the Social Construction of Political Actors in Mexico', paper presented at the American Educational Research Association annual meeting, Chicago, 3–7 April.

TORRES, C.A. (1991) 'State corporatism, educational policies, and students' and teachers' movements in Mexico', in GINSBURG, M. (Ed) *Understanding Educational Reform in Global Context*, New York, Garland, pp. 115–50.

WEILER, K. (1988) *Women Teaching for Change*, Albany, NY, State University of New York Press.

ZEICHNER, K. and GORE, J. (1990) 'Teacher socialization', in HOUSTON, W.R. (Ed) *Handbook of Research on Teacher Education*, New York, Macmillan, pp. 329–48.

Chapter 13

Transforming Teacher Education in Papua New Guinea: A Framework for Sustainable Professional Development in Community Teachers Colleges

Clarrie Burke

At this time the education system in Papua New Guinea is responding to a major government review of education at all levels. The *Education Sector Review* (Department of Education 1991) is currently having a major determining effect on the reformulation of policy and planning, which is reshaping the structure and operation of the school system at all levels. This has resulted in a high priority being placed on breaking the cycle of low teaching standards leading to low pupil performance and underachievement in the primary school system. Apart from improving education for primary school leavers, the policy is intended to enhance the quality of students entering secondary schools, and to have a 'flow-on effect' to various forms of postsecondary education.

For some years the key to raising primary school standards has been considered to lie in improving the professional capability of primary teachers' college lecturers, who in turn, would contribute significantly towards appropriate preservice and in-service professional development of primary teachers (AIDAB 1989; McNamara 1989). The rise of this position has coincided with the shift that has taken place in teacher education philosophy in Papua New Guinea away from the centralized, bureaucratic, standardized emphasis on 'basic skills' and the 'skilled technician', towards a more devolved, institutional-based approach to 'critically reflective practice' and 'meaningful teaching'. This represents a significant shift in the political socialization of teacher educators and teachers in Papua New Guinea. The approach is considered appropriate to the recently extended preservice teacher education course for primary teachers from two to three years and to the educational needs and priorities outlined in the *Education Sector Review* and the *National Higher Education Plan* (Commission for Higher Education 1990).

In recognition of the need for improved professional development of teachers college lecturers to enable them to carry out the changes in philosophy, policy and approach, the Australian government has provided 'tied aid' in the form of an Aus$3 million grant over five years, through the establishment of the Papua New Guinea Community Teachers College Lecturers Professional Development Project, 1990–94 (AIDAB 1989). The project is managed by Queensland University of Technology.

This chapter examines the transformative approach — and the inherent political (re)socialization — adopted by the project. The approach derives from the contemporary social, economic and political context, and the recent national and international teacher education imperatives and pedagogical trends shaping this developing country. Arising from this analysis of contextual and educational issues is the framework of sustainability in which the project has been set, such that when the project is completed, the perspectives and orientations that have been driving it will be maintained in a self-sustaining professional development network of community teachers colleges.

The Papua New Guinea Context

A relatively young nation, Papua New Guinea is characterized as a developing country in a state of rapid economic and social transition. The population is nearly four million, and it is predicted that this will reach five million by the year 2000. Because of this rapid rate of growth, half of the population will be under 18 years of age by that time (Commission for Higher Education 1990). Lacking a unifying monoculture the people are nonetheless identified as Melanesian. The country is geographically and demographically diverse, comprising numerous and contrasting, predominantly rural (82 percent) ethnic groups. Urban migration is on the increase and squatter settlements now ring the major cities and other urban centers. The people speak over 700 distinct vernacular languages and dialects. Two lingua francas (Tokpisin and Motu) provide the means of communication for the majority of people across the country. English is the accepted national language for business and formal education within the country, and is the medium of participation in the modern world.

Papua New Guinea became an independent country in 1975. In his pathfinding book, *Papua New Guinea: Which Way?* Samana (1988), a political activist, former provincial premier and subsequently national Minister of Education, describes the inherited form of government as 'a highly centralized bureaucracy, modelled along the lines of the Australian civil service, built purposely for the colonial administration and totally unsuited to Papua New Guinea's situation' (p. 65). The approach to parliamentary democracy comprised 'a poor blend of British–Westminster and Australian styles of colonial administration, with overcentralized and monolithic administrative structures . . . all outside the experience of human organization and human relations of PNG societies' (p. 63). After independence the centralized colonial structure of the former Australian administration was abandoned in favor of a system of government which gave greater recognition to regional interests and 'the avenue by which people can exercise their power to develop themselves' (p. 74). The new administration was characterized by centralized policy functions of the national government which serve the national interest, coexisting with decentralization of operations to provincial governments (largely functioning within preexisting provincial boundaries), to provide for local ethnic and developmental needs and circumstances.

Several political parties exist, which are pragmatically rather than ideologically or ethnically based. No sufficiently dominant ethnic grouping or political bloc currently exists which can impose its purpose and orientation on the people generally, or parliament in particular, in a concerted and enduring manner. This reflects the extreme diversity and lack of cohesion among traditional groupings. Consequently, Papua New Guinea governments and oppositions tend to comprise loose and shifting coalitions. One effect is that governments are subjected to frequent votes of no confidence in parliament. Despite the tendency towards unstable coalition governments in recent years, the processes of parliamentary democracy has survived in a relatively stable manner.

Since independence the country has relied heavily on foreign aid (AIDAB 1993a). Papua New Guinea is the largest recipient of Australian development assistance, receiving almost one quarter of Australia's total aid program (AIDAB 1993b). This is provided by means of a bilateral agreement in the form of unconditional budgetary assistance, as well as jointly programmed project assistance, to support locally-determined priority areas of economic and human resource development. Apart from its post-colonial ties and commitments Australia's relationship with Papua New Guinea derives from economic and strategic defense links in the region. Substantial aid is also provided by Japan, which quickly recognized the investment and trade potential of this resource (mining and petroleum) rich country, and by Germany, which has enduring ties rooted in its earlier colonial history in the region, once known as German New Guinea. Germany has had substantial missionary interests in the past, and in recent years has made significant contributions to building and resource development programs in Catholic teachers colleges in the region of its former colony.

Other significant contributors to bilateral aid are the United Kingdom and New Zealand, whose interests lie in mining and petroleum exploration, and trade and agricultural development respectively. Considerable multilateral aid is provided by international aid agencies, such as the World Bank and the Asian Development Bank, for projects in key industries and social services which promise to support the country's economic and social development in a self-sustaining way.

Despite this dependency on foreign aid, there is no indication that Papua New Guinea is uncompromisingly aligned with a particular international capital or foreign governments. While Australian aid constituted nearly 40 percent of the total budget during the 1980s, there is little to suggest that Papua New Guinea has been beholden to, or politically dominated by, Australia during the post-independence period. This aid notwithstanding, severe economic constraints within the country in recent years have seriously slowed progress toward social improvement.

On the World Bank ranking, Papua New Guinea is classified as a 'lower middle-income' country, and is placed at fiftieth poorest out of the 120 countries listed. However, while it is not considered among the 'poorest of the poor', Papua New Guinea's educational status is actually viewed as below average for the 'low income countries' (Department of Education 1991).

While this World Bank assessment is indicative of present conditions, it belies the country's unrealized potential to generate substantial revenue from its considerable, and as yet largely undeveloped mineral, petroleum and agricultural resources. However, future socioeconomic prospects will largely depend on the negotiation of favorable conditions in terms of national ownership and foreign capital distribution. Potential natural wealth aside, severe economic constraints in recent years have all but stifled economic growth. In the short term these restrictive economic conditions will seriously limit possibilities for social development. Given the prevailing economic conditions, it is apparent that Papua New Guinea's relative status on such social indicators as education is unlikely to rise significantly above its present 'below average' ranking for low income countries, unless strategic developments in education are made a high priority in national planning (and perhaps supported by aid from foreign governments or international organizations) during the oncoming era of natural resource development. Clearly there is a desperate need for substantial improvements in educational provisions across the board, but the country's present capacity to provide is far from adequate.

Under present circumstances there is provision for about two-thirds of Papua New Guinean children aged 7 to 12 to attend primary school. Participation rates drop sharply in lower (16 percent) and upper (1 percent) secondary. Tertiary enrollments are limited by 'the very small number of Grade 12 matriculants from the four national high schools, where number and output have not increased for nearly 10 years' (Curtin 1989, p. 45).

Asian Development Bank estimates indicate that only 4 percent of primary school leavers, and 35 percent of secondary school leavers may expect to gain secure wage employment. Employment prospects for those leaving technical colleges with a Pre-Employment Technical Training qualification are much more restricted by the very limited number of new apprenticeships likely to be offered in the next few years. Each year, therefore, tens of thousands of school and college leavers have to be accommodated either by the rural subsistence sector (self-employment) or by informal activities in urban areas. However, workforce demand for university graduates contrasts markedly with this. In this case the shortfall of university graduates has led to the call for a substantial increase in output to meet the needs of the economy (Commission for Higher Education 1990). Realization of this need in effect means that continued dependence on foreign development assistance aid can be expected for some years to come, particularly to enhance the output of suitably qualified university graduates.

Given this predicament, in recent years changing governments have adopted quite different approaches to education development. The conflicting perspectives are a major contributing factor to the tensions and dilemmas in formulating and implementing education policy positions (Avalos and Neuendorf 1991). One line of thought has it that in Papua New Guinea, 'where occupations in the modern sector are limited, the need arises for policies of "educational relevance" which direct education to be useful to the villager and his or her community' (Avalos and Neuendorf 1991, p. 3). Thus education priorities and policies have given rise to 'an education strategy linked less to economic ends, and more to a concept of the person who finds realization in his or her local community or village' (Avalos and Neuendorf 1991, p. 3). At best, however, some of the more forward-looking developments in education policy have viewed preparation for life in the village, and experiencing the effect of the modern system of education as complementary, rather than antithetical, to contemporary Papua New Guinea social and economic needs. This has been referred to as 'dependent modernization'. It reflects the goal of 'integral human development' in the national interest as proclaimed in the national constitution which is characterized by its liberating, humanitarian ideals and goals.

The contrary position advocates that 'a potentially rich country such as Papua New Guinea needs to have [a cadre] of sufficiently educated population if it is to take control of its resources and put them to use efficiently for national development' (Avalos and Neuendorf 1991, p. 3). Basic to this view is greater government intervention in, and regulation of, national development by (re)-structuring the public sector along centralist lines.

Consistent with the policy of the World Bank, a medium-term limited expansion of the secondary and higher education area is planned, while a higher priority has been given to improving teaching standards in the primary or community education sector (Department of Education 1991). In proposing the means to this end the *National Higher Education Plan* (Commission for Higher Education 1990) recently recommended that, in a 'rational and cost-effective manner', community teachers colleges should have more autonomy in the development of institutional policy, financial and educational management, and improving the quality of graduates through an extended (from two to three years) primary preservice teacher education program.

The movement towards institutional autonomy and enhanced quality reflects the ideals of 'national sovereignty' and 'self-reliance', emphatically stated as a goal for the country in the national constitution. What this means in the context of community teachers colleges is that for teachers to assume their role of preparing self-reliant people, their own status and quality of training needs to be recognized and improved. This is not only a matter of extending the quantitative, and upgrading the qualitative aspects of courses, but a shift in the way teachers come to perceive themselves as professional people:

> For teachers to assume their role for preparing self-reliant people, their own status and quality of training needs to be recognized and improved . . . While lengthening of training from two to three years is a key aspect of the reform, more important is that the content and style of training be geared towards the preparation of teachers who feel themselves as autonomous professionals with at the same time a mission towards the children and the communities which they serve. (Avalos and Neuendorf 1991, pp. 10–11)

Ad hoc attempts by community teachers colleges in the 1980s towards autonomous college-based decision making were not well received by the education bureaucracy. There has been a long history of central control in the administration of teacher education, particularly in the area of curriculum development and practices. However, by the mid-1980s the seriously deteriorating social and economic conditions forced a policy response from the government. The *Matane Report* (1986) called for reform of the teacher education system and the devolution of responsibility for college curriculum decision making. A scenario for the improved preparation of primary teachers along these lines was provided by the recommendations of the National Teacher Education Research Project Task Force commissioned by the government (McNamara 1989).

Thus, the education bureaucracy, which in the past has tended to use its power to impose hegemonic mindsets on lecturers, and thereby inhibit any predisposition to political participation in program, institutional and social change, has come under serious challenge from many quarters. The assumptive right of the bureaucracy to exercise 'power-over' (Kreisberg 1992) relations with colleges, involving domination and subordination of the institutions, is increasingly being called to question. The reflected 'passive reactive model' (Baker 1972) which has characterized the centralized, standardized approach and minimized participation in and by the colleges, is in the process of giving way. The call in recent times has been for a redirection in the political socialization within community teachers colleges toward what Kreisberg (1992, p. 85) refers to as 'relationships of co-agency', in which 'people find ways to satisfy their desires and to fulfill their interests without imposing on one another . . . where there is equality: situations in which individuals and groups fulfill their desire by acting together [in a] jointly developing capacity.' This approach reflects more actively involved, mutually supportive, 'power-with' (Kriesberg 1992) relations among stakeholders, and increased institution-based decision making and responsibility. The trend has tended to radicalize the discourse and problematize some of the taken-for-granted constraints related to traditional structural relations in Papua New Guinea teacher education.

It is within this context that in 1989, the Australian International Development Assistance Bureau (AIDAB) conducted a review of Australia's project support of teacher education in Papua New Guinea over the past 15 years. The conclusion reached was that 'the [teacher education] programs of study have not in general produced lecturers who have significantly influenced the teachers college workplace' (AIDAB 1989). In the light of this, and in an effort to consolidate its support for teacher education in Papua New Guinea, AIDAB called tenders (sent out requests for proposals) for the design and implementation of a professional development project for community teachers college lecturers. The project was to develop a reconceptualized framework that addressed previous degree programs offered in Australia to Papua New Guinean College lecturers, and the range of in-country in-service programs that had been conducted with AIDAB support. The goal was to provide an approach which would enable college lecturers to be more autonomous and self-generating in developing their college programs. This goal reflects AIDAB's desire to complement devolutionary moves indicated above, but more particularly, to reduce the dependency in teacher education support from the Australian government.

Rethinking the Pedagogical Approach

The introduction of the *National Objectives for Teachers College Courses* in 1979 was aimed at providing 'guidelines' to clarify and specify the nature and purpose of the particular areas of study in teachers colleges (Department of Education 1979). The approach stemmed from the adoption of a psychology of learning which was based on the Tyler (1949) classical objectives model. In recent times considerable criticism (including from the colleges themselves) has been levelled at the standardized, uncritical, reproductive manner in which the national objectives have been interpreted and applied to colleges (Avalos 1989; McNamara 1989). Though proposed as 'guidelines', a departmental notice conveying the intent of the national objectives implied uniformity and lockstep. Colleges were advised that they were 'institutions carrying out the same work [and should] keep in step with each other so that their graduates can be employed at a known level of skill anywhere in the country' (Department of Education 1977, p. 4). By this means teacher educators have encountered a message which reflects the 'passive–reactive' model of 'political socialization' at the national level that they are increasingly coming to resent. Lecturers comment that the resentment stems from the idea that a centrally-administered, standardized national curriculum reflects a distrust of and lack of confidence in decisions being made locally. It conveys to lecturers the message that teacher education needs not only to be orchestrated nationally, but inspected by the department. It reflects for lecturers a form of in-country 'intellectual colonization' which employs 'power-over' relations with colleges in the form of hierarchical and bureaucratic domination and central control. This clearly contradicts another 'political' message — the more 'power-with', socially democratic, negotiated means and ends set out in the national constitution and the national philosophy of education. The underlying utilitarian mindset leaves little room for social constructs in the discourse of intellectual development in teacher education. It rests on the questionable assumption that if you standardize the recipe for technical efficiency in teacher education, and centralize the administration, then this will improve schooling in the national interest. This particular instrumentalist approach to teacher education has been criticized as both miseducative and 'ideologically suspect' (McLaughlin 1988). It has been argued that the approach is, in effect, a form of political socialization contributing (albeit unwittingly) towards processes of reproduction and maintenance of social, economic and cultural inequities in wider Papua New Guinea society — a condition that runs contrary to key declarations in the national constitution.

In practice this approach has led to concentration on technical aspects, resulting in a delimited view of teaching that is uncritical, highly specified, atomistic, and given to regimented rote teaching/learning methods devoid of contextual relevance. A National Teacher Education Research Project Task Force commissioned by the government concluded that 'because curricula are based on the achievement of a large number of behavioral objectives . . . students tend to have a very formal perception of teaching' (McNamara 1989, p. 2). In this way 'techniques and styles in teaching become perverted to ends in themselves rather than a means towards some clear educational purpose' (McLaughlin 1989, p. 4). The net effect is a stereotyped, 'stepwise' approach to teaching which predisposes students to be and to become passive and reactive, and denies opportunities to stimulate diagnosis, analysis and interpretation in their college courses. From this perspective Papua New Guinean teacher education is open to the criticism of operating, for the most part, within a limiting perspective characterized as 'technical rationality', which Zeichner (1981) concludes 'gives legitimacy to narrowly defined roles for teachers'. The narrowness and formality of the approach has been a matter of considerable concern to lecturers themselves:

> Teaching methods generally used here are chalk and talk or simulated lessons — in a word, spoonfeeding. Students are being trained, not educated. We are happy if they can perform satisfactorily in a classroom, but we fail to use a methodology that might allow them to see beyond this. (McLaughlin 1990, p. 31)

Preoccupied with and constrained by technical proficiency, lecturers tend to model teacher education strategies in mechanical, unproblematic and ritualistic ways. The end result, as Avalos (1989) reported in a study of second-year students across all colleges, is a stereotyped, taken-for-granted teaching style, uniformly applied by aspiring teachers, regardless of the college they attend.

Research indicates that lecturers, and in turn student teachers, are perfectly capable of generating their own hypotheses, setting up their own classification systems, producing their own ideas and taking decisions for themselves, if they are given the opportunity (McLaughlin 1989). A major inhibiting factor, however, is rote style teaching, and the rote style learning that derives from it.

Given the need that has been established for political (re)socialization which fosters autonomy, critical analysis and adaptability in teaching and learning, a further underlying consideration is that improvement in the quality of education in Papua New Guinea should 'grow out of a PNG reality'. As McLaughlin (1989, p. 12) concludes, the development of teacher educators can be deemed effective when it 'promotes those critical faculties for educators to assess the Papua New Guinea context, identifies problem areas and generates appropriate Papua New Guinea solutions which Papua New Guineans can implement intelligently.' This calls for 'curriculum procedures which involve lecturers in the intelligent analysis of their own situation' (McLaughlin 1990, p. 32). It calls for lecturers to research their own traditional ways of knowing, not to romanticize their culture and past, but to protect against 'intellectual colonization'. Thus Papua New Guinean lecturers can deal critically with the present realities of teachers colleges in order to improve them. In this case professional 'socialization is not merely the transfer from one group to another [lecturer–student teacher] in a static social structure, but the active creation of a new identity through a personal definition of the [teaching/learning] situation' (Reinharz 1979, p. 74).

Within the Papua New Guinea context there exists, therefore, an urgent need for teacher educators, not only to recommit to an appropriate pedagogy to suit present national ideals, demands and circumstances, but also to consider how such a commitment ought to be acted out in a sustainable manner in the institutional context — in terms of approach to institutional management, course development and delivery, in staff–student interactions, and in intra/inter-college support networks.

The Project Response: Beyond Critical Reflection to Transformative Action

In developing the perspective and framework to underpin its approach, the project has drawn upon responses gained during the preliminary 'environmental scan'[1] conducted by the project management team in 1990. Guided by the findings of the environment scan the project has applied an approach to problems based on the concept of meta-cognition (Biggs 1988). The 'meta-cognitive' approach contrasts with the unreflective, 'formalistic' approach (Guthrie 1990) which has been applied in the past, in that it takes the learners' perspective about problems into account, causes them to reflect critically on what they know and need to know, and goes on to provide the basis for the development of 'responsible self-direction and action'.

This brings into question the critical interrelationship between action and reflection. The two are inextricably connected in praxis. According to Freire (1972), praxis represents the dynamic interplay between reflection and action, between theory and practice. Thus, praxis may be viewed as a continuing developmental cycle of reflective activity in which action is informed by critical reflection, and critical reflection, in turn, informed by the action that ensues.

Praxis has two major implications for the nature and processes of teaching and learning in the college context which can guide sustainable professional development. First, lecturers need to question critically their approach to college functioning. When teachers adopt a reflective attitude toward their teaching, actually questioning their own practices, then they engage in a process of rendering problematic or questionable those aspects of teaching generally taken for granted (Smyth 1986). Second, within the concept of praxis, student teachers and lecturers should be seen to co-constitute the teaching/learning situation. By means of 'critical and liberating dialogue' (Freire 1972) and negotiation, both parties, as collaborative participants, draw upon their joint experience. This experience is regarded as problematic, however. As a result of this process, critical awareness of the world, the place of people and problems within it, begin to emerge. The need to search for answers, and to act upon them ensues. In this way the possibility of genuine self-initiated learning is enhanced.

This is the basis for transformative education in that it reflects the dynamic interplay between experience, critical reflection and professional action as an ongoing cycle. It is, in effect, a process of political socialization that employs a critical pedagogy of reflective practice, based on transformative praxis — a self-renewing political process of personal and educational reconstruction.

The process involves an 'active curriculum' in which the student is viewed as an inquirer, and in which contemporary issues and problems that significantly affect students' lives, however controversial, are critically examined and better informed. Thus critical reflection and informed teacher education practices actively involve lecturers and student teachers as a community of inquirers who collectively critique the nature, purpose and effect of their academic knowledge and pedagogical practice and, in turn, act upon the institutional culture and wider community in which they participate. This approach embraces Aronowitz and Giroux's (1985) concept of the transformative intellectual, who 'helps to critically analyze various interests and contradictions within [education and] society and collaborate[s] with others in articulating emancipatory possibilities and working toward their realization' (cited in Ginsburg 1988, p. 202).

The transformative approach adopted by the project calls for the integration of the lecturer, his or her professional activity and his or her goals into an ongoing cycle of personal and professional development, and institutional and social change. Such integration is one way of addressing the context of existing community teachers colleges. The aims are:

1 to enable the multidimensional requirements for professional development to be addressed by building on the whole context of lecturers' work and relating this to personal action;
2 to allow automatically lecturers to address their prior notions and development as the first phase of their development;
3 to recognize the distinctive learning needs of lecturers by integrating their actions with their goals;
4 to promote the cognitive and affective changes required of lecturers by enabling them to consider their whole working context, including their attitudes towards it;
5 to build a supportive environment for lecturers to sustain their work; and
6 to facilitate ongoing development by offering both challenge and support to lecturers.

The Project Model

Elliot (1992a) has argued that lecturers have been bound into existing practices through a model of curriculum which divorces them from crucial decisions about their curricula, and from information and actions that would enlighten their practice. The project mode of professional development has been developed to enable the lecturer in the colleges to reach beyond the situations and conditions that constrain them. A central tenet of the 'relationship of co-agency' inherent in the model involves lecturers so that, collaboratively, they can constructively and comparatively (across colleges and internationally) examine the very structures and sociopolitical contexts that limit and/or enhance curriculum, pedagogy and evaluation practices. This is, in effect, a process of political resocialization consistent with the literature referred to earlier (Matane 1986; AIDAB 1989; McLaughlin 1989; McNamara 1989; Commission of Higher Education 1990; Avalos and Neuendorf 1991).

It is through this participative, critically reflective and comparative approach that college lecturers develop a discourse that moves them, where necessary, outside their context to see issues of educational 'relevance' and 'modernization' from other perspectives. Such an outcome is in keeping with Narakobi's (1991) desire to 'transcend, to live a little bit outside one's traditions and to examine the role of tradition in a new and modern society'. For this purpose workshop facilitators (as 'outsider' project participants) engage in a dialogue with lecturers that pays due regard both to surrounding institutional, cultural, political and economic realities of Papua New Guinea life, and also to ideas that are international, and flow across cultural and national backgrounds. In turn, with 'insider' knowledge, the lecturers can apply the sociopolitical approach modelled in project workshops in their approaches to teacher education in their own college contexts.

The model has drawn from 'collaborative action research' in that 'each group represented in the process shares in the planning, implementation, and analysis of the research [and development] and that each contributes different expertise and a unique perspective' (Nodie Oja and Smulyan 1989, p. 1). Thus, all stakeholders are actively involved in the ongoing cycles of problem definition, plans and strategies, incorporating reflections on outcomes (Kemmis 1981). The underlying purpose is to enable participants to come to understand their context through multiple perspectives, and through this, develop strategies to address problems which they consider are significant in their context (Pope and Denicolo 1990).

To facilitate the process of action planning and research, special activity guides were prepared employing 'situational analysis', based on the conceptualizations of Skilbeck (1976) and Maxwell (1985). Situational analysis in the workshop setting is a form of 'environmental scanning'. It comprises a detailed critical analysis of pertinent 'inside factors' which are controlled by the institution, and 'outside factors' which tend to be out of the institution's control (Pfeffer and Salancik 1978), that is, those wider contextual forces and trends that relate colleges to the wider national (and global) educational, social, political and economic policies and structures. In this way action planning in the workshops calls upon lecturers to identify the best 'fit' between lecturers, institutions and their wider environment, and to take creative initiative to implement their action plans. The process in practice is iterative, takes note of the political nature of professional life, and builds on the nature of political decision making. With this in mind, upon their return to their own college contexts all lecturers are required to plan and conduct workshops for other lecturing staff as a contribution towards staff development and institutional strengthening, as well as proceeding with the post-workshop action research (derived from their workshop action plans) in their field of specialization.

The project's approach assumes that not only should lecturers and, in turn, teachers be encouraged to function at the level of reflective practice, and with heightened social and political awareness, but there must also be sustained benefit to the colleges in terms of present teacher education imperatives and realities. An emerging outcome of the project has been the formulation of an approach to sustainability that links course offerings to post-course activities. This is a key feature of the project and distinguishes it from other similar international projects that have foundered at this point (Crossley 1984; Hickling-Hudson 1988).

Application on the Model

There are two specific and separate instances in which this model has been applied within the project in order to promote professional development of community teachers college lecturers. On the one hand, lecturers study in Australia at Queensland University of Technology, which collaborates with University of Papua New Guinea, in order to gain a BEd from that university. On the other hand, lecturers have the opportunity to participate in a range of in-country in-service professional development workshops facilitated by Queensland University of Technology personnel and selected in-country resource personnel in order to develop and sustain their work, and to strengthen the institutions in which they are engaged.

Both these components are guided by principles and questions that call for participation of stakeholders and reflect 'power-with' dispositions and relations. The principles underpin the project approach and involve joint planning, negotiated curriculum, collegiality, coordination and supportive networking among project stakeholders. Key questions seek to access lecturers' views on the purpose, priorities and intent of their role(s) and to problematize issues. The questions include: What kind of schooling and society have the community teachers college lecturers come to value? What experiences need to be provided that will critically review the lecturers' level of awareness of their own political socialization, and process of program development and delivery? What orientations, knowledge and skills do lecturers need to develop to facilitate their work as teacher-educators, as they confront teacher education imperatives and address issues of educational relevance and modernization in contemporary Papua New Guinea society?

Consistent with these principles and questions, opportunities were provided for lecturers to participate in reflective, collaborative learning experiences in which they are encouraged to:

1 view their professional world of teacher education in a more problematic way;
2 critically examine what they are currently doing, and why; and
3 explore a range of alternative means, and then judiciously arrive at a preferred option by which they may bring about program, institutional and/

or broader educational change collectively, at policy, structural and procedural levels.

The approach to professional development can be illustrated in terms of processes adopted in the two components of the project: in-country workshops and coursework in Australia.

In-Country Workshops

In the two-week, in-country workshops Queensland University of Technology workshop facilitators engage in collaborative pre-workshop negotiations with community teachers college lecturers in order to address their areas of need and concern. Some four weeks before the workshop the selected lecturers are asked to consider the purposes of the workshop and list the sorts of things (for each purpose) that they wish to gain from it. They are also asked to describe briefly their particular college context in terms of their present position regarding developments in the subject area addressed by the workshop.

In general lecturers' preworkshop expectations have tended to be confined to the 'what' and 'how to' practicalities of program development and delivery. Needs are largely expressed in utilitarian terms in relation to becoming a more technically competent lecturer. Analysis of the expectations of the Community Development[2] workshop, for instance, revealed this instrumentalist view in the form of three major areas of need and concern, and a number of themes/questions lecturers wished to pursue within each area:

A   Understandings of the concept of Community Development.

   1   What is the place of Community Development in the course?
   2   What are the possibilities?
   3   How do we assess the specific needs in the colleges and their communities?
   4   How do we stress diversity and encourage adaptability in the course?

B   Expertise in the area of curriculum design, implementation and evaluation.

   1   What strategies can be used for implementation and evaluation?
   2   How can we design a work program?
   3   Is there opportunity to develop sample units?

C   Orientation to developing the newly introduced preservice course.

   1   In what respects should the Community Development program in the new three-year course differ from the past two-year program?
   2   What should student teachers be able to do, given the raised level and expanded content in the new program?
   3   What does this mean in terms of the kinds of resources (texts and aids) now needed? (McPherson *et al.* 1991)

The process employed during workshops is consistent with the concept of transformative praxis. This is well illustrated in the case of the 'Assessment and Evaluation' workshop (1993). Early on in the 'Assessment and Evaluation' workshop lecturers were engaged in reflective (meta-cognitive) learning experiences based on the principles and questions referred to earlier. During this time they collectively critiqued their own present thinking on, and problematized their college's approach to assessment and evaluation. Both during and after the process lecturers spoke of a heightened awareness that assessment and evaluation were more 'multi-dimensional' and 'interpretative' than they had previously believed. Several remarked critically that a 'certain dogmatism' had developed around a 'single traditional, uncritically accepted, system approach' in the colleges. Closer examination revealed a 'rhetoric–reality gap' between stated policy guidelines and the actual experience of implementing assessment and evaluation procedures with the students. Others commented that their own (personal) previously taken-for-granted positions had been rendered problematic, and were more 'socially decontextualized' and open to question than they had realized.

The raised consciousness prompted the group to revisit, in a critically reflective way, the 'nature of the assessment and evaluation problem' in its broader educational, systemic and social contexts. Lecturers began asking themselves what *they* saw as salient issues, and how they perceived themselves to be constrained. Eventually the group came to see the problem in terms of structural relations, and requiring systemic change at the level of policy. This called for, in part, the use of situational analysis, which, in turn, gave rise to the need to search for 'better answers' and more 'knowledge and theory'. This was to ensure that the emerging collective position would be an informed one. The facilitator's task was to assist the group to access the needed input from multiple perspectives, and to raise questions and issues (in Socratic manner) without providing answers. Considerable discussion of this input (both human and material resources) occurred as lecturers sought to develop a 'defensible position', a consequence of which was the emergence of a predisposition to act. This culminated in a commitment by the group to formulate a course of action that would address the questions and issues now before them, and incorporate the agreements that had been reached about the nature, function, principles and procedures for assessment and evaluation in the colleges.

There were two aspects to the development of the course of action. The first had to do with ownership of the process and product — the product being a comprehensive statement in the form of a discussion/proposal paper entitled 'A Policy for Assessment and Evaluation in Community Teachers Colleges', which included principles of policy and principles of procedure. The second aspect related to what was needed to advocate policy change by identifying strategic policy decision making points and key stakeholders in the teacher education structure where the discussion paper would be addressed.

To this end individual action plans were prepared for follow-up in-service workshops with colleagues in the colleges upon return, and for project workshop participants to address college governing bodies on the matter. In addition to this action it was resolved that arrangements be made to consult with the senior Department of Education official overseeing teacher education, with the request that the discussion paper be tabled at the next meeting of the community teachers college principals' conference.[3] By the time of the conference, principals had already become familiar with the discussion paper through the post-workshop activity of participants. The paper was duly tabled and the advocate was a deputy principal — a workshop participant who attended the conference.

The outcome was that the 1993 principals' conference decided to draw upon the proposed model and outcomes of the Assessment and Evaluation workshop as a device for reviewing/examining current policies and practices. The conference resolved that the assessment document be considered as 'a document to be applied to all colleges . . . [and to] be used as a basis for ongoing development, culminating in Education Department-organized professional development workshops in the area' (Project Coordinating Group Minutes 1993, p. 2). Thus the first phase of transformative praxis (i.e. the initial cycle of reflective activity in which critical reflection has led to action) has been played out for the most part. The stage is set now for the next stage of the ongoing development cycle of reflection and action to occur. Thus the proposal to view assessment and evaluation more contextually and developmentally (as an integral part of teaching and learning) could have far reaching effects on models and perspectives of teaching and learning in the colleges, the nature of student–staff relationships, and the methods of these *tertiary* institutions. In this way student teachers would be encouraged to reflect upon their own teaching situations and contexts. The proactive, informed and consultative manner by which lecturers processed their proposal could have far reaching effects in terms of interdependence in structural relations and approach to policy formulation.

The above examples serve to illustrate how, during these workshop experiences, lecturers have been called upon to see themselves not only as skilled practitioners, but also as political actors in a process that is critically reflective, action-oriented, consultative, transformative and sustainable in their field of teacher education. Moreover, there is evidence that their students in community teachers colleges are being encouraged to adopt at least some aspects of such a critically reflective stance. According to a report on several colleges visited by a senior Department of Education official:

> [T]he importance of more critical and interdependent work by the students has been accepted in the colleges . . . staff were convinced of the need to develop critical reflectivity [about broader educational and social contextual issues as well as technical issues] . . . the maintenance of reflective journals [to this end] by students seems to have assumed a large role in all colleges. (Doyle 1992, p. 3)

Favorable comment was also made in the report on the level of growth and mutually supportive actions taken by lecturers following professional development workshops conducted by the project.

To achieve such outcomes in all in-country workshops, and to promote the transformative perspective fundamental to the project, joint responsibility for co-planning and key linkages with selected national (in-country) resource persons is required. National (in-country) resource persons are identified by the National Department of Education (Staff Development and Training Division) and the University of Papua New Guinea, in consultation with the particular workshop coordinator — a member of the project management team. As Elliott (1992b), a workshop coordinator, commented in his review of the extensive preworkshop planning: 'we are anxious to have a model whereby the [in-country] resource persons are well integrated into the Project. . . . [I]t seems the best way to move towards a shared perspective for the workshop amongst the personnel involved.'

The planning stage of the workshops provide useful case studies of the tensions inherent in a project that seeks to develop a critical and creative response to the traditional educational climate in which the lecturers have worked. On the one hand, lecturers express concern about past power-over relationships which give rise to passive–reactive attitudes and which stress the need to concentrate on a core of essentials in a standardized, centralized national teacher education program. On the other hand, the workshop facilitator (including in-country resource persons) sensitive to the findings in the environmental scan and the views of workshop participants, as well as the Papua New Guinea literature referred to, have emphasized the transformative co-agency, power-with, perspective, arguing that 'the intention is not to provide specific detail on program content in the [workshop themes], but critical and contextual curriculum understandings for participation to enable them to develop programs back in their own college settings' (Elliott 1992b).

Evaluations of specific workshops have been completed. For example Lucas *et al.* (1993) report specific data concerning the Mathematics and Science workshop consisting of immediate and delayed ratings by participants of the workshop effectiveness, participants' reports on the effectiveness of their action plans and college principals' perceptions of workshop effectiveness. Their conclusion was that the workshop was not only effective in improving the participants' substantive understandings in the area but that 'for a significant number of lecturers, the ideas and strategies introduced during the workshop continued to influence performance after a period of three months' (Lucas *et al.* 1993, p. 11). In general terms, evaluation from six workshops completed in 1991–92 indicates that:

1 all lecturers are able to complete key aspects of action planning after returning to their colleges;
2 networks of communication are sustained in many cases so that there is greater sharing of professional work within and across the colleges; and
3 lecturers are, in most cases, meeting the challenge of implementing the workshop-developed plans to initiate change in their own colleges.

The Australian Coursework Component

While studying in accredited courses at Queensland University of Technology community teachers college lecturers are called upon to participate in a specific tutorial arrangement, the application tutorial. This arrangement encourages participants to engage in cycles of research and development through personal action.

In analyzing the participants' experiences Elliot (1992a) has noted the dissonance they experienced regarding a number of ideas with which they are confronted during their study in Australia. Such dissonance arises because each experiences a difficulty of considering professional knowledge in a context that is educationally and sociopolitically different from that in which they might hope to apply such knowledge at a later time. While considering knowledge out of its context is one way of promoting dissonance and promoting professional development, there is the attendant danger that such knowledge may be regarded as 'cargo' (Lawrence 1969) to be 'uncritically transplanted upon a Papua New Guinea context' (McLaughlin 1989, p. 1). In this case the danger is that lecturers may seek to accept uncritically this new knowledge during cognitive reorganization. In order to work against such a 'passive–reactive' possibility, the model incorporates actions with future goals in similar fashion to the in-country workshops. Lecturers are called upon to:

1 prepare an action plan for how the knowledge that they are considering in their courses is problematic in their Papua New Guinea college context and may be used as the basis for change in practice, pedagogy, curriculum or administration;
2 establish collegial intercollege networks to ensure that they have support for themselves when they return home from the course by making contact with other lecturers in Papua New Guinea and solicit their opinions about the issue with which they were grappling; and
3 enact the action plans on return to the college and continue to correspond with Australian workshop facilitators to discuss progress with their research.

In general the approach has proved a promising platform for conceiving and implementing professional development programs for the lecturers. In terms of the criteria noted by Zuber-Skeret (1990, p. 153) the lecturers are:

1 developing critical attitudes towards not only their own work but also the sociopolitical context in which that work is set;
2 incorporating ongoing research into their work;
3 accepting autonomy, responsibility and accountability for the professional actions in which they engage; and
4 evaluating themselves in an ongoing manner in the networks of lecturers that are formed.

Summary and Conclusion

This chapter has presented a critical analysis of imperatives impacting on community teachers colleges within the socioeconomic and political context of Papua New Guinea today. It has been developed to elucidate the approach (including political dimensions) that has been taken to professional development by the Papua New Guinea Community Teachers College Lecturers Professional Development Project (1991–94).

The approach to political (re)socialization adopted by the project has been developed to facilitate critical and liberating dialogue with a view to developing critical self-awareness and responsible self-direction in furthering developments in teacher education. Herein a key goal is an understanding of, and responsibility for, appropriate knowledge jointly produced, rather than knowledge as a predetermined commodity to be transmitted from the 'knowing' (project teaching team) to the 'unknowing' (college lecturers as course participants) in a passive–reactive manner. By means of action research, opportunities are provided for the views and experience of both parties to be brought forward in a problematic way, for deliberation and potential transformation, rather than one which simply imposes one view of the world of teaching (etc.) and invalidates another. In the final analysis, lecturers as the key element in the ongoing growth cycle inherent in the notion of sustainable development, take responsibility for ensuring that program development and college policy and practice, meet educational 'relevance' and 'modernization' criteria for contemporary Papua New Guinea society.

To this end the project is in the form of negotiated professional development experiences. The approach is designed to enable Papua New Guinean lecturers (and in turn, their student teachers) to develop the requisite analytical skills and conceptual tools to reflect critically upon and transform their specialized academic area(s), and the taken-for-granted traditional college context. In this context learning is not entirely a psychological process. It is also about building context. The learning process involves problematizing issues and contextualizing the discourses using multiple perspectives. It seeks to address policy — its (re)formulation and implementation. The key to this is dialogue with key stakeholders in the teacher education system, in ways that have potential for consensus, mutual support and restructure in directions that increasingly provide for devolution of responsibility for decision making at the level of individual college, and intercollege networks. Clearly this calls for an ethic of cultural sensitivity, and a framework of social responsibility. It requires of Papua New Guinea lecturers an awareness of their own capacity and limitations, and recognition of the need for ongoing professional development through local initiatives.

A distinctive contribution of the approach taken by this project is that it continues past the stage where many other similar programs end. It is the serious consideration given and the coordinated negotiated approach taken to the post-course phase that distinguishes the project's response to teacher education needs in the 1990s in Papua New Guinea. The significance of the project also lies in its potential to provide a general approach to transformative education, and a curriculum model applicable to an emerging literature on self-sustaining professional development. To this end the contextual analysis, underlying principles, goals, processes and outcomes of the project:

1 provide a generalized applicability to a range of diverse professional development settings for teacher educators elsewhere;
2 have an applicability to a range of social and cultural contexts both in developing and developed countries; and
3 provide the basis of development and evaluation of a wide range of international professional development assistance projects.

Notes

1 The 'environmental scan' was conducted in Papua New Guinea, in March 1990, by the project director (the writer) and the in-service coordinator. The purpose was to obtain information regarding the perceptions of lecturers of community teachers colleges, the college principals, University of Papua New Guinea Department of Education staff, (Government) Department of Education officials, and Australian International Development Assistance Bureau (AIDAB) officials, about professional training needs of lecturers from 1991–94.
2 'Community Development' is a strand in the new three-year primary teachers preservice program.

3   The principals' conference is an annual meeting which, in addition to college principals, brings together other key stakeholders in teacher education from the Department of Education and University of Papua New Guinea to review policy and
planning in the colleges.

References

AUSTRALIAN INTERNATIONAL DEVELOPMENT ASSISTANCE BUREAU (AIDAB), CENTRE FOR
PACIFIC DEVELOPMENT AND TRAINING (ACPAC) (1989) *PNG Community Teachers
College Lecturers Professional Development: A Project Review and Design Study*, Can-
berra, Department of Foreign Affairs and Trade, ACT.

AUSTRALIAN INTERNATIONAL DEVELOPMENT ASSISTANCE BUREAU (AIDAB) (1993a) *Australia and Papua New Guinea: A Developing Partnership*, Canberra, National Capital
Printing.

AUSTRALIAN INTERNATIONAL DEVELOPMENT ASSISTANCE BUREAU (AIDAB) (1993b) *The
Papua New Guinea Economy: Prospects for Sectoral Development and Broad Based
Growth* (International Development Issues No. 30), Canberra, AIDAB.

AVALOS, B. (1989) 'TERP Unit 3: The Characteristics and Problems of the Practice
Teaching Component in College Training' (draft), Waigani, Research and Evaluation Unit, Department of Education.

AVALOS, B. and NEUENDORF, L. (Eds) (1991) *Teaching in Papua New Guinea: A Perspective for the Nineties*, Port Moresby, University of Papua New Guinea Press.

BAKER, D. (1972) 'Political socialization parameters and disposition', *Polity*, **3**, 4, pp.
586–600.

BIGGS, J.B. (1988) 'The role of metacognition in enhancing learning', *Australian Journal
of Education*, **32**, 2, pp. 127–38.

COMMISSION FOR HIGHER EDUCATION (1990) *National Higher Education Plan*, Port
Moresby, Education Printshop.

CROSSLEY, M. (1984) 'Strategies for curriculum change and the question of international transfer', *Journal of Curriculum Studies*, **16**, 1, pp. 75–88.

CURTIN, T. (1989) 'The evaluation of human capital: A comment on recent literature
relating to Papua New Guinea', *PNG Journal of Education*, **25**, 2, pp. 41–55.

DEPARTMENT OF EDUCATION (1977) *Curricula for Educational Institutions in Papua New
Guinea* (Education Gazette 22/77), Port Moresby, PNG Department of Education.

DEPARTMENT OF EDUCATION (1979) *National Objectives for Teachers College Courses*, Port
Moresby, PNG Department of Education.

DEPARTMENT OF EDUCATION (1991) *Education Sector Review: Executive Summary and
Principal Recommendations*, Port Moresby, PNG Department of Education.

DOYLE, D. (1992) 'What's Happening in the Colleges?' paper presented at the Faculty
of Education 13th Extraordinary Meeting: Participating in Educational Change,
Possibilities, Issues and Experiences, University of Papua New Guinea, Port
Moresby, September.

ELLIOTT, R. (1992a) 'Moving from Domestication to Internationalization: Teacher Education in Papua New Guinea', paper presented at the ICET Conference, Paris,
July.

ELLIOTT, R. (1992b) 'Report on Curriculum Understandings Workshop', Port Moresby
In-service College, Brisbane, Queensland University of Technology.

FREIRE, P. (1972) *Pedagogy of the Oppressed*, New York, Herder and Herder.

GINSBURG, M.B. (1988) *Contradictions in Teacher Education and Society: A Critical Analysis*, London, Falmer Press.

GUTHRIE, G. (1990) 'In defense of formalistic teaching', in RUST, V. and DALIN, P.
(Eds) *Teachers and Teaching in the Developing World*, New York, Garland Publishing, pp. 219–32.

HICKLING-HUDSON, A. (1988) 'Toward communication praxis: Reflections on the pedagogy of Paulo Freire and educational change in Grenada', *Journal of Education*, **170**, 2, pp. 9–38.
KEMMIS, S. (1981) *The Professional Development of Teachers Through Involvement in Action-Research Projects*, Geelong, Deakin University.
KREISBERG, S. (1992) *Transforming Power: Domination, Empowerment and Education*, Albany, NY, State University of New York Press.
LAWRENCE, P. (1969) *Road Belong Cargo*, Melbourne, Melbourne University Press.
LUCAS, K., SWINSON, K. and TULIP, D. (1993) 'Effective professional development for teacher educators in Papua New Guinea', *Journal of Science and Mathematics Education in Southeast Asia*, **16**, 1, pp. 57–69.
MCLAUGHLIN, D. (1988) *Teacher Education by Teacher Educators in Papua New Guinea*, Waigani, Research and Evaluation Unit, Department of Education.
MCLAUGHLIN, D. (1989) *Basic Spills in the Basic Skills. National Examinations in Teacher Education in Papua New Guinea*, Port Moresby, University of Papua New Guinea.
MCLAUGHLIN, D. (1990) 'A curriculum for teacher education: Some preliminary considerations', *Papua New Guinea Journal of Education*, **26**, 1, pp. 29–35.
MCNAMARA, V. (1989) *The Future Direction of Community School Teacher Education*, Unit 4 Task Force Report, Waigani, Teacher Education Research Project, Department of Education.
MCPHERSON, I., BURKE, C., ELLIOTT, R. and WILKINSON, M. (1991) 'Summary Statement of Community Development In-service Workshop', Brisbane, Queensland University of Technology.
MATANE, P. (Chairman, Ministerial Review Committee) (1986) *A Philosophy of Education for Papua New Guinea*, Waigani, Department of Education.
MAXWELL, T. (1985) 'The Illumination of Situational Analysis by Frame Factor Theory', *Curriculum Prospective*, **5**, 1, pp. 47–52.
NARAKOBI, B. (1991) 'Education and development', in B. AVALOS and L. NEUENDORF (Eds) *Teaching in Papua New Guinea*, Port Moresby, University of Papua New Guinea, pp. 19–27.
NODIE OJA, S. and SMULYAN, L. (1989) *Collaborative Action Research: A Developmental Approach*, London, Falmer Press.
PFEFFER, J. and SALANCIK, G. (1978) *The External Control of Organizations: A Resource Dependence Perspective*, New York, Harper and Row.
POPE, M. and DENICOLO, P. (1990) 'Developing Constructive Action: Personal Construct Psychology, Action Research and Professional Development', in O. ZUBER-SKERET (Ed) *Action Research for Change and Development*, Brisbane, CALT, Griffith University, pp. 119–40.
PROJECT COORDINATING GROUP (1993) 'Papua New Guinea Community Teachers' College Lecturers' Professional Development Project', minutes of meeting held in Port Moresby, 19 November.
REINHARZ, S. (1979) *On Becoming a Social Scientist*, San Francisco, CA, Jossey-Bass.
SAMANA, U. (1988) *Papua New Guinea: Which Way?* Victoria, Australia North Carlton, Arena.
SKILBECK, M. (1976) 'School-Based Curriculum Development and Teacher Education', mimeograph, Paris, OECD.
SMYTH, J. (1986) *Reflection-in-Action*, Geelong, Deakin University Press.
TYLER, R. (1949) *Basic Principles of Curriculum and Instruction*, Chicago, IL, University of Chicago Press.
ZEICHNER, K. (1981) 'Reflective teaching and field-based experience in preservice teacher education', *Interchange*, **12**, 1, pp. 5–24.
ZUBER-SKERET, O. (1990) 'Action research as a model of professional development', in ZUBER-SKERRITT, O. (Ed) *Action Research for Change and Development*, Brisbane, Australia, Griffith University, pp. 141–67.

Part 4

Implications for a Transformative Agenda in Teacher Education

Chapter 14

Transforming Teacher Education, Schooling, and Society: Lessons Learned and Political Commitments

Beverly Lindsay and Mark B. Ginsburg

Born with a veil, and gifted with a second-sight . . . It is a peculiar sensation, this double-consciousness . . . One ever feels [one's] twoness . . . two souls, two thoughts, two unreconciled strivings; two warring ideals in one dark body, whose dogged strength alone keeps it from being torn asunder. (Du Bois 1903, p. 45)

Our task is to free the structure . . . These [educational] institutions are just an epiphenomena as far as . . . participation is concerned. I say no . . . The first and major responsibility of the intellectual is to struggle over ideas. We didn't create the artificial distinction between mental and manual [the doing], but it is there, and needs to be transcended. It is to be transcended by breaking the pattern of society that entrenches such a distinction. Therefore the first level of struggle for the intellectual is in his [*sic*] own sphere of operation. (Rodney 1990, p. 113).

As we pondered the ideas and thoughts we would like to impart in the final chapter, the works of pioneering scholar-activists came to mind. The influence of progressive scholar-activists were foremost because we are interested in the fusion, the integration, the linkages that occur among the formal educational system and educators *and* that of sociopolitical and economic realities of the larger society. Thus, we reflected on the works of scholar-activists who helped set the tone for the beginning of the twentieth century and beyond as well as those scholar-activists whose work and lives in the last part of the century have made an impact. Scholars who embodied these views include W.E.B. Du Bois for the first illustration and Walter Rodney for the second. Because of their views, they were often challenged and in the final analysis 'cast aside' by many for their perspectives and actions. Du Bois, an African American, died in exile in Ghana at 95 years of age. Rodney, who lived throughout the Caribbean, England, and Tanzania, was assassinated in Guyana (his birthplace) for his political views and activities.

Hence, the beginning quotations are presented. The first reflects how individuals give meaning to and engage in comprehensive activities in various realms of their professional and personal lives. The second emphasizes the salience of ideas that are central to educational institutions and individuals therein who are involved in the larger society, while at the same time not ruling out intellectuals from engaging in political action other than in the realm of ideas. Throughout this chapter, therefore, we interweave the ideas derived from quotations of Du Bois and Rodney.

While the various chapter writers discuss the political dimensions of teacher education based upon their diverse research interests, scholarly backgrounds and teaching specialties, discernable motifs emerged. As we are steered across six continents, some of the distinguishing motifs that emerge include *inter alia*: the processes of policy formation and modifications; the relative participation (or non-participation) of teacher educators in policy development and political processes; the historical antecedents of contemporary policies and programs for schooling and teacher education; the views of preservice and in-service teachers toward their roles as political actors; the perceptions of potential and current teachers of the political and socialization features within educational settings; and the overt and hidden characteristics of the curriculum in teacher education programs.

What we as a group of scholar activists have attempted to do in this volume is move beyond the identification of cross-national motifs pertaining to teacher education. We critically examine dynamic and empirical motifs while integrating them with theoretical and conceptual frameworks, thereby helping us fathom the comprehensive interactive aspects of policy formation, socialization, and society. What we now wish to offer are some concluding reflections designed for current and subsequent analyses and actions for those integrally involved with teacher education, schooling and society.

Thus the following components of this chapter will be concerned with further elucidation of macro, micro, and phenomenological conceptual frameworks *vis-à-vis* policy dimensions and political socialization affecting teacher education and teachers as witnessed in the various chapters. We shall observe interactive, yet distinct and independent, effects among macro, micro, and phenomenological issues depending upon country-specific and individual characteristics. This is undertaken to help clarify the political structures that affect the world of teachers (Smith 1987, 1990, cited in Ritzer 1992, p. 339). Yet we recognize that a single grand response or meta-theory will be not be offered; instead we hope to further the debate and struggle over ideas and practices, leading to concrete proactive solutions to grave political issues.

In addition, we devote special attention to political realities and structural conditions that maintain the status quo. We then explicate how changes and ultimately transformations are undertaken so that concrete policies and practices for teacher education, including the construction of the formal and informal curriculum and forms of individual and collective political actions, alter the world of teachers and teacher educators in various societies.

The Multiple Levels of Analyses

Although several working constructs were presented for the term policy, an overarching definition encompasses policies as the plans of action to accomplish some goals of the government (national, regional/provincial/state, and local) or organizations. Political or legislative, judicial, or executive actions are usual bases for public and educational policies that are often influenced by political, social and economic or fiscal realities. Within educational settings, policies are overall procedures or methods designed for program implementation. This implementation is often based upon a comprehension of the major national or state/provincial policies (macro-level) and of individual organizations or systems (micro-level). In a somewhat ideal sense, policies are based upon underlying philosophical premises as part of the social and cultural milieu (Lindsay 1988). Formal (or *de jure*) policies exist as a result of official documents, laws or practices. Informal (or *de facto*) policies exist in and by fact, and although they do not have formal legal status, they often carry as much weight as formal ones. That is, *de facto* conditions exist as part of the institutional, local, regional or national cultures often with the same or greater impact as formal policies (Klein 1987; LaMorte 1987; Lindsay 1994).

To recognize the focuses and dimensions of macro and micro-level public and educational policies is to comprehend the level of 'development' or 'modernization' of various countries (see Horowitz 1972; Rodney 1972; Marable 1983; Wallerstein 1989; Amin 1990a, 1990b; Carnoy and Samoff 1990). Thus the initial several chapters, focusing on England, Australia and the United States, highlight some of the complex dimensions of policies in 'developed' or 'modern' nations. These countries collectively espouse, via their constitutions and other official documents, the ideals of democracy and equality — or at least equality of opportunity. Mass primary and secondary education are ostensibly designed to meet these ideals. On the surface, the formal policies and subsequent programs are designed to ensure democracy and perpetuate or ensure equality via diverse means. Yet apparent contradictions exist when authentic democracy and equality are not available to all, particularly in school settings.

In Australia and England, macro-level issues entail the development and modification of policies at the national or the state level. Deer *et al.* (Chapter 3) assert that in Australia centralization and devolution are twin tendencies. For schools, curriculum is heavily influenced by the state governments, which provide approximately 90 percent of the funding, while decisions about how to implement the curriculum and, increasingly, personnel decisions are the responsibility of institutions. In higher education, the twin tendencies of centralization and devolution involve the national government and, until recently, several types of institutions. The national government's move to amalgamate colleges of advanced education, colleges of further education and universities, often located hundreds of miles apart and with little in common in terms of institutional culture and historical antecedents, leads to serious challenges for teacher educators. Within England, a perpetual struggle continues over the control of teacher education and training. Local autonomy, external accountability, and funding formulas and allocations are closely linked to the national public policies regarding the provision of services and entitlements. What can be observed in England is a struggle — over defining the needs and how to meet the needs of diverse constituents — between an increasingly active and powerful central Conservative Party government and a group of teachers and teacher educators, whose professional authority and status as monopoly providers is being undermined. The identification of national priorities and how to achieve them in a postmodern era is at the heart of the matter for England and Australia. Problems that were not prominent, even 15 or 20 years ago, such as England's declining industrial base and international economic and political stature, are at the forefront. For both nations, the international economic down-turn is paramount. Thus one immediate reality, according to Deer *et al.* is that 'education is now seen as a branch of economic policy, rather than a mix of social, economic, and cultural policy.'

Popkewitz's chapter on the United States focuses less attention on national and global economic dynamics, but he does make clear how debates about school-ing and teacher education reflect a discourse infused by certain forms of economic rationality. Moreover, we need only observe the popular media (for example, daily issues of the *Washington Post* and the *New York Times*, or broadcasts by the Cable News Network [CNN]) to see the linkages between education and socio-economic conditions. In the US as in England, there is a fascination with the 'marketization' of education in the form of school choice and voucher plans as well as private firms being hired to manage public 'charter' schools. As Popkewitz notes, furthermore, disparities and different forms of regulation are present from the historical period to contemporary discursive practices and other endeavors, for example, systemic school reform, constructivist psychologies to reorder concep-tions about teaching, and the Teach For America program designed for rural and urban schools. Conditions of teaching and education in rural (as discussed by Spatig) and urban schools frequently represent salient contradictions regarding espoused and actual policies. Hence national and state policies appear contradic-tory and lack coherence, unless we clearly recognize that in the United States, as in many western nations, macro-level policies make reference to one set of prin-ciples while actually advocating and implementing others. Through the analysis of the political dimension in teacher education programs and related organizations, contradictions can be analyzed with the aim of beginning to make differences in such programs through participatory empowerment processes.

Therefore the micro-level analyses become important as witnessed in Spatig's chapter on university-based teacher education program in Appalachia. An overarching theme, critical reasoning, was to permeate the institutional policies and practices in this teacher preparation program. Yet, for the most part, the students did not know of the theme, which had been formally adopted half-way through their four-year degree program, or they did not lend much credence to it. Instead, various teacher educators and students usually focused on 'whatever works, appearance over substance, and a fragmented approach to teaching'. Since critical reasoning apparently had not been effectively incorporated into program realities, students completed the program with few changes in their approaches to teaching and simply reproduced knowledge via parts of the curriculum and continual socialization from the educational, home and community milieux.

Of especial concern about critical reasoning not being institutionalized in the program's curriculum and pedagogy was the apparent contradiction between teacher-educators' involvement in articulating it as a program theme and their limited success in placing it at the core of a program within a two-year period. It may not be surprising that a theme such as critical reasoning developed — or at least formally adopted — by faculty to meet external accreditation requirements is not strongly evidenced in the university and school-based experiences of stu-dent teachers. Nevertheless, this analysis does suggest a serious implication of university instructors, student teaching supervisors, and cooperating teachers them-selves being oblivious to or failing to draw attention to macro-level university-wide, state, and national policies and political realities affecting their profession and those intending to enter it. Thus their oblivion and failure means students are not exposed to critical political dimensions integrally affecting their professions and do not know how to assume proactive postures.

The formation of macro-level policies in 'developing' countries sometimes appears daunting. Colonial legacies are coupled with the influences of 'developed' nations, thereby enabling international and transnational economic and political priorities and policies to affect national development policies. Banya's chapter on Sierra Leone and Lindsay's on South Africa discuss how funding decisions of international organizations affect national policies in developing nations. That is, policies, programs and practices, developed for national concerns to address the needs of the domestic infrastructure, including that for education and teacher education, are heavily affected by the 'superstructures'[1] of other nations. The participative involvement, even under the best of circumstances in developing nations, is usually tempered by this international distribution of economic and political power.

The struggle over ideals to guide developing societies must constantly encompass the role of teaching, teachers, teacher education, and schooling since quality education is generally seen as at the core of development. Developing nations, as we have witnessed in the illustrations pertaining to Burkina Faso, China, Mexico, Papua New Guinea, Sierra Leone, South Africa and Sri Lanka, wrestle with various ideological principles to help set the educational and teacher preparation paths leading to enhanced quality of life for all. In Sri Lanka and Burkina Faso, for example, there are tensions (during some periods) and cooperation (at other times) among the national ministries, teachers' unions, and other groups. Thus teachers have been the catalysts for change leading to the formation of new policies, while in other eras they resist change and perpetuate prevalent conditions or serve as change agents in accord with directions determined by state or economic élites. In the case of South Africa, teachers and teacher educators have been catalysts for change. Yet, until very recently, the majority of educators have largely sought to effect teacher education and postsecondary education from outside the official policy making arena. This is because *de jure* and *de facto* policies of the former government not only proscribed their involvement, but also prevented them from obtaining sound academic and research skills which are so vitally needed in the formation of long-range policies for a new nation.

Central to the policy debate among various developing nations are issues pertaining to the philosophical bases for teacher education and other components of the educational system, the processes or mechanisms for achieving comprehensive goals, and the rationales and descriptions of functions for teacher education whether in teacher colleges, colleges of education or related postsecondary entities, or universities. Paine's discussion of teacher education in China captures some of the national policy debate that employs metaphors to portray ideals and philosophical views. Red and expert is the most widely cited illustration of the (perhaps) universal tension between the goal of preparing teachers to socialize students to view the existing political economy as legitimate and the goal of developing students' knowledge and skills so that they can be productive workers. The dilemma often occurs for teacher-educators and others to interpret 'accurately' these metaphors as national political postures shift. Paine's chapter suggests that the dilemma currently facing teachers and teacher-educators in China is whether either a 'nationalizing' (red) or a 'modernizing' (expert) discourse can mobilize sufficient commitment to teaching in the face of relatively declining material and symbolic resources being provided to those who enter the 'profession'.

The intersections between macro and micro-level analyses are aptly illuminated in the ethnographic presentations by Raghu regarding Germany and Ginsburg pertaining to Mexico. Raghu analyzes the roles of the church, as a major social institution, in conveying and perpetuating gender roles via official religious policies. Such policies are subsequently translated in the curriculum and related features of a Catholic university in Germany. The intersection is further evinced in the symbiotical relations between Catholic university administrators, faculty, and students *and* the state. For students in particular, the university ensures that matriculants are eligible to take state examinations that are requisites for subsequent teaching positions, which are also determined by the state.

The more extensive ethnography by Ginsburg specifically focused on how individual students (micro-level focuses) view macro-level social, political and economic problems. Thus interactive relations were salient nexuses between the two levels of analyses as students articulated their views of how macro-level national (and international) sociopolitical and economic conditions influenced the schools and local communities in which they do and will work and live. They then noted the relative influence (or lack thereof in some instances) of the formal and hidden curriculum of the *Escuela Normal Superior Veracruzana* (ENSV) on their views and upon their plans for involvement in societal problems outside the formal work environment.

Reading Ginsburg's, Spatig's, Popkewitz's and Paine's chapters leads us to still another level of analysis — the phenomenological. With the phenomenological approach, we are concerned with the meanings that individual teachers, teacher-educators, students and professionals give to policies, events and circumstances. How one interprets, internalizes, or alters social and political conditions and meanings is critical (Du Bois 1903, 1940; Berger and Luckmann 1967; Schutz 1967; Bateson 1989).[2] Thus, as Popkewitz discusses, the participants in Teach For America came to attribute to their students various characteristics, and these attributions (whether valid or invalid) became the basis for the novice teachers' curricular decisions, strategies for interactions with students, and explanations of existing inequalities in schools and society.

Paine's chapter provides an intriguing examination of the use and promulgation of metaphors at the national and state levels in China *and* their interpretations by individuals. She indicates that the Communist Party and the state articulate metaphoric ideas concerning comprehensive roles for teacher education and teachers to achieve economic, political, and social development. Teachers, according to Paine, often used one kind of language to express views of national and state level policies, and still another language when describing teacher education and components thereof in which they are integrally involved. This and other illustrations are indexes of blurred metaphors which appear contradictory, in terms of messages being conveyed and policy guidelines.

On the one hand, this seeming contradiction may indicate the need for clarification or integration, at the macro-level, since individual teachers express dissonance and because metaphors change periodically. While the changes in metaphors may occur, teachers' status, power, and material rewards may remain below that of many with comparable educational backgrounds and professional responsibilities. Chapters on Burkina Faso, China, England, and Sri Lanka portray these difficulties confronting teachers, which may dissuade individuals from entering or remaining in the field and which may limit their capacity effectively to carry out the professional (and civic) responsibilities.

On the other hand, individual teachers may continue to function effectively because they ignore the metaphors or construct their own phenomenological interpretations of the metaphors. There may be clarity for individuals, although dual or blurred metaphors may be operating simultaneously. For example, teachers may envision red experts, experts who are red, or simply experts. This type of interpretation or reinterpretation is often witnessed in various cultures (from indigenous groups in Liberia to African Americans to authors engaged in creative expressions) as anthropologists and sociologists have documented (Cole 1988; Bateson 1989, 1991) so that individuals continue to exert power and control over their lives. Making unique meanings is central to oneself as an individual or part of a cultural group. A second sight or double-consciousness may be operative — even or especially in the face of serious challenges to one's status, power and livelihood.

The Status Quo, Alternative Changes, or Transformation

A central purpose of this section is to articulate how despite the status quo, alternative changes or transformations are evinced. Various situations discussed in this volume provide insight regarding equilibrium or the status quo. For societies, states and institutions to survive (and progress), various constant features are maintained via socialization or other forms of regulation. Schools are a most extensive institution for socialization, and the roles that curriculum and teacher behavior play in this regard are noted by several authors. Teachers as reproducers of knowledge and power relations (Spatig focusing on the US) or change agents for the state (Ginsburg on Mexico and Tatto and Dharmadasa on Sri Lanka) perpetuate that which exists. Ginsburg, Raghu, and Spatig note how students' experiences with the broader ideological and structural context as well as the formal and hidden curriculum of teacher education programs, respectively, in a Mexican normal school, a German Catholic university, and a state university in Appalachia (West Virginia), often reproduce existing educational and social conditions. Efforts to hold teachers and teacher educators *accountable* to institutional and state authorities, as witnessed in Deer *et al.*'s and Landman and Ozga's respective discussions about Australia and England, may also preserve the status quo.

Perhaps the most prominent example of reproduction of the political status quo *vis-à-vis* teacher education was presented by Banya in his discussion of Sierra Leone. Extending a rural teacher education program to urban areas was done by senior government officials to maintain and enhance their political bases. A creative response to requests from various urban constituents was a political façade. In the case of Sierra Leone and other developing nations, such façades, although they may attract needed resources from international organizations and bilateral agencies, have deleterious effects because depressed educational areas remain or further decline. Other notable examples were evident in chapters on Mexico and South Africa. In short, changes to modify or alter are often designed to appear responsive to problems.

A certain degree of ingenuity or adeptness is required to enable teacher educators and others to participate in proposing alternatives and changing existing conditions. Thus some teacher education students in the ethnographies cited in Germany and Mexico and the actions of organized teachers in Burkina Faso and Sri Lanka certainly did (or had the potential to) change sociopolitical and economic circumstances. German students designated as socialist and radical feminists in Ragu's study and Mexican students with conflict perspectives in Ginsburg's ethnography plan some level of active 'political' involvement to bring about change at the micro and macro-levels, although like the US students described by Spatig, they face tremendous ideological and structural barriers to effective individual or collective action.

The amalgamation of colleges of education and universities, along with issues of centralized versus decentralized decision making and funding allocations have promoted Australian teacher-educators to become politically involved, both to preserve positive aspects of the status quo in teacher education, which they view threatened by national government intervention, and to collaborate with state and economic élites in promoting needed changes. In 'advanced' or 'developed' societies, such as Australia, England, Germany and the United States, the state and major social institutions encourage — or at least tolerate — the active participation of educators and others in the change process usually so long as actions fit within fairly wide parameters. Active involvement in the change process leads to alterations, while preserving various basic features and goals of the institutions and society. The activities of individual teachers, groups, unions, professional associations, and the like can include protesting policies, modifying the curriculum, challenging education administrators and government officials, and engaging in formal and informal political exercises. We should note, however, that as in England in recent years educators' participation in policy making, etc., may be delegitimized as state and economic élites seek to characterize educators as narrowly pursuing their own self-interests and using their 'provider monopoly' to block 'needed' reforms.

In newly independent and 'developing' nations, engaging in change may be seen as central to the national development and educational processes. Teachers and teacher-educators in Burkina Faso, Papua New Guinea, South Africa and Sri Lanka were encouraged, at various times, by the government and education officials to 'break with the past' and establish systems that address indigenous needs. Simultaneously, components of former systems can be retained if officials believe that such preservations provide the view that everyone has opportunities to participate fairly. For example, in Mexico and Sri Lanka formal assessments for student teachers and others were designed with merit criteria as the basis for advancement or promotion. Yet in these countries (and indeed in developed nations), demographic characteristics (such as race or ethnicity, class, or gender) often affect a person's or group's academic and social achievement. To quote the frequently used statement, 'the anointed ones' can participate; for others it is an illusion of fair participation in educational and social ventures.

When viewing changes designed to modify existing conditions, we assert that authority and accountability are key terms. Authority from policies and officials *and* accountability to such entities are the modes of operations. Teachers and teacher-educators in Sri Lanka and Burkina Faso were supposed to be accountable to government authorities which often led to tensions between the groups. Contradictions and dissonance still result for individual teachers and others because what is espoused is often not what is evident in *de jure* and *de facto* policies and programs. The double-consciousness, the two thoughts, the two warring ideals are then present for individuals. The challenge is to understand the double-consciousness, and to move forward so that the gap between the stated and the real is narrowed (in the short run) and eliminated in the long run.

Moving forward means undertaking various endeavors for authentic transformations. As Deer *et al.* point out, forays into the political arena by the Australian Council of Deans of Education (ACDE) is one avenue for initiating transformations — at least in teacher education, if not in schooling and society — via active participation in decision making. The activist role being pursued by the ACDE may represent one form of political engagement by teacher-educators, which Landman and Ozga bemoan has recently been lacking in the English context. The ACDE is attempting to address contradictions and discrepancies pertaining to teacher education and postsecondary education caused by government policies and funding levels. The statements of radical feminists and those with conflict perspectives as reported by Raghu and Ginsburg, respectively, are another means for potential active involvement in authentic transformations. Certainly the strikes and other political demonstrations initiated by South African, Sri Lankan, and Burkinabè teachers are still other examples. Collective actions by teacher-educators, teachers, unions, and other bodies can lead to productive partnerships among the stakeholders thereby producing transformations, although such actions are not always viewed by élites in such a positive light.

Authentic transformations may also occur, as Burke discusses, by teacher-educators' integral involvement with the structure policy and curricula of their institutions. For example, although much of the external funding was provided by the Australian government for the community teacher education project in Papua New Guinea, indigenous educators continually shared responsibility in professional development for community teacher college lecturers. Power-with rather than power-over was central to the enterprise. A critical issue, however, is still present: the continuation of the power-with framework. While collaborations between stakeholders is under way to address sustainable development as an ongoing institutional process, it will be worth monitoring in the future whether government officials and others may overtly or covertly exert measures to change this framework, particularly if these teacher-educators (and/or their students) become oriented to changing more fundamental aspects of existing educational and societal relations.

Earlier in this chapter, we discussed how authority and accountability are used for modifications or alterations, rather than transformations. We add a third component — autonomy — and then redefine concepts for authority and accountability. Autonomy enables teacher-educators and teachers to engage in independent actions in light of their professional (and personal) views and experiences. This independence may (or should) also mean authority and accountability to other teachers, students, parents, and the community to establish progressive sociopolitical and economic structures. In essence, horizontal rather than vertical communications, interactions, and decision making would be the norm.

The struggle over ideals, ideologies and discursive practices is at the core of transformations — a point emphasized particularly by Burke, Paine, Popkewitz, Spatig, and Tatto and Dharmadasa. This 'first level' (Rodney 1990) of struggle does not ignore or negate the need for simultaneous political action to challenge directly the reality of the unequal distribution of power and economic resources as observed in all of the countries discussed in this volume. Indeed, as outlined in Chapter 1, issues of power and material resources as well as resources constituted through symbols are at the core of politics.

One place to begin is to struggle to have ideas embedded in the curriculum; the structure of teacher education programs and institutional policies should be consistent with what is espoused. For example, following from Spatig's findings, we need to avoid adopting slogans — such as critical reasoning — to characterize teacher education programs when we do not effectively work to institutionalize curricular components and pedagogical practices which reflect and encourage such a potentially transformative process. In reference to Raghu's analysis, we need to ensure that illustrations in textbooks and lectures portray male and female instructors teaching boys and girls, that in teacher education institutions females and males occupy similar statuses as instructors and administrators, and that staff model active involvement in school-level (and community-level) political decisions and other actions (see also Burke and Ginsburg).

New definitions and constructs for the same terms may emerge, or new terms, ideals, and explications may be introduced to introduce innovative policies and program development (Rodney 1990; Morrison 1992). A synthesis of terms, fused metaphors, and new analogies can also become the new normative reality. As Bateson (1989, 1991) reveals, 'our own metaphors' are the creative process of fusing metaphors which can be analogous to painting or composing jazz, producing a novel work from disparate and contradictory elements. A lucid example, often observed in primary and secondary schools, is that of students giving new meanings and forms to traditional words. For example, to African American students 'bad' means good and a 'clean teacher' is someone who is smartly dressed. In a newly independent country such as South Africa, traditional terms such as democracy and economic development are being redefined to include all ethnic and racial groups in a fair participative manner. Former white power holders, Afrikaners and English descendants, are ensured of some seats and participation in parliamentary processes despite their excluding black (and other non-white) South Africans for centuries under the guise of separate development. Authentic democracy can be the reality in a new South Africa.

Lessons Learned for Progressive Political Commitments

The discussion and analysis offered in this and preceding chapters serves as one forum for integrating the scholarly work of academicians involved, in some fashion, with the preparation of teachers. Based upon the preceding pages, we offer summary remarks and recommendations to enhance the linkages between our endeavors in the academy and those of teachers (and other citizen workers) wherever they work and live.

An ultimate goal is to help ensure that all the stakeholders in the educational enterprise and related sociopolitical realms have opportunities to participate equally in policy formation and decision making. That is, to create a context in which they share in the rights and responsibilities as well as the benefits of social life in institutions, communities, nations and the world in a manner to avoid acting primarily to serve narrowly-defined self or group interests. Transparent processes, an often used term in the new South Africa, are those that have open and maximum input, discussion, and dialogue by all stakeholders. Transparency also encompasses a lucid comprehension of the multiple levels of sociopolitical and phenomenological analyses *and* the complex web of interactions among those involved and/or implicated by educational and other policies and practices. Moving beyond divergences for common ground is integral to the process.

As educational and political goals are achieved, new problems and conflicts will likely emerge. Recognizing salient trends at the macro and micro-level is critical since progressive change (or its reversal) is an ongoing phenomenon. What is new becomes old and may need to be altered or recreated. The 'current' old and the 'new' old structures and ideas which preclude the participation of all educators and other stakeholders must be challenged continually. While some may live within the veil and be effective via a double-consciousness because their dogged strength keeps them from being torn apart, ultimately the veil which blinds others must be ripped asunder.

Notes

1 For a more detailed discussion of infrastructures, superstructures, dependency, and development, see Rodney (1972) and Amin (1990a, 1990b).
2 We recognize that there is a considerable body of literature on phenomenology and the social sciences. Countless works from the literary world and other humanities provide numerous illustrations of phenomenological interpretations. What we wish to emphasize is the fusion (to use a term from the jazz genre) from several disciplines to elucidate how people give different and novel meanings to phenomena.

References

AMIN, S. (1990a) *DeLinking: Towards a Polycentric World*, London, Ved Books.
AMIN, S. (1990b) *Maldevelopment: Anatomy of A Global Failure*, London, Ved Books.
BATESON, M.C. (1989) *Composing A Life*, New York, Plume.
BATESON, M.C. (1991) *Our Own Metaphor*, Washington, DC, Smithsonian Institute Press.
BERGER, P. and LUCKMANN, T. (1967) *The Social Construction of Reality*, Garden City, NY, Anchor.
CARNOY, M. and SAMOFF, J. (1990) *Education and Social Transition in the Third World*, Princeton, NJ, Princeton University Press.
COLE, J.B. (Ed) (1988) *Anthropology for the Nineties: Introductory Readings*, New York, Free Press.
DU BOIS, W.E.B (1903, 1969) *The Souls of Black Folk*, New York, Signet Classic.
DU BOIS, W.E.B. (1940) *Dusk of Dawn: An Autobiography of a Race Concept*, New York, Harcourt, Brace, and Company.
HOROWITZ, I.L. (1972) *Three Worlds of Development: The Theory and Practice of International Stratification*, 2nd edn, New York, Oxford University Press.
KLEIN, S.S. (1987) 'The Role of Public Policy in the Education of Girls and Women', paper presented at the annual conference of the American Educational Research Association, Washington, DC, 20–24 April.
LAMORTE, M. (1987) *School Law: Cases and Concepts*, Englewood Cliffs, NJ: Prentice Hall.

LINDSAY, B. (1994) 'Legislation and minority rights in higher education: American and Kenyan case studies', in TULASIEWICZ, W. and STROWBRIDGE, G. (Eds) *Education and the Law: International Perspectives*, London, Routledge, pp. 3–28.

LINDSAY, B. (1988) 'Public and higher education policies influencing African-American women', *Higher Education: The International Journal of Higher Education and Educational Planning*, **17**, 3, pp. 563–80.

MARABLE, M. (1983) *How Capitalism Underdeveloped Black America*, Boston, MA, South End Press.

MORRISON, T. (1992) 'Introduction: Friday on the Potomac', in MORRISON, T. (Ed) *Raceing Justice, En-Gendering Power: Essays on Anita Hill, Clarence Thomas, and the Construction of Social Reality*, New York, Pantheon Books, pp. vii–xxx.

RITZER. G. (1992) *Contemporary Sociological Theory*, 3rd edn, New York, McGraw-Hill.

RODNEY, W. (1972) *How Europe Underdeveloped Africa*, Dar es Salaam, Tanzania, Tanzania Publishing House.

RODNEY, W. (1990) *Walter Rodney Speaks: The Making of an African Intellectual*, Trenton, NJ, Africa World Press.

SCHUTZ, A. (1967) *The Phenomenology of the Social World*, Evanston, IL, Northwestern University Press.

SMITH, D. (1987) *The Everyday World as Problematic: A Feminist Sociology*, Boston, MA. Northeastern University Press.

SMITH, D. (1990) *The Conceptual Practices of Power: A Feminist Sociology of Knowledge*, Boston, MA, Northeastern University Press.

WALLERSTEIN, I. (1989) *The Modern World-System III*, San Diego, CA, Academic Press, Inc.

Notes on Contributors

Kingsley Banya is Chairperson and Associate Professor of Curriculum Theory in the Department of Educational Leadership and Policy Studies at Florida International University, Miami, FL. He has worked extensively on research and development projects in Africa and the United States, and has written on curriculum issues, educational change, and multicultural education. He is author of *Implementing Educational Innovation in the Third World: A West African Experience* (Mellen Research University Press, 1993).

Clarrie Burke was a teacher and school administrator in Papua New Guinea and now is Associate Professor in the School of Cultural and Policy Studies, Faculty of Education, Queensland University of Technology (Australia). His scholarly interests are in philosophy of education, teacher education, and decentralization reforms.

Christine E. Deer is Professor and Head of the School of Teacher Education at the University of Technology, Sydney (Australia), a position she has held since 1990. Her research interests include the professional development of teachers and curriculum studies, particularly curriculum implementation and change. She has published widely on these topics both nationally and internationally.

Martial Dembélé — a citizen of Burkina Faso — is a PhD candidate in Curriculum, Teaching and Educational Policy at Michigan State University, East Lansing, MI, having completed his masters degree in Social and Comparative Analysis in Education at the University of Pittsburgh, PA. He specializes in teacher education and teacher learning. He works as a research assistant for the National Center for Research on Teacher Learning, where he has been involved, since fall 1991, in a cross-national study of mentoring among teachers. Besides mentoring and learning to teach, his interests range from teacher organizational activity, educational biographies, teacher research, collaborative action research, to issues related to the use of mother tongues as languages of instruction in former colonies.

K.H. Dharmadasa, Chief Project Officer of the Department of Educational Research of the National Institute of Education, Sri Lanka, is presently a doctoral student in Educational Psychology at the Auburn University, AL. His research interests focus on teacher education, secondary education, and primary education. He has participated in a number of collaborative research projects sponsored by the United Nations Development Program, the United Nations Educational Scientific and Cultural Organization, and the United States Agency for International Development.

Mark B. Ginsburg is Professor of Comparative Sociology of Education in the Departments of Administrative and Policy Studies and Sociology and a Senior Associate in the Institute for International Studies in Education at the University of Pittsburgh, PA. His scholarly work focuses on social inequalities and the politics of teachers' work and teacher education. His books include: *Contradictions in Teacher Education and Society* (Falmer, 1988), *Understanding Educational Reform in Global Context: Economy, Ideology and the State* (Garland, 1991), and *The Politics of Educators' Work and Lives* (Garland, 1995).

Susan Groundwater-Smith is Associate Professor of Professional Development at the University of Technology, Sydney (Australia). Her academic focus is on curriculum theorizing and evaluation and assessment in education. This has led her to take an increasing interest in policy development and implementation.

Maeve Landman is Principal Lecturer in Education and Director of the Bachelor of Education (honors degree program) at the University of the West of England, Bristol. Previously she taught in primary and secondary schools in an alternative education project in London. Her research interests include the structures and processes of the governance of higher education, special educational needs, and feminist methodologies.

Beverly Lindsay is Dean of International Education and Policy Studies at Hampton University, VA. She is also Professor of Higher Education and Administration at the University of Georgia, Athens, GA. Her scholarly work focuses on public and higher educational policies in cross-national settings as well as on social and educational planning in developing nations. Her books include: *Comparative Perspectives of Third World Women: The Impact of Race, Sex, and Class* (Praeger, 1980, 1983) and *African Migration and National Development* (Pennsylvania State University Press, 1985).

Robert Meyenn is Professor and Dean of Education at Charles Sturt University Bathurst, New South Wales (Australia). He has been president of the NSW Teacher Education Council, a member of the board of Australian Deans of Education, and the NSW Ministerial Advisory Council on Teacher Education and the Quality of Teaching (MACTEQT). His research interests include rural education, education policy analysis and third world education.

Jenny Ozga is currently Professor of Educational Policy in the Department of Education at Keele University (United Kingdom). Before that she was Dean of Education at Bristol, University of the West of England. She has worked for the Open University for many years, and also taught management and administration at Strathclyde University after a period as Senior Administrative Officer in the Education Department of the National Union of Teachers. She was (and still is) a teacher, and her research interests are in teachers' work and educational policy.

Lynn Paine is Associate Professor in the Department of Teacher Education and the Department of Sociology at Michigan State University East Lansing, MI. Her research has focused on teachers, teaching, and teacher education, as well as the connections between educational policy and practice in comparative perspective. She has undertaken extensive fieldwork in China focused on these topics.

Judith Parker is Associate Professor and Head of the School of Teacher Education at Charles Sturt University, Bathurst, New South Wales (Australia). She is an executive member of the NSW Teacher Education Council and her present research interests are policy developments in teacher education and secondary english curriculum.

Thomas S. Popkewitz is Professor of Curriculum and Instruction at the University of Wisconsin-Madison. His work centers on the political sociology of educational reform, educational sciences, and professionalization. He completed a study of educational reform in the United States (*A Political Sociology of Educational Reform*, Teachers College Press, 1991) and an eight-country study of teacher education (*Changing Patterns of Regulation*, State University of New York Press, 1993). His current work includes investigations of knowledge/power relations in teacher education and an international study of social relations in which discourses of professionalism occur.

Rajeshwari Raghu — a citizen of India — completed her doctorate in the Social and Comparative Analysis in Education program area at the University of Pittsburgh, PA. Her dissertation, 'Development of Teachers as Political Actors in a Private German University: How Teachers Anticipate Their Contribution to Preserving/Transforming Gender Relations', explores the political socialization experiences of prospective teachers.

Linda Spatig is Associate Professor of Educational Foundations at Marshall University in Huntington, West Virginia (United States). Her research focuses on schooling, teacher education, and social inequalities, particularly with respect to gender and social class.

Maria Teresa Tatto is an Assistant Professor in the Department of Teacher Education at Michigan State University, East Lansing, MI. She has coordinated and participated in national-level research studies in Asia, Latin America, and the United States. Her areas of specialization include evaluation research and policy analysis, effectiveness and cost of secondary and higher education, teacher education and student learning, and the relationship between educational policy and practice.

Author Index

Tatto, Maria Teresa 12–13, 99–120, 158, 271, 273, 279
Taylor, William 141, 160

UNDP 124, 137
UNESCO 3, 19, 144, 160
USAID 162, 168, 174

Weiler, Kathleen 177, 196, 198, 215, 235, 242
Whitty, Geoff 28, 38, 39
World Bank 122, 137

Yeatman, A. 42, 53

Zeichner, Kenneth 9, 19, 199, 215, 216, 242, 249, 261

Subject Index

accountability 23, 42, 116, 272, 273
Afghanistan 238
African National Congress (ANC) 165, 166, 172
Afrikaners 162, 165, 274
aid agencies, bilateral/multilateral 8, 103, 131–135, 168, 245
alchemies of school subjects 67, 69
Apartheid 13, 162–166, 171
Appalachia 14, 177–196, 271
'appearance versus substance' theme 186, 187
Australia 11, 15, 24, 40–53, 168, 243, 244, 245, 248, 253, 257, 267, 271–273
Australian Council of Deans of Education (ACDE) 45, 273
autonomy/authority, of teachers 65, 99, 100, 111, 116, 117, 132, 148, 179, 272, 273
Azanian People's Organization (AZAPO) 165

Bantu Education Act (1953) 162, 163
bantustans 164, 173
Benin 141
bilateral/multilateral aid agencies 8, 103, 131–135, 168, 245
blurred genre/metaphor 77, 93, 270
Britain/England/United Kingdom 11, 12, 23–39, 102, 103, 106, 109–112, 114–116, 124, 125, 127, 244, 245, 265, 267, 268, 270–273
Bunumbu Project 127–133
Burkina Faso 5, 13, 140–161, 269, 270, 272, 273

Canada 131, 137, 168
capitalism 7, 101, 126
center societies 7, 15
centralization 42, 58, 107, 127, 179, 218, 231, 257
China 5, 12, 76–98, 135, 269, 270
church/religion 14, 16, 55, 56, 58, 71, 72, 99, 106, 107, 109–111, 113–116, 118, 127, 134, 145, 197, 198, 200, 201, 211–214, 245, 270
civil society 4, 16
collaborative action research 252
cold war 136, 137
colonialism/colonization 8, 13, 99, 106, 110, 115, 124, 143, 145, 245, 250, 269
Common School Movement 179

Communist Party 77, 103, 104, 270
community teachers colleges 15, 244–261
conflict theories/perspectives 100, 223–225, 234
consciousness raising 225, 228, 234–236, 238, 253
contradictions 7, 199, 213, 217, 235, 267, 270, 273, 274
constructivist psychologies 12, 55, 61, 63–67, 69
corporatism 14, 219
Côte d'Ivoire 141, 143
Council for the Accreditation of Teacher Education (CATE) 28–35
critical reasoning/reflection 14, 183, 184, 189–191, 193, 250–253, 258, 259, 268, 274
curriculum, formal/official 10, 14, 15, 208–212, 222, 231, 234, 270, 271
curriculum, hidden 10, 14, 15, 208–212, 222, 231, 234, 270, 271

decentralization (devolution, deconcentration) 42, 58, 116, 220, 237
Department of Employment, Education and Training (DEET) 40, 44, 45, 48, 49
dependency, economic and cultural 218, 245
deprofessionalization 11, 23
deskilling 26, 37
developed countries 3, 6, 8, 122, 269, 272
developing countries 3, 6, 8, 122, 143, 269, 272
development, economic 88, 107, 129, 130, 137, 143, 218
'discipline/control in the classroom' theme 185, 186, 189, 194
discourse 46, 49, 54, 56, 60–63, 71, 76–78, 85, 87, 88, 95, 101, 108, 268, 269
discursive practices 54, 58, 67, 69, 78
distance education 113, 118

East Germany 200
economic development 88, 107, 129, 130, 137, 143, 218
economic hardship 13, 143–144, 155
educational reform 5, 24, 54, 60, 70, 99, 109, 115, 144–145, 200
electoral politics 228–229, 239–240
elites, economic 14, 15, 16, 269